BUTLER'S
LIVES OF THE SAINTS

BUTLER'S LIVES OF THE SAINTS

The Third Millennium

Paul Burns

BURNS & OATES
A Continuum imprint
LONDON • NEW YORK

To the memory of Pope John Paul II,
18 May 1920–2 April 2005.

Burns & Oates
A Continuum imprint
The Tower Building
11 York Road
London SE1 7NX

15 East 26th Street
New York
NY 10010

www.continuumbooks.com

First published 2005
Reprinted 2005

British Library Cataloguing-in-Publication Data
A catalogue record for this book is available from the British Library.

ISBN 0-86012-382-0 (hardback)
ISBN 0-86012-383-9 (paperback)

Typeset by Fakenham Photosetting Limited, Fakenham, Norfolk
Printed and bound by MPG Books Ltd, Bodmin, Cornwall

CONTENTS

INTRODUCTION

This volume continues the tradition of saints' Lives in English established by the Revd Alban Butler (1710–1773) in his *The Lives of the Fathers, Martyrs, and Other Principal Saints: Compiled from Original Monuments and other Authentick Records; illustrated with the Remarks of judicious modern Criticks and Historians*, published in London in seven volumes between 1756 and 1759. His approach is shown in the words "authentick", "judicious", "criticks", and "historians": he was endeavouring to present true historical studies, not pious legends. His great intuition was that saints should be seen more as examples than as intercessors: "Example instructs without usurping the authoritative air of a master ... In the lives of the saints we see the most perfect maxims of the gospel reduced to practice." The same principle was followed in the third major revision of his work, published in twelve volumes, one for each month of the year, from 1995 to 2000, and described as a "new full edition." The present work is the first supplement to that edition, covering canonizations and beatifications enacted from late 1999 to the end of 2003. It differs from the scope of the new full edition in that (barring accidents) it contains all the new saints and blessed of its short span, whereas the new full edition covered only a selection of the 10,000 and more belonging to two millennia.

The long pontificate (exceeded only by that of Pius IX) of Pope John Paul II has produced an unprecedented flurry of beatifications and canonizations, a process that has continued into the closing years of his pontificate. Many of the great saints from the Middle Ages, when the Vatican took control of the process of declaring a person a saint, waited centuries for their canonization. (Those that were "fast-tracked," such as Thomas Becket, tended—whatever their obvious sanctity—to be useful to the papacy in its continual struggle with secular rulers.) In the late twentieth century the founder of Opus Dei, Josemaría Escrivá de Balaguer, died in 1975, was beatified in 1992, and canonized in 2002. There was an even shorter interval, just over six years, between Mother Teresa of Calcutta's death in September 1997 and her beatification on 19 October 2003, and it is unlikely that her canonization will be long delayed. Promoters of both causes deny that any particular pressure has been applied to secure a rapid outcome in order to please large and well-organized bodies of supporters or followers: and indeed in an age of speedy exchange of information it is only natural for this process—like almost any other—to take less time.

The number and speed of beatifications and canonizations is generally agreed to be the result of conscious policy on the Pope's part. Outside Europe, Catholicism is expanding, changing, and facing various threats; in western

Europe it is losing congregations and struggling to retain its voice in public affairs; in eastern Europe—so dear to John Paul's heart—it is either re-emerging after decades of suppression under Communism, or already losing its character of popular resistance movement and succumbing to consumer capitalism. In all these situations, the Pope's policy has been to provide local examples to strengthen the people's faith. In calling attention to local figures, especially in the Developing World, he has been outstandingly successful. Canonization ceremonies have drawn crowds that even Live Aid pop concerts would envy: while the canonization of a popular European saint such as Padre Pio can draw 300,000 pilgrims to Rome (which is quickly and relatively cheaply reached by road, rail, or air), as did the beatification of Mother Teresa, this cannot compare with the 500,000 who travelled to Guatemala City in Central America's totally different conditions for the canonization of St Peter de Betancur, let alone the 5,000,000 who celebrated that of St Juan Diego at the shrine of the Virgin of Guadalupe outside Mexico City. In terms of providing local examples to fortify the people's faith, the outcome is perhaps less successful—or one just has to accept that there are many sorts of faith within the "catholic" Church and that the Western, enlightenment variety does not represent the majority. So, as a Vatican news service reports, "Since John Paul II canonized Brother Pedro [de Betancur], the church where he is buried is crowded with the faithful ... Pilgrims and tourists arrive daily from all over the country, as well as from Honduras, El Salvador and Mexico ... Faithful who were interviewed said they visit the church in thanksgiving for favours received through the saint's intercession." They do not say that they are determined to follow Brother Pedro's example of providing practical assistance to the poor and the sick. No doubt many of these pilgrims are the poor and the sick: is there any evidence that Brother Pedro's example is leading them to campaign for their rights to social justice, as a "liberation" response would indicate?

The Vatican is certainly not blind to these differences in response: time and again, in his homilies at the ceremonies, Pope John Paul II expressed his hopes and fears in relation to the situation obtaining in the countries from which the particular new saint or blessed comes. So in Bulgaria and Ukraine he has pointed out the virtues of Orthodoxy and appealed for improved ecumenical relations; in Poland he has—in somewhat pessimistic terms, it has to be said—appealed for the retention of traditional values in the face of rapid social change; in Italy the preferred example seems to be that of extolling "family values" in a country still reacting against Mussolini's policy of *natalismo* (designed to provide ever more Italians to wage war) and which now has the lowest birth rate in Europe—unlikely to be the case due to "natural" means alone.

Western liberal ways of thinking come up against other, apparently more "primitive" ones, in other areas. Catholic commentators would in general now explain the "evil spirits" of the gospel miracle stories as psychological damage, yet Mother Teresa's process came up against a problem that was (attempted to be) explained in terms that have not changed from those used in the first century: "Mother Teresa was not exorcized, Archbishop says: priest simply told to pray over her," headed the story in the Vatican news service, which continued:

> Mother Teresa of Calcutta did not undergo the rite of exorcism, says Archbishop Henry D'Souza of Calcutta, denying statements attributed to him by the international press. Rather, a priest was simply asked to pray over her during a troubled period in 1996, the archbishop said. Speaking to the Catholic agency UCA News, the archbishop said that the faulty news of the exorcism was due to a conversation he had with reporters, who asked if holy people can experience abandonment by God. He told the story of Mother Teresa, while she was in the Woodlands Hospital in 1996. She was found to be very perturbed, suffering from doubts and profound fears. She was hospitalized because of heart problems, and was unable to sleep. Archbishop D'Souza thought that perhaps an evil spirit was trying to steal her interior peace and confidence in God. So he asked Father Rosario Stroscio, 79, a Salesian priest of Sicilian origin, to pray over her, with a prayer used for exorcisms. However, it was not an exorcism as such.

Past and present also co-exist uneasily in the role of "miracles" in the saint-making process. Alban Butler and his contemporary Charles Fell[1] were criticized at the time for the relatively ruthless way they dealt with miracles, which before then had played a prominent part in standard Lives of saints. Fell argued that working miracles in one's lifetime was no proof of holiness, citing the gospel reference to those who claim to have worked many wonders and will still be cast out at the last judgment (see Matt. 25). In this he has been supported by later church thinking, which now looks above all for "heroic virtue" exercised over a period of years. Fell has also of course been supported by the onward march of sciences, medical and other, which now leave less and less room for inexplicable phenomena in our lives. Fell distinguished between miracles supposed to have been worked during a saint's life on earth and those worked after their death through their intercession. The official Church makes the same distinction and insists (with rare exceptions) on one posthumous miracle for beatification and another for canonization. These are usually otherwise inexplicable cures of someone who has prayed to the candidate or been "touched" by him or her—perhaps with a relic. Some remain quite inexplicable even in the light of modern medical knowledge. One of the most popular recent canonizations, that of Padre Pio (see 23 Sept.) in June 2002, was made possible by the "cure" of a girl from Scotland, Danielle O'Connor, who suffered from a rare chromosome defect at birth, which left her profoundly physically and mentally disabled. When she was twenty-one months old, her doctors removed her from all life-support systems, wrapped her in a blanket, and gave her back to her parents to die peacefully. A stranger touched the baby with a rosary and a relic of Padre Pio. Ten years later, she was reported as being not only alive but alert, if frail-looking.[2] Until some other explanation is found, this and similar cases are still understandably regarded—by the child's parents and the official Church— as miracles worked by the candidate for sainthood. Such occurrences, however, fall by definition outside the life of the saint concerned and so are not discussed here (though several are mentioned in tracing the progress of a cause).

Pope John Paul II beatified and canonized more individuals (though often in large groups) than all his predecessors since the papacy reserved the process to itself in the twelfth century. There are those who say that the idea of canonization is being devalued by sheer quantity: the altar is feeling a little "crowded," as one cardinal observed.[3] There are also continued accusations of "political" bias and some evidence that the official Church is drifting away from popular sentiment. The founder of Opus Dei, whose members tend to be middle class and concerned with their own salvation, is canonized in almost record time, while the martyr-archbishop Oscar Romero, concerned for the fate of his people, and killed by those who would regard themselves as Catholic, is not—though almost universally hailed as "St Romero of America." The twentieth century has been the century of martyrs, but those beatified or canonized have overwhelmingly been clergy, put to death by Nazi or—more often—communist regimes, not the thousands of lay people murdered or "disappeared" by "national security" regimes as a result of their struggle for the "Kingdom of God" rather than for the visible Church. The Vatican takes care to point out that the martyrs of the Spanish civil war (nearly all priests killed in the revolutionary left-wing uprising immediately preceding Franco's rebellion), for example, cannot be seen as political figures and died purely because they represented the Church: but the Church was inevitably politicized by its dominant position in society.

Karl Rahner, writing in a 1983 volume of *Concilium* on the subject of martyrdom, pleaded for the concept to be broadened. He defined the "classical" concept as "the free, tolerant acceptance of death for the sake of the faith, except in the course of an active struggle as in the case of soldiers." He questions the exclusion of active struggle "for the Christian faith and its moral demands (including those affecting society as a whole)." Jesus, the model for death "passively endured," he points out, in fact "died because he fought," and his death "must not be seen in isolation from his life." Oscar Romero died "while fighting for justice in society," yet his own homilies show him as freely and toler- antly accepting his own death: "Why should he not be a martyr?" Countless Christians die deaths that "can be foreseen and accepted as the consequence of an active struggle for justice and other Christian realities and values." Why should their deaths too not be seen as those of martyrs? In support, Rahner cites St Thomas Aquinas, who "says that someone is a martyr through a death that is clearly related to Christ if he is defending society (*res publica*) against the attacks of its enemies who are trying to damage the Christian faith." Such an enlargement of the concept, he concludes, "has a very down-to-earth practical significance for a Christianity and a Church that mean to be aware of their responsibility for justice and peace in the world;" it should therefore be the concern of a theology of liberation.[4] There are exceptions, such as—to mention only martyr-bishops—Archbishop Gerardi in Guatemala, Archbishop Isaías Duarte in Colombia, Archbishop Minzihirwa in the Democratic Republic of Congo, but as a whole the Church does not take up major crosses in order to say what it says or to do what it does, unlike the situation some years ago. Nor does it canonize these and many other martyrs of our times—which would lead it into conflict with their murderers, who are still alive. *Concilium* returned to the subject in its 2003/1 volume, *Rethinking Martyrdom*, to which readers interested in pursuing the question further are referred.

There are numerous martyrs among those canonized and beatified during the four years covered here, twelve as individuals but most of them in groups ranging in number from two to 233. The largest group is those of the Spanish civil war; other large groups are from China, Brazil, and Mexico. Those who suffered under Soviet puppet regimes in eastern Europe during and after the Second World War have group entries as Martyrs of Ukraine and of Bulgaria, besides individual entries. Most died in the twentieth century but some, generally beatified earlier and now proceeding to canonization, go as far back as seventeenth-century Latin America. All, most as priests but others as nuns or catechists, were representatives of the institutional Church, so no shift in the direction of "Kingdom values"—which many will also have upheld—is yet discernible.

This "official" martyrdom continues in the twenty-first century. At the end of the beatification ceremony of several martyrs on 20 October 2002 the Pope paid homage "to the men and women missionaries—priests, men and women religious, and laity—who spend their energies on the front line in service of Christ, at times even paying for their witness with blood." According to the Vatican Congregation for the Evangelization of Peoples, in 2001 thirty-three Catholic missionaries were killed in Asia, Africa and Latin America while working to spread the Gospel, and reports of deaths in various parts of the world indicate comparable numbers in subsequent years.

Pope John Paul II also declared his purpose of evening up the disproportion between numbers of men and women saints and blessed, and here there is discernible change, if not radical. From the tenth century to the end of the reign of Paul VI in 1978, 82 per cent of canonizations and 79 per cent of beatifications had been of men; of the entries in this book, the proportion of men has gone down to 72 per cent. By contrast, the proportion of clergy to laity does not appear to have altered significantly. Figures from the same period as above show that 81 per cent of canonizations and 65 per cent of beatifications were of clergy[5] (I am taking "clergy" here as excluding—correctly—non-ordained religious of both sexes). Without making an exact comparison, 86 per cent of the entries here are for clergy and religious together (which actually seems a more recognizable division), with only fifteen out of 163 being lay people in the normally accepted sense of the word. There is at least one significant gesture toward recognizing the holiness of married life—so constantly preached but so little upheld in the form of a model of sanctity. While husband and wife have previously become saints in the history of the Church, usually as martyrs, the beatification of Luigi and Maria Beltrame Quattrochi on 21 October 2001 marked the first time a married couple has been beatified together. The occasion was all the more remarkable because three of their four children were present at the ceremony. It was certainly a good indication that holiness is not restricted to religious and priests: but, as the figures show, more are needed to constitute a trend.

Another underlying aim of the selection of candidates for beatification or canonization has been to extend the geographical spread of examples for the faithful of what is now truly a universal Church. The many journeys Pope Paul II has made have often incorporated a ceremony raising a local figure to the altars. As with the gender balance, the entries here reflect a partial shift of emphasis, but there is still a preponderance of "Old Europe:" Italy has by far the most with forty-one, followed by Spain with nineteen (though if all the martyrs of the civil war are counted individually this figure leaps to over 250); France—perhaps regarded as having had more than its fair share in the past—is way behind with four, followed by Belgium and Malta with three each, Germany and Portugal with two each, the Netherlands with one (who was born in Germany), and one from Sweden. From "new" (in the sense of eastern) Europe, Poland has six (including a group of eleven martyrs), Ukraine four (though one is a group of over twenty martyrs), Slovakia three, and Bosnia, Bulgaria (a group of three), Croatia, (present day) Czech Republic, Hungary, and Slovenia one each. With boundaries changed through wars, allocation of a country in this region is not precise, but taken as a whole they add up to a concerted effort to bring peace to a troubled region—and to remind it of its inheritance of faith before it goes the way of consumerist and secular western Europe, now the Vatican's main *bête noire*. From the Middle East there is one from Lebanon and one from Armenia. Moving to the New World, there are five from Mexico (one a group of twenty-five), three from Colombia, two each from Argentina, Brazil (one a group of thirty), Canada, and the U.S.A., and one each from Guatemala, Nicaragua, Peru, and Puerto Rico. Not all of these were born locally: several came from Europe, but if they did their main work in their adopted country they are considered to belong to that. From Asia there are three from India—including Mother Teresa, Albanian by birth but Indian by adoption—and two from China (one a European but on the same principle), then one each from the Philippines, Thailand, and Vietnam. From Africa there are two from Sudan (one of whom moved to Italy and the other from Italy), and one each from Uganda and Madagascar.

Most of the new saints and blessed here were born in the nineteenth century, and many also died in it. This places them within a period characterized by a particular view of the Church, of papal authority, and of devotions. It was a period of withdrawal into an institution set apart, defined as a "perfect society"—meaning something complete in itself, rather than "perfect" in the usual sense—in reaction against the Enlightenment, the French Revolution, certain scientific advances, and most of what can be summed up under "the world." It was a Church familiar to Catholics now in their sixties and above, but perhaps strange to those who are younger.[6] Virtually all those recorded here from this period are described in Vatican documents as having a spirituality rooted in the Eucharist and in devotion to the Blessed Virgin and to the Sacred Heart. (To those who associate the word "Eucharist" primarily with the participatory post-Vatican II Mass, the term as used here may seem strange: what is referred to is rather devotion to the Blessed Sacrament in the tabernacle or exposed on the altar in services such as Benediction.) To emphasize this "spiritual life" in entry after entry struck me as stating the obvious to the point of tedium, so I have tended to take it for granted and concentrate on what their devotional life inspired them to do, taking my cue from a typical woman religious of the period: "From the altar of the Lord I go to my work. I take up my duties in the ward. I am not afraid of anything; I seek to begin everything with joy. I can proclaim the Lord's message better by my example than by my words, just as we have to recognize Christ himself in the way he lived his life." This is not only a perfect illustration of the "Butler" principle enunciated at the start of this introduction, but also shows why so many of the lives recorded here are not just "more of the same," as I feared when approaching this work, but individual nuggets well worth mining.

This volume, as will be obvious to those familiar with the new full edition of *Butler's Lives*, is by comparison light on bibliographical references. This is partly because there is little written in English on most of the "new" saints and blessed (and most readers of this volume are not likely to be linguists), and partly because what is available on the internet has increased many-fold in both quantity and quality since 1999, when the last of the twelve volumes was written. Vatican sources, mainly the Patron Saints Index and the biographical account in the *Osservatore Romano* appearing at the time of beatification or canonization, have become more factual, and the English of the weekly English edition of the *Osservatore Romano* has improved greatly. (It would of course be presumptuous to imagine that people at the Congregation for the Causes of Saints have learned from the new Butler volumes, but it is a suspicion.) These have therefore been my main sources: where they have been the only ones there are no references at the end of an entry, as repetition seemed unnecessary. I have selected and re-written in every case, but there are only so many ways in which one can say "He/she was born in …," so there are bound to be some verbal equivalences. As a general principle I have added geographical indications, using the *Times Atlas of the World*, in which most of the towns mentioned, though not villages, can be found. Canonized saints included here often have an entry as "Blessed" in one of the *Butler* volumes, and I have drawn on those entries, usually expanding somewhat. I am grateful to the revisers of those volumes for this accessible source material. I should like to express particular thanks to Andrew Krasinski for his translation from the Polish of source material on BB Joseph Bilczewski and Sigmund Goradowski, for whom Google failed to produce the usual sources in English.

Finally, a note on the liturgical status of new Blessed and saints.[7] There are four stages in the canonization process: Servant of God, Venerable, Blessed, and Saint, of which the last two entitle the "candidate" to liturgical commemoration. The blessed are generally entitled to local veneration, the Saints to universal, but initially limiting the cult to places closely associated with the person is recommended for both categories. Inclusion in a diocesan calendar may be the next step, followed by inclusion in a national calendar, but both of these require permission from Rome, and for the national calendar, two-thirds of the country's bishops have to agree in secret ballot. Religious Orders or Congregations may celebrate their members in their own chapels. We are a long way from the canonization by spontaneous acclamation of the first millennium, but then as the altars become more "crowded" (n. 3 below), it becomes more and more difficult to find space in calendars. Since the calendar reform of 1969, there are four grades of commemoration: Optional Memorial, Memorial, Feast, and Solemnity. The blessed are usually confined to the first, occasionally progressing to the second; saints may be in any one of the four ranks but need to have the status of an apostle to rate a Feast, and of a St Peter, St Paul, or St John the Baptist to rate a Solemnity, which is usually reserved for feasts of Our Lord or Our Lady. Even towering figures such as St Jerome and St Ignatius Loyola only have Memorials. Most of the candidates in this book, with rare probable exceptions such as Mother Teresa, seem likely to remain at the local Optional Memorial level even when canonized. They are nonetheless worthy, often inspiring, and occasionally even entertaining.

P.B.

8 February 2005: Memorial of St Josephine Bakhita

Notes

1. Fr Charles Fell published a four-volume collection in 1728–29, in which he expressed the same purpose as Butler: "The Lives of Saints are nothing less than the Law of God reduced to Practice; a rich Collection of illustrious Examples of the Force of the divine Grace and the Fidelity of such as have been favoured with it." Quoted in Peter Doyle, "Charles Fell, Miracles and the Lives of Saints," in *Analecta Bollandiana* 119, June 2001.

2. Reported by Tracy McVeigh in the British *Observer*, 16 June 2002.
3. Cardinal Silvio Oddi, described as a "veteran Holy See diplomat," quoted by Viviane Hewitt in the *Catholic Herald*, 20 April 1996.
4. Karl Rahner, "Dimensions of Martyrdom: a plea for the broadening of a classical concept," in J. B. Metz and E. Schillebeeckx (eds.), *Martyrdom Today* (Concilium, March 1983), pp. 9–11.
5. Figures are from tables in P. Delooz, "The Social Function of the Canonisation of Saints", in *Models of Holiness* (Concilium, 1979), pp. 14–24, here p. 21. The division between clergy and laity is not defined, but I am taking "laity" to include non-ordained religious.
6. A brilliant evocation of this world can be found in Eamon Duffy, *Faith of Our Fathers* (Continuum, 2004), in which the Professor of the History of Christianity in the University of Cambridge not only provides a fascinating overview of "the Catholic metaphysic" but makes clear which historical developments are worth keeping and which are not.
7. Taken from Vatican News Service, *Zenit*, 21 December 2004, answer to a question by Fr E. McNamara, Professor of Liturgy at the Regina Apostolorum Pontifical University, citing *Notification of Congregation for Divine Worship and the Sacraments*, 20 September 1997.

ABBREVIATIONS AND SHORT FORMS

A.A.S.	*Acta Apostolica Sedis. Commentarium officiale.* Rome, 1908–.
Atlas	*The Times Comprehensive Atlas of the World.* London, 1967; new ed. 2000.
Bibl.SS	*Bibliotheca Sanctorum*, 12 vols. Rome, 1960–70; *Prima Appendice* (Suppl. 1). Rome, 1980; *Seconda Appendice* (Suppl. 2). Rome, 1990.
Butler	Various. *Butler's Lives of the Saints*, new full edition, ed. Paul Burns, 12 vols. Tunbridge Wells and Collegeville, Minnesota, 1995–2000.
C.E	C. Herberman (ed.). *The Catholic Encyclopedia*, 17 vols and index. London and New York, 1907–14.
Diz. Inst. Perf.	G. Pellica and G. Rocca (eds). *Dizionario degli Institute di Perfezione*, 10 vols. Rome, 1974–.
Doc. cath.	*Documentation catholique.*
J.E.H.	*Journal of Ecclesiastical History* (1950–).
LThK	*Lexicon für Theologie und Kirche*, 2d edn. Freiburg, 1957–68.
Orders	Peter Day. *A Dictionary of Religious Orders.* London and New York, 2001.
Oss.Rom.	*Osservatore Romano.* Vatican daily newspaper, in Italian, with summarized weekly editions in other languages.

JANUARY

1

Bd Valentine Paquay (1828–1905)

This model religious and priest in the style of his age came from the province of Limburg in the Flemish-speaking eastern part of Belgium. He was the fifth of eleven children of Henry Paquay and Anna Neven and was born in Tongeren on 17 November 1828 (the Flemish form of his name is Valentijn). After elementary school he moved to a secondary school in Tongeren run by the Austin Canons, from where he entered the seminary in St-Truiden, a few miles to the west.

His father died suddenly in 1847, and his mother agreed to him joining the Franciscans. He began his novitiate in Tielt, over in western Belgium, in October 1849, making his profession a year later, followed by a theological course starting in Beckheim and finishing at the Franciscan convent in St-Truiden. He was ordained in Liège on 10 June 1854 and spent the rest of his life in Hasselt, twenty miles north west of Liège. He served as guardian and vicar of the province and also twice as provincial, in 1890 and 1899, and for twenty-six years as director of the Franciscan Secular Order of Hasselt.

In the mould of the Curé d'Ars (St John Vianney, 1786–1859, declared patron of all parish clergy in 1929; 4 August), the fame of whose holiness would have been well known to him, Fr Valentine spent long hours in the confessional and became known for seeing right into the hearts of his penitents, who came from long distances to confess to him. He also gained a reputation not only as a simple direct preacher but as someone who spoke words of wisdom wherever he went. His devotions were those of the time: the Sacred Heart, the Blessed Sacrament of the altar, and the Virgin Mary, especially as Immaculate, as he had been ordained in the year the dogma of the Immaculate Conception was defined. The Eucharist was at the heart of his life as a priest, and he encouraged the faithful to receive Communion frequently: in this he was somewhat in advance of his time. He died in Hasselt on 1 January 1905, aged seventy-seven, and was beatified with four others in the last beatification ceremony of 2003, on 9 November.

Bd Sigmund Gorazdowski, *Founder* (1845–1920)

Sigmund (Zygmund) Gorazdowski was born on 1 November 1845 in Sanok, in the extreme south east of Poland, which is now less than twenty miles from the border with Ukraine but was at the time of his birth part of the Austro-Hungarian Empire as the crown land of Galicia (see The Martyrs of Ukraine; 7 March). He was the second of the seven Gorazdowski children and grew up in harsh conditions that contributed to serious chest illnesses from an early age. After grammar school in Przemysl he studied law at Lvov University but became convinced he had a vocation to the priesthood and abandoned these studies in his second year to enter the Senior Seminary of the Holy Ghost—Latin-rite in a predominantly Greek Catholic area—in Lvov (now the regional capital of western Ukraine, spelt L'viv in Ukrainian, Lwów in Polish, and Lvov in Russian and common Western usage). He managed to complete his theological studies despite his poor health, went through an intensive two-year course of treatment for his chest ailment, and was ordained priest in Lvov Cathedral on 25 July 1871.

In the first six years of his priesthood he worked as a parish priest and administrator in five towns or villages in the region, followed by an appointment to the church of St Martin and Our Lady of the Snows in Lvov and then to the parish of St Nicholas in Lvov, where he spent the next forty years, almost the rest of his life. As a young priest he was noted for his outstanding pastoral care and his total dedication. During a cholera epidemic in Wojnitów he helped the sick with complete disregard for his own health and placed the dead into their coffins with his own hands despite the serious danger of infection, winning fame beyond the Christian community as a holy man.

His concern for the spiritual development of his flock led Fr Gorazdowski to produce and publish a "People's Catechism," of which he edited several editions. He himself undertook the work of teaching the catechism in many schools. He also wrote *Educational Norms and Principles*, addressed to parents and teachers, and further books and articles on pastoral, educational, and social issues. In addition, he started the Bonus Pastor institute for priests.

In the charitable sphere he was active in a variety of areas, including serving for long years as secretary to the Institute of Poor Christians. Learning the details of the very difficult moral and economic situations in which many of the inhabitants of Lvov for various reasons found themselves led him to fund directly many Christian charitable works. In 1882, with the help of a charitable society, he began a refuge for beggars in which they could undertake voluntary work. The effectiveness of this house became clear when many of the inmates stopped begging and returned to working for a living, with a renewed belief in their own worth. Also in 1882 Fr Gorazdowski's involvement with the poor led to the establishment of the Lvov People's Kitchen, where the poor of the town or impecunious students could get a daily meal for a nominal sum or often for nothing.

Gorazdowski was the instigator of the Lvov Institute, a hospice where the incurably sick and chronic invalids, rejected by hospitals, received appropriate care for body and soul. Other ventures included a teacher training college, where he built a dormitory for poor students, and the Child Jesus Institute for single mothers and abandoned babies, responsible for rescuing many mothers and over 3,000 children from death. He also founded the Catholic school of St Joseph, with lessons given in Polish and German, and co-founded the Union Institute, providing help to the poor and sick, and the Benevolent Society. On 17 February 1884 he founded the Congregation of Sisters of Mercy of St Joseph, to carry on the work of these charitable institutions.

Fr Sigmund Gorazdowski died on 1 January 1920, renowned throughout Lvov as "Father of the poor and priest of the homeless," and was buried in the city's Lyczakowski cemetery. He was beatified together with Bishop Joseph Bilczewski of Lvov (see 20 Mar.), with whom he had worked closely on his charitable ventures, at Lvov racecourse on 26 June 2001, during Pope John Paul II's pastoral visit to Ukraine. "His extraordinary charity," the Pope said in his homily, "led him to dedicate himself unstintingly to the poor, despite his precarious health ... His creativity and dedication in this area were almost boundless."

❖

The Sisters of Mercy of St Joseph today work in Poland, France, Germany, Italy, Brazil, Congo, and Cameroon, teaching and serving those in need of all sorts of help: the poor and abandoned, children, the sick, the elderly, lonely, and homeless.

2

Bd Marie-Anne Blondin, *Founder* (1809–1890)

The daughter of Jean Baptiste Blondin and Marie Rose Limoges, born on 18 April 1809 at Terrebonne (now a suburb of Montreal) in the province of Quebec, she was christened Esther. She grew up illiterate like the rest of her family, and found work as a domestic servant, working first for a merchant in her village and then at the convent of the Sisters of the Congregation of Notre Dame (founded in Montreal by St Margaret Bourgeoys in 1653). There she learned to read and write and entered the novitiate, but ill health forced her to leave.

Esther was then invited by another former novice, Suzanne Pineault, to teach in the parochial school of Vaudreuil. A few years later she was appointed *directrice* (Head), and the school began to prepare teachers for rural schools, becoming known as the Blondin Academy. At the time virtually all education was in church hands, but there was a strict rule that girls could be taught only by women and boys only by men. This meant that parishes either had to run two schools or discriminate, with the result that many simply had none. She saw that teaching boys and girls in the same school was the only solution and sought permission to found a new religious Congregation to put this radical idea into practice. The bishop and the government supported her, and the Congregation of the Sisters of St Anne was founded in Vaudreuil on 8 September 1850. Esther became the first superior, taking the names Marie-Anne in religion.

The venture flourished, and increasing numbers prompted a move of the motherhouse to Saint Jacques de l'Achigan (now Saint Jacques de Montcalm) three years later. There, like so many other nineteenth-century women pioneers (and St Margaret Bourgeoys two centuries earlier), she fell foul of interfering male clergy—this time in the person of the Congregation's chaplain, an ambitious young priest named Fr Louis Adolphe Maréchal, who tried to take over the Sisters' financial and spiritual affairs and to sabotage Marie-Anne's work at every turn. He had her removed from her position as superior general and forced her to leave the motherhouse. She was appointed Head at another convent school, but four years later Maréchal had her recalled to the motherhouse and publicly humiliated her, banning her from any administrative role for the rest of her life—a further thirty-two years. Reduced, as she said, to a *zéro*, she carried out menial tasks, working in the laundry and the ironing room. Her Sisters several times elected her superior, but she never even tried to accept the position. The Congregation spread in her lifetime all over Canada, to Alaska and the Yukon, to New York, Boston, and elsewhere in the eastern States of the United States.

Marie-Anne died of natural causes at Lachine, near Montreal (where the motherhouse had moved in 1864), on 2 January 1890, at the age of eighty. In 1917 a new chaplain at the motherhouse began asking those who had known her about her life and gave a series of conferences on her. This began the process of her posthumous rehabilitation. In 1950, the centenary year of the foundation, Archbishop Emile Léger of Montreal opened the diocesan cause for her beatification. Pope John Paul II declared her venerable in 1991; a miracle was accepted as authentic in 1999, and she was beatified on 29 April 2001. The Pope in his homily called her "a model of a life given to love and inspired by Christ's death and resurrection" but somewhat underplayed the injustice she suffered, saying merely that "she would humbly accept the Church's decisions and until her death did menial tasks for her Sisters' good."

A biography by Eugène Nadeau, OMI, *Martyr of Silence* (1956), brought to light many concealed aspects of Anne Marie's life. Several studies in French are listed on the Sisters of Sainte Anne website.

By the end of the nineteenth century the Sisters were working in Florida, West Virginia, Missouri, and Maryland. Farther afield they run missions in Haiti, Chile, and Cameroon. Besides their educational work, they take care of the sick and the elderly, with special ministries to AIDS sufferers and the handicapped: *Orders*, pp. 10–11.

4

Bd Manuel González García, *Bishop and Founder* (1877–1940)

Manuel was the fourth of five children born to Martín González Lara, who worked as a carpenter, and his wife Antonia. The family was poor and devout. One of Manuel's cherished childhood memories was to have been part of the *seises*, the group of choristers of Seville Cathedral who dance in the sanctuary on the feasts of Corpus Christi and the Immaculate Conception. He surprised his parents by applying to take the examinations to enter the diocesan seminary, which he passed. He financed his years of study by working as a domestic servant.

He was ordained on 21 September 1906 by Cardinal Marcelo Spinola of Seville (beatified in 1987). The following year he was sent to preach a mission in Palomares del Río, a small town just south west of Seville, where the sacristan gave him such a horrifying account of the sort of reception he might expect that he almost fled. Instead he prayed at the foot of a crucifix. The figure was probably one of the super-realistic polychrome wood figures of the kind carried in Seville's Holy Week processions, as he commented that, "The look of Jesus Christ in those figures is a look that gets nailed into your soul and is never forgotten. It came to be a sort of starting point for me to see, understand, and grasp the whole of my priestly ministry." In 1905 Manuel was posted to Huelva, near the "Coast of Light" west of Seville, where he had to work patiently and hard to revive religious feeling among a very indifferent population. He did what he could for the poor and for children, for whom he started schools. He wrote his reflections on his years there in the first of his many books, *Lo que puede un cura hoy* ("What a priest can do today"), which became a standard manual for parish priests.

In a region of decrepit and abandoned churches and shrines, Manuel came to see Jesus in the Sacrament of the altar as the most abandoned of the poor and began to beg people to become the "Marys of those abandoned tabernacles" in imitation of the women who stayed at the foot of Jesus' cross. This appeal gave rise to the movement of "Work for tabernacles and calvaries," whose purpose was to "respond with reparational love to the love of Christ in the Eucharist." This lay movement was followed by a Congregation of priests, the Eucharistic

Missionaries, in 1918; a corresponding Congregation of religious sisters, the Eucharistic Missionaries of Nazareth, in 1921; the Auxiliary Missionaries of Nazareth in 1932; and a movement for young people, the Eucharistic Youth of Reparation, in 1939. The expansion was carried forward largely by the diffusion of a magazine he started, *El granito de arena* ("The little grain of sand"), and this encouraged him to seek papal approval for his foundations. This was granted by Pope St Pius X (21 Aug.) in November 1912.

Pius' successor, Benedict XV, appointed Manuel as auxiliary bishop of Málaga in 1916 and diocesan bishop in 1920. He celebrated his appointment by giving a banquet for 3,000 poor children, at which the city authorities—who would usually have been the beneficiaries—and priests and seminarians served the children. He spent time studying the conditions in his diocese and decided that the main cause of the sorry state of the Church was the quality of its priests. He saw the current diocesan seminary as beyond redemption and embarked on building a new one, in which the Eucharist was to be, "in the pedagogical order, the most effective stimulus; in the academic, the first teacher and the first assignment; in the disciplinary, the most vigilant inspector; in the ascetical, the most living model; in the economic, the great provider; and in the architectural, the cornerstone." The priests this institution was to produce would be "hosts in union with the consecrated Host," who would "give and give themselves to God and for the sake of their neighbour in the most absolute and irrevocable way."

The dream was not to become reality. Málaga was one of the most anti-clerical and republican areas of Spain, and with the coming of the Republic this active bishop became a marked man. A direct attack was made on him on 11 May 1931, when the bishop's residence was set on fire and he was forced to take refuge with supporters, then to move to Gibraltar so as not to jeopardize their lives. From there he moved to Madrid and governed his diocese as best he could from there. In 1935 he was appointed bishop of Palencia, in northern Castile, an area that remained under Nationalist control during the civil war (1936–1939) and free from revolutionary anti-Church violence. He spent his last years, in declining health but still active, as bishop of the diocese. He wrote regularly throughout his years of ministry, his many books inspiring love of the Eucharist, guiding young priests, encouraging lay people to pray, and instructing catechists.

Manuel died on 4 January 1940 and was buried in Palencia Cathedral. The words of his final wish were inscribed on his tomb: "I ask to be buried next to a tabernacle so that my bones, after my death, like my tongue and my pen in life, can always be saying to those who pass by, 'There's Jesus! There he is! Don't leave him abandoned!'" Pope John Paul II promulgated his heroic virtue in 1998 and approved the miracle required for his beatification on 20 December 1999. His beatification took place on 29 April 2001. The Pope in his homily held him up as a model of Eucharistic faith whose example is still relevant to the Church today.

❖

Manuel's complete works were re-issued in a uniform edition in 2001. Titles include *El abandono de los Sagrarios acompañados; Oremos en el Sagrario como se oraba en el Evangelio; Artes para ser apóstol; La gracia en la educación,* and *Arte y liturgia.* Information from *Oss.Rom.,* Spanish weekly edition, 29 April 2001.

5

St Genevieve Torres Morales, *Founder* (1870–1956)

Born in Almenara in eastern Spain, twenty miles north of Valencia, Genevieve (Genoveva) was the youngest of six children, of whom four had died by the time she was eight, when both her parents also died, leaving her caring for her one surviving elder brother, José. She was obliged to abandon her brief schooling, though she continued to attend catechism classes on Sundays. José was somewhat taciturn and aloof, so her childhood was solitary as well as hard. Accustomed to spiritual reading from the age of about ten, she had an early sense that life should consist of doing God's will.

Genevieve suffered a major trauma when she was thirteen: a tumour in her left leg led to gangrene, and the limb had to be amputated. The surgery was done at her home, without anaesthetic: the pain was terrible, and the wound never healed properly. Besides having to walk with crutches, she suffered recurrent pain from it for the rest of her life. The fact that she lived to eighty-six is a tribute to her determination. She spent the nine years 1885–1894 living at the *Casa de la Merced* ("Mercy Home") orphanage run by the Carmelite Sisters of Charity in Valencia. She continued with her spiritual reading, which would have included the Spanish Carmelite classics of St Teresa of Avila and St John of the Cross, moving deeper into understanding and practice of a "spiritual life," so that she could write quite technically of her progress: "I loved freedom of heart very much, and worked and am working to achieve it fully ... It does the soul so much good that every effort is nothing compared with this free condition of the heart." She asked if she could join the Carmelites but was told that her health made this impossible.

She left the orphanage in 1894 and, with two other women who supported themselves by working, took a small house in Valencia, which they opened to some homeless women, sharing with them a life of poverty and prayer. Having identified such women as representing a category in special need and yet not cared for specifically by any organization, she spent the next seventeen years helping them as she could. Then, in 1911, Canon Barbarrós of Valencia Cathedral suggested that Genevieve should start a community to help poor, homeless, and abandoned women achieve independence. With his help, and that of the Jesuit Fr Martín Sánchez, she began a community in Valencia. The original three women took in four others as resident guests. The appeal of the venture was soon proved, with more recruits arriving, and a clear need to open similar houses in other parts of Spain led to the next being founded in Zaragoza. Women who wanted to help others came as well as those in need of help, and they formed the Congregation of the Sacred Heart of Jesus and the Holy Angels, known as *Angélicas*. Those who could pay for their keep and care did so; those who could not were equally welcome. Prayer, especially before the reserved Blessed Sacrament, was an essential ingredient of life for all.

Community members started to wear religious dress in 1912, and in 1915 they began to take private vows. In December 1925 the archbishop of Zaragoza established them as a Congregation of diocesan right, which enabled Genevieve and eighteen companions to make public vows. Genevieve was duly elected as the first mother superior. The work spread, despite setbacks under Republican governments from 1931 and disruption during the civil war of 1936–1939. Mother Genevieve, whose personal desire was for quiet solitude and whose health and disability made travel difficult for her, spent the rest of her life in the service of the growing Congregation, which received papal recognition in 1953.

Genevieve died of natural causes in Zaragoza on 5 January 1956, venerated during her lifetime for her activities and her spiritual writings. The diocesan cause of her canonization was rapidly mounted, and she was beatified by Pope John Paul II on 29 January 1995, and canonized in Madrid's Plaza de Colón as one of a group of five Spaniards on 4 May 2003. In his homily the Pope described her as "an instrument of God's tender love for lonely people in need of love, comfort, and physical and spiritual care."

10

St Léonie Aviat, *Founder*, 1844–1914

Léonie was born on 16 September 1844 in the town of Sézanne in the Champagne region, sixty miles east of Paris, where her parents, Théodore Aviat and Emilie Caillot, were shopkeepers. At the age of eleven she was sent to board at the Visitation (the Order founded by St Jane de Chantal; 12 Dec.) convent in the historic city of Troyes, thirty miles away to the south east. There she found two great spiritual guides in the persons of the superior, Mother Marie de Sales Chappuis, and the chaplain, Fr Louis Brisson. She spent five years at the school and emerged with both a well-developed sense of the social problems of the time (when rapid industrialization was drawing large numbers of young girls in from rural areas to work in mills in the cities), and a conviction that she had a religious vocation. As she was only sixteen, Mother Chappuis and Fr Brisson advised her to wait until God's will became clearer.

Léonie's parents were unconvinced by the vocation, and set about preparing her for marriage. They introduced her to a suitable and wealthy young man, but she remained adamant that she would be a religious. Her father asked her to wait until she was twenty-one before any final decision was made. Her own desire became a conviction when she took her mother's spectacles for repair to a factory in Sézanne. She saw a workroom full of young women and knew that her life must be devoted to helping and guiding young workers in such situations.

Some years earlier, in 1858, Fr Brisson had started an initiative, the *Oeuvre Saint François de Sales*, to house, educate, and train the young girls who were coming into Troyes, attracted by work (however low-paid), but with nowhere to stay and no protection against the exploitation—sexual and otherwise—that threatened them. He had found volunteers to help, but no one with real dedication and ability. Léonie was exactly the right person, and he enlisted her collaboration when she was on a retreat at the convent in 1866. On 16 April she took over the administration of the foundation, known from then on as *Oeuvre ouvrière* ("work for [female] workers"). Two years later she and a companion from school were clothed in what had become the germ of a new Congregation, formally known as the Oblate Sisters of St Francis de Sales (though still generally referred to as *Oeuvre ouvrière*). She took the saint's name (adapted to the female *Françoise*, [Frances]) as her name in religion, made her religious profession in October 1871, and was elected superior general the following year.

The Congregation grew rapidly under her guidance, opening youth clubs and homes where girls could receive practical training as well as education in the faith. Frances' whole emphasis was on working for others: she taught the dignity of work, even at this lowly level; she encouraged the girls to save something each week, even from their very meagre wages, opening a small savings bank for them; she provided hobbies and pursuits, showing a pedagogical enlightenment well in advance of her time. Her inspiration was the fact that Jesus had worked during his time in Nazareth, a favourite theme of Fr Brisson, who taught that oblates resembled the saviour and his mother by their work. "Jesus the worker" was to live in the oblates and act through them. The inspiration was handed on, and girls from "Fr Brisson's home" then became apostles to others in their places of work. The foundation expanded to provide free elementary schools and fee-paying boarding schools. Frances moved to Paris to organize one of the latter, and stayed there to run it for eight years, accepting the wrench away from the *Oeuvre oeuvrière* and the working girls she had come to love as the will of God.

She returned to Troyes to find Fr Brisson under suspicion from the diocesan authorities—a not uncommon phase in the lives of innovative founders, particularly those who concern themselves with the welfare of young women—and for a time their disapproval extended to her too, forcing her to give up her post as superior general. The foundation recovered the respect it deserved, however, and after being re-elected in 1893 she spread the work farther afield, to other countries in Europe and "mission territories" in South Africa and Ecuador. The next wave of troubles came not from Church but from State, when in 1903 laws were passed depriving religious Congregations of their property. Some of the houses and schools closed altogether, but she managed to keep some operating by requiring the Sisters to wear lay dress and so disguise their identity. She herself was forced into exile in April 1904 and settled in Perugia, moving the motherhouse there and continuing to work on the Constitutions. A great sadness was the death of Fr Brisson, who had been too old to leave France, on 2 February 1908.

Pope Leo XIII had given provisional approval to the Oblates for ten years in 1890, the period being extended on account of the troubles in France. The final approbation of the Constitutions came from Pope St Pius X (21 Aug.) in 1911. Frances died after a short bout of bronchial pneumonia on 10 January 1914. She was already regarded as "the saint" in Perugia, and people flocked past her open coffin for a last look at her. The main precept she left her Sisters was, "Let us work for the happiness of others." Pope John Paul II beatified her in 1992 and canonized her on 25 November 2001. After her death the Oblates of St Francis de Sales spread to the United States, where they currently staff three schools. The miracle that opened the way to her canonization took place in Springfield, Illinois, in March 1992, when a girl named Bernadette McKenzie Kutufaris recovered from an incurable spine condition, "tethered spinal cord syndrome," during a novena to Mother Frances de Sales Aviat.

Fuller than usual biographical information is available at oblatosamlat. cybereme.net; there is a detailed account of the miracle at County Press online. com, for 2 June 2003. Further information can be obtained from the Salesian Center for Faith and Culture, De Sales University, Center Valley, Pennsylvania 18034.

Bd María Dolores Rodríguez Sopeña Ortega, *Founder* (1848–1918)

Dolores' father, Tomás Rodríguez Sopeña, a qualified lawyer apparently unable to find work in Madrid because he had qualified at too young an age, moved to Vélez Rubio, a town in the northern part of the province of Almería in south-eastern Spain, where he found work as estate manager for the marquis of Vélez. Dolores was born there on 30 December 1848. (Her mother's name was Nicolasa Ortega Salomón, which by Spanish custom would normally make her surnames Rodríguez Ortega, not Rodríguez Sopeña Ortega, but she gave the name Sopeña to various foundations, so it seems advisable to retain it.) Her father was then appointed magistrate in various towns in the Alpujarras area south of Granada, and in 1866 he became an attorney in the provincial capital of Almería. His position meant that Dolores "came out" in society, which she did not appreciate, being already more inclined to apostolic rather than social activities. She looked after a leper and two girls suffering from typhoid, keeping this secret from her parents, though her mother and she together visited the sick under the auspices of the St Vincent de Paul Society.

In 1869 her father was posted to Puerto Rico. He went there with one of his sons (Dolores was one of seven siblings), while his wife took the others to Madrid. There Dolores taught the catechism to women prisoners, hospital patients, and Sunday school pupils. In 1872 the family moved to join her father and brother in Puerto Rico. She became close to the Jesuits there, taking one, Fr Goicoechea, as her spiritual adviser. Still in her early twenties, she started the Association of the Sodality of the Virgin Mary, as well as primary schools for poor children, where she taught reading and writing in addition to the catechism. The following year her father was nominated State Attorney in Santiago de Cuba (Cuba was still a Spanish colony), and the family moved there, to a society torn apart by religious schism. This restricted Dolores' activities to visiting patients in a military hospital, but once the schism was resolved she immediately took up her apostolic endeavours once more, starting three "Instruction Centers" in poor *barrios*, where she taught and provided medical care. She asked to join the local community of the Sisters of Charity but was rejected on account of her poor eyesight (the consequence of an eye operation when she was eight).

Her mother died in Cuba, and her father, not wishing to remain there, asked to take retirement. In 1877 the family moved back to Madrid, where Dolores took up her former activities as well as looking after the house and her father. He died in 1883, and she felt free to explore her own religious vocation once more. A new spiritual director advised her to enter a Visitation convent, but ten days there were enough to convince her that the contemplative life was not for her, and she returned to her activities in the wider community. In 1885 Dolores opened what she called a "Social House," where people in various sorts of need came to seek resolution of their problems. A visit to a recently released woman prisoner led her to the slum district known as *Las Injurias* ("The insults"), where she was shocked by the level of deprivation. She took to visiting families there every week and encouraging friends to come with her. The group became organized into what she initially called "Works of the Doctrines" (Spanish *doctrinas*, indicating a mission territory rather than just "doctrine") and later the "Workers' Centre." The bishop of Madrid encouraged her to found an association of lay people—which still operates as the "Sopeña Lay Movement"—

and with approval from the civic authorities she extended the *doctrinas* into eight other districts of Madrid. Then in 1896 she broadened their activities to other parts of Spain, travelling endlessly (199 journeys in four years) around a harsh land where communications were still very undeveloped.

Dolores was in Rome for the Jubilee Year of 1900, and while she was there the archbishop of Toledo (the primatial see of Spain) suggested that she develop her lay association into a religious Institute. She began living in community with eight companions in Toledo in October 1901; they were known originally as the *Damas del Instituto Catequista* ("Ladies of the Catechetical Institute") and as such were approved by the Holy See in 1905, with direct approval coming from Pope St Pius X two years later. Dolores became superior general and added the María before her name. She was careful, however, not to place her social work solely in the hands of religious; nor did she, in the anti-clerical climate of the time, make her religious overtly so. She started a civil association, officially approved by the government in 1902, to parallel the religious one. This has flourished and become an integral part of the voluntary sector in many parts of Spain, as OSCUS (*Obra Social y Cultural Sopeña*). She also decided that members of the Institute would not wear habits, enabling them to approach all classes without building a wall of prejudice.

Behind all this activity and organization lay a deep feeling for the dignity of all as brothers and sisters in Christ. Her inner convictions lent her a fearlessness that took her unhesitatingly to rough *barrios* where most angels—certainly female ones—would definitely have feared to tread in that period.

The communities spread to other cities in Spain, concentrating on the newly industrialized areas where social problems were most acute. She was re-elected superior general at the first general chapter, held in 1910. In 1914 the first house outside Spain was opened in Rome, and in 1917 the first in America appeared. Mother María Dolores died in Madrid on 10 January 1918, already widely seen as a saint. The decree of heroic virtue was promulgated on 11 July 1992, and on 23 April 2002 a miracle attributed to her intercession was certified, clearing the way to her beatification on 23 March 2003. The Pope in his homily said that, "She wanted to respond to the challenge of making Christ's redemption present in the world of work. For this reason, she gave herself the goal of 'making all one single family in Jesus Christ.'"

The three institutions she founded—the Catechetical Institute, the Lay Movement, and the Social and Cultural Work—are all still active and operating in Spain, as well as in Argentina, Chile, Colombia, Cuba, the Dominican Republic, Ecuador, and Mexico.

11

St Thomas of Cori (1655–1729)

Francesco Antonio Placidi was born in the town of Cori, thirty miles south-east of Rome, in the Latina coastal region of Italy, on 4 June 1655. His family were peasant farmers, and both his parents had died by the time he reached the age of fourteen, leaving him as the sole male in the family and so the only breadwinner. He shepherded sheep for eight years, until both his sisters had made suitable marriages. He was then free to pursue his desire to become a Franciscan friar.

He entered a local convent, where he had got to know the friars, and was then sent to the Holy Trinity Convent in Orvieto on 7 February 1677, taking the name Tommaso (Thomas) in religion. After five years of preparation he was ordained priest in 1683 and given a licence to preach. His obvious gifts earned him the post of vice novice-master immediately after his ordination. He ministered in the diocese of Subiaco, a mountainous area east of Rome, to such good effect that he became known as "the apostle to the *Sublacense,*" as the locality was known.

Thomas' sermons were collected into a manuscript volume. He became an expert spiritual director—he often had to be deterred from spending "from morning to night" every day in the confessional—and he was in constant demand to attend to the sick and the dying. He improved public morality and had a gift for resolving personal conflicts. He refused to accept Mass offerings and summed up all the other virtues in his radical practice of poverty. Humble and patient to an exceptional degree, Thomas encouraged humiliations by his brother friars, bore an ulcer in his leg that would not heal for forty years and—more important for him—constant aridity in prayer, despite being described as "a man who became prayer."

Thomas soon became part of the Hermitage or Recollection movement within the Order, effectively yet another wave of reform seeking ever stricter observance of the original Rule and spirit of St Francis (4 Oct.), as each previous attempt seemed doomed to lapse into what was seen as the more lax Conventual way of life. Dating from as far back as St Bonaventure (d. 1274; 15 July), the movement flourished at different times in different provinces. In the latter half of the seventeenth century, these hermitages (*ritiri* in Italian) became widespread in Italy thanks to the efforts of Bd Bonaventue of Barcelona (d. 1684), who established the first houses in the city of Rome itself. Building on his example, Thomas founded one in the town of Civitella (since re-named Bellegra, a hilltop village, now of some 3,000 inhabitants, in the Subiaco area), followed by another at Palombara, in the Sabine hills near Rome. He lived at Bellegra from 1684 to the time of his death, except for six years as Guardian of the convent at Palombara. He wrote Constitutions for both houses, thus establishing yet another branch of the Franciscan family. In 1756 these Constitutions were extended to all the Order's hermitages by rule of the general chapter held at Murcia in Spain. They were very strict in spirit, enjoining a life of contemplation and religious observance.

Many eminent Franciscans, including future saints, spent time at the hermitage of Bellegra, which became a powerhouse of Franciscan spirituality. At times Thomas was deserted by brethren who found his Rule too strict, but he waited patiently for them to return or for others to arrive. He preached tirelessly, in simple and direct style, choosing humble venues in preference to the great churches that were offered to him. He died on 11 January 1729, at the age of seventy-four. The cause of his beatification was soon introduced, in 1737, and he was beatified in 1786. He then had to wait over 200 years to be canonized, which he finally was by Pope John Paul II on 21 November 1999.

❖

The original manuscript of the Constitutions is kept at Bellegra. On the Hermitage movement see L. Iriarte de Aspurz, OFM Cap., *Franciscan History*, English translation 1982, pp. 59–75, 169–75. Bellegra, suppressed in the eighteenth century, has been extensively enlarged since 1929 and is now a very popular retreat centre: details in G. M. Grasselli and P. Tarallo, *Guida ai Monasteri d'Italia*, 8th edn 1996, p. 298, and on various websites accessed (some more in theory) under Bellegra.

12

St Bernard of Corleone (1605–1667)

Born Filippo Latino in the Sicilian town of Corleone (now of *Godfather* movies fame) in February 1605, he was the fifth of six siblings. His father was a shoemaker, renowned for his charity to the poor of the town, who imbued his children with the same spirit. At the time, Sicily was under Spanish occupation. Corleone had succumbed after fierce resistance, and these circumstances developed another side to Filippo's character: the Spaniards encouraged the young men of the town to learn military skills, presumably with the intention of recruiting them into their army, and Filippo became an expert swordsman, ready to defend his reputation by challenging to a duel anyone who denied his reputation as the most expert swordsman in the whole of Sicily. His final duel was with a certain Catino, who fell to the ground, causing Filippo, who believed he had killed him, to seek sanctuary from justice in the Capuchin convent.

There he had time and peace to reflect on his past ways, which led him to apply to join the Capuchins as a lay brother. Admitted to the novitiate in nearby Caltanissetta, he received the habit on 13 December 1631, taking the name Bernardo in religion. From then on, his life was one of prayer and penance. He adopted a personal style of austerity beyond the normal call of the Order, living habitually on three pieces of bread a day, dipped in brackish water, and sleeping on a board. It was said that he never ate a proper meal during the thirty-seven years he spent as a friar. He scourged himself regularly, as was the spiritual fashion at the time, regarding his body as "brother ass" in the Franciscan tradition. He espoused a humility that made him kneel to address his superiors and even his fellow brethren. He cooked for the brethren, nursed those who were sick, and endeavoured to help all in any way he could.

Bernardo moved to the nearby convent of Bivona, where an epidemic laid all his brethren low, leaving him the only one healthy and ministering to all their needs. When he too was affected, he withdrew to the parish church, sat under a statue of St Francis and, it is said, refused to move until he was cured so that he could return to helping his brethren. St Francis duly obliged, and Bernardo returned to his ministry of service. This story is authenticated by a Dr Caracciolo, the local doctor responsible for attending the brethren when they were sick. Bernardo also developed a reputation for curing sick animals, on which the local families depended for their survival.

Toward the end of his life he was rewarded with a vision of the Lord, who dipped a piece of bread in the wound in his side and gave it to Bernardo, thereby conveying a sense of the joys of paradise to him. He died at the age of sixty-two, on 12 January 1667. A fellow friar who was by his bedside claimed that he died in ecstasy, repeating the word "Paradise" and counting the blessings of a religious life well lived. His fame of holiness preceded his death, and at his funeral crowds gathered in the hope of obtaining a relic. Miracles were attributed to him after his death, and he was beatified by Pope Clement XIII in 1768, already just over a hundred years after his death. He then had to wait a further 223 years for canonization, on 10 June 2001—possibly not a record, but a very long period, especially given the fact that he was a member of an influential Order with many saints among its number. Perhaps the facts of, and the legends that accrued around, his somewhat violent youth militated against the final step, until new criteria made his thirty-seven years of prayer, penance, and service a more than long enough period of "heroic virtue" to erase what had gone before.

Bd Nicholas Bunkerd Kitbamrung (1895–1944)

Thailand's first missionary priest of local origin was one of six children, born in the Nakhon Chaisiri district, and brought up as a Christian. Through contact with overseas missionaries, he decided to become a priest and studied first at the junior seminary of Hanf Xan and then at the major seminary of Penang, followed by a theology degree course at an international college in Malaysia. He was ordained in Bangkok in 1926 and engaged in pastoral work, first at Bang Kok Khneuk and then, from 1928, at Phitsanulok.

In 1930 he was despatched on a special mission to northern Vietnam, then part of French Indo-China, with the purpose of bringing Catholics who had lapsed from practice of their faith back into communion with the Church. He spent seven years there and was then posted to the district of Khorat. When the war for independence from the French broke out in 1940, Fr Nicholas was accused of spying for the French. This was probably at least partly as a result of a general perception that Christianity was allied to the colonial power: "The Thai people misunderstood the Church: they saw it as part of French culture and began to persecute foreign missionaries as well as Thai priests and laity. Schools the Church had opened were closed, many churches destroyed, local Catholics were hunted down" (*Fides* agency, quoting "a local Catholic," 5 May 2000). Fr Nicholas was arrested on 12 January 1941 and, after nine months in prison, was tried and sentenced to fifteen years. There he still managed to minister to his fellow prisoners, catechizing and baptizing sixty-eight of them before the conditions of deprivation contributed to him contracting tuberculosis, leading to his death on 12 January 1944.

The cardinal archbishop of Bangkok, with five other Thai bishops, forty priests and some 300 faithful of the diocese travelled to Rome for the beatification ceremony on 5 March 2000, the first of the Jubilee Year. The cardinal remembered seeing Fr Nicholas "when he returned home to visit his family in Nakhon Pathom. And I believe he was genuinely holy." Pope John Paul II described him as "a man of prayer ... outstanding in teaching the faith, in seeking out the lapsed, and in his charity toward the poor." One of the concelebrants at the Mass, Fr John Bosco Sukhum Kitsanguan, was a great-nephew of Fr Nicholas: he relates that an uncle encouraged Nicholas to enter the seminary and his mother consented only because she thought he would soon be back.

15

St Arnold Janssen, *Founder* (1837–1909)

The founder of the Divine Word Missionaries was born on 5 November 1837, the second of ten children of Johann Janssen and his wife, Anna Katharina. His birthplace was the small German town of Goch, near the Rhine and just over the border from Holland, about half way between Arnhem and Düsseldorf. He later described his parents as "plain and simple;" his father was a small farmer, who also engaged in transportation. The family atmosphere was strongly religious: his father, a strong patriarchal figure, would read the Sunday's Gospel, plus a commentary on it, and examine the children rigorously on the catechism; his mother was more given to her private prayer and devotions.

Arnold was sent to a new middle school opened in Goch: the first principal knew the family and recognized Arnold as a child who would benefit from further education. Arnold felt a calling to the priesthood, and after a year and a half moved on to the minor diocesan seminary in Münster, followed from the age of eighteen by philosophical and theological studies at Borromeo College in Münster, which had been established the previous year. He sped through his philosophy course in a year, leaving him, at nineteen, too young to enter the major seminary, so he trained to be a teacher for a year at the university of Bonn. This led to the offer of a teaching post in Berlin, but he turned that down and returned to Münster to complete his theology. He was ordained a diocesan priest on 15 August 1861 and sent to teach in a secondary school in Bocholt, also just on the German side of the border with Holland, about twenty miles north-east of his birthplace. He spent the next twelve years there, specializing in mathematics and natural sciences and gaining a reputation for being strict but just. He was also appointed diocesan director of the Apostleship of Prayer, which focused largely, in the manner of the time, on devotion to the Sacred Heart.

In due course Arnold felt the need for wider horizons. Attendance at the General Convention of Catholic Organizations in Germany and Austria at Innsbruck in 1867 led to an increased interest in the mission fields, and in particular to the part he felt the German Church should play in evangelization. He decided that developing this should be his life's work, and in 1873 resigned from his teaching post. To provide himself with a living, he became chaplain to the Ursuline Sisters at Kempen, but his main concern was the launch of a new magazine, which would be a vehicle for his own ideas on missionary work as well as reporting from mission fields. The first number of this, the *Little Messenger of the Sacred Heart*, was published in July 1874 (and publication has never ceased). But the cultural climate in Germany was inimical to such initiatives, with the ruling party passing laws to bring all aspects of Church life under civil control, followed by Chancellor Bismark's unleashing of his *Kulturkampf*, more stringent laws which led to the expulsion of many priests and religious and the imprisonment of some bishops. No mission seminary was permitted in Germany, and Arnold decided that if there was to be a German missionary apostleship, as he was convinced there must be, it would have to be outside Germany. He raised funds through the magazine and, realizing that if the project was to take shape, he would have to organize it, looked for a site across the border in Holland.

Arnold managed to buy a dilapidated old tavern, named Ronck Villa, at Steyl, on the banks of the river Meuse (Maas in Dutch); with some encouragement—especially from the apostolic vicar of Hong Kong, Bishop Raimondi—and, despite some discouragement from local ecclesiastical authorities, established his first seminary there in 1875. By September there were nine residents, plus Arnold's brother Wilhelm, the Capuchin Br Juniper, who came from Germany to serve as cook, and 8 September 1875 is taken as the date of foundation of the Divine Word Missionaries. The community adopted the motto, *Vivat cor Jesu in cordibus hominum* ("May the heart of Jesus live in the hearts of men"). Arnold defined the twin objectives of the seminary as the training of missionaries and the cultivation of Christian sciences—to which some objected as a dilution of the missionary endeavour.

Restoration of the decrepit building and training of missionaries got under way in parallel. Within five years the foundation at Steyl had grown to many times its original size. Arnold was of the view that whatever was necessary could and should be undertaken, financed by money "already there, in the pockets of good people who will give it to you at the proper time," this became a self-fulfilling prophecy. More support services were needed, and in 1876 the Sisters of Divine Providence (founded in France in 1762 by Bd John Martin Moye and expelled from the country during the French Revolution), who had recently been expelled from Germany, came to take charge of the kitchens and the laundry. A printing press was installed to print the *Little Messenger*, which did provide a steady source of income to support growth. Another magazine, *Stadt Gottes* ("The City of God," still the largest illustrated Catholic family magazine in Germany) joined it in January 1876, distributed by thousands of volunteers throughout Germany, and the printing works grew, always keeping abreast of technical advances. It obviously did not need to be staffed by priests, and a parallel Congregation of lay brothers, the Divine Word Missionary Brothers, was founded. They were always the special object of Fr Arnold's attention, and by 1900 they outnumbered the priests. A further activity was the establishment of an "apostolic school," a sort of mission high school, which took in poor children without charging for their lodging.

The first two missionaries set out for China in March 1879. One of these was Joseph Freinademetz, who was to be beatified and canonized with Arnold (see 28 Jan.). Joseph came from northern Italy (then under Austrian rule), so the community was an international one from the start. The other was John Baptist von Anzer, who went on to become a bishop. Fr Janssen had pinpointed the Far East as a priority at the first general chapter in 1886, at which he was elected superior general: he defined the purpose of the Order as "proclamation of the Word of God on earth, through missionary activity among those non-Catholic peoples where this activity appears more successful. Hence we have in mind in the first place the non-Christian people especially in the Far East"—a very characteristic tempering of his blind faith with practical consideration of outcomes.

In the 1880s further Divine Word missionaries spread throughout China, which Arnold called "that great land of Jesus' longing," and their outreach was extended to Togo in 1892, Papua New Guinea in 1896, Japan in 1907, and Indonesia in 1912. Requests for missionaries began to come from Latin America also, and Divine Word missions were founded in Argentina in 1889, Ecuador in 1893 (but later abandoned), Brazil in 1895, and Chile in 1900. In the 1880s young women, not content with domestic roles, also applied to be trained as missionaries, and the first sixteen postulants of a Congregation for them, the Holy Spirit Missionary Sisters, were clothed in 1892. Four years later this produced a contemplative offshoot, the Sisters Servants of the Holy Spirit of Perpetual Adoration, led by Maria Helena Stollenwerk, the co-founder of the Missionary Sisters (beatified in 1995). Their purpose was to pray ceaselessly for the Church and especially for the two missionary Congregations. The Missionary Sisters first went overseas, to Argentina, in 1895.

Arnold never lost sight of his secondary aim for the seminary, the development of Christian sciences, and his missionaries were trained in disciplines such as linguistics and ethnology. Their learning bore fruit in the magazine *Anthropos* and in a corresponding Institute devoted to the natural sciences, whose members are Divine Word Missionaries from all over the world. A foundation was made in Rome, to which priests were sent to study theology, and another in Vienna, for which Arnold had to become an Austrian citizen. The Prussian government undid the prohibitions of Bismark and asked him to establish mission seminaries and staff missions in German colonies (which then included parts of present-day Poland and Austria): there is now a Polish province with its motherhouse in Silesia. Just before his death, Fr Janssen approved the extension of the Order's mission to the United States, leading to the building of St Mary Mission Seminary in Techny, Illinois, near Chicago.

Arnold was still active and healthy at the age of seventy, but he then developed a form of creeping paralysis that forced him to slow down in the last year of his life. He died on 15 January 1909, having achieved amazing feats by trust in the will of God and a remarkable ability to harness volunteers to carry out what he saw as that will—which was in effect anything they could accomplish. The diocesan process for his beatification was opened in 1933, and the apostolic process in 1943. He and Fr Freinademetz were beatified by Pope Paul VI on 19 October 1975, World Mission Sunday. In his homily the Pope said, "In Arnold Janssen the Church honours an indefatigable apostle of the Good News of Jesus Christ ... His life and work, rooted in his profound faith, were devoted especially to the missionary mandate of Christ: 'Go out to the whole world; proclaim the God news to all creation.'" At their canonization on 5 October 2003, Pope John Paul II said that Arnold Janssen "zealously carried out his priestly work, spreading the Word of God by means of the new mass media, especially the press," adding, "Obstacles did not dismay him."

❖

Butler, January, 2d edn, pp. 110–12, citing H. von Fischer, *Arnold Janssen* (1919); S. Kausbauer, *Arnold Janssen, Mensch von Gott für unser Zeit* (1936); and F.-J. Eilers and H. Helf, *Arnold Janssen, 1837–1909: A Pictorial Biography* (1987). On the Sisters of Divine Providence see *Orders*, p. 116; on the Missionary Sisters and the Holy Spirit Sisters, *ibid.*, pp. 194, 195. The Divine Word Missionaries website is informative.

The press at Steyl continued to grow and develop, first with powered letter-press, then rotogravure, and now the latest computer-assisted technology.

There are over 6,000 Divine Word Missionaries working in sixty-five countries, plus over 3,800 Missionary Sisters in thirty-five, and 400 Holy Spirit Sisters in ten. A further U.S. seminary was opened in St Louis in 1923, to train African-American priests for mission; six of its more than 100 ordained priests went on to become bishops. The mission extended to Vietnam in the 1980s (with the first Vietnamese priest ordained in 1985), and to Russia in 2003.

16

Bd Juana María Condesa Lluch, *Founder* (1862–1916)

Born into a wealthy family in Valencia, on the east coast of Spain, Juana María became one—among many beatified recently—of those devout and idealistic young nineteenth-century women who were appalled at conditions in their industrializing countries and set out to find a practical remedy. In the virtual absence of civic social welfare and before trade unions had come into their own, help for those least able to help themselves had to come from those prepared to devote their lives to the cause of the oppressed, and this effectively meant members of religious institutions founded for the purpose.

Juana María was well educated in a pious Catholic family whose piety was directed outward to the needs of others. As a teenager she felt deeply for the plight of workers who left the countryside (where they were usually landless and at best seasonally employed) to seek work in the factories of the large cities. There the work was routine and lacking in any human dignity. Women began to join the workforce and were even less protected than the men, besides being prey to sexual predation. By the time she was eighteen Juana María already felt a vocation to found a religious Congregation of women dedicated to helping such workers and their families. Cardinal Antolín Monescillo, the archbishop of

Valencia, told her she was too young to found a Congregation, but by 1884—when she was still only twenty-two—she had persuaded him to allow her to open a shelter to receive workers arriving in the city, where they were given not only food and a roof but spiritual formation too. This was followed by a school for their children. Other like-minded young women came to work with her, and her conviction that they should have a formal place in the Church grew. She finally received diocesan approval in 1892, and her Congregation came into being as the Handmaids of the Immaculate Conception, Protectress of Workers. Juana and her companions made their first vows in 1895, and the Congregation grew rapidly and spread to other cities in Spain, working as "handmaids of the Lord" wherever they saw the most acute need. The first Sisters took final vows in 1911, by which time Juana had only five years of life left to her, dying at the age of fifty-four on 16 January 1916.

The Congregation was approved provisionally in 1937, and formally in 1947. Juana María was beatified on 23 March 2003, when Pope John Paul II said of her that she was "prepared to dedicate herself totally to the love of God, founding the Congregation of the Handmaids of Mary Immaculate who, faithful to her charism, continue to be involved in the advancement of working women."

18

St Jaime Hilario, *Martyr* (1898–1937)

Manuel Barbal Cosan was born in the village of Enviny, in the foothills of the Pyrenees in the province of Lérida in northern Spain, on 2 January 1898. His parents worked as hill farmers and were devout Catholics. He wanted to become a priest and at the age of thirteen entered the seminary of La Seu d'Urgell. An ear infection that was to trouble him throughout his life forced him to abandon his studies for the priesthood, but in 1917 he joined the novitiate of the La Salle Brothers in Irún, taking the names Jaime Hilario (James Hilary) in religion.

Jaime worked as a catechist and teacher in Catalonia and in the Toulouse region of south-west France, during which time his literary gifts became apparent in contributions to numerous Christian journals; but his increasing deafness forced him to abandon teaching. He moved to Cambrils, near Tarragona on the coast of Catalonia, and worked in the garden of the Order's training house there. On the outbreak of the Spanish civil war on 18 July 1936 he took refuge in nearby Mollerosa but was arrested as a religious and taken to Lérida prison, from where he was sent back to Tarragona for trial. He was held on board a prison ship, the *Mahon*, with other priests and lay Christians, and refused the services of a lawyer, since he was going to tell nothing but the truth. He was condemned to death by the "People's Tribunal," on no grounds beyond his religious status—the only religious in a group of twenty-four and the only one not to have his sentence mitigated. On learning of the sentence, he wrote to his family:"God be blessed; I'll pray for all of you in heaven. What more could I desire than to die for no other crime but that of being a religious and for having made my contribution to the Christian education of children … I accept the sentence with joy … I shall die for God and my country. Farewell, I shall be waiting for you in heaven."

He was shot in a wood known as the Mount of Olives next to Tarragona cemetery at 3.30p.m. on 18 January 1937. His last words to his executioners were, "My friends, to die for Christ is to reign." To the horror of the picket (though some may have aimed wide), he remained standing after two volleys had been fired at him. Its members fled in terror while their commander, with a furious oath, despatched him with five pistol shots to the temple. He was associated with the other La Salle martyrs (Cyril Bertrand and Companions.; 9 Oct.) in their beatification ceremony in April 1990 and canonization on 21 November 1999.

Sources as for SS Cyril Bertrand and Comps. (9 Oct.). Quotation from letter above from Patron Saints Index, www.catholic-forum.com/saints/saintjef.

20

Bd Maria Cristina Brando, *Founder* (1856–1906)

The daughter of Giovanni Giuseppe Brando and Maria Concetta Marrazzo, a wealthy couple living in Naples, she was born on 1 May 1856 and christened Adelaida. Her mother died when she was only a few days old, and her father remarried, producing three more children with his second wife. She was educated at home, attended daily Mass, expressed a determination to become a saint, and showed an early inclination to enter religious life.

Adelaida's first attempt was early in her teens, when she tried join the Sacramentine Nuns in Naples but was prevented by her father. He then consented to her entering the Poor Clare convent of the Fiorentine, but she twice had to withdraw on account of illness, being nursed back to health at home. She did then join the Sacramentines as she had originally wished, taking simple vows in 1876 and the name María Cristina of the Immaculate Conception. Again her health forced to return home, however, and she was forced permanently to abandon this vocation. Her half-sister Concetta had also joined and then left the Poor Clares, and the two of them went to live as boarders with the newly-founded Teresian Sisters in their house at Torre del Greco near

Naples, while, together with other like-minded young women, they reflected on past failures and discerned a new way ahead. The result was the foundation of a new Congregation, originally known as the Pious Institute of the Perpetual Adoration of the Blessed Sacrament, with Maria Cristina as first superior. Encouraged by Ludovico of Casoria (see Bd Julia Salzano; 17 May) they moved to Casoria, north of Naples, where numbers grew quickly. The objective, besides perpetual adoration, was "the Christian education of young girls, through spiritual exercises, boarding schools, day schools, and nursery schools."

By 1892 there were seventy-six Sisters, and they acquired larger premises in Casoria. Maria Cristina built a cell next to the church, which she called her "*groticella*" (little grotto) and where she spent every night on a chair so as to be nearer to the Blessed Sacrament. She took her temporary vows in 1897 and permanent vows in 1902, the year before the Congregations received official approval from the Holy See and adopted the final form of its name, Sisters Expiatory Victims of Jesus in the Blessed Sacrament.

Maria Cristina died in Casoria on 20 January 1906, having suffered from bronchitis and heart problems for many years. Pope John Paul II beatified her, together with her fellow Casorian Julia Salzano, on 27 April 2003. Love of God and love of neighbour, she had said, were "two branches that stem from the same trunk," and the Pope commented on this in his homily: "Her desire to take part in Christ's passion, as it were, 'overflowed' into educational works, for the purpose of making people aware of their dignity and open to the Lord's merciful love."

❖

On the Sacramentine Nuns (Religious of the Blessed Sacrament and Our Lady) see *Orders*, pp. 52–3; on the Teresian Sisters, *ibid.*, p. 377.

22

Bd William Joseph Chaminade, *Founder* (1761–1850)

He was the second youngest of fifteen children born to Blaise Chaminade and Cathérine Bethon, a deeply religious couple living in Périgueux, capital of the Périgord region of south-west France. Three of his brothers also became priests. His second name, Joseph, was his confirmation name, which he preferred to Guillaume (William). He entered the junior seminary at Mussidan, some twenty miles south-west of Périgueux, in 1771, at the age of ten. He spent the next twenty years there, progressing from student to priest in 1785 and working as teacher, steward, and chaplain.

He moved to Bordeaux in 1790, after the outbreak of the Revolution. The following year he refused to take the oath of allegiance to the Civil Constitution of the Clergy and was forced into hiding. William carried on a clandestine mission during the Terror, in a manner for which his clerical formation under the *ancien régime* had in no way prepared him. In collaboration with (Venerable) Marie-Thérèse Charlotte de Lamourous, he founded the *Miséricorde* in Bordeaux, a house to shelter and reconcile "fallen" women. In 1795 he was given diocesan responsibility for priests who had taken the constitutional oath but later repented of having done so, and over the next two years he helped fifty of these priests become reconciled to the Church.

His activities, which placed his life in constant danger, forced William into exile in Zaragoza in northern Spain in 1797, where he spent three years. Zaragoza, where the great shrine of Our Lady of the Pillar stands (built on the basis of a legend telling of St James' vision of Mary carrying the Christ-child followed by angels bearing a pillar), helped him to develop his doctrinal appreciation of Mary in the story of salvation and so established the doctrinal basis for his subsequent foundations. He returned to Bordeaux in 1800 and immediately began the formation of what is now the Marianist Family, beginning with a group of mostly young lay people, a new embodiment of the Marian Sodality he had started before his exile. He concentrated his ministry on them for some time, in the process antagonizing many of the traditionalist French clergy, who saw the task for the Church after the persecution and turmoil of the Revolution as rebuilding the structures, re-establishing the customs, and reclaiming the privileges of the Church under the *ancien régime*. For them restoration of hierarchy, clergy, and parish life was a far higher priority than initiatives to develop lay spirituality. But Chaminade saw his Sodality members as "the amazing and attractive reality of a people of saints" and the spearhead of efforts to re-christianize France. He received support for his approach from the Vatican, being given the title of Missionary Apostolic in 1801.

For the next fifteen years William carried on his mission through the sodalities, which spread from Bordeaux throughout France through affiliated groups. Members kept their secular occupations but devoted what time and effort they could to the apostolate. Then some sought a more permanent commitment, and in response he founded the Institute of Daughters of Mary Immaculate at Agen in 1816, followed by the Society of Mary (or Marianists, as they became generally known) in Bordeaux in 1817. Both institutes grew rapidly in France, exercising their apostolate through teaching at primary and secondary level and starting schools to provide apprenticeships to various trades. Fr Chaminade also started a network of teacher training colleges to form instructors in the faith, but this was forced to close after the revolution of 1830, which brought back an anti-clerical regime under King Louis-Philippe (of the House of Orleans). The Marianists spread to Switzerland in 1839 and then to the U.S.A. in 1849, the year before the founder's death.

Chaminade's inspiration was the early church community in Jerusalem, the perfect model of a Christian community involving all sorts of people. The Gospel, he believed, could be lived "in the full force of its letter and spirit" as well in his own day as in primitive times. He was ahead of his times in proposing a vision of the role of lay men and women in the Church (which had to wait for its endorsement until the Second Vatican Council). The fall of Napoleon and the Bourbon restoration that followed it had brought back the clerical privileges that the traditionalists hoped for, and he faced a further period of resistance to his missionary work from conservative forces in the Church. His response to them, given in 1824, can be summed up in the words, "The levers that move the moral world somehow need a new fulcrum" (cited by David Joseph Fleming, S.M., superior general, in his circular to all Marianists on the occasion of William's beatification). His devotion to Mary never wavered, and in 1839 he addressed a letter to all the retreat-masters of the Order, expressing the conviction that "a great victory in our day" was reserved to her. He saw Mary as "the way that leads to her Son," and his devotion to her was "quintessentially Christocentric" (Fleming)—and, therefore, in the central tradition stemming from the fourth-century definition of Mary as *theotokos* ("God-bearer": to assert the divinity of Christ against the Arians). For him, Mary stands at the side of her Son working for the salvation of the world, a view far removed from sentimental self-focused devotion. "Jesus," he wrote, "made Mary the companion of his labours, of his joy, of his preaching, of his death. Mary had a part to play in all the glorious, joyful, and sorrowful mysteries of Jesus."

In the 1840s, the last decade of his life, William suffered his sharpest trials when many of his followers turned against him, including some of his first and most gifted recruits, who left the society. Many others remained faithful to his vision, and several of these were at his bedside when he died peacefully in Bordeaux on 22 January 1850.

He was beatified on 3 September 2000, together with two popes and another founder, Archbishop Thomas Reggio. In his homily Pope John Paul II said that his example should show the faithful "ever new ways of bearing witness to the faith" and that "his concern for human, moral and religious education calls the entire Church to renew her attention to young people."

J. Stefanelli, S.M., *Chaminade: Pragmatist with a Vision* (2000); E. Cárdenas, S.M., *Perfil espiritual de G.-J. Chaminade* (2000); B. Manciet, *G.-J. Chaminade, la sainteté pas à pas* (2000); R. Bichelberger, *Prier quinze jours avec G.-J. Chaminade* (2000). The Marian Library/International Marian Research Institute, Dayton, Ohio, 45469–1390, issues regular bulletins. For the Martyrs of the French Revolution see *Butler*, January (2d edn, 1998), pp. 23–7.

The Marianists, like most religious Orders, have seen their numbers fall in the decades since the Second Vatican Council, from some 3,250 to about 1,500, of whom 25 per cent work in Africa, Asia, and Latin America, a significant increase in Third World involvement since the 1960s. Members have been killed in Brazil, Colombia, and Nigeria. Numbers in the Marianist Lay Communities have, on the other hand, shown an increase, with many thousands more looking to these communities as motivators of their spiritual life. The first foundations in the U.S.A. were at Dayton, Ohio (Marianist) and Somerset, Texas (Marianist Sisters), both in 1849.

Bd Ladislaus Battyány-Strattmann (1870–1931)

Ladislaus (László) Battyány was the sixth of ten children, all boys, born into an ancient family of Hungarian nobles. He was born in Dunakiliti, in north-western Hungary, on 28 October 1870. His family moved to Austria when he was six, and his mother died six years later. From an early age Ladislaus had set his heart on becoming a doctor, but his father wanted him to grow up to manage the family estates. In compliance with his father's wishes, he studied agriculture at the university of Vienna, but as part of a broad curriculum that also embraced chemistry, physics, philosophy, literature, and music. This already extended his time as a student to six years, and then in 1896 he seems to have persuaded his father of the direction he should take and began to study medicine, in which he graduated in 1900. Halfway through his medical degree course he married Countess Maria Teresa Coreth, with whom he went on to produce thirteen children. They were both devout and devoted, attending Mass every day and saying prayers as a family.

As a child Ladislaus had declared that he would treat the sick and poor free of charge, but his first venture was to build a small private hospital in Kittsee, with twenty-five beds. He worked there first as a general practitioner before going on to specialize in ophthalmology, in which he was to become an inter-nationally recognized expert. The hospital treated wounded soldiers during the First World War, when it was enlarged to 120 beds.

In 1915 he inherited the castle of Körmend in western Hungary (just a few miles from the Austrian boundary, due east of Graz) from an uncle, with which went the title of Prince and the second part of his surname, Strattmann. He moved there with his family in 1920 and turned one wing of the castle into a specialist ophthalmology unit. Here he was able to put his childhood ideal into practice and treat the poor with no fee other than a request to pray an Our Father for him. He provided medicines free and was also known to give money to those most in need. He regarded his medical skill as a gift from God and part of God's own healing process, and presented each discharged patient with an image of Christ and a book of spiritual reading.

In 1930 Ladislaus was diagnosed with cancer of the bladder and admitted to the Löw Sanatorium in Vienna. No treatment proved effective, and after fourteen months of increasingly painful suffering he died on 22 January 1931. He bore the pain with joy "for Christ," accepting it as a gift in the same way he had previously accepted "so much joy in my life," as he wrote to his daughter Lilli. He was beatified on 23 March 2003, cited by the Pope as an "example of family life and of generous Christian solidarity."

23

Bd Nicholas Gross, *Martyr* (1898–1945)

A married man with seven children, this principled opponent and victim of the Nazi regime was born on 30 September 1898 in Niederwenigern near Essen, in the Ruhr valley coal-mining and industrial complex in north-western Germany. His father was a colliery blacksmith. Nicholas (Nikolaus) attended the local Catholic school for seven years, after which he worked in a plate-rolling mill, as a grinder, and as a miner, spending five years working underground at the coalface. At the age of nineteen he joined the Christian Miners' Trade Union; the following year he became a member of the Centre Party; and the next the *Antonius Kappenverein KAB* ("St Antony's Miners Association"), which provided an important Catholic voice in social affairs. When Nicholas was twenty-two he became its secretary for young people, and the next year he was appointed assistant editor of the union's paper, *Bergknappe*. He had furthered his education in what little spare time he had.

Nicholas married Elizabeth Koch, also from Niederwernigern, and they went on to have seven children. He was a loving and attentive husband and father, and his concern for his family in the difficult social and economic conditions of Germany in the 1920s was at the heart of his wider social concerns and activities. Early in 1927 he became assistant editor of the St Antony's Association newspaper, the *Westdeutschen Arbeiterzeitung* ("West German Workers' Paper"), and was soon promoted to editor-in-chief, which involved the family moving to Cologne. In this position he gave steady guidance to Catholic workers on social and political matters, and he soon saw a real menace to the values of a civilized and ethical society in the rise of the Nazi party. Some years before it took power, in 1930, he wrote in an editorial: "As Catholic workers we reject Nazism not only for political and economic reasons, but decisively also, resolutely and clearly, on account of our religious and cultural position."

Soon after Hitler came to power, his labour minister called the paper "hostile to the State." Nicholas tried every subterfuge to keep it published: he changed the title and became skilful at implying rather than stating criticism of the regime. In November 1938, however, the newspaper was finally closed down.

At great personal risk, he managed to continue publishing an underground edition, and he also set out his moral stance against the Nazis in a series of pamphlets. Two of these, "The Great Tasks" and "Is Germany Lost?" fell into the hands of the Gestapo and became powerful weapons for the prosecution at his trial. In 1940 he was subjected to interrogations and searches of his house, but nothing conclusively indicating treason was found.

His Catholic principles led Nicholas to join the resistance movement against Hitler. Reminded by the head of the KAB that as the father of a large family he had responsibilities and should look out for his own safety, he replied, "If we do not risk our life today, how then shall we seek one day to justify ourselves before God and our people?" He was clearly aware of preparations for the abortive plot to assassinate Hitler on 20 July 1944, though his association took no active part in it. He was arrested some three weeks after its failure, on 12 August, and taken to Ravensbrück prison and then to Berlin-Tegel, where he was evidently tortured, as his wife could see when she twice managed to visit him. He prayed constantly, and asked his wife and children in letters (at least some of which have survived) to pray for him every day. The verdict, though, was inevitable, and on 15 January 1945 he was condemned to death for treason, the Chairman of the People's Court declaring: "He swam along in treason and consequently had to drown in it." He was hanged at Berlin-Plotenzee gaol on 23 January 1945. His body was cremated and the ashes scattered on a sewage farm: the Nazis were careful not to allow any sort of remains to become the focus for veneration as a martyr.

His cause was promoted by the diocese of Essen and led to his beatification (with no need for a miracle to be proved, as he was a martyr) with six others in St Peter's Piazza on 7 October 2001. The Pope said that his example "teaches us to obey God rather than men," and continued: "Our time urgently needs convinced Christians, who listen to the voice of their conscience and have the courage to speak out when it is a question of the transcendence of the human person." "The righteous," he quoted from the prophet Habakkuk, "live by their faith" (2:4).

The last letter Nicholas wrote to his wife and children, two days before his death, appears in full (in German) on www.albertusmagnus.de/text/gross (linked from Patron Saints Index, though the link to further information appears to be a dead end).

28

St Joseph Freinademetz (1852–1908)

One of the first two Divine Word (SVD, for *Societas Verbi Divini*) Missionaries (see St Arnold Janssen; 15 Jan.) to go to China, Joseph (Guiseppe) Freinademetz was born on 15 April 1852 in Oies, a tiny hamlet in the Dolomite Alps. Now in northern Italy, in the Trentino-Alto Adige region, the area was at the time known as South Tyrol, part of the Austro-Hungarian empire. The local dialect and Joseph's first language was Ladino, in which he was known by the diminutive Seppl and his surname means "half way up the mountain." His parents, John Matthias and Anna Maria, who were peasant farmers, had him baptized within hours of his birth. They had thirteen children, of whom four died in infancy.

From the ages of six to ten Joseph attended the local school, where teaching was in Ladino. He was then taken under the wing of a local weaver named Matthias Thaler, who spotted his exceptional intelligence and enrolled him in a German-speaking school in the nearby city of Bressanone ("Brixen" in German), where he persuaded various kind-hearted women to provide the child with board and lodging. After two years he moved on to the Imperial Royal Grammar School, from where he won a choral scholarship to the cathedral school. He sang solo in the cathedral choir and rapidly learned Italian, Latin, and some French to add to his German. He finished his college course in 1872, passing with distinction, and went straight to the diocesan seminary, where he studied philosophy and theology and was ordained on 25 July 1875. Appointed curate at San Martino di Badio, very close to his birthplace, he earned the affection and respect of the parishioners for his affectionate manner and the quality of his preaching. Joseph, however, found the life too easy and dreamed of overseas mission. He had heard of Fr Arnold Janssen's foundation of the SVD and wrote to him in Steyl in 1877. Janssen came to Bressanone to see him and secured the permission of his diocesan bishop to take him to join the new Society. Joseph was overjoyed, despite the chaotic conditions he found in the old inn at Steyl: "Becoming a missionary," he wrote, "is not a sacrifice I am making to God. It is a grace He is offering me."

Joseph and John Baptist Anzer left Steyl on 2 March 1879, after a service in which Arnold Janssen had urged them to "face the future, then, with confidence. In this dark night you walk hand in hand with a living God, and our prayers will accompany you." They travelled via Rome, where they received Pope Leo XIII's blessing on their mission, embarked on a steamship at Ancona, and arrived in Hong Kong five weeks later (it was the vicar apostolic of Hong

Kong, Bishop Raimondi, who had made the first request for missionaries to Fr Janssen). Joseph and John Baptist stayed there for two years while they prepared themselves for their mission to the interior of China. They were destined for southern Shandong (Shantung, in earlier spelling convention), where Bishop Cosi had reserved a mission territory exclusively to the SVD, though they would remain under diocesan jurisdiction. They arrived there in 1881, and Joseph, who had studied Chinese in Holland, now had to learn a new dialect in order to be able to make himself understood by the local people. The province had twelve million inhabitants and had once been evangelized by Jesuits under Adam Schall, but over the course of two centuries Christians had been reduced in numbers by persecution to 158, most living near the village of Puoli. The two missionaries set about building a chapel there in 1882, and were joined by two others.

They divided tasks among them, and Joseph spent most of his time as a wandering preacher. He soon saw the need for cultural adaptation and adopted Chinese dress. Unlike earlier missionaries he concentrated on the peasants, not the upper classes. Progress was slow, with not much evidence of enthusiasm for a new faith, difficult journeys, and constant attacks by bandits. The bishop did not help either: he was always asking for new foundations, and for him to move on before he had a chance to establish a sound community in any one place. Joseph persevered, however, and within six years had over a thousand catechumens spread over thirty villages. He realized the need for local catechists, to be followed by Chinese priests. He felt sufficiently encouraged to write an account of his mission titled *Triumph of Grace*, and after four years had mastered enough of the local language to be able to produce a volume of sermons in it. The basic difficulty was the identification of Christianity with European powers, which—while intermittently waging war on China—declared the missionaries under their protection but were obviously powerless to protect all of them in different situations, so in practice the degree of freedom or persecution they encountered depended on the attitude taken by the local mandarin and his henchman the magistrate. On one occasion in southern Shandong, fifteen Chinese Christians were killed and many more forced to flee their homes when a local magistrate declared war on the "religion of the Europeans." Two of the SVD missionaries were killed in disturbances occasioned by war between China and Japan in 1894.

John Baptist Anzer was summoned back to Steyl in 1885 for the first general chapter of the Society, due to begin in May 1886, and he appointed Joseph administrator of the South Shandong mission during his absence, which meant that he had to spend most of his time in Puoli. Anzer was appointed bishop of the diocese during his stay in Europe; he returned to Puoli in a great procession and appointed Joseph pro-vicar and superior of several districts, which enabled him again to travel to his beloved villages, but also forced him to concentrate more on encouraging the missionaries than on evangelizing the peasants directly. Appointed visitator, he visited every SVD member in the region in the summer of 1896. The need for an indigenous clergy prompted the building of a seminary, of which Joseph was made rector. He moved it from Puoli to the larger settlement of Tsining, where the first two Chinese priests were ordained for the mission in 1896. He also opened a retreat house, where all the SVD missionaries made an annual retreat.

By 1898 the rigours of Joseph's life and the local conditions were taking their toll. He developed laryngitis and was ordered to Japan for a rest. There was little chance that he would rest for long enough, and he returned only partly cured. In 1900 he refused an invitation from Fr Janssen to return to Steyl for the celebration of the twenty-fifth anniversary of the SVD. This was in view of the difficult situation brought about by the Boxer Rebellion, during which he and his missionaries were forced to flee (though persecution was less in South Shantung than in other provinces, where hundreds of European missionaries and their Chinese helpers were put to death). Joseph was nevertheless able to write home: "In spite of the persecutions, we have had such a harvest as never before." He managed to restore the community in Puoli and stayed there during the troubles, despite orders from the German authorities (who had taken over "protection" duties from France) to take refuge on the coast at the port of Tsingtao. He did send a group of orphans there, writing to the local mission-aries: "They are absolutely destitute. Please have the kindness to do something for them. With conditions as they are we must not hesitate to incur a few extra expenses in order to save what can still be saved ... I think it would be better to sell the horses."

His next move was to build a new retreat house at Taikia, and he was appointed first provincial superior, responsible for the religious life of all the missionaries in his province. As the Boxer Rebellion subsided and China's policy shifted toward westernization, Christians were left in peace and the numbers of converts increased, but Joseph saw danger in the identification of Christianity with the Europeans, mostly traders, who were flocking to the country: "The greatest scourge for us, as well as for the Chinese, are the crowds of morally inferior Europeans without any religion who swarm all over China ... There is no doubt that our heathen Chinese are a hundred times better than these dregs of mankind." Of the Chinese, by contrast, he wrote: "I have come to love my Chinese. I take China and its people and its language as my native country ... I would die for them a thousand times over ... I want to be still Chinese in heaven."

Bishop Anzer went to Europe once more in the spring of 1903, leaving Joseph in charge of the diocese as his vicar, residing at Yenchowfu. The day after being received in audience by Leo XIII, Anzer died suddenly. The general supposition was that Joseph would replace him as bishop, though he dismissed the idea, saying, "A mitre does not fit on a blockhead." He had had enough of admin-istrative responsibility, and his health was failing. In the event another SVD missionary, Fr Henninghaus, was chosen. Whenever he was out of the country he left Joseph as diocesan administrator.

Joseph was serving his sixth tour of this duty in late 1907, when an epidemic of typhus broke out. He went on visiting his communities and inevitably caught the disease, from which he died at Taikia, the diocesan seat, on 28 January 1908. He was buried by the twelfth station of the Way of the Cross that had been built there, and this soon became a place of pilgrimage. Popular agitation for his cause to be opened began in his native region (by then of Italy) in around 1935. In 1947 his one-time pupil Cardinal Tien wrote to the vice-postulator of the cause: "Of all the missionaries of China I know of no holier one than Father Freinademetz." The apostolic cause was introduced in 1951, and he was beatified with Arnold Janssen on 19 October 1975 and canonized with him on 5 October 2003. In his homily on the latter occasion Pope John Paul II said of him: "With the tenacity typical of mountain people, this generous 'witness of love' made a gift of himself to the Chinese peoples of Southern Shandong. For love and with love he embraced their living conditions, in accordance with his own advice to his missionaries: 'Missionary work is useless if one does not love and is not loved.' "

Butler, January, 2d edn, pp. 214–17, citing F. Bornemann, *Der selige P. J. Freinademetz, 1852–1908: Ein Styler China-Missionar* (1976), partially translated into English, *As Wine Poured Out: Blessed J. F. SVD, Missionary in China 1879–1908* (1984); H. M. Prince, *Fu Shenfu, the Luck-Priest* (1962; a popular account). For a general account of the martyrs of China see *Butler*, Feb., pp. 175–84, with bibliography. See also Divine Word Missionaries website.

30

Bd Columba Marmion, *Abbot* (1858–1923)

The future abbot of Maredsous in Belgium was born in Dublin on 1 April 1858. His father, William Marmion, was Irish, and his mother, Herminie Cordier, French. They had lost two boys in infancy and saw the third, christened Joseph Aloysius, as a special gift from God, whom they "promised" back to God. He entered the archdiocesan seminary at the age of sixteen and went on to study theology at the Propaganda Fide College in Rome, where he was a brilliant student. He was ordained in Rome on 16 June 1881 and at first intended to be a missionary in Australia. Then a visit to the "newborn" abbey of Maredsous, an offshoot of Beuron Abbey in Germany, inspired him with its atmosphere of liturgical renewal, and he asked if he could join the community there. The

Dublin vicar general, however, made him postpone any thought of becoming a Benedictine, and summoned him back to Ireland.

After a short spell as parish priest of Dumdrun Joseph was appointed professor at the major seminary of Clonliffe. He also acted as chaplain to a convent of Redemptorist Sisters and to Mountjoy Prison in Dublin. His experiences there, where he worked to infuse some sense of meaning into the lives of men and women often incarcerated for life, with no expectation of release, were influential in his later development of a theology of hope. He seemed to be well on the ladder of ecclesiastical preferment in Dublin, but in November 1886 he asked the archbishop for permission to become a monk at Maredsous, which was granted.

He was received by the first abbot, Dom Placidus Walter, and joined the novitiate under the severe rule of the novice-master, Dom Benoît d'Hondt. Already ordained priest and nearly thirty years old, he shared the novitiate with a group of young men some ten or more years younger than himself, while at the same time having to adjust to a new language and a new culture. He made his simple profession in 1888, taking the name Columba in religion, after his distinguished predecessor St Columba of Iona (*c.* 521–597; 9 June), likewise an "exile for Christ" in the Irish tradition. He was solemnly professed in 1891and became assistant novice-master. He also taught in the school attached to the monastery and began to preach in nearby churches.

Columba was then ordered to join a group of monks in the foundation of the abbey of Mont-César at Louvain, south-east of Brussels and site of a great Catholic university where monastic and clerical students went to study theology and philosophy. Appointed prior, he was responsible for the spiritual welfare of all the young monks there. At the same time he was much in demand as a spiritual director and giver of retreats, both in Belgium and in Great Britain. He became confessor to Mgr Joseph Mercier, the future cardinal-archbishop of Malines-Brussels (and Pope St Pius X's staunch ally in the anti-Modernist "crusade").

The second abbot of Maredsous, Dom Hildebrand de Hemptine, was appointed first abbot primate of the Benedictine Confederation by Pope Leo XIII in 1893. This forced him to spend much of his time in Rome, and he eventually decided he could no longer effectively also act as abbot. Columba was elected to succeed him in 1909. By this time Maredsous had grown to a community of over a hundred monks. It ran a School of Humanities, a School of Applied Arts, and numerous workshops. Its intellectual eminence was assured by the publication of the *Revue Bénédictine* and other works, and it was renowned for research into the origins of the Faith. The Belgian government asked him to open a mission in Katanga, but the monastery chapter refused on the grounds of its many other responsibilities. Abbot Columba was probably disappointed by this decision and continued to take a close interest in the mission to Katanga, which was entrusted to the newer foundation of Saint-André in Bruges. He also continued to give retreats in Britain, and his reputation there encouraged the Anglican Benedictine monks of Caldey Island, off the coast of South Wales, together with their sister foundation for nuns at Milford Haven in Pembrokeshire, to seek his aid when the whole community decided to convert to Roman Catholicism in 1913. He took care of the canonical procedure as well as acting as their spiritual mentor.

During the First World War Abbot Columba arranged for the young monks of Maredsous to be evacuated to Ireland for their safety. He personally oversaw the creation of a refuge for them in Ireland in 1916, but first his absence from the abbey, then the different climate in which the monks continued their formation in Ireland, caused misunderstanding and a rift among the Belgian Benedictines that began to undermine his health. In 1920 he was forced to order the secession of the monasteries of Maredsous, Mont-César, and Saint-André into a separate Benedictine Congregation, called "of the Annunciation." It was hardly a triumphant outcome, though his personal reputation as a spiritual and doctrinal authority survived intact. He caught influenza during an epidemic early in 1923 and died in the evening of 30 January.

Columba distilled his many years of teaching, guiding, and directing spirituality into a great trilogy of books: *Christ, Life of the Soul* (1917); *Christ in His Mysteries* (1921); and *Christ the Ideal of the Monk* (1922). These were enormously influential in the formation of Catholic clergy and religious, including many of the Fathers of the Second Vatican Council, for four decades. Pope Benedict XV recommended them as representing "the pure teaching of the Church." They provide a thorough course of Christology and did much to enhance devotion to Christ in the mysteries of his life, as they unfold in the christological feasts of the liturgical year. Marmion had originally been attracted to Maredsous by the beauty of its liturgy, and he became a great promoter of liturgical reform, one of the first writers to use the expression "liturgical movement" (in the context of encouraging greater participation by the faithful in the Church's liturgy).

His spirituality is inevitably of its time and place, formed in the later decades of the nineteenth century, characterized by deep devotion to the Sacred Heart, to the Blessed Sacrament, and to Mary. The Dublin Columba grew up in was dedicated to traditional Roman devotions: Forty Hours, novenas, pilgrimages, and the like. His writings form a bridge between this popular Catholicism and centuries of monastic wisdom, learned but at the same time accessible to all, a unique blend of devotion and theology. His ultimate sources of inspiration are St Paul and St John the Evangelist, but he had also made a thorough study of St Thomas Aquinas' *Summa theologica* in his student days in Rome and kept returning to him as a sure source, together with the Bible as a whole and the Rule of St Benedict. His immersion over many years as a monk in prayer, above all the prayer of the Church as expressed in the Divine Office, suffuses all his writings: as Dom Mark Tierney writes, "They are born in prayer and of prayer."

By the time of his death Columba was, according to the postulator of his cause, Dom Olivier Raquez, widely regarded as a great monk "devoted to the quest for God," and the impetus for his eventual canonization was immediate, including supporters such as the future Pope Paul VI. The cause was officially opened in 1955; from 1957 to 1961 the diocesan process gathered evidence from forty-five witnesses, while his complete works were published and sent to Rome for examination, earning a positive report in 1973. In 1983 the requirements for advancing causes were modified, including the need for a "Statement on the Life and Virtues" prepared according to academic norms based on documentary evidence. This meant, in Columba's case, that much of the earlier documentation had to be revised. The "statement" finally appeared in 1994 in the form of two volumes, the first a biography, the second containing supporting documents. The sudden, permanent, and inexplicable cure from cancer in 1966 of an American woman, who had been advised by the monks of Marmion Abbey to pray for Dom Columba's intercession, was included in the dossier as the necessary miracle in 1996, and was formally accepted in Rome in January 2000. Dom Columba was beatified in Rome by Pope John Paul II on 3 September 2000, in a ceremony that also included two popes, Pius IX and John XXIII.

❖

M. Tierney, Abbot N. Dayez of Maredsous, and Dom O. Raquez, OSB, at www.paginecattoliche.it/BeatoColumbaMarmion.

Marmion Abbey in Aurora, Illinois, formerly the Catholic high school, was staffed by Benedictine monks from St Meinrad Abbey in 1933, changing its name to "Marmion" after Abbot Columba; it became a dependent priory in 1943 and an independent abbey in 1947. Monasticism on Caldey Island dates from the sixth century but was suppressed at the Reformation. In 1906 Anglican Benedictines bought the island and built a new monastery in Italianate style. Having converted in 1913 they were forced to sell and move in 1925. The island was bought by the Cistercian Order, which sent monks from Scourmont in Belgium in 1929. The community currently has some twenty monks and is financially secured by the sale of perfume and other local products.

FEBRUARY

1

Bd Louis Variara, *Founder* (1875–1923)

Louis (Luigi) was born in Viarigi in the Asti province of the Piedmont region of northern Italy on 15 January 1875. He was a weak baby and not expected to live, so he was baptized the same day. His father, Pietro, had been deeply impressed by St John Bosco (31 Jan.), who had preached a mission in Viarigi in 1856. This persuaded him that Louis, the son of his second marriage, should be educated at Don Bosco's Oratory of Valdocco in Turin. He took him there on 1 October 1887, just four months before Don Bosco's death but not too late for the boy to catch a glimpse of the man whom his pupils revered as a saint. Louis wrote of the occasion: "Then suddenly he looked at me in a most kindly way, and his eyes held my attention. I really don't know how to describe my feelings at that moment. That day was for me one of the happiest of my life. I was sure I had gazed on a real saint, and that that saint had read in my soul something known only to God and himself."

He (fairly naturally) decided that he was destined for the Salesian life and joined the novitiate on 17 August 1891. Don Bosco's successor, Bd Michael Rua (6 Apr.) whispered to him as he made his final profession, playing on his name, "*Variara, non variare*" ("Variaria, don't vary"). He studied philosophy at Valsalice, and in 1894 met Fr Michele Unia, who had for some years been working in the leper colony of Agua de Dios in Colombia. He told Br Louis that the place needed some Salesian cheerfulness ("*allegria*"), and when he discovered that Louis was a fine musician with a good singing voice, he decided he would be the ideal person to return with him to the colony. Louis agreed willingly, calling it "a magnificent grace, a grace I treasured as a gift from Mary, Help of Christians." The journey took seventy days, by steamship to Barranquilla on the north coast of Colombia, then by sail up the Magdalena River, and finally on mule.

There were 2,000 residents in the colony: 800 lepers, the most serious cases confined to the *leprosarium* but most living in huts, and their families. Fr Unia died just over a year after his return, and Br Louis took over the running of the colony. The atmosphere was one of depression, but he soon changed that: he opened an Oratory; he taught the children to play musical instruments; he made them act in plays and reviews; he formed a choir that performed with the instrumentalists in the chapel on feast-days; he was "mother and father" to the children, and no aspect of care was too repugnant for him. Gradually a feeling of hope took hold in the colony. He also gave catechism classes, while learning the local language and continuing the theological studies he needed for ordination. He was ordained in 1898, the first Salesian to be ordained in Colombia, and added the function of wise confessor to all his other tasks. He formed members of the Children of Mary Sodality into a religious association, originally just to help in the apostolate within the colony. There was no Congregation in the Church that would accept lepers or their children. In 1901 he could write: "I have never been so happy to be a Salesian as I have this year, and I bless the Lord for sending me to this leper colony, where I have learned not to have heaven stolen from me."

Louis' happiness was not to last, however. He fell victim to the "bitchiness" that affects so many new religious endeavours: the superior of the Presentation Sisters who also worked at Agua de Dios did not approve of his idea to start a Congregation that would take lepers; she gave false reports to the archbishop of Bogotá, who complained to the Salesian provincial, who transferred Fr Luigi from Agua de Dios to two other places in Colombia and then allowed him back again. The effect on morale in the colony was disastrous. Other Salesians also had doubts about the proposed Congregation and worked against it: the concept of those "unfortunates" to whom they ministered actually becoming ministers in their own right was probably simply too radical for them. Also, no Salesian had yet started a religious Institute, and this young innovator was not yet thirty ... But Louis persevered: he saw the need for an orphanage in the colony and went to Bogotá to raise money, asking that every healthy child contribute a centavo for the sick children in Agua de Dios. The money poured in, and he was able to buy land and start building. Then the so-called "One thousand days' war," a bloody civil conflict, interrupted the work. This was followed by an outbreak of yellow fever.

Building work eventually resumed, and then no religious would take charge of the orphanage, so the foundation of his Congregation became a necessity. The first aspirants wrote to Don Michele Rua, who succeeded Don Bosco as "Rector Major" of the Salesians worldwide, to tell him of their purpose: "Our aim will be to take care of our fellow lepers. In our Congregation we will serve God, offering ourselves as willing victims of expiation under the protection of the Sacred Heart of Jesus and that of Mary Help of Christians. It will not be a great undertaking, but this small Congregation will be for us like an oasis of happiness in the desert that surrounds us." Fr Rua supported the venture, telling Louis by letter in 1908: "Try to increase the number of your Sisters, and always keep the religious authorities well informed of everything. Your institution is a fine thing; it ought to progress and develop." His successor, Fr Paolo Albera, whom Louis saw on a visit to Italy in 1911, also expressed his support, and the

Sisters, known as the Daughters of the Sacred Hearts of Jesus and Mary, became an active community. Nevertheless, they could not gain official approval (which was not granted until provisionally in 1965, and finally fully in 1983).

Louis had four years back in Agua de Dios but was then sent to Bogotá. There he developed sores, which led everyone to suppose—erroneously—that he had contracted leprosy, and he was sent back to Agua de Dios. A few months later he was transferred to Barranquilla. He was told to stop writing to the leper Sisters and to consider himself no longer responsible for them: again, false accusations had been made about his relations with them. This must have been devastating for him, but he accepted it as part of his "share in the cross of Jesus." After two miserable years in Barranquilla he was sent to Táriba, just over the border in Venezuela and 5,300 feet up in the Cordillera de Mérida, the north-eastern end of the Andes chain. The climate caused his health to decline sharply, and his doctor ordered his transfer to Cúcuta, on the other side of the mountains in Colombia, where the climate was more bearable. A Salesian Lay Brother, Rodolfo Faccini, cared for him in his family home, but he never recovered. He died on 1 February 1923, at the age of just forty-nine. He was buried in Cúcuta and in 1932 his remains were taken back to his beloved Agua de Dios, where they are still, in the chapel of his Sisters. He was beatified on 14 April 2002, in the same ceremony as two other Salesians from Latin America, the Nicaraguan-born Sr María Romero Meneses (see 7 July) and the naturalized Argentinian "coadjutor" Artemide Zatti (see 15 Mar.).

Informative sites at www.salesianmissions.org and www.donbosco.asn.au, on which most of the above, including quotations, is based. Contact: Salesian Missions, 2 Lefevre Lane, PO Box 30, New Rochelle, NY 10802–0030; e-mail info@salesianmissions.org.

The Daughters of the Sacred Hearts of Jesus and Mary survived and flourished. Today they have 400 members—some of them lepers—with fifty houses in Colombia and Venezuela and others in Bolivia, Brazil, Dominican Republic, Ecuador, Equatorial Guinea, Italy, Mexico, and Spain.

2

Bd Maria Mantovani (1862–1934)

Maria Domenica was the eldest of the four children of Giovanni Mantovani and his wife, Prudenza Zamperini. She was born on 12 November 1862 in the lakeside village of Castelleto di Brenzone, a community of some 900 souls half way up the eastern side of Lake Garda in the province of Verona, and spent her childhood there, attending elementary school for only three years and then helping her parents in the hard life of small farmers. Her devout parents taught her the elements of the faith.

When she was fifteen years old, a new curate arrived in the parish. He was Fr Joseph (Giuseppe) Nascimbeni (beatified in 1988; 22 Jan.), who succeeded as parish priest when the current incumbent died in 1884 and spent the rest of his life there, dying in 1922. He revitalized the life of the parish and found Maria Domenica to be an enthusiastic collaborator. He encouraged her to teach the catechism to other children as well as to visit the sick and join in parish activities. On the feast of the Immaculate Conception in 1886, she made a private vow of virginity before a statue of the Virgin and asked for guidance as to how she could best serve God and Our Lady in religion.

It was to be a further six years before any definite project emerged. In 1892 the bishop of Verona advised Fr Nascimbeni that a new Congregation for women could do useful work, and Maria assisted him in founding the Little Sisters of the Holy Family, acting as co-founder and becoming its first superior general as Mother Maria of the Immaculate, universally known simply as "Mother." The purpose was to promote the development of parish life in villages through religious instruction of adults and catechism classes for children, and to help people in need both spiritually and materially. There were only four Sisters originally, but numbers grew rapidly and other houses were opened, first in other parts of Italy and then in South America (to support the great number of Italians emigrating there). Maria never moved from Castelletto and the mother-house was established there.

For the next forty years Maria guided the Congregation, with Fr Nascimbeni during his lifetime and then on her own for the twelve years by which she outlived him. She died of natural causes in Castelletto on 2 February 1934, and was beatified by Pope John Paul II on 27 April 2003. In his homily the Pope said of her:"This praiseworthy daughter of the region of Verona ... was inspired by the Holy Family of Nazareth to make herself 'all things to all people,' ever attentive to the needs of the poor ... What a fine example of holiness for every believer!"

❧

For Joseph Nascimbeni see *Butler*, Jan., pp. 150–1 (2d edn, 160–1). The house where Maria was born is now an "ethnographic museum" devoted to her memory, furnished as it would have been in her youth and maintained by civic and religious authorities together: for information e-mail centrostudi@pssf.it. The Little Sisters presently work in Italy, Switzerland, and Albania; in Africa; and in Argentina, Brazil, Paraguay, and Uruguay.

6

Bd Alphonsus Mary Fusco, *Founder* (1839–1910)

The founder of the Baptistine Sisters was born in Angri in the province of Salerno, south-east of Naples (see also Bd Thomas Mary Fusco; 24 Feb.). His parents, Aniello Fusco and Giuseppina Schiavone, had been married for four years and had no children when they prayed at the tomb of St Alphonsus de'Liguori (then Bd; 1 Aug.) in Pagani. There a Redemptorist priest (acting in the role of Gabriel?) told them:"You will have a son; you will name him Alfonso; he will become a priest and will live the life of Blessed Alfonso."Alphonsus was born the following year (in which Bd Alphonsus de'Liguori was canonized), followed by four more children.

He made his First Communion and received Confirmation at the age of seven, and by the time he was eleven had decided that he wanted to be a priest. He entered the diocesan junior seminary in Nocera in November 1850 and was ordained thirteen years later, on 29 May 1863. He was appointed to the collegiate church of St John the Baptist in Angri and quickly became known as a zealous priest who loved the liturgy and was gentle and caring with the penitents who flocked to his confessional.

Alphonsus had had a dream at the seminary in which Jesus called him to establish an orphanage for boys and girls once he was ordained. He had made a start by opening his own house as a free elementary school—the first in Angri—in 1870. His fellow-priests had not supported him in this venture, and its continuance was difficult, but then in 1877 a childless widow, Donna Raffaella Graziano, gave him a somewhat dilapidated house she owned. The project took more definite shape through his meeting with Maddalena Caputo, a determined young woman looking for a suitable religious life. In September 1878 Fr Fusco met her and two other young women and planned what became the Congregation of the Baptistine Sisters of the Nazarene. The young women vowed poverty, union with God, and care of poor orphans, and they set about converting the house, called"Casa Scarcella,"into an orphanage, which became known as the "Little House of Providence." Fr Fusco became director of the Institute, and Maddalena, now Sister Crocifissa, became the first superior. More postulants joined them, and the first orphans arrived.

As seemed to happen inevitably with new religious foundations of the period, disputes arouse, and Fr Fusco found many of the Sisters turning against him, persuading the bishop to ask him to resign, and locking the doors of their house in Rome against him—showing their desire to break away and become a separate Congregation. The hardest aspect to bear was that Sister Crocifissa was one of the main instigators of the revolt. She had objected to the proximity of the orphans to the Sisters' quarters in the Scarcella house, and her grievances seem to have mounted from there, even though Fr Fusco then found other premises to act as a craft and technical school, taking many of the orphans away. (This school included a printing press, on which he printed many of the devotional pamphlets he wrote.) The climax came when Cardinal Respighi, vicar of Rome, told him: "You have founded this community of good Sisters, who are doing their best. Now withdraw!" There was little he could do except pray, which he did, and wait for vindication, which came in time. He was in fact a wise and gentle director, caring for his Sisters and the orphans in equal measure. More houses in Italy opened in response to requests, first in the Campania region, then throughout Italy.

He died after a short illness on 6 February 1910, and news of the death of "the father of the poor" and "the saint" spread quickly through the town. Pope Paul VI declared him venerable on 12 February 1976. In February 2000 a four-year-old Zambian boy, Gershom Chizuma, caught malaria, which progressed to a third-degree coma with *status epilepticus*, confirmed as cerebral malaria, which was almost inevitably fatal. Doctors and family despaired, but a Baptistine Sister, Livia Caserio, with two others, persuaded his mother and grandmother, who were Seventh Day Adventists, to ask for Fr. Fusco's intervention. They placed a picture of him under the boy's pillow and all prayed. The next morning he regained consciousness and went on to make a complete recovery, with no mental or physical ill effects—unknown in cases of cerebral malaria. This cure was accepted as miraculous on 3 March 2000, and Pope John Paul beatified Alphonsus Mary Fusco with six others (including Fr Thomas Mary Fusco) on 7 October 2001. The Pope described him as a "Don Bosco of southern Italy" and spoke of his "passionate desire to dedicate his life to the service of the neediest, especially of children and young people."

There are several biographies in Italian; for a list see www.alfonsomariafusco.org/biogra. There is also a more detailed account of his life on the same site.

The Baptistine Sisters expanded to the U.S.A. in 1906 and now also work in Korea, the Philippines, India, South America, Poland, Malawi, Madagascar, and Zambia. They care for the aged (men and women), conduct retreats for children, and look after children at any sort of risk and those excluded from society: *Orders*, p. 28, and the Congregation's website.

7

Bd Rosalie Rendu (1786–1856)

Born in the mountainous region of France bordering Switzerland, at Confort in the Gex district (just ten miles north of Geneva), she was the eldest of four girls, born on 9 September 1786 and christened Jeanne Marie. Her parents were middle-class, property-owners on a modest scale, and committed Catholics. The French Revolution broke out when Jeanne Marie was three, and they made their house a refuge for priests who refused to take the oath of loyalty to the State required by the Civil Constitution on the Clergy (12 July 1790), letting it be known that they were extra hands hired to work on their farms. Jeanne Marie received her First Communion from one of these priests in the basement of the family house. After the revised "Liberty-Equality Oath" promulgated in August 1792, priests who refused to swear and remained in France were in danger of their lives.

Her father died on 12 May 1796, followed by a younger sister two months later, and her responsibilities helping her mother in the home increased. When the Revolutionary Directorate was overthrown in 1799, with Napoleon becoming "first consul" (effectively dictator) and subsequently emperor, Church–State relations were gradually normalized, leading to the Concordat between Napoleon and Pius VII in 1801. Religious Orders in France were able to operate openly once more, and Jeanne Marie spent two years as a boarder at the Ursuline school in Gex. Nearby was a hospital in which the Daughters of Charity cared for the sick, and she began to help them. Their novitiate had been re-opened in 1800, and on 25 May 1802, aged nearly seventeen, Jeanne Marie joined the Congregation at their motherhouse in Paris, taking the name Rosalie in religion. She plunged into a life of rigorous asceticism, to such a degree that her health suffered severely. After a period of recovery she was sent to the Daughters' house in the slum district of Mouffetard, then one of the poorest in Paris. She was to work there for fifty-four years, becoming the area's local saint.

Home visits bringing help to the destitute and diseased were the staple activity of the Daughters. In any spare time Rosalie taught the catechism and literacy to girls attending the local free school. She made her religious profession in 1807 and in 1815 became superior of the house in the rue des Francs Bourgeois. Her work over the years encompassed a free clinic, a pharmacy, a school, an orphanage, a child-care centre, a youth club, and a retirement home. She assembled a competent team of co-workers to administer all these, and her reputation grew in the capital and beyond, attracting donations from rich and poor alike. She sustained her activity with an intense prayer life and was often to be found on her knees in the chapel or in her office, but she said that she found God in the homes of the poor and that she never prayed as well as she did in the street.

The Daughters of Charity's house in the Rue de l'Epée de Bois, to where Sr Rosalie had moved, became a focus for prominent people committed in various ways to develop a network of charity to help the poor at a time when State provision was non-existent. Rosalie, who was appointed Justice of the Peace for the area, advised law and medical students from the nearby university of the Sorbonne, and her advice was equally heeded by professors and others. A study club calling itself the History Conference had been meeting since 1819 at the home of Emanuel Bailly, professor of philosophy and editor of *Le Tribune Catholique*. Its aim was to spearhead a religious renaissance in France, and one of its most influential members was Frédéric Ozanam (beatified in 1997; 8 Sept.). He and a group of others started a "Charity Conference" in 1835, to function as the organizing arm of the planned network of charity. Ozanam was one of those who came to Rosalie—by then known as "the mother of the poor"—for advice, and she was instrumental in developing the Conference into what became the Society of St Vincent de Paul, a lay institute to work alongside the Vincentian priests and the Daughters, using the same methods based on home visits to ascertain precisely what actual needs were. In this, Rosalie acted as instructor and adviser and so played a prominent part in the foundation of the SVP, teaching its members not merely to dispense aid but to help the poor find work so that they could help themselves; not to blame the poor for their condition; and to remember that their behaviour toward the poor, always respecting their dignity, was more important than the material help they could give.

Paris erupted in revolution in 1830 and 1848. Rosalie was caught up in the conflict in both years. In 1830 she rescued General Montmahaut, whom she knew to be a benefactor of the poor, when he lay seriously wounded in the Place de l'Hôtel de Ville. She also rebuked the Chief of Police, who came in person to arrest her for helping wanted persons to escape, telling him that as a Daughter of Charity she helped unfortunates whoever they might be and sending him away empty-handed. The following year she sheltered the archbishop of Paris and a group of his priests when a mob set fire to his residence. In 1848 she saved an officer from being shot at a barricade, telling the insurgents, "We do not kill here!"

In 1852 Emperor Napoleon III (president of the Second Republic from 1848 to 1852, emperor from 1852 to 1870), who with his wife Eugénie was to be a visitor to the house on Rue de l'Epée de Bois, awarded Rosalie the Cross of the Légion d'Honneur for her charitable work. At first she refused to accept any personal recognition, but the superior general of the Vincentians and Daughters of Charity, Fr Etienne, eventually persuaded her to do so. Two years later her sight began to fail, and the last two years of her life brought progressive blindness. She died on 7 February 1856 after a short final illness.

Rosalie was declared Venerable on 24 April 2001, then the sudden, inexplicable cure from progressive motor-neurone disease of Sr Thérèse Béquet, aged thirty-two, on 1 February 1952 as the entire community prayed to Sr Rosalie, led to her beatification, which took place in St Peter's Square on 9 November 2003, the last such ceremony of that year. Pope John Paul II said of her in his homily: "In an era troubled by social conflicts, Rosalie Rendu joyfully became a servant to the poorest, restoring dignity to each one by means of material help, education, and the teaching of the Christian mystery … Her secret was simple: to see the face of Christ in every man and woman." The ceremony was attended by hundreds of members of the Vincentian family, men and women, from all over the world.

On the French Revolution see *Butler*, Jan., pp. 23–7; on Frédéric Ozanam, *ibid.*, Sept., pp. 71–5. In addition to Vatican sources there is an informative website from the Daughters of Charity: www.filles-de-la-charite.org/en/rosalie_rendu (in English).

Bd Pius IX, *Pope* (1792–1878)

The longest-serving pope in history, and one of the most important and controversial, Giovanni Maria Mastai-Ferretti was born on 13 May 1792 at Senigallia in the region of Le Marche on the Adriatic coast of Italy, the earliest Roman settlement on that coast. His parents, Gerolamo Ferretti and Caterina Solazzi, were both from families of the local nobility. He was a somewhat delicate child, suffering from what appeared to have been epileptic fits; though these ceased as he grew older, they seem to have left him with an excitable disposition. He received a classical education at the Piarist college in Volterra for seven years from the age of ten, then went to Rome, where he studied philosophy and theology for three more years. His health then appears to have obliged him to leave Rome and his studies for a time, but he returned in 1814 and asked to join the pope's Noble Guard. He was refused on the grounds of his health but was admitted to the Roman seminary to study theology. His fits left him, and he was ordained priest on 10 April 1819.

After serving for two years as spiritual director of the orphanage known as "Tata Giovanni" he was sent by Pope Pius VII (1800–23) to Chile, as auditor to the apostolic delegate. He returned to Rome in 1825 and was appointed canon of Santa Maria in via Lata by Pope Leo XII (1823–29), who also made him director of the San Michele Hospital. Two years later, a mere eight years after his ordination, he was consecrated archbishop of Spoleto. There he first became involved in the ongoing struggles between the Austrian empire and nascent Italian nationalist forces, when 4,000 of the latter, fleeing from the Austrians, threatened to occupy Spoleto. He persuaded them to lay down their arms and the Austrian commander to pardon them, then gave them money to return to their homes. In 1832 Pope Gregory XVI (1831–46) moved him to the larger diocese of Imola, where he remained as bishop until his election to the papacy. Gregory publicly created him cardinal priest of Santi Petro e Marcellino on 14 December 1840.

Gregory's rule had become increasingly conservative, absolutist, and intransigent. His secretary of state, Cardinal Lambruschini, saw even railways and gas street lighting as sinful threats to good order in the Papal States. Gregory carried out a lavish program of architectural and engineering works and patronized learning, but he left the States virtually bankrupt and effectively a police state. When he died, many cardinals in the conclave looked for someone with decidedly more liberal views to replace him. Mastai-Ferretti seemed to answer the needs of the liberal camp and was elected by three votes over the required majority at the fourth scrutiny. (The Austrian government sent the cardinal archbishop of Milan with a veto against his election, but he was delayed and arrived too late.)

The new pope was crowned on 21 June 1846 and took the name Pius in commemoration of his first benefactor, Pius VII. He was a popular choice: he was known for his charity to the poor, his warm heart, and his wit, and he was generally greeted with joy. He was far more open than his predecessors: he increased the number of audiences and charmed his visitors, who returned to their countries to disseminate their favourable impressions, which contributed to growing adulation of the person of the pope and so contributed to increasing centralization in Church affairs. He was also presumed to support Italian nationalism: all Italian demonstrations against Austrian occupation were accompanied by cries of "Long live Pius IX!" The French lawyer, writer, and reformer Frederick Ozanam (now Bd.; 8 Sept.) saw him as "a messenger of God sent to complete the great work of the nineteenth century, the alliance between religion and liberty."

Despite his years of study (which took place at a time when schools and colleges were disrupted in the aftermath of the Napoleonic wars), Pius was not highly educated and lacked the analytical skills needed to see the way ahead for the Church in new conditions. His basic instincts tended to be anti-liberal, but he was constantly torn between opposing advice from left and right, and at first he seemed to fulfil the liberal reformers' expectations. He granted an amnesty to political exiles and prisoners in the Papal States, which earned him the accusation from reactionaries of being in league with the Freemasons and a revolutionary Roman organization known as the Carbonari. It soon became apparent, however, that while he approved of limited political reform—such as establishing an advisory council, a civic guard, and a cabinet council—he was a jealous guardian of the Church's privileges. This emerged in his first encyclical, *Qui pluribus*, "On Faith and Religion," dated 9 November 1846, in which he attacked what was to become a familiar litany of the evils of the age: oppression of Catholic interests, secret societies, sects, indifference, false philosophy, the press, and so on. This, however, was ignored because of his popular reputation.

On the political front, Pius was engulfed by a radical movement he could not control. Street riots in early 1848 forced him to grant a constitution with lay ministers for the Papal States, but when the mob demanded that he declare war on Austria he was caught in the dilemma of his dual role as monarch of the Papal States and "Father of Christendom" as pope. He had supported the formation of a league of Italian States against Austria, but this was effectively taken over by Piedmontese ambitions. A speech on 29 April 1848 was probably amended by Cardinal Antonelli to stress that he could not declare war against Catholic Austria and to omit any expression of sympathy for the nationalist cause. Overnight, the "liberal" pope became the "anti-nationalist" pope—with as little justification.

Denounced as a traitor to his country, Pius was besieged in the Quirinal Palace, from which he escaped in disguise with the help of the Bavarian and French ambassadors on 24 November 1848. He handed over the administration of the Papal States to Count Pellegrino Rossi, who was promptly assassinated by radicals. Pius took refuge in the Neapolitan port of Gaeta, with the intention of sailing to France. Invited to stay by the King of Naples, he remained there for seventeen months. He formally dissolved the government of the Papal States and placed Cardinal Antonelli at the head of a new administration, with the tile of pro-secretary. He was joined by many cardinals, while in Rome the mob seized control and proclaimed a democratic republic, with Giuseppe Mazzini at its head, and the abolition of the temporal power of the papacy. Rome for the first time became the focus of the *Risorgimento*. Pius appealed to foreign forces to restore his sovereignty: France, Austria, Naples and Spain. French troops put down the rebellion (or new democracy) and Pius returned to Rome in April 1850 determined to maintain the status quo and equating the fate of the Church with that of the Papal States. It was the end of his "liberal" period, and though it was Antonelli more than he who was to drive forward the repressive policies of the next twenty-five years, his own convictions showed in the placing of books by Rosmini and others, his former liberal advisers, on the Index of Forbidden Books in May 1849. Roger Aubert describes the restored papal authority as "reactionary and inept."

From then on Pius' papacy became one long struggle against the ideological "enemies" of the Church (as bastion of truth) and the political enemies of the Papal States (as emblem of the sovereignty of the Church). The latter were embodied in the movement for Italian unity, beginning with the reconquest from the Austrians of Piedmont in the north. The leaders were Victor Emmanuel, king of Sardinia (to which Piedmont nominally belonged) from 1849, and his prime minister, Cavour, who by the end of the 1850s had driven the Austrians from

Piedmont and begun a process that was to lead to the dissolution of the Papal States. Pius had been forced to rely on French and Austrian troops to maintain order in Rome and papal cities farther north, but when the French emperor Napoleon III concerted with Cavour to end Austrian occupation and promote the unification of Italy, Pius was left without protectors. The Italian provinces north of Rome were annexed one by one, peaceably or otherwise, until by 1860 the Papal States had been reduced to Rome and the area immediately surrounding it. Finally, in 1870 (with France under Prussian domination),Victor Emmanuel seized Rome and made it the capital of a united Italy, leaving Pius famously "the prisoner of the Vatican," the only area left under his control as temporal ruler (under a set of "guarantees" he refused to accept). This in fact led to a rush of sympathy for him and eventually to a huge extension of the influence of the pope worldwide, but Pius may be excused for not seeing it in those terms at the time. On the wider political scene his policy was to defend the interests of the Church against often-hostile States by signing concordats. Some of these—with Spain, Portugal, Costa Rica, Guatemala, Nicaragua, San Salvador, Honduras, Haiti, Venezuela, and Ecuador—lasted; others—with Würtemburg, Baden, Russia, and Austria—were abrogated relatively quickly.

As a temporal ruler Pius inevitably devoted much of his time to what would now be accepted as secular politics, but his main concern (though he would not have accepted the distinction) was with the religious health of the Church. Here again he saw the Church as a citadel under siege from all sides: liberalism in all its forms, secular and religious; rationalism; naturalism; freemasonry; socialism; communism ... the intellectual counterparts of the radicals who were undoubtedly attacking church structures wherever they took power in Italy and elsewhere. His opposition to the whole tenor of the age was expressed most forcefully in his encyclical *Quanta Cura*,"Condemning Current Errors," with its attached "Syllabus of Errors," 80 in number, dated 8 December 1864, the tenth anniversary of the proclamation of the dogma of the Immaculate Conception. This, rather than the declaration of papal infallibility six years later, may be seen as marking the high point of ultramontanism and the aggrandizement of the papacy, largely setting its course for almost a hundred years, until the Second Vatican Council ushered in a new relationship between Church and world. As late as 1911, the *Catholic Encyclopedia* could say of the "Syllabus" that, "It has done an inestimable service to the Church and to society at large by unmasking the false liberalism which had begun to insinuate its subtle poison into the very marrow of Catholicism."

Pius' pontificate was more obviously successful in ecclesiastical affairs. He was responsible for the restoration of the hierarchy in England and Wales in 1850, appointing Bishop Nicholas Wiseman, then vicar apostolic of the London District of the English Mission, cardinal and first archbishop of Westminster. The Roman triumphalism of Wiseman's first pastoral, issued "From the Flaminian Gate" (in Rome), aroused fears of papal aggression in many British subjects,

47

including the prime minister, Lord John Russell. The fears were spread by a campaign in *The Times*: effigies of the pope and the cardinal were burned on Guy Fawkes' day, and Wiseman adopted a more conciliatory tone to avoid outright persecution of Catholics. Three years later, Pius restored the Catholic hierarchy in the Netherlands. He was also responsible for the erection of more than forty dioceses in the United States over the period from 1847 to 1874; and, as noted above, for a number of concordats with various European and American governments. In the central government of the Church he reduced the importance of the college of cardinals—which in any case no longer had the Papal States to govern—while making its composition more international. Papal nunciatures and Roman Congregations (the Curia) assumed greater importance, but they tended to be headed by mediocre figures who "favoured everything that was old, from dress to opinions, from labels to theology" (Cochin, 1862). More positively, Pius insisted that all priests should have a seminary education, which improved the spiritual formation of the clergy and enabled them to cope with the external expansion of the Church, largely through emigration from Europe to North and South America and to Australia. Missions increased greatly, largely through the work of Cardinal Barnabo, whom Pius appointed prefect of the Society for the Propagation of the Faith.

He also considerably developed the devotional life of the Church, with a strong emphasis on Mary, especially through the promulgation of the doctrine of the Immaculate Conception as dogma through the apostolic constitution *Ineffabilis Deus* of 8 December 1854. The belief was ancient and popular, spread from Britain to the Continent in the Middle Ages mainly by St Anselm (21 Apr.) and John Duns Scotus (8 Nov.; "Who fired France for Mary without spot," as Hopkins wrote). The feast—as the Conception of Mary—became obligatory for the Roman rite in 1708, and Pius' declaration of the *Immaculate* Conception was made after a process of consultation with the bishops, who advised him that it was opportune. It appeared to receive supernatural confirmation four years later with the apparitions of a "Lady" who said she was the Immaculate Conception to Bernadette Soubirous at Lourdes. His other great devotions were to the Sacred Heart, extending the feast-day to the whole world in 1856 and consecrating the Catholic world to the Sacred Heart in 1875; and to the Eucharist, as embodied in the Blessed Sacrament.

This intensification of popular piety was at least in part a healthy corrective to the rather cold "deism" promoted in the eighteenth century. Encouragement of frequent communion showed Christ as the incarnation of divine love. Pius promoted the devotion of Perpetual Adoration of the Blessed Sacrament, the purpose of which was personal atonement for the injuries inflicted on Christ. This need for atonement was then extended to public authorities and produced the idea of Eucharistic Congresses. In France, veneration of the Sacred Heart was to become associated with concern for the "prisoner of the Vatican" and memory of the national defeat by the Prussians in 1870. The whole popular devotional movement developed, though, without intellectual roots. Pius showed little interest in learning or research, and Rome lacked good libraries, so that in 1863 the German historian Anton Döllinger could say, with justification, that the German school of theology was defending Catholicism with rifles, while the Roman school was doing so with bows and arrows—a situation that largely persisted until at least the 1940s.

The idea of a council as the means of settling the problems besetting the Church in the modern world was suggested to Pius as early as 1849, but it was slow to mature, taking shape after he consulted a group of cardinals in 1864. Four preparatory commissions were formed; the project was announced in June 1967; and then a year later, on 29 June 1868, Pius issued the Bull *Aeterni Patris* convoking the Vatican Council. It had been proclaimed as an "ecumenical council," and Orthodox, Anglican, and Protestant leaders were invited to "submit" to Rome in order for them to be able to take part. Not surprisingly, none accepted this clumsy invitation. The Council's main task was to produce a Dogmatic Constitution on the Church, and Chapter 11 of the draft dealt with the question of papal infallibility, again an ancient doctrine but never systematically defined. Curial preparations aroused liberal suspicions that the council Fathers were going to be presented with a *fait accompli*, and even that the *Syllabus of Errors* was to be made the basis for deliberations. Promulgation of the personal infallibility of the pope was seen as confirming the teaching of the great Scholastics, as expressing reverence for the person of Pius IX, as sending a warning to democratic societies that a central authority was always necessary, and as encouraging potential converts looking for assurance—an aspect stressed by Cardinal Manning of Westminster (who headed one election committee for the commission and managed to exclude the names of those he suspected of opposing the definition). A minority of bishops saw all these aspects as indications of its inopportuneness. The first achievement of the council was the approval of the dogmatic constitution *Dei Filius*, a solid document dealing with God, revelation, and the faith. Outside the chamber, papal infallibility was the chief concern. Despite an effective minority opposition group led by Lord Acton, Pius personally decided, on 1 March 1870, to include a formal definition of papal infallibility in the draft constitution on the Church. "Infallibilists" and "antis" did all they could, by methods open and underhand, to influence public opinion and the press one way and another. Secular governments were concerned that a definition would be used to encourage the Church to interfere in their legitimate spheres of action. The debate threatened to become more and more acrimonious and to last at least a year; Pius therefore, despite the opposition of three out of five council presidents, decided to take it out of the dogmatic constitution and deal with it separately as soon as *Dei Filius* had been promulgated. It thus became the subject of a small constitution of its own, devoted entirely to the position of the pope, which was thereby divorced from the broader question of the nature of the Church.

Discussion opened on 13 May 1870, and the debate, inside and outside the chamber, was intense and passionate, to the distress of most of the Fathers, who were generally moderates looking for a formulation between the two extremes. But Pius, increasingly impatient and influenced by ultramontanist advisers, refused a strong minority request for amendments to the proposed wording that would imply the need for close cooperation between the pope and the Church. Rather than vote against the proposal in the presence of a pope who set such personal store by the outcome, some sixty bishops, led by Dupanloup of Orléans (who earlier may or may not have asked for the secular powers to intervene to prevent a definition), retired to their dioceses. The final version, including the tendentious phrase *"ex sese, non autem ex consensu Ecclesiae"* ("of himself, and not from the consensus of the Church"), was solemnly approved by virtually all those present on 18 July 1870. Most of the Fathers then left Rome to escape the summer heat.

Two months later Garibaldi's troops entered Rome and effectively put an end to the council, which Pius formally adjourned *sine die* on 20 October. It was to be ninety-four years before its successor, convened by Pope John XXIII, produced a very different dogmatic constitution on the Church, redressing the balance by considering its hierarchical structure after its composition as "people of God." On 13 May 1871 Pius refused to accept the Italian government's terms for his occupancy of the Vatican—now the only remaining part of the former Papal States—expressed in the "Guarantee Law," but he did remain there, a self-declared prisoner. His health declined, and he died on 7 February 1878.

The process for his beatification opened in 1907 under his successor but one, Pius X, but made little headway, with no evidence of popular devotion to him in his home province of Le Marche. The three succeeding popes all tried to revive it, with little success; then under John Paul II he was proclaimed "venerable" in 1985. The process again stalled until in 1999 a miracle attributed to his intercession was confirmed, and the pope consulted the Italian bishops, who—somewhat unexpectedly—endorsed his beatification, which took place, in the same ceremony as that of Pope John XXIII, on 3 September 2000. It was an extraordinary combination, which "liberal" Catholics tended to see as a deliberate attempt to overshadow the pope who "opened the windows" of the Vatican on the world by the one who closed them against the world. This was expressed in an editorial in *The Tablet* of 8 July 2000, hoping for a last-minute change of heart (with Archbishop Oscar Romero replacing Pius IX), calling the beatification "the work of a small group of ultra-conservatives," and asking what benefit the example of Pius IX could be to the modern world. Therein lies the problem, which cannot be overlooked in a work that takes its cue from Alban Butler's "Example instructs without usurping the authoritative air of a master ..." So, "For whom, to what degree and with what qualifications is this blessed or saint a model?" (O'Malley).

Misgivings in both Catholic and Jewish circles focused on the case of Edgardo Mortara, kidnapped from his Jewish home in Rome by papal police on 23 June 1858, because he had been baptized by a Catholic maid when he was dangerously ill as an infant. Pius personally refused to give the child back to his parents, on the grounds that it was not right for a Christian child to live in a Jewish household, and made him a personal ward. (He was eventually ordained a priest.) Another counter-indication was his restoration and application of the death penalty in the Papal States. Wider grounds for objection revolve around the impossibility of separating the man (who left little or no record of his inner spiritual life) from the pope who was the last monarch of the Papal States, about whom an enormous amount of information is available and of whom reasoned—rather than the earlier highly impassioned and partisan— judgments have eventually been made (by Mortara and Aubert in particular). The overall conclusion seems inescapable that Pius' most positive legacy to the Church was the loss of the Papal States, against which he fought for thirty years and which he considered "impious" even to mention as a possibility. Even with this outcome, he left a "bulwark church" (O'Malley) that lasted almost a century until the walls came down with Vatican II's pastoral constitution on "The Church in the World Today." Can one really argue that Pius IX was the pope that was needed in his day, as John XXIII was the one needed in his? Both completely overturned initial expectations of them; beyond that it is difficult to find anything that justifies their sharing in the same beatification ceremony.

Several biographies were published in English around the time of his death: see the *CE* entry. The principal modern study is G. Martina, SJ, *Pio Nono*, 3 vols (1974, 1986, 1990); see also R. Aubert, *Le pontificat de Pie IX, 1846–1878* (vol. XXI of Fliche–Martin, *Histoire de l'église*, 1952), with good bibliography, there is no English translation of either of these, but Aubert also contributed the relevant chapters to H. Jedin, (ed.), *History of the Church*, vol. 8, *The Church in the Age of Liberalism* (English translation 1981; see also abridged edn, vol. 3, pp. 218–385). Original English studies include E. E. Y. Hales, *Pio Nono* (1954, n.e. 1962); and F. J. Coppa, *Pope Pius IX* (1979). *How the Pope Became Infallible* (1981) is a synopsis of A. B. Hasler, *Pius IX (1846–1878); Päpstliche Unfelbarkheit und 1. Vatikanisches Konzil*, 2 vols (1977), discussed also by Martina in *Archivum Historiae Pontificiae* 16 (1978), 341–550. Further refs in *ODCC* (1957), p. 1029. On the beatification see K. Woodward, *Making Saints* (1990); *The Tablet*, 8 July 2000, p. 915; and J. W. O'Malley, "The Beatification of Pope Pius IX" in *America*, 26 Aug. 2000, online at www.americamagazine.org/articles/Omalley-pius9. On the Mortara incident see D. L. Kertzer, *The Kidnapping of Edgardo Mortara* (1997).

The line from Hopkins is from his "Duns Scotus's Oxford," in *Poems of Gerard Manley Hopkins*, 3d edn, ed. R. Bridges and W. H. Gardner (1948). The website of the Holy Cross Seminary in Australia (Opus Dei) praises the Syllabus of Errors and its remedy of prayer compared to the "optimistic humanism" of the Second Vatican Council and its reliance on the better side of human nature.

The most familiar portrait photograph shows Pius at the time of the Vatican Council and is shown in Patron Saints Index at www.catholicforum.com/saints/saintp01. An engraving based on it appears in, *inter alia*, A. C. Ewald, *The Life and Times of William Ewart Gladstone*, 5 vols (n.d.). An image showing a rather more severe face, with a pronounced Roman nose, is in the Perry-Castañeda library at the university of Austin, Texas. A bronze bust by T. Saulini, *c.* 1850, shows him in papal robes with insignia, including the tiara and keys, on the collar. This was reproduced as a bronzed uniface electrotype commemorative medal. Another medal, by F. Speranza, 1870, shows him facing right, with the reverse depicting Christ asleep in the boat with his terrified apostles in the storm, a clear image of the barque of Peter tossed by the waves of nationalism, liberalism, etc.

8

St Josephine Bakhita (1869–1947)

Her real name is unknown, as the trauma of being kidnapped at the age of nine (or possibly a few years younger) made her forget it completely. She is the first Sudanese to be canonized, and the first saint from Africa since the early centuries when northern Africa was an integral part of the Roman Empire and therefore fertile territory for the early expansion of Christianity, representing a major part of Christendom before falling to the Muslims in the seventh century.

Her exact date or place of birth are not known either, but Josephine is assumed to have come from the village of Olgossa, twenty-five miles northeast of the township of Nyala in the Darfur region of southern Sudan. Her parents were relatively wealthy and she had three brothers and two sisters, one of which was her twin. An uncle was the village chief. Darfur at the time was part of the British-Egyptian Protectorate of Sudan. The slave trade had been banned in 1856, but the ban was not rigorously enforced and marauding bands of slave-traders regularly carried off children to sell as slaves, mainly in the Arab markets of North Africa, the trade with America having been effectively halted. Josephine's elder sister was seized in this way while she was at home minding the youngest child while the rest of the family were working in the fields. Josephine herself described (many years later) what then happened to her:

> I was approximately nine years old when I, one early morning, walked around the fields, a bit far away from home, with a companion. Suddenly we saw two

strangers appear from behind a fence. One of then told my companion, "Let the small girl go into the forest to pick me some fruits. Meanwhile, you continue on your walk." ... I, of course, did not suspect anything and hurried to obey, which my mother had taught me to do. Once we were in the forest, I saw two persons behind me. One of them briskly grabbed me with one hand, while the other one pulled out a knife and held it to my side. He told me, "If you cry, you'll die. Follow us."

She was given the name Bakhita (meaning "fortunate one"), kept in a "hole of a room" for a month, and then sold to a slave-merchant, who force-marched her and a group of other slaves for eight days. She and another young girl managed to escape from a slave-market and head for open country, but they were soon tricked and sold again. After another forced march they came to the city of El Obeid, where Bakhita was sold to an Arab chief. She was to be a maid to his daughter, but she somehow offended his son, who beat her so severely she took a month to recover. Her worst owners, however, were the fourth, in the household of a Turkish general in Khartoum, where the mistress had her tattooed by the excruciating traditional method of making incisions with a knife and rubbing salt into the cuts for a month to cause raised welts. The pain was extreme, and Bakhita records that she thought she would die. She was then bought by the Italian vice consul, Callisto Legnani, who treated her well, so that she knew kindness for the first time since her capture. His family were forced to flee from Sudan in 1885 when the Dervish forces of Mohammed Ahmed, known as The Mahdi (Muslim Messiah), advanced from El Obeid on Khartoum (where they famously killed General Gordon). Legnani offered to free Bakhita and leave her in Sudan, but she begged him to take her to Italy with his family, and he eventually agreed.

The party was met on arrival in Italy by the wife of a friend, Augusto Michaeli, who had escaped from Sudan with them. Signora Michaeli asked to be given one of the African servants they had brought, and Bakhita was chosen. She lived with them for three years, in the village of Zianigo, near Mirano Veneto in the region of Venice. She acted as nanny to a daughter, Alice, known as Minnina, of whom she became very fond. At one point she returned to the Sudan for a year with the family.

Signor Michaeli then acquired a large hotel at Suakin, on the shores of the Red Sea, and his wife went with him to manage it. Minnina and Bakhita were entrusted to the care of the Canossian Sisters (originally Servants of the Poor, founded by St Magdalen of Canossa, 1774–1835, canonized in 1988; Apr. 10), who ran the Institute of Catechumens in Venice. Here she came to know the Christian religion and found a God whom "she had experienced in her heart without ever knowing who he was." Signora Michieli returned to collect her daughter and Bakhita, to take them to Suakin, but Bakhita, who was by then legally of age, refused to go back to Africa, choosing rather to stay with the Canossian Sisters. In this she was supported by the cardinal patriarch of Venice, to whom Signora Michaeli—who evidently still regarded her as some sort of slave—had appealed. On 9 January 1890 she was baptized and given the name Josephine (Giuseppina, together with Margarita and Afortunata, the last translating "Bakhita") and received First Communion and Confirmation from the cardinal patriarch himself.

Josephine joined the Institute in 1893 and took her final vows on 8 December 1896, after being questioned and then welcomed into the Order by the new patriarch of Venice, the future Pope Pius X. She lived as a Canossian Sister for just over a further fifty years, moving from Venice to Schio in 1902, working variously as cook, seamstress, embroiderer, sacristan, and doorkeeper, all of which duties she carried out with unusual attention to detail. She became a much-loved figure to all who came to the Institute for help, as well as to the pupils at the school, and was known as "Sor Moretta" (little brown sister). Children especially were apparently charmed by the lilting intonation of her Italian. She was encouraged to start writing her memoirs in 1910, and they were eventually published in 1930. Her writing demonstrated the physical and spiritual path she had trodden and made her a celebrated figure in Italy. Josephine longed to be a missionary and take the gospel back to her own people. Instead, in 1935 this shy and reserved former slave girl found herself travelling around Italy delivering lectures on her experiences and collecting donations for the Sisters. From 1936 to 1938 she was doorkeeper at the missionary novitiate in Milan, where she was able to welcome young women arriving to train as missionaries. She then returned to Schio, where she stayed for the duration of the Second World War (1939–45). During her later years she was confined to a wheelchair and in constant pain. She remained resigned and cheerful, saying that she was "As the Master desires."

As her last days approached, Josephine was feverish with pneumonia and tormented by images of her former slavery, begging those caring for her to "Loosen the chains … they are so heavy." She finally died peacefully, with the words "Madonna, Madonna" on her lips. Her body lay in state for three days, with thousands passing the bier to pay their last respects.

In response to popular devotion, the diocesan process for her beatification was started in 1959, twelve years after her death. Pope John Paul II beatified her on 17 May 1992. The following year he welcomed her relics in Khartoum Cathedral, with the words, "Rejoice, all of Africa. Bakhita has come back to you: the daughter of the Sudan, sold into slavery as a living piece of merchandise, and yet still free: free with the freedom of the saints." He canonized Josephine on 1 October 2000, calling her "our universal sister" and declaring her patron of Sudan. As the first African-born saint of modern times, her canonization was intended as a symbol to extol African Christianity and African women, and to make reparation for European and Christian involvement in the history of slavery. According to the editor of the Spanish missionary journal *Mundo negro*, "Bakhita taught us the path of liberation. The path she followed and that led her from slavery to freedom still has to be walked by so many people who are subject to a variety of forms of slavery."Actual slavery, in fact, still continues in the Sudan, in much the same form as Bakhita experienced it, with marauding gangs from the government-controlled north seizing women and children in the largely Christian south of the country and the Dafur region in the west.

K. Jones, *Women Saints: Lives of Faith and Courage* (1999), pp. 188–92, citing M. L. Dagnino, *Bakhita tells her Story* (1991, 3d edn 1993); Mother Agnes, FDCC, *The Lucky One* (1970); *Vita più Speciale: Communicazioni di Vita Canossiana* no. 3 (1992); Christian Service International Report, Oct. 1998. J.-L. Lisalde in *Mundo negro* Oct. 2000, cited on afrol.com/archive/josephine_bakhita. There is one well-known photograph of her (though its origin seems to be unknown), reproduced in *Women Saints* and on the Patron Saints Index, which also contains numerous quotes from her memoirs. See also *Bibl.SS*. Suppl. 1, 114; *A.A.S.* (1993), p. 224.

20

BB Francisco (1908–1919) and Jacinta (1910–1920) Marto

Two of the three shepherd children who experienced visions of the Virgin Mary at Fátima in Portugal in 1917 died young as a result of the epidemic of Spanish flu that swept the world in late 1918, killing more people than died in the Great War of 1914–18; the third, their cousin Lucia Santo, lived to the age of 97, dying in February 2005. It was she who wrote the account of the apparitions—including the famous three "secrets"—on which the huge devotional enterprise covered by the word"Fátima"depends.

Francisco was born on 11 June 1908 and Jacinta on 11 March 1910, both in the little village of Aljustrel, just outside the town of Fátima in Portugal, seventy miles north-east of Lisbon. Their parents, Manuel Pedro Marto and his wife Olimpia de Jesús, were peasant farmers, and the children spent their time minding sheep with their older cousin. None went to school. Francisco is said to have been the more serious of the two, loving nature and music, while his sister was more playful and active. Both were placed in the company of their cousin, who was devout and taught them to pray, partly to avoid"bad company."

The story of the apparitions resembles the earlier sequence of appearances to Bernadette at Lourdes, with the difference that visions of the Virgin Mary were preceded by those of a messenger, an angel who announced that he was the protector of Portugal and the angel of peace. He appeared to them three times, taught them prayers, and on his last appearance brought a host and chalice, giving the host to Lucia, who had made her First Communion, and the consecrated wine to Francisco and Jacinta. The first apparition of the Virgin took place on 13 May 1917, when she asked them to pray the rosary and make sacrifices for the conversion of sinners, promising to return six times. They evidently told others of their experience, as crowds grew larger for each appearance. They took the appeal to make sacrifices with great seriousness, giving their food to people needier than themselves, denying themselves water on hot days, and tying tight cords round their waists—until told by Our Lady to stop doing this. Otherwise their lives went on normally, and Lucia started going to school, in response to another request from Our Lady. Francisco and Jacinta walked there with her but did not attend school. Francisco, told that he would not be in this world for long, did not consider it worth while to learn to read and spent the school hours praying in church, from where the girls collected him on their way home.

By the third appearance, on 13 July 1917, the crowds had grown to 4,000, but only the three children saw anything. According to Lucia's account, the Virgin showed them a terrible vision of hell and asked them to pray the rosary daily and make sacrifices to atone for the sins of the world, foretelling that then the war would end but that if men went on offending God another worse one would break out in the pontificate of Pius XI. She asked for the world to be consecrated to her Immaculate Heart and promised that if this were done Russia would be converted and there would be peace. (This took place between the February and October revolutions in Russia: the "revelations" had a strongly anti-socialist and anti-Communist tone.) On 13 August, the three had been arrested and locked up to force them to reveal the "secret" communicated in July, which they resolutely refused to do. Released two days later, they saw the Virgin again on 19 August. Once more, she told them to pray and make sacrifices and to return on 13 September, which they did, with a crowd of 30,000. They were told to continue praying the rosary so that the war would end, and to come back in October, when Our Lady would bring (somewhat confusingly) "Our Lord, Our Lady of Sorrows and Carmel, and St Joseph and the Child Jesus to bless the world." She would also perform a miracle "so that all would believe." On 13 October, a crowd of 70,000 gathered, in torrential rain. Our Lady asked them to build a chapel in her honour as Virgin of the Rosary, then said, "Let there be no more offences against God Our Lord, who is already very offended." Lucia's account continues:

> And opening her hands she made them reflect the sun and, as she rose up, the brightness of her own light continued, projecting itself on the sun [which by then had broken through the clouds]. And I called for everyone to look at the sun. The miracle of the sun then took place, promised three months earlier, as a proof of the truth of the apparitions of Fátima. The rain stopped and the sun spun on itself three times, throwing out flashes of light of all colours in all directions. At a certain height it seemed to detach itself from the firmament and fall on the crowd. All were astounded. The journalists from the secular press who had come incredulous

to ridicule the apparitions took photos and bore witness to that miracle in the papers. After ten minutes of marvel the sun returned to its normal state.

This was the last of the apparitions to the three children together. Somehow they seem to have returned to a normal life for over a year. In the autumn of 1918 both Francisco and Jacinta were struck down with Spanish flu. Both developed complications, and neither recovered. Francisco died five months later, on 14 April 1919, the day after making his First Communion. Jacinta lingered on for nearly another year, developing pleurisy, which led to a huge abscess in her chest. She underwent an operation in a Lisbon hospital, but this failed to cure her and she died in the hospital on 20 February 1920.

Lucia entered religious life and continued to receive further instructions and promises. A vision in 1925 encouraged the devotional practice of "five first Saturdays," in reparation for the sins of the world, to which St Pope Pius X had attached indulgences in 1905. In 1929 she was asked to arrange for the consecration of the world and especially Russia to her Immaculate Heart. It was not until 1940 that she received permission to communicate this wish to Pope Pius XII, and not until 1984 that Pope John Paul II consecrated the world to the Immaculate Heart of Mary "together with all the bishops," as the Virgin had collegially requested—both Pius XII and Paul VI had done so on their own. On 8 October 2000 John Paul II again consecrated the world and the third millennium to the Immaculate Heart of Mary, with Sr Lucia leading one of the mysteries of the rosary from her cell on the world's television. The first two "secrets" were revealed shortly after the Second World War, and the third, long rumoured in popular Catholic circles to predict the end of the world, was known to a privileged few in the Vatican and eventually made public in 2000, with a cautious commentary by Cardinal Ratzinger. It turned out to be a somewhat gnomic pronouncement in language derived from the Apocalypse, involving a pontiff understood to be John Paul II, who has consistently stressed the role of Mary in the salvation of the world.

Francisco and Jacinta were declared Venerable in April 1989 and beatified by Pope John Paul II in Fátima on 13 May 2000, the eighty-third anniversary of the first apparition, an event expressly connected with the Great Jubilee celebrations and the birth of the new millennium. They are the first non-martyr children to be beatified. There is no avoiding the fact that the language of the "revelations" strikes a note very different from anything characteristic of Mary and Jesus in the Gospels, and seems to respond more to the political concerns of the time (providing an important "prop" to the authoritarian, anti-socialist "New State" regime of Antonio d'Oliviera Salazar in Portugal from 1928 to 1968); but this has not prevented Fátima from growing steadily in popularity as a pilgrimage centre, now attracting four million pilgrims each year.

✤

The most detailed accessible web account is provided (in Spanish) by the Florida-based Sisters of the Pierced Hearts of Jesus and Mary at www.corazones.org/santos/francisco_jacinta.

The third Visionary of Fatima, Sr Lucia de Jesus dos Santos, died on 13 February 2005, aged 97. She had spent 57 years in virtual seclusion in the Carmalite convent in Coimbra. She last visited the shrine at Fatima when Pope John Paul II beatified her cousins on 13 May 2000. Details of her correspondence with the Pope and of the "secrets" of Fatima, with a commentary by Cardinal Ratzinger (now Pope Benedict XVI), can be found at www.zenit.org/english/archive/documents/fatima/eng.

24

Bd Thomas Mary Fusco, *Founder* (1831–1891)

Tommaso Maria was the seventh of eight children born to Dr Antonio Fusco and his wife Stella Giordano, who came from a family of Italian nobles. He was born on 1 December 1831 near Salerno, on the coast thirty miles south-east of Naples. His mother died of cholera when he was six, and his father, a doctor, four years later. Thomas was educated by his father's brother Giuseppe, a priest and primary school teacher, who died in 1847, the year Thomas entered the diocesan seminary of Nocera. He was ordained in 1855, at the age of twenty-four.

Thomas opened a school for children in his own house in the mornings and in the evenings organized prayer groups for young people and adults in the parish church of Pagani, where St Alphonsus de'Liguori (1 Aug.) had preached and ministered 130 years earlier. In 1857 he entered the Congregation of Missionaries of Nocera and became an itinerant missionary in southern Italy. In 1860 he was appointed chaplain at the shrine of Our Lady of Mount Carmel in Pagani and developed associations for lay men and women. Two years later Thomas started a school of moral theology in his own house, where he trained priests to become better confessors, and founded the Priestly Society of the Catholic Apostolate, designed to train and supply priests to carry out local missions. This was to receive papal approval in 1874. The plight of an orphan girl inspired him to another foundation in 1873: the Daughters of Charity of the Most Precious Blood, which started with the clothing of three postulants on the feast of the Epiphany and an orphanage with seven girls to care for.

In 1874 Thomas was appointed parish priest of San Felice e Corpo di Cristo, the principal church in Pagani, a post he was to hold until 1887. He wrote books of moral theology and developed a great devotion to the Precious Blood. He became the victim of a slander campaign by a fellow priest envious of his reputation: his bishop had said to him at the time of his second foundation,

"Have you chosen the title of the Most Precious Blood? Well, may you be prepared to drink the bitter cup." He bore the trial with patience and was eventually vindicated. His health failed from a chronic disease of the liver, and Thomas died peacefully on 24 February 1891.

His cause was started in 1955 and, once the decree of heroic virtue was published in April 2001, moved very swiftly. A miracle produced by his intercession was recognized in July, and he was beatified on 7 October the same year. "By virtue of faith he knew how to live in the world the reality of the Kingdom of God in a very special way," the Pope said in his homily.

25

Bd Maria Adeodata Pisani (1806–1855)

This Benedictine nun is chronologically the earliest of the three Maltese beatified in Malta, on 9 May 2001, by Pope John Paul II on the last leg of his journey "in the footsteps of St Paul," which had taken him to the Holy Land, Syria, and Greece. The other two are Bd Ignatius Falzon (1 July) and Bd George Preca (26 July). A brief outline of their background seems appropriate here.

The British took informal possession of Malta in 1800, ruling it as a protectorate. In 1813 a first Constitution was drawn up in London, making Malta and Gozo a Crown Colony, ruled by a Governor. This stipulated religious freedom for the island's Roman Catholic population, though some ancient privileges of the Church were removed in subsequent years (including control of the press). Malta was a strategic staging post between Britain and its possessions in the Middle East, and its importance increased with the Crimean War of 1853–56 and the opening of the Suez Canal in 1869. The island was transformed into a fortress, and British sailors and soldiers were a constant presence in Valletta, the capital.

Education had for centuries been exclusively in the hands of the Church and had proved extremely ineffective, with an illiteracy rate of over 90 per cent. Even religious knowledge was virtually non-existent, with a folk religion based almost entirely on popular custom. Both Ignatius Falzon in the nineteenth century and George Preca in the twentieth were to recognize and address all these issues. Most of the British servicemen and their families were Anglican, and it was Anglicans who first made parts of the Bible and a catechism in Maltese available to their Catholic hosts. During the Second World War, Malta endured a siege and bombardment by the Axis forces that earned its inhabitants collectively the highest British civilian decoration, the George Cross. In the post-war period it became independent and began a gradual process of modernization (and secularization) as it assimilated itself to the conditions of the European Union, which it joined in 2004.

Maria Teresa Pisani came from a mixed Maltese-Neopolitan family and was born in Naples on 29 December 1806, where she spent the first nineteen years of her life. Her father, Baron Benedetto Pisani Monpalao Cuzkeri of Frigenuini, was a wealthy Maltese nobleman who developed a drink problem that split the matrimonial home. Maria Teresa's mother fled, entrusting the young Maria Teresa to the baron's mother, who took good care of her but died when she was only ten. She was then sent to the smartest boarding school in Naples, where she stayed for seven years. Her father took part in an attempted uprising in Naples in 1821 and on its failure was sentenced to death. As he was a British citizen, however, the sentence was commuted to one of banishment, and he was sent back to Malta, where he continued his dissolute way of life. Maria Teresa and her mother also returned in 1825, to the same town, Rabat, but not to the paternal home.

Her mother tried to prepare her to make an advantageous marriage, but Maria Teresa declined anyone she proposed. She went to daily Mass and evening prayers, and it was when praying one day before an image of Our Lady of Good Counsel (a title deriving from an icon venerated in Gennazzano, south-east of Rome) that she decided she had a vocation to religious life. Her parents were shocked and persuaded her to wait a year before making a final decision. She obeyed but remained determined and on 16 July 1828 entered the Benedictine monastery of St Peter in Medina as a postulant. She joined the novitiate six months later, taking the names Maria Adeodata in religion. The following year she signed a Notarial Act renouncing her (vast) inheritance, after which she was solemnly professed. She spent the rest of her relatively short life, a further twenty-five years, in the monastery. Known for her exceptional humility and charity, she never put herself forward for any position of authority, preferring relatively humble tasks such as sacristan and infirmarian, where she could feel closest to Jesus in the sacrament and in the sick.

Maria Adeodata was then appointed novice-mistress, a position she held for four years and which inspired her to write a spiritual treatise, "The Mystical Garden of the Soul that Loves Jesus and Mary," and several other works of spiritual formation, as well as a number of prayers for liturgical use, these last written in the Maltese she had struggled to learn. In 1851 she was elected abbess and as such endured a difficult two years, with new members of the community objecting to her proposed reforms (aimed at a closer observance of the Rule) and some envy of her reputation for saintliness. After her term as abbess her heart, never very strong, weakened, and her health inexorably declined, while she tried to play a normal active role in community life. On 25 February 1855 she dragged herself to chapel for conventual Mass and had to be carried back to bed after receiving Communion. She died soon after. The news of her death spread immediately all over the island, in the words, "The saint has died." She was buried in the monastery crypt the following day.

Maria Adeoata's cause was initiated in 1892, and a cure of the mortally sick

Benedictine abbess of Subiaco in 1897 was approved as a miracle due to her intercession; but then the cause languished due to lack of funds and political difficulties between Malta and Italy. It was taken up again by the community of St Peter's in 1989 and moved relatively swiftly to her beatification on 9 May 2001. At the ceremony, the Pope spoke of his special concern to see religious life fully adapted to the teaching of the Second Vatican Council on its special witness to the modern world, and asked Blessed Maria Adeodata to intercede in this cause, while commending"to all consecrated men and women the example of personal maturity and responsibility which was wonderfully evident in [her] life."

❖

Maltese history from Fr J. Bezzina,"An Historic Note,"introduction to biography of Ignatius Falzon in *Franciscan News*, Malta, 24 April 2001; life mainly from "Footsteps of St Paul," issued by archdiocese of Malta: ewtn.com/footsteps/ BL_Maria_Adeodata_Pisani.htm.

26

St Paula Montal Fornés, *Founder* (1799–1889)

Her life spanned almost the whole of the nineteenth century, a century in which Spain oscillated violently between revolution and reaction, liberal secularism and conservative Catholicism. Paula Montal Fornés steered a steady course, devoting her life to providing a sound Christian education for girls, first in her native Catalonia, then throughout Spain, and founding a new Congregation, the Daughters of Mary, Sisters of the Pious Schools (*Hijas de María, Religiosas de las Escuelas Pías* in Spanish).

She was born on 11 October 1799 in Arenys de Mar, on the Mediterranean coast twenty miles north-east of Barcelona, and spent her childhood there, the eldest daughter of a modest and pious family. Her father died when she was ten, and as the eldest she found herself helping her mother look after the younger siblings and so denied any chance of receiving an education. This made her determined to fulfil her vocation by providing just what she—and indeed most girls in Spain at the time—had lacked.

When Paula was thirty she moved north to Figueras, near the border with France, together with a lifelong friend, Inés Busquets. They opened a school for girls that provided a broader curriculum than that generally on offer for boys. Their aim was to offer an education that was fully human because it was fully Christian. They saw the subordination of women in Spanish society as a basic cause of family breakdown and many other social ills, and set out to make the advancement of women through education their apostolate. After thirteen years in Figueras they opened a second school in Paula's home town of Arenys de Mar, followed in 1846 by a third in Sabadell, inland from Barcelona. There Paula was helped by two Piarist Fathers (the Order founded by St Joseph Calasanz in 1617, formally the Order of Clerks Regular of the Pious Schools) to found a Congregation for women based on the Piarist model and with the spirituality of St Joseph Calasanz (25 Aug.; declared patron of Christian schools in 1948) as its inspiration. They helped her draw up a canonical structure, and on 2 February 1847 Paula and three companions made their profession as Daughters of Mary, Sisters of the Pious Schools. She added "of St Joseph of Calasanz" to Paula as her name in religion.

Between 1829 and 1859 Paula personally founded seven schools in the area around Barcelona and collaborated in a further four, including one in the city itself. Her last foundation was at Olesa de Montserrat, a small, poor town at the foot of the mountain on which the famous monastery of Montserrat stands. She spent the last thirty years of her life there. By the time she died, at the age of ninety, of natural causes on 26 February 1889, she had instructed the first 130 Sisters of the Congregation; these then numbered 346, teaching in nineteen schools spread throughout Spain. The process for her beatification began in Barcelona in 1957; Pope John Paul II beatified her on 18 April 1993. After the cure of an eight-year-old Colombian girl living in a violent area of Medellín was ascribed to her intercession that same year, the canonization process was able to move forward, and the ceremony took place on 25 November 2001. Her purpose had been to "Save the family, educating the young girls in a holy fear of God," as the pope quoted in his homily.

There are currently over 800 Sisters of the Pious Schools, working to educate some 30,000 students in 112 countries. Local addresses on diocesan websites.

27

Bd Caritas Brader, *Founder* (1860–1943)

Maria Josefa Carolina Brader was born in Kaltbrunn, in the easterly Canton of Sankt Gallen in Switzerland, on 14 August 1860. Her parents were Joseph Sebastian Brader and Maria Anna Carolina Zahner, and she was their only child. Maria showed academic promise as a child, but instead of going on to university she joined the Franciscan convent of Maria Hilf at Alstätten in

October 1880. She took the lengthy religious name Mary Charity—hence Caritas—of the Love of the Spirit and made her final vows in August 1882. This was then a cloistered convent, and she spent her first years as a nun teaching in the secondary school it ran, which she herself had attended.

A new dispensation then made it permissible for cloistered nuns to undertake apostolic work outside their convents, and many bishops in mission territories appealed to convents in Europe to send nuns to help in their areas. One such was Bishop Pedro Schumacher of Portoviejo in Ecuador, a Missionary of St Vincent de Paul, who wrote to Maria Hilf asking for volunteers. The superior herself, Mother Maria Bernarda Bütler (beatified on 29 Oct. 1995), decided to go with five others, including Sr Caritas, who was among the first to volunteer. They were based in Chone, in the coastal zone just south of the Equator, and for five years Sr Caritas worked as a teacher and catechist of children.

In 1893 she was moved to Túquerres, in Colombia, just over the border from Ecuador and high in the Andes. Her mission territory covered coastal zones, tropical jungle, and high plateau. The local people were generally extremely poor, and conditions could be dangerous. Sr Caritas loved them and sought out the most remote and excluded, those least likely to have had the gospel preached to them. She saw the need for more missionaries if such vast areas were ever to be properly evangelized, and with the backing of a German missionary, Fr Reinaldo Herbrand, she set about founding a new Congregation, of which she became first superior. Known as the Franciscan Sisters of Mary Immaculate, their first members were young women from Switzerland following the example of the first six, but part of the purpose was to appeal to local girls, and Colombian vocations were soon numerous.

Now Mother Caritas ("María Caridad" in Spanish-speaking Colombia), she looked back to her own academic prowess at school and encouraged her Sisters to gain worthwhile academic qualifications, telling them that the better educated they were, the more they would be able to do "for our holy religion and the glory of God." Above all, however, she inculcated the Franciscan spirit of poverty: her Sisters were to live as poorly as the poor to whom they ministered. She was superior general of the new Congregation from its inception in 1893 to 1919, and then for a further period from 1928 to 1940, during which time she visited recent foundations in the U.S.A. She was eighty years old by the time she relinquished the position for the second time, and she lived a further three years, dying on 27 February in Pasto, the principal city of that region of southern Colombia.

She was immediately venerated as a saint, and pilgrims began flocking to her tomb. She was declared venerable in 1999, and after the unexpected survival and recovery of a girl from Pasto, born hydrocephalic, following prayers to Mother Caritas was declared miraculous in 2002, she was beatified in the first such ceremony of 2003, on 23 March.

MARCH

2

St Angela of the Cross Guerrero González, *Founder*
(1846–1932)

Born in Seville on 30 January 1846, christened María de los Angeles, and affectionately known as Angelita, she was one of fourteen children, of whom eight died in infancy. Hers was a pious family, and both her parents worked in the convent of the Trinitarian Fathers, her father as cook and her mother as laundress. She was brought up in the traditional *Sevillana* atmosphere of devotion to Our Lady under the guise of the various "Virgins" to whom many parish churches were dedicated. She made her first Communion when she was eight and was confirmed a year later.

Her father died when she was still young, and Angelita had to abandon her schooling and work to help support the family. She began work as a cobbler, making expensive shoes for society ladies and for clergymen in a workshop run by Antonia Maldonado. Antonia was a remarkable woman, who insisted that the working day should include time for praying the rosary and reading Lives of saints. Angelita went beyond this piety and began giving her Friday meal to the poor, asking other employees to contribute a little of their own. She was also found one day in a state of ecstasy, suspended above the floor. Antonia, recognizing that there was something exceptional about her, asked Canon José Torres Padilla, a holy priest and trained theologian, originally from the Canary Islands, to talk to her, and Angelita eventually told him of her desires and experiences. He became her spiritual director and remained so, guiding her throughout her life and as director of the Institute she was to found under his guidance until his death in 1878.

In her late teens Angelita wanted to enter a contemplative Order, and first tried the Discalced Carmelites in the Santa Cruz district of Seville. But her health was frail, and their regime was harsh, so they rejected her. Fr Torres steered her to direct care for cholera victims during an epidemic. She tried her vocation again in 1868, with the Daughters of Charity in Seville; this time she was admitted, and the nuns sent her to Cuenca and Valencia in an effort to improve her health; but this failed, and they too decided they had to let her go. She returned to work at Antonia's cobbler's workshop and during this period, urged by Fr Torres, wrote a lengthy account of her spiritual pilgrimage and aspirations.

She realized the concrete form her vocation could take when she heard friends criticizing a wealthy woman who gave food and medicines to the poor while encouraging them to remain content with their lot. All very well for her, was the general consensus, and Angelita had the intuition that she had to become poor with the poor—original in the days before the Second Vatican Council and liberation theology changed the perceptions of so many religious as to their place in society. Three other like-minded women joined her on 2 August 1875 and began community life with her in Seville. They personally consecrated themselves to God and vowed love and service of the poor, venturing out day and night from the rented room that was their convent to give what assistance they could, especially to the sick. Angelita became superior as Mother Angela of the Cross, and they called themselves the Sisters of the Company of the Cross. They were to lead a contemplative prayer life in their room whenever they were not answering calls from outside.

More women came to join them, and they had to find larger premises. Mother Angela insisted that these had to remain poor and even stipulated the details of decoration and furnishing: "A house where total silence reigns, its walls white and everything very clean; no furniture in the corridors, only at intervals some small cheap pictures of the Stations of the Cross with a crucifix above."A second community was founded in Utrera, south-east of Seville, in 1877, and a third in Ayamonte, near the coast next to the Portuguese border, the following year. A further twenty-three were established in Mother Angela's lifetime. The Sisters of the Cross addressed all the problems of the poor: the uprooting caused by industrialization, leading to crowding into insanitary slums; the lack of welfare provision by the State or yet through trade unions; and the (at least seasonal) lack of work for the remaining landless rural poor.

Poor though they made themselves in their material circumstances, Angela recognized that the Sisters were not truly poor compared to the real economically poor, and made sure that they remained conscious of this fact and the privilege it was for them to serve the truly impoverished. They were to tell themselves, she wrote: "I who have been called by God, who has shown me that in this virtue is the source of all wealth, I work not only for God but also for myself, and I do not succeed in practising total poverty. I hardly notice I need something but I find a way of meeting that need. I have no more than the merest vestige of poverty in comparison with the poor." They were to imagine themselves crucified on an imaginary cross facing that of Our Lord on Calvary so that they could be united with him in reaching out with his love and compassion. If the message sounds harsh, there was nothing gloomy about her: she was said to be"immersed in Easter joy."

Angelita lived (like Genoveva Torres, canonized with her) to the age of eighty-six, universally known as"Mother of the Poor." She died in Seville on 2

March 1932 and was beatified in Seville by Pope John Paul II on 5 November 1982 and canonized by him in Madrid, in the presence of the king and queen of Spain, on 4 May 2003. "Love for and sensitivity to the poor," the Pope said in his homily, "prompted [her] to found her Company of the Cross for the most deprived with a charitable and social dimension that made an enormous impact on the Church and society of Seville in her day."

❖

Butler, March, pp. 17–19, citing *Ecclesia*, 13 November 1982 and biography in Spanish by J. M. Javierre.

3

St Teresa Verzeri, *Founder* (1801–1852)

The first of seven children of Antonio Verzeri and Countess Elena Pedrocca-Grumelli, Teresa Eustochio was born on 31 July 1801 in Bergamo, north-east of Milan in northern Italy. Her mother had wanted to become a nun but had been dissuaded by her aunt, Mother Antonia Grumelli, a Poor Clare, who had told her that she was destined by God "to become the mother of holy children." One of her sons, Girolamo, was to become bishop of Brescia.

Antonio Verzeri died while Teresa was still a child, and her early formation in the life of the spirit was by her mother, aided by Canon Giuseppe Benaglio, vicar general of the diocese of Bergamo, who became a close and influential friend of the family after Antonio's death. After studying at home, Teresa entered the Benedictine monastery of Grata at the age of sixteen. Anti-clerical laws forbade the clothing of religious until they reached the age of twenty-four, so she returned home for a time, on Benaglio's advice. She went back to Grata in 1821, to find the community disturbed by the prevailing laws and its observance growing lax. Some of the nuns, including Teresa, pressed for reforms, but others opposed them, and in the end she felt the situation too unsettling to continue there and, again on Benaglio's advice, left once more. He had told her that he was planning to gather a community of women who would teach while at the same time living a contemplative life. Teresa was attracted by this idea, but it was slow to take shape, and she decided that the cloistered life was what suited her after all, and entered Grata a third time, in 1828. She was now over twenty-four and was clothed in the habit, but this coming and going had not endeared her to the rest of the community, and she was assigned the most menial tasks, whereas before she had been given charge of the formation of postulants. She suffered great spiritual aridity and doubts about her vocation and consulted

Canon Benaglio once more. He in turn discussed her case with St Magdalen of Canossa (founder of the Daughters of Charity; 10 Apr.), who advised that Teresa should leave Grata for good.

Benaglio's venture began to take shape, with Teresa and his other choice, Virginia Simoni, living together in a country house in Gromo and giving courses of religious instruction to young women. They were joined by Teresa's sister Antonia and Katarina Manghenoni, and the four formed the nucleus of a new Institute when they made their simple vows before Canon Benaglio. Its initial purpose was the religious formation of young people. The first years were hard for Teresa, elected first mother superior and still subject to doubts and temptations, but she proved to be an inspired educator and the Institute was strengthened by the arrival of new recruits, including her three sisters and then also her mother. It took the name of Daughters of the Sacred Heart, and its Rule and Constitutions, drawn up mainly by Teresa and Benaglio, were approved by the bishop of Bergamo in 1842. Its objectives were extended to include schools for poor children, visits to sick women, houses of rescue for women at risk of being forced into prostitution, and the conducting of retreats for laywomen, which became a prime function, conducted in accordance with the *Spiritual Exercises* of St Ignatius of Loyola (31 July).

Teresa still had periodic doubts, which did not endear her to the bishop. She wondered whether they should merge with the Society of the Sacred Heart, founded in 1800 by St Madeleine-Sophie Barat (25 May), which had a retreat centre in Turin, but eventually decided that there was need for both. After various further difficulties, Teresa and her companions made their final vows in 1841. Provisional papal approval followed shortly, with final confirmation in 1847, when the pope authorized the opening of a house in Rome. Canon Benaglio had died in 1836, but Teresa found a new supporter in Ludovico Pavoni (beatified in 1947), a canon of Brescia Cathedral and founder of the Sons of Mary Immaculate. He printed the Constitutions of her Institute—at some risk to his own safety in a time of rampant anticlericalism—and supervised the alterations needed to an old convent she acquired in Brescia.

Teresa opened the house in Rome in 1848, and her last years were ones of relative personal peace, growth in holiness, and progress in her foundation. She wrote a three-volume *Book of Duties* for the Daughters of the Sacred Heart, in which she told them (some years before the revival of devotion to the Sacred Heart in the second half of the nineteenth century): "To you and to your Institute Jesus Christ has given the precious gift of his Heart, for from no one else can you learn holiness, he being the inexhaustible source of true holiness" (vol. III, p. 484). She also set forth her educational principles, stating that the young should be allowed "a holy freedom so that they may do willingly and with full agreement that which, oppressed by command, would only be accomplished as a burden and with violence," and that education had to be suited to individual needs, adapted "to the temperament, the inclinations, the circumstances of each person … and be according to the capacity of each" (III, pp. 347 and 349). Besides these volumes and one of *Duties*, she wrote over 3,500 letters to her Sisters, which have survived.

Teresa Verzeri died of cholera in Brescia on 3 March 1852, victim of an epidemic that swept northern Italy, and was buried in the chapel of the mother-house in Bergamo. She was beatified by Pope Pius XII in 1946 and canonized by Pope John Paul II on 10 June 2001. In his homily at the canonization ceremony the pope referred to her spiritual trials and sense of "the absence of God," despite which she clung unshakeably to faith and "confidence in the provident and merciful Father," an example for the present times, in which God seems absent to so many amidst widespread violence and suffering.

❖

Butler, March, pp. 32–4. Biographies of Teresa Verzeri have appeared only in Italian, as have several volumes of her letters. Quotations from the "Book of Duties" (*Libro dei Doveri*) appear in the brief biography issued by the Vatican News Service on the occasion of her canonization.

The Daughters of the Sacred Heart are active in Albania, Argentina, Bolivia, Brazil, Cameroon, the Central African Republic, and India, caring for the poor and oppressed in the spirit defined by their founder: "universal charity that excludes no one but embraces all; generous charity that does not draw back from suffering, is not alarmed by contradiction, but rather, in suffering and opposition, grows in vigour and conquers through patience" (*Duties*, I, p. 58).

St Katharine Drexel, *Founder* (1858–1955)

The history of the Church has seen many women from wealthy and socially prominent backgrounds give up the prospects of brilliant marriages to devote themselves to a life of charity and service, but perhaps not since St Melania the Younger in the fourth century has a saint made a financial contribution to compare with that of Katharine Drexel. She was enabled to do this through her father's extreme wealth and carefully crafted will, which divided the income from his estate—$15.5 million, worth about $250 million today—among his daughters.

Born in Philadelphia on 26 November 1858, she was the second of three daughters of Francis Drexel, the eldest being Elizabeth. Her mother, Hannah, died a few weeks after giving birth to her, and two years later her father married Emma Bouvier, who was the mother of the third child, Louise. Francis' father had been a portrait painter from the Austrian Tyrol, who had emigrated to seek his fortune in America. He became a classic American success story, first brokering the many local currencies that were still in circulation, then opening a bank. This made a fortune out of the California Gold Rush and lent gold to the Union government during the Civil War. The Drexels came to occupy a very prominent place in Philadelphia society.

They were also devout Catholics with an unusual degree of social conscience. Francis and Emma opened their house to poor people three days each week, and Emma ran a dispensary for the sick poor from the house. The girls were brought up with a strong sense that their wealth was to be used to benefit those less fortunate. At the same time they received a thorough general education from tutors at home, designed to enable them to take their proper place in society. Katharine accompanied the family on her first trip to Europe at the age of fifteen: she already had firm likes and dislikes, pronouncing Westminster Abbey "gloomy," and becoming indignant when she found Fr John Gerard's cell at the Tower of London closed to visitors. She made her society début in 1878, when she was twenty, but took part in the social round without evident enthusiasm.

Two years later her stepmother became seriously ill, and Katharine nursed her until she died three years later. Francis took his daughters on another tour of Europe, and this time Katharine was impressed when she visited the house of St Catherine of Siena, her name-saint. She returned believing she had a vocation to the contemplative life, but was dissuaded by Fr James O'Connor, a friend of the family, who had earlier first alerted her to the injustices done to the American Indians. She and her sisters accompanied their father on a journey by private rail car to the developing north west, where the family bank, Drexel and Co., was considering investing in the North Pacific Railroad.

Francis died in 1885, and his daughters found themselves equal sharers in the income from $15.5 million. If one daughter died, her share of the income was to be added to that of the survivors, while eventually the capital was to go to their children. In the event, none of the sisters had children, and Katharine lived the longest, so all the income came to her. But not the capital: in such an event, this was to benefit various religious charities and Institutes—excluding, as it was not yet in existence, her own foundation.

Katherine began to help Indian missions financially through the Benedictine Bishop Martin Marty, who had braved Chief Red Cloud by going to parley with him after the chief had threatened to kill the next white man he saw. Katharine and her sisters went to Europe again and were twice received in audience by Pope Leo XIII; she asked him to send more missionaries to the Indians, and he replied, "Why not become a missionary yourself, my child?" O'Connor, by now vicar apostolic of Nebraska, invited her to visit the missions of the north west again, and her first-hand experiences there convinced her what her mission was to be. She intended to found a new Order, but first she had to serve a novitiate in an existing one, so in May 1889 she began a six-month postulancy with the Sisters of Mercy in Pittsburgh, prompting a headline in a Philadelphia paper: "Miss Drexel Enters a Catholic Convent—Gives Up Seven Million."

In November 1889 she made her profession to Archbishop Patrick Ryan of Philadelphia, taking the names Mary Katharine in religion. She added a fourth vow to the usual three: "To be the mother and servant of the Indian and Negro races." She made her solemn vows on 12 February 1891, by which time twelve postulants had come to the convent with the intention of joining her in her new Order. A few months later the foundation stone of its first house, at Bensalem, was laid by Archbishop Ryan. Katharine had made two more journeys west and wanted to stay there, but O'Connor and Ryan persuaded her of the need for a secure foundation. In January 1895 she took her final vows and the new Congregation came into being, named the Sisters of the Blessed Sacrament for Indians and Negroes, with a Rule taken largely from that of the Sisters of Mercy.

Slaves had been freed by the Emancipation Proclamation some thirty years earlier, but any meaningful civil rights for blacks were still decades away, and the Sisters met considerable prejudice, sometimes violent, lasting at least into the 1930s. Katharine's income, large though it was, was constantly stretched, and she could never do as much as she wanted to. By the turn of the century she was spending $50,000 a year on schools and making donations to twenty-six dioceses. She personally economized in every little way she could: on her many long train journeys she spent hours in the relatively uncomfortable but cheaper day coaches and used the money saved to tip the black porters. She re-used envelopes and sewed her shoelaces back together when they broke.

In 1900 Katharine visited the Navajos in Arizona and established a mission for them: a year later virtually no work had been done on the buildings and she had to chivvy the contractors. In 1904 she was planning to open a school for black children in Nashville, Tennessee, strongly supported by the black population, who saw education as their way out of poverty, but equally opposed by the white authorities. Three years later she had to go to Rome to negotiate revisions to the Constitutions of her Congregation: these were making no progress by correspondence, and a determined Italian missionary by the name of Frances Xavier Cabrini (canonized in 1946; 22 Dec.) told her the only way to make progress was to go in person. The Vatican officials knew her as a generous benefactor, and it took her only a month to agree the revisions required; in 1913 final approval was agreed, including a change from "Negroes" in the title to "the coloured population."

In the same year, the Georgia Legislature tried to enact a law prohibiting white teachers from teaching black children, in an effort to stop the Sisters opening a school in Macon. Katharine herself tramped the streets looking for premises for convents, schools, or missions from Harlem to St Louis. In 1915 the archbishop of New Orleans asked her to make a foundation for a school. She bought the abandoned campus of the former Southern University for $18,000 and established Xavier Preparatory School. Vandals smashed all the windows, but it grew into Xavier Academy and finally Xavier University, the first Catholic university in the South for coloured students, soon supplying graduates to teach in the many rural schools the Sisters had founded.

In Beaumont, Texas, in 1922, Klansmen nailed a notice to the door of their new school: "We want an end of services here … We will not stand by while white priests consort with nigger wenches in the face of our families. Suppress it in one week or flogging with tar and feathers will follow."The following day a threat to dynamite the building was issued, but a week later a violent thunderstorm destroyed the Ku Klux Klan headquarters and lightning killed their local leader, so heaven appeared to be with the Sisters.

In the late 1920s Katharine was able to purchase a new site in New Orleans to expand Xavier University: she prudently used an agent to make the purchase in order to prevent suspicion. By the time the new buildings were completed, in 1932, the site and construction had cost $656,000: "What a waste!" a priest observed—in Latin—at the dedication ceremony. (Katharine never heard this remark, as she refused to sit with the dignitaries and watched from a window in the science block.) Another priest, from Pennsylvania, thwarted a plan to which she had contributed to build a new church for both blacks and whites, so that the blacks ended up with the old church while the new one became "whites only."

Examples such as these prove that Katherine was well before her time as a campaigner for social justice for African and Native Americans: one of her Sisters who helped document the cause for her canonization said of her that "Way back in 1891 she was a pioneer for the most downtrodden and the poorest of the poor. She didn't have a prejudiced molecule in her body, never mind a bone. She believed that everyone was a child of God." The Benedictine archivist of Belmont Abbey, North Carolina, commented: "We do Katharine Drexel a disservice if we view her only in terms of her money. She had a real social policy to go with it … It's just magnificent to have her recognized by the Church. It's such a tribute to all progressive thinkers in issues of social justice." Just as she would rather give an extra tip to a railroad porter than see the money go on luxury for herself, so she resented the proportion of her income (some 35 per cent) taken by federal taxes, and in the 1920s she successfully lobbied Congress to pass an amendment that exempted from income tax an organization giving more than 90 per cent of its income to charity. Known as "The Philadelphia Nun Loophole," this unfortunately became a device employed by large corporations with creative accountants and less charitable intentions than hers.

She made a yearly visitation of all her foundation until 1935, when she was seventy-six and suffered a severe heart attack. Told to take life more easily, Katharine refused to have money spent on a wheelchair but allowed the Sisters to fix wooden wheels to the legs of a convent chair. She then lived for another twenty years, which meant that her foundations received income for twenty years longer than they might reasonably have expected. Because her sister Louise died in 1945, for ten years the entire income from the Drexel Trust was hers to spend—which she did, on new foundations in California, Indiana, Louisiana, and elsewhere. She devoted her time to the prayer and meditation for which she had previously longed and found no time.

Katharine finally died on 3 March 1955 at her Congregation's motherhouse at Bensalem, Pennsylvania. She had given more than $20 million to schools, hospitals, mission stations, and Xavier University. She was beatified by Pope John Paul II on 20 November 1988 and canonized by him in Rome on 1 October 2000. Her legacy lives on not only in the 245 Sisters working in twenty-one States and in Haiti, but in a Church that without her might well have been far less committed to social justice. She died in the decade that saw the start of the Civil Rights movement, of which she had been a precursor—though her conscious purpose was the evangelization of the African and Native American people of her country.

K. Jones, *Women Saints: Lives of Faith and Courage* (1999), pp. 268–74; *Butler*, March, pp. 200–2; P. Finney, "The Legacy of St Katharine Drexel," *St Antony Messenger* October 2000 and at www.americancatholic.org/Messenger/Oct2000. There are two full-length biographies: K. Burton, *The Golden Door: The Life of Katharine Drexel* (1957); Sr C. R. Duffy, SBS, *Katharine Drexel: A Biography* (1996).

4

Bd John Antony Farina, *Bishop and Founder* (1803–1888)

John was born on 11 January 1803 in the village of Gambarella in the northern Italian province of Vicenza, which was at the time under the domination of the Austro-Hungarian Empire. His parents were Pietro and Francesca Bellame, and he received his early education from his father's brother, who was a priest: there was a lack of public schools in rural areas. At the age of fifteen he entered the diocesan seminary of Vicenza, where he proved a dedicated and outstanding student: when he was twenty-one he was teaching in the seminary while still studying for his theology course.

Ordained on 27 January 1827, John soon received the diploma enabling him to teach in primary schools. He taught in the seminary for eighteen months, was chaplain of San Pietro in Vicenza for a time, and was active in a number of cultural, spiritual, and charitable organizations in the town, as well as becoming director of its public primary and secondary school. In 1831 he started the first free school for girls; and five years later he founded the Institute of the Sisters

Teachers of St Dorothy, Daughters of the Sacred Heart. This was for "teachers of proven calling, consecrated to the Lord and wholly devoted to the teaching of poor girls." The category was soon expanded to include daughters of "good families," deaf-mute, and blind girls; and then the ministry was extended to cover care of the sick and old people in hospitals, hospices, and their homes. The Institute received papal approval from Pope Gregory XVI in 1839.

In 1850 John was elected bishop of Treviso, and he was consecrated on 19 January 1851. He introduced a number of pastoral initiatives, particularly the establishment of associations in each parish to care for the needy, so that he became known as "the bishop of the poor." He spread the practice of spiritual exercises, provided assistance to sick and poor priests, improved religious education for both clergy and laity and catechesis for young people. John had to contend in all his reforms with the cathedral Chapter, who opposed him at every turn and eventually prevented him from holding a diocesan synod. On 18 September 1858 he ordained Giuseppe Sarto, the future Pope St Pius X (21 Aug.).

After ten years in Treviso John was transferred to Vicenza, a larger city and diocese, where, free of his conservative colleagues in Treviso, he embarked on a wide agenda of administrative reform, including re-instituting the diocesan synod (which had not been held for nearly 200 years), and pastoral, educational, and charitable initiatives. He visited the whole diocese, including mountain parishes that could be reached only on foot or on mule. He encouraged devotion to the Eucharist, the Sacred Heart, and the Virgin Mary. In 1869–70 he took part in the First Vatican Council, at which he voted for the definition of papal infallibility.

John's later years brought a combination of recognition for all his pastoral work and false accusations by those who had resisted his reforms. He bore the latter with resignation, assured that he had always followed his conscience and worked for the wider salvation of his people. His health declined sharply after a serious illness in 1886, and he died of a stroke on 4 March 1888. He was revered as a saint in church and civil circles, and people were asking favours through his intercession less than ten years after his death. In 1978 Sister Inés Torres Codova, an Ecuadorian member of the Sisters Teachers, suffering from apparently incurable cancer, recovered after she and her companions prayed to their founder. This was accepted as a miracle on 7 July 2001 and cleared the way to his beatification on 4 November. Pope John Paul II in his homily summed up "His long pastoral ministry ... as a vast pastoral activity totally dedicated to the doctrinal and spiritual formation of the clergy and the faithful."

The Sisters Teachers of St Dorothy have their own saint in Mary Bertilla Boscardin, who joined the Institute in Vicenza in 1907, heroically nursed wounded combatants in the First World War, and died of cancer in 1922. She was beatified in 1952 and canonized by Pope John XXIII in 1961. *Butler*, Oct., pp. 144–5.

7

The Martyrs of Ukraine (died between 1935 and 1973)

Pope John Paul II made a controversial visit to western Ukraine from 23 to 27 June 2001, during the course of which he beatified two Roman Catholics, Archbishop Joseph Bilczewski (1860–1923; 20 Mar.) and Fr Sigmund Gorazdowski (1845–1920; 1 Jan.), on 26 June, and twenty-seven Greek Catholic martyrs and one nun, Sister Josaphata Hordashevska (1869–1919; 7 Apr.) on the following day. The controversy surrounding the visit and the beatifications stemmed from the very complex (and hardly ecumenical) situation of the various Christian Churches in Ukraine, understanding of which calls for an attempt at a historical summary.

Christianity in what is now Ukraine dates from 988, when Prince Volodymyr the Great made Byzantine-Slavic rite Christianity, under the jurisdiction of the patriarchate of Constantinople, the national religion of Kyvian-Rus, as his country then was. This Church remained in communion with Rome after the Great Schism of 1054 (which divided the Greek East from the Latin West), and for centuries worked to try to restore unity. A Decree of Union was signed at the Council of Florence in 1439, but Orthodox synods refused to ratify this, and in 1448 the new Moscow *metropolia* announced its self-governing status (autocephaly). It became a patriarchate in 1589, at a time when Greek Orthodoxy and Constantinople were under Turkish dominance.

In 1596 the Kyvian Church, subject to pressure from both Protestant reformers and Catholic counter-reformers, decided to accept the jurisdiction of the Roman Catholic Church. This was ratified at the Council of Brest, which marks the beginning of the Ukrainian Greek Catholic Church (UGCC), or Uniate Church of Ukraine. Parts of this Church, however, refused to accept this and in 1686 preferred the jurisdiction of the Moscow patriarchate, after the ruler of Moscow had seized control of central and eastern Ukraine. Over the next 200 years, the Tsarist Empire repressed the UGCC and made forced conversions to Russian Orthodoxy. After the Russian Revolution in 1917 a Ukrainian Autocephalous Orthodox Church (UAOC) came into unofficial existence, under conditions of repression by the Soviet authorities.

At the time of the Union of Brest, the whole of Ukraine had been part of the Polish-Lithuanian Commonwealth. Western Ukraine then became part of the Austrian Empire as the crown land of Galicia, and the Hapsburg emperors upheld the UGCC against Russian Orthodoxy. With the break-up of the Austro-Hungarian Empire (as a result of the First World War), western Ukraine was briefly independent but was then assigned to southern Poland under the Treaty of Versailles. Stalin occupied the country in September 1939 under the terms of the Nazi-Soviet pact.

As the Communist government intensified its persecution of Christian Churches, Orthodox, Greek Catholic, and other religious representatives were assassinated or deported to labour camps, and the Churches were forced underground. Some hoped for better conditions under the Nazis with the abrogation of the Nazi-Soviet pact in June 1941, but were soon disabused as they watched the mass murders of Jews. By summer 1944 the Red Army had reoccupied Ukraine, and Metropolitan Josyf Slipyj of Lvov and all the UGCC hierarchy were soon to be arrested. At the "Synod of Lvov," convened at gunpoint in March 1946, the Union of Brest was revoked and the UGCC "rejoined" to the Russian Orthodox Church.

Between 1946 and 1989 the UGCC, forced to function as a "Church of the catacombs," was the largest banned Church in the world, as well as forming the largest single group of internal social opposition to the USSR. With the waning of Soviet power in the 1980s, the UGCC emerged from the underground, and new communities of the UAOC were created in 1989. Religious freedom was declared with Ukrainian independence in 1991, ending conflict between Church and State but leaving a number of Churches in competition with each other (and all subject to further competition from Islam and new religious movements).

Religious communities in Ukraine are now 97 per cent Christian, divided almost equally between Orthodox on one hand and Catholic and Protestant on the other. Of the three main Orthodox groups, the Ukrainian Orthodox Church–Moscow Patriarchate (UOC–MP) is by far the largest, followed by the Ukrainian Orthodox Church–Kyvian Patriarchate (UOC–KP) and then the UAOC. Of the two Catholic groups, the UGCC is about the same size as the UOC–KP, while the Roman Catholic Church is less than a third the size of this, though growing. There are tensions not only between Orthodox and Catholic, but also within Orthodoxy and within Catholicism. The Orthodox Churches, whatever their divisions, are opposed to Catholic proselytism in any form, and the UGCC is at best wary of Latin Catholicism, and at worst given to seizing its churches. This was the religious quagmire into which the Pope stepped in June 2001. He was at least careful not to suggest any fusion between Rome and the UGCC, by separating the two Roman Catholic from the Greek Catholic beatifications. It is the twenty-seven martyrs of the latter who are considered here, in chronological order of their deaths; the date of 7 March chosen for the group is that of the death of the first to suffer.

❖

Leonid Feodorov was born in St Petersburg on 4 November 1879. Brought up Russian Orthodox, he studied at the Petersburg Spiritual Academy but abandoned his studies and went abroad, converting to Roman Catholicism in Rome. He studied in Agnani, Rome, and Freiburg and was ordained a Greek Catholic priest in 1911. In 1913 he became a Studite monk (the tradition of St Theodore the Studite, 759–826; 11 Nov.) in Bosnia. He returned to Russia at the beginning of the First World War, only to find himself exiled to Siberia for being a Catholic. He was released in 1917 and appointed head (*exarch*) of the Russian Greek-Catholic Church. He was imprisoned again by the Bolsheviks in 1923 and served ten years in gulags and exile, which destroyed his health, so that he is considered a martyr even though he was not actually killed for his faith (as is the case with many of this group). Leonid died on 7 March 1935.

Mykola Konrad, born in the Ternopil region (*oblask*) of western Ukraine on 16 May 1876, completed his studies in philosophy and theology in Rome and was ordained priest in 1899. He taught at two Ukrainian high schools and in 1929 founded the first association of Catholic students, named *Obnova* (Renewal). In 1930 the great archbishop of Lvov, Andrey Szeptyckyj, who guided the UGCC from 1901 until his death in November 1944 (but has not yet been beatified, possibly at the request of the Polish hierarchy), appointed him to the Lvov Theological Academy. Mykola later served as parish priest near the town of Yaniv, until he was seized and killed by the NKVD (the Soviet Secret Police) on 26 June 1941.

Volodymyr Pryima was born in the Yaroviv region, north-west of Lvov, on 17 July 1906. He graduated from a school for cantors and became the cantor and director of music in his local church. He took an active part in parish activities and was highly respected as a principled and upright man. A married man with two young children, he was with Mykola Konrad on the night of 26 June 1941 and was killed with him. It was a week before local people found their bodies. Volodymyr had been stabbed many times in the chest with a bayonet.

Andrii Ischak came from Mykolaiv in the Lvov region. Born on 20 September 1887, he studied theology at the University of Lvov and then at Innsbruck in Austria. He received a Ph.D. in theology and was ordained priest in 1914. He served as a parish priest, and from 1928 combined this with teaching dogmatic theology and canon law at Lvov Theological Academy. Russian soldiers retreating from the advancing German army (Hitler had by then abrogated the Nazi-Soviet pact of 1939) seized him but then let him go. Andrii refused to go into hiding and two days later was taken from his home to an overgrown place where he was shot in the stomach and knifed. He died on the same day as the previous two martyrs: 26 June 1941.

Severian Baranyk was born on 18 July 1889 and then entered the Basilian monastery in Krekhiv in 1904. Ordained in 1914, by 1932 he had become prior of the monastery in Drobobych, from where he was taken by NKVD members to the local prison on 26 June 1941. He was never seen alive again. When the

Germans arrived they allowed the locals to dig, with their hands, in a huge hole filled with sand in the prison yard. Fr Baranyk's body, swollen, black, and covered with marks of torture, was one of many dragged out. The sign of the cross had been slashed on his chest.

Yakim Senkivsky, born in the Ternopil region on 2 May 1896, studied theology in Lvov and was ordained in 1921. Two years later, he became a novice in the Basilian monastery in Krekhiv; as he was already a priest, he was assigned to parish work for several years. After a spell at the monastery of Onufry in Lvov, where he was chaplain of the Marian Society, ministered to young people, and started a Eucharistic Society, he was appointed abbot of Drobobych. Yakim too was arrested on 26 June 1941, and several witnesses state that he was boiled to death in a cauldron in the prison on 29 June. Those who knew him testify to the way his humility, dignity, and openness to everyone earned him the respect and affection of the whole town.

Zenovii Kovalyk was born near Ternopil on 18 August 1903, and joined the Redemptorists. After studying philosophy and theology in Belgium he returned to Ukraine, where he was ordained in September 1937. He served on the mission in Volyn (in the north-west) until he was arrested in his church, where his impressive sermons pulled no punches about his views on Communism, on 20 December 1940. Zenovii was taken to Lvov, where he was imprisoned for six months, horribly tortured, and finally executed in a mock crucifixion in a street in June 1941.

The only martyr under the Nazi regime, which replaced the Soviet one in late June 1941, was **Emilian Kovch**, born near Kosiv, in south-western Ukraine, on 20 August 1884. He studied in Rome, was ordained in 1911, and served as field chaplain to the Ukrainian Galician army after the First World War and then as parish priest in Przemysl. During the Second World War he worked to save many Jews from death (for which he was recognized as a "Righteous Ukrainian" by the Jewish Council of Ukraine in 1999). Arrested by the Gestapo at the end of 1942, he spent fifteen months in a concentration camp, during which he heroically strove to keep inmates of all nationalities from despair, refusing an offer of freedom on the grounds that he "couldn't imagine what would happen here without me"—he was the only priest in the camp. Emilian was burned to death in the ovens of Majdanek death camp on 25 March 1944.

Soviet power was restored in the summer of 1944, and priests, religious, and faithful alike feared for their lives. **Tarsykiya Matskiv**, one of three religious Sisters in this group of martyrs, was born in the Lvov region on 23 March 1919. She joined the Sisters Servants of Mary Immaculate (founded by Josaphata Hordashevska, also beatified in the same ceremony), taking her first vows in December 1940. Her convent was surrounded by Russian troops on 17 July 1944. Not knowing this, Tarsykiya opened the door in response to a knock, expecting a priest to say Mass, but found a soldier who shot her without warning—simply "because she was a nun," it was later said.

77

Vitalii Bairak, born on 24 February in the Ternopil region, became a Basilian monk and was ordained in 1933. He replaced Yakim Senkivskyi (see above) as abbot of Drobobych after the latter's death. He was arrested in September 1945 and sentenced to eight years' imprisonment. Vitalli was severely beaten in the prison and died from his injuries just before Easter 1946, the first post-war victim of Soviet persecution in this group.

Hryhorii Khomyshyn, born on 25 March 1867 near Ternopil, graduated from the seminary in Lvov and was ordained in 1893. He went on to study theology in Vienna for five years, being awarded a doctorate in 1899. Archbishop Szeptychkyj appointed him first rector of the seminary (in 1904) and then bishop of Ivano-Frankivsk, the region directly south of Lvov. He was bishop for over forty years. Arrested by the NKVD in 1939, he was released, then arrested again in 1945, when he was taken to the Lukianviska prison in the capital, Kiev. There he faced a sadistic interrogator who beat him nearly to death with copies of his own books. Hryhorii died in the prison infirmary on 17 January 1947.

Born into a family of railway workers in the Zakarpatsk region, in the extreme west of Ukraine, on 14 April 1911, **Theodore Romzha** studied at the Gregorian University in Rome. After a short spell as a village pastor he taught philosophy and became spiritual director at the seminary of Uzhorod, of which he was consecrated bishop in September 1944. He refused to cooperate with the Soviet plan to detach the UGCC from the Vatican and incorporate it into the Russian Orthodox Church. The authorities decided to assassinate him, and his horse-drawn carriage was rammed by a military vehicle on 27 October 1947. He was badly shaken but did not die. Soldiers then beat him unconscious. Theodore was taken to hospital, where he was poisoned by Soviet collaborators on 1 November.

Josaphat Kotsylovsky was born in the Lemkiv region on 3 March 1876, studied for a theology degree in Rome, and was ordained in October 1907. He was appointed vice rector and professor of theology at the diocesan seminary of Ivano-Frankivsk, then in 1911 joined the Basilian novitiate. Archbishop Szeptyckyj, who had been in captivity in Russia but was released in 1917, consecrated him bishop of Przemsyl in September. He was first arrested in September 1945, released, then arrested again and imprisoned in Kiev. Transferred to the nearby concentration camp at Chapaivka, Josaphat died there on 17 November 1947.

Nykyta Budka was born near Zbarazh, north-east of Ternopil, on 7 June 1877, studied in Vienna and Innsbruck, and was ordained in 1905. He concerned himself with Ukrainian emigrants and in 1912 was appointed first bishop for Ukrainian Catholics in Canada, where he stayed until 1928. Back in Lvov, he became vicar general of the metropolitan curia. He was arrested in April 1945 and imprisoned with other bishops, then transferred to a camp in Kazakhstan, where he died on 1 October 1949. The camp guards took all bodies out of the camp and left them in the woods to be eaten by wild animals. A group of prisoners went to try to find Nykyta the next day but found nothing more than his shirt sleeve—his clothes had been left on his body as a sign of respect.

Yet another of this heroic generation of bishops, **Hryhorii Lakota** was born in the Lvov region on 31 January 1883 and studied theology first in Lvov and then, after his ordination in 1908, in Vienna, where he gained his Ph.D. He was appointed auxiliary bishop of Przemysl in May 1926. He served there for twenty years, until his arrest in June 1946, when he was sentenced to ten years in prison. He was exiled to a gulag in Vorkuta, north of the Arctic Circle in Siberia, where he did all he could to comfort the other inmates. Hryhorii died near there on 12 November 1950.

Archbishop Szeptyckyj's younger brother, **Klymentii**, was born on 17 November 1869 near Yavoriv in south-western Ukraine. He had a successful lay career, studying law in Munich and Paris and receiving a doctorate from the University of Krakow. He became a legate in the Austrian parliament and a member of the National Council. He then renounced all this and became a Studite monk, studied theology in Innsbruck, and was ordained in 1915, going on to become prior and then abbot of his monastery, in Univ. He too was arrested and sentenced to imprisonment after the Second World War, during which he had given assistance to many Jews. Klymentii was exiled to the extreme east of the Soviet Union, Vladimir on the coast of the Sea of Japan, where he died in a camp on 1 May 1951.

Mykola Tsehelskyi came from the Ternopil region, and was born on 17 December 1896. He graduated in theology from Lvov University and was ordained in April 1925. Married, with three children, he was arrested in October 1946 for refusing to convert to Orthodoxy and was sentenced to ten years. He was deported to Mordovia, in west-central Russia, while his wife and children were sent thousands of miles farther north-east, to Chytynskaya, north of China. Mykola died from illness and camp conditions on 25 May 1951.

Ivan Ziatyk was born near Sianok on 26 December 1899, and studied for the priesthood at Przemysl. Ordained in 1932, he joined the Redemptorists three years later. He taught dogmatic theology and scripture, and during the Nazi occupation (1942–44) was acting superior of the monastery in Ternopil and then in Lvov. He was arrested in 1950, accused of "preaching the ideas of the pope of Rome," and eventually sent to a camp near Irkutsk, north of Mongolia on Lake Baikal. After surviving seventy-two interrogations and being left to die in the cold after being drenched with water, Ivan died in the camp infirmary on 17 May 1952.

The second of the Sisters in this group to die was **Olympia Olha Brida**, born in the Lvov region in 1903. She became a Sister of St Joseph (a Congregation with many branches, all tracing their foundation to the initiative of six young women in France in 1650), and in 1938 was appointed superior of their house in Khyriv. This was attacked several times by Soviet agents, but she carried on catechizing and ministering until she was arrested in 1950. Olympia was exiled for life to the Tomsk region of Siberia, together with Sister Lavrentia (below), where she endured inhuman conditions, which brought about her death on 23 January 1952.

Lavrentia Herasymiv, also from the Lvov region, was born on 31 September 1911 and took her first vows in the Congregation's house in Tsebliv in 1933. She went to Khyriv in 1938 with Sister Olympia and was arrested and exiled with her. She had tuberculosis when she arrived in Tomsk and was forced to share a room with a paralyzed man behind a partition. Lavrentia died on 28 August 1952.

Petro Verhun was born in Horodok in the Lvov region on 18 November 1890, and was ordained in 1927. Archbishop Szeptyckyj appointed him pastor and later apostolic visitor of Ukrainian Catholics living in Germany. When the Red Army occupied Berlin he was arrested and sentenced to eight years' hard labour in Siberia. He gathered other Ukrainians around him in the camp and encouraged them by his example, rising above the awful conditions with amazing serenity: "Finally, I don't need anything. I feel that my head is tending little by little to my eternal rest," he wrote in a letter. Petro died on 7 February 1957.

Oleskii Zarytskyi was born in the Lvov region in 1912, studied at Lvov Theological Academy, and was ordained in 1936. After twelve years as a much-loved parish priest, he was arrested and sentenced to ten years in the camps for refusing to convert to Orthodoxy. He was rehabilitated as part of the thaw that followed Stalin's death in 1953, and in 1957 returned to western Ukraine. Oleskii slipped back into Russia and Kazakhstan to minister to Ukrainians in exile and was arrested again for "vagrancy" and sent to a camp near Karaganda, in east-central Kazakhstan, where he died on 30 October 1963.

Mykola Charnetskyi was born in the Ivano-Frankivsk region in 1884. He studied for the priesthood at the local seminary and then in Rome, and was ordained in 1909. He completed a doctorate in dogmatic theology in Rome and was appointed professor at the seminary in Ivano-Frankivsk. He joined the Redemptorists in Lvov in 1919, and in 1926 he became apostolic visitor to Greek Catholics in northern parts of western Ukraine. He was consecrated bishop in Rome in 1931 and continued his apostolic ministry until he was arrested in 1946. Mykola spent ten years in various camps and places of exile, and was terminally ill when he was allowed back to western Ukraine in 1956. He died in Lvov on 2 April 1959.

Semeon Lukach, also from the Ivano-Frankivsk region, was born in 1893, studied at the local seminary, and was ordained in 1919. The following year he was appointed professor of moral theology at the seminary. Consecrated bishop in secret in 1945, he was arrested in October 1949 and sentenced to ten years' hard labour. He served half this time and was allowed back to western Ukraine in 1955, but he was re-arrested in 1962 and sentenced to five years. Semeon developed tuberculosis of the lungs in the camp and was released and taken to his local village, where he died on 22 August 1964.

Ivan Sleziuk, born on 14 January 1896, had a similar history: seminary, ordination in 1923, secret consecration in 1945, arrested and sentenced to ten years' hard labour, released in 1955, and re-arrested with Bishop Semeon in 1962. Released in 1968, he continued to administer the eparchy of Ivano-Frankivsk but was subjected to frequent summons to "conversations" with the NKVD, from the last of which he never recovered. Ivan died on 2 December 1973.

Vasyl Velychovsky, born on 1 June 1903, also in the Ivano-Frankivsk region, studied at the seminary of Lvov and joined the Redemptorists in 1925. After serving as a missionary in the northern region of Volyn, he became prior of the monastery in Ternopil, where he was arrested in 1945. His sentence was originally death, but this was commuted to ten years in the camps. He survived these and returned to Lvov in 1955. In 1963, Metropolitan Josyf Slipyj (1892–1984), successor to Andrey Szeptyckyj and leader of the UGCC throughout its "catacomb" years, secretly consecrated him archbishop in a hotel in Moscow (from where he was being exiled to Rome) and designated him his successor. He in turn consecrated new underground bishops in 1964. Vasyl was arrested again in 1969, imprisoned for three years, then deported from the USSR. He went to Canada, dying in Winnipeg on 30 June 1973 of a heart disease acquired in prison. His successor, Volodymyr Sterniuk, one of those he had secretly consecrated, led the Church "out of the catacombs" after the break-up of the Soviet Union in 1989 and Ukraine's independence in 1991.

Metropolitan Szeptyckyj had prophesied on his deathbed in 1944:

> Our Church will be ruined, destroyed by the Bolsheviks, but you will hold on, do not renounce the faith, the Catholic Church. A difficult trial will fall on our Church, but it is passing. I see the rebirth of our Church: it will be more beautiful, more glorious than of old, and it will embrace all our people. Ukraine will rise again from her destruction and will become a mighty state, united, great, comparable to other highly-developed countries. Peace, well-being, happiness, high culture, mutual love and harmony will rule here. It will all be as I say. It is only necessary to pray that the Lord God and the Mother of God will care for our poor tired people, who have suffered so much, and that God's care will last forever.

Post-Soviet Ukraine may not be quite the paradise he foretold, but these martyrs are witnesses to faith sustained in hope throughout long years under the worst tyrannies of the twentieth century. The Pope in his homily referred to those of other denominations who had also been martyred for their faith, and he was direct about the troubled history: "During the last centuries too many stereotyped ways of thinking, too much mutual resentment, and too much intolerance have accumulated. The only way to clear the path is to forget the past, ask forgiveness of one another and forgive one another for the wounds inflicted and received, and unreservedly trust the renewing action of the Holy Spirit."

The historical summary is from a speech by Prof. Oleh Turiy of the Institute of Church History of Lvov, delivered in Freising, Germany, on 15 September 2000. This and related essays, plus brief biographies, which form the basis of those above, are on the very informative www.papalvisit.org.ua/eng. The final quotation is from the same source, citing an interview with Fr Yosyf Kladochni. Most towns, although not villages, mentioned can be found in *Atlas* (1999), Plates 39–45 (Lviv and Kyiv have here been westernized to the more familiar Lvov and Kiev).

The persecutions in the Ukraine have been thoroughly examined in books from refugee sources. The following is a selection of titles in English from the bibliography on www.holycross-edu/departements/history/vlpomar/persec: W. Dushyck, *Martyrdom in Ukraine* (1947); M Schudlo, *Ukrainian Catholics* (1951); P. Isair, *Persecution of the Ukrainian Greek Catholic Church* (1961); G. Luznycky, *Persecution and Destruction of the Ukrainian Church by the Russian Bolsheviks* (1966); J. Slypyj, *The Church of the Martyrs* (1981); E. Tremblay, *The Ukrainian Paradox* (1982); *Martyrology of the Ukrainian Churches* (1985); C. Korolevsky, *Metropolitan Andrew, 1865–1944* (1993); Can. Inst. of Ukrainian Studies, *The Ukrainian Greek Catholic Church and the Soviet State, 1939–1950* (1996).

15

Bd John Balicki (1869–1948)

John (Jan) Adalbert Balicki was born in the province of Rzeszów in south-eastern Poland, into a poor but devout family, on 25 January 1869. After a good schooling in Rzeszów he went to the diocesan seminary of Przemysl, just to the east, in September 1888 and was ordained there four years later, on 20 July 1892. After a spell as assistant priest in the parish of Polna he was sent to Rome to read for a degree in theology at the Gregorian University. He profited from his time there not only academically but also spiritually, reflecting on his studies in long hours of prayer and visiting the tombs of the apostles and the houses associated with later saints.

On John's return to Przemysl in 1897 he became professor of dogmatic theology in the diocesan seminary, serving also as prefect of studies until 1900. He continued as professor for thirty years, and then in 1927 was in addition appointed vice rector and, in the following year, rector. As such he had to present candidates for ordination to the bishop, a task to which he devoted the most scrupulous attention, to ensure that those he put forward were indeed worthy. By 1934, when he was sixty-five, his health obliged him to resign as rector and professor, and for the next five years he confined his activities to hearing Confessions and giving spiritual advice.

A few days after the outbreak of the Second World War (in September 1939), Przemysl was split between German and Russian occupying forces, the Germans holding most of the city while Soviet troops occupied the old centre. Most of the clergy opted to move to the German zone, but Fr Balicki stayed in the Soviet sector, hoping to be able to re-start the seminary at some future date. He escaped arrest but was not permitted any overt activity and was obliged to move into a room in the house to which the bishop had also been forced to move. He stayed there after the partitioning of the city came to an end in October 1941 (as a result of Hitler's invasion of Russia in the summer) and for the rest of his life, which ended before the post-war Communist regimes began their outright persecution of the Church. He died in hospital from pneumonia brought on by advanced tuberculosis on 15 May 1948.

John's reputation for holiness spread first throughout Poland and then wider through Polish emigrants. In 1975 the then Cardinal Wojtyla of Kraków wrote to Pope Paul VI praising John Balicki as a model for priests. As Pope John Paul II he beatified him in Kraków with three other Poles on 18 August 2002, saying that his life "was marked by his service of mercy. As a priest, his heart was always open to the needy. His ministry of mercy, besides offering his help to the sick and the poor, found a particularly energetic expression in the confessional, where he was filled with patience and humility, always open to bringing the repentant sinner back to the throne of divine grace."

Bd Artemide Zatti (1880–1951)

One of three sons of a poor family, Artemide was born in Reggio Emilia, in northern Italy, on 12 October 1880. By the time he was nine he was having to help support his family by working as a day-labourer for a wealthy neighbour. In 1897 the family, along with many thousands of Italians, emigrated to Argentina. They settled in Bahía Blanca, on the coast about 400 miles south-west of Buenos Aires, where an uncle already had a steady job. Life for the family improved considerably. Artemide, aged seventeen, worked first in a hotel, then in a tile factory. The local parish church had been established in 1890 by Salesians (founded by St John Bosco, 1815–88; 31 Jan.), and Artemide, encouraged by the parish priest, Fr Carlo Cavalli, soon felt drawn to the Salesian way of life.

He entered their seminary, Casa de Bernal, when he was twenty. He was older than the other "aspirants" but well behind them in studies, owing to his lack of early education. He worked hard alongside youths of eleven to fourteen and did his best to catch up. He was willing to do anything and was asked to undertake a number of tasks. These included looking after a young priest with tuberculosis, and he unfortunately caught the disease. Fr Cavalli had kept in touch from his parish, and he was influential in having Artemide moved to the Salesian house in Viedma, about 100 miles south, in the province of Rio Negro, where the climate was better and there was a mission hospital. The infirmarian there, Fr Evaristo Garrone, saw that Artemide would make an excellent hospital administrator were his health to permit this. He suggested that he pray to the Virgin Mary for a cure, promising to serve the sick for the rest of his life in return. He did so, and the tuberculosis vanished. His promise meant that he had to give up his ambition to become a priest, but he never expressed any resentment at this loss.

Artemide took final vows as a Salesian Brother in February 1911, by which time he had also qualified as a pharmacist. When Fr Garrone died two years later, he took over the complete running of the hospital, and dedicated himself totally to the service of the sick, in the hospital and in the locality, travelling around on a bicycle, which he said made it easier for him to meet people: he sold a car he was given. His days normally began at 4.30 a.m. and ended at 11 at night, though he would respond to calls at any hour of day or night. He was both administrator and pharmacist, would accept no personal payment, and gave any offerings to the hospital, following Fr Garrone's principle that "Those who have little, pay little, and the ones who have nothing pay nothing." His reputation grew and people started coming to consult him from all across Patagonia. Taking Matthew chapter 25 *au pied de la lettre*, he referred to his patients as "Jesus." He worked without holidays or rest days—the only respite he had, it was said, was when he was sent to prison for five days after a prisoner he was treating in hospital escaped. He combined all this with scrupulous attention to the liturgy and the common life of the community and, true to the spirit of Don Bosco, was unfailingly cheerful. His obvious goodness had the effect of confirming others in their faith.

A report on the hospital made by Fr Berutti, a member of the Salesian Superior Council, on an official visit to Patagonia, described it as "a miracle of Providence" and said that "Brother Zatti is a man sent by God ... The hospital is a prodigy of God's care; I cannot understand how it can actually carry on" (included in the "information process" of his cause). In 1950 Artemide (aged seventy) fell off a ladder he was climbing to mend a leaking water tank on the hospital roof and required medical treatment himself; after some months doctors realized that he was showing symptoms of advanced liver cancer. He carried on working for as long as he could but after two months of serious illness died on 15 March 1951.

Crowds from Viedma and nearby Carmen de Patagones flocked to his funeral, and his tomb in the Salesian chapel in Viedma soon became a focus of veneration. The diocesan process was started in 1979, and its findings were forwarded to Rome in 1981. In the same year his remains were moved to the church of the Sacred Heart in the parish of St John Bosco in Viedma. He was declared Venerable in 1997, and a miracle attributed to his intercession was accepted on 9 March 2000, clearing the way for his beatification, which took place on 14 April 2002. In his homily Pope John Paul II said of him: "His almost fifty years in Viedma represent the history of an exemplary religious, careful to accomplish his duties in his community and totally devoted to the service of those in need."

❖

There is a biography in Spanish: N. A. Noriega, *Artemides Zatti* (n.d.).

The city of Viedma was founded in 1779; ecclesiastically, it formed part of the archdiocese of Buenos Aires. In 1876 *Propaganda Fide* gave all five provinces of Patagonia to the Salesians as mission territory, and Don Bosco sent the first priests out. A Salesian was appointed first bishop-vicar apostolic in 1884. The diocese of Viedma was established in 1934, and Salesians have been four of its five bishops to date.

17

Bd John Nepomucene Zegrí y Moreno, *Founder* (1831–1905)

Juan Nepomuceno was named, like the pioneering bishop of Philadelphia, John Nepomucene Neumann (1811–60; 5 Jan.), after St John Nepomuk, the fourteenth-century confessor to Queen Sophie of Bohemia, who was drowned on the orders of her dissolute husband, King Wenceslaus IV. Juan was born in Granada in southern Spain to Antonio Zegrí Martín and Josefa Moreno Escudero, who brought him up to be devout and sensitive to the needs of the poor. He wanted to become a priest in order to serve the poor, and accordingly entered the seminary of San Dionisio in Granada, and was ordained in the cathedral in June 1855. He served in two parishes in Granada, carrying out his duties, as he said in a homily, "like a good shepherd, going after lost sheep; like a doctor, healing sick hearts wounded by faults and binding them with hope; like a father, who visibly provides for all of those who, suffering from abandonment, must drink from the bitter chalice and receive nourishment from the bread of tears."

Juan's career progressed rapidly in ecclesiastical terms: he was appointed synodal judge in Granada, then canon of Málaga Cathedral, visitor of the religious Orders in the diocese, and spiritual director of the seminarians. He was then summoned to Madrid to become preacher and royal chaplain to Queen Isabel II (1830–1904; queen 1843–68). After she was deposed he returned to Málaga, and in March 1878 he founded the Congregation of the Sisters of Charity of the Blessed Virgin Mary of Mercy, whose purpose was to work for the spiritual and material advancement of the poor. The foundation spread rapidly throughout Spain. Following the general understanding in the Church at the time (determined to distinguish itself from a nascent socialism dedicated to changing the structures of society), Fr Zegrí declared that "charity is the only answer to all social problems." He told his Sisters to "heal wounds, repair evils, comfort sorrows, dry tears; do not, if possible, leave even one person in the world abandoned, afflicted, unprotected, without religious education and assistance."

This noble goal did not prevent some of the Sisters from accusing him of improper behaviour. The case was referred to Rome and no less a weapon than a Pontifical Decree was launched at him, barring him from contact with the Congregation he had founded. This unjust situation lasted six years, until a further Pontifical Decree reinstated him, though in practice he still kept away from his "daughters," who were not disposed to accept Rome's second verdict. This state of affairs lasted until he died on 17 March 1905, "like Jesus, alone and abandoned." Some of the Sisters had kept a true memory of events, but it was not until twenty years after his death that he was again officially recognized as the founder of the Congregation.

He was declared Venerable by Pope John Paul II in 2001 and beatified by him on 9 November 2003, with four others, in a ceremony that brought the number of Blessed declared by this Pope to 1,320. In his homily, the Pope called him "an upright priest of deep Eucharistic piety," made no mention of the rift with his Congregation, and simply said, "Today this Institute, following in the footsteps of its founder, continues its dedication to witness and promote redemptive charity."

20

St María Josefa of the Heart of Jesus Sancho de Guerra, *Founder* (1842–1912)

The first Basque woman to be canonized was born on 7 September 1842 in Vitoria (Gasteiz in Basque), capital of the province of Alava in the Spanish Basque Country. She was the eldest daughter of a chair-maker named Bernabé Sancho and his wife Petra de Guerra. She was baptized the following day, confirmed at the age of two (as was customary at the time), and made her First Communion when she was ten. Her father died when she was seven, and she spent three years, from the ages of fifteen to eighteen, receiving a further education in Madrid. On her return to Vitoria she told her mother that she wanted to enter a religious Order.

Maria's first choice was the contemplative Conceptionist convent in Aranjuez, but she developed typhus and had to cancel the plan. Recovered, she felt that an active religious life was her true vocation and was drawn to the Handmaids of Mary Serving the Sick, founded in 1855 by Maria Soledad Torres Acosta (1826–87; 11 Oct.; canonized 1970), with whom she discussed her vocation.

The outcome of these conversations, as well as discussions with confessors and with Archbishop Antony Mary Claret (1807–70; 24 Oct.), then fretting in Madrid as confessor to Queen Isabel II, was that she left the Institute before being professed, in order to found a new one. This was to specialize solely in visiting the sick poor in hospitals and in their homes. Three other Handmaids went with her, with the permission of the cardinal archbishop of Toledo.

The new foundation was named Religious Servants of Jesus of Charity, with its first house founded in Bilbao in 1871. María Josefa was then twenty-nine and was to spend the next forty-one years as superior. Her spiritual vision was based on devotion to the Blessed Sacrament and the Sacred Heart and was to issue in total dedication to the sick, accompanying them to the point of their death, with "help of the heart" more important than giving food and medicine. Several communities were established, and she visited all of them regularly until a long illness confined her to the motherhouse in Bilbao, either in bed or in a wheelchair.

By the time of María's death on 20 March 1912, there were over 1,000 Sisters in forty-three houses in Spain and elsewhere. She was originally buried in the municipal cemetery in Bilbao, but her reputation for sanctity grew steadily, and her remains were transferred to the motherhouse chapel, where they lie still. The diocesan process was begun in 1951; her cause was formally introduced in Rome in 1972; the "Decree on her Virtues" was promulgated in 1989; and she was beatified on 27 September 1992 and canonized on 1 October 2000. In his homily at the ceremony the pope welcomed pilgrims from the Basque Country, "where she lived and died," from other parts of Europe, and from the Philippines. In a thinly-veiled reference to ETA, he prayed: "May María Josefa of the Heart of Jesus help the Basque people to banish violence for ever and may Euskadi be a blessed land and a place of peaceful and fraternal coexistence, where the rights of every person are respected and innocent blood is no longer shed."

❖

Today there are 1,050 Sisters working in Spain, other countries of Europe, South America, the Caribbean, and the Philippines. They have broadened their original mission to include day care centres for the aged, pastoral health care, and clinics for AIDS sufferers.

María Josefa wrote a "directory of aid" as a guide to the Institute, published as *Directorio de asistencias de la Congregación Religiosas Siervas de Jesús de la Caridad* (1930). See also M. A . Velasco, *Servants of Jesus: A History of Love and Hope* (2000); P. B. Aristegui, *Beata María Josefa del Corazón de Jesús* (1992); *idem*, *Consejos y máximas de nuestra venerada madre fundadora* (1994).

For St María Soledad Torres Acosta see usual Vatican sources. She spent thirty-five years as superior of her Congregation, and by the time of her death on 11 October 1887 there were forty-six houses around the world. For St Antony Mary Claret see *Butler*, October, pp. 164–7.

Bd Joseph Bilczewski, *Bishop* (1860–1923)

Joseph (Józef) Bilczewski was born on 26 April 1860 in Wilamowice near Kety in eastern Galicia, which was then part of the Austro-Hungarian Empire. He attended primary school in Wilamowice and later in Kety, followed by grammar school in Wadowice, from which he matriculated with distinction in June 1880. He then entered the Holy Ghost Seminary in Kraków and was ordained there by Bishop Dunajewski on 6 July 1884, being appointed parish priest of nearby Mogile. From 1886 to 1888 he continued his theological studies in Vienna, Rome, and Paris. On his return to Poland he was appointed parish priest in Kety and then in Kraków. In 1890 he presented his doctoral dissertation at the Jagellonian University of Kraków on "Christian Archaeology in Relation to the Church and Dogma." (In his homily at the beatification ceremony, Pope John Paul II referred to his "burning passion for revealed truth, [which] led him to make theological research an original way of translating the command to love God into practical behaviour.") Joseph was professor of dogmatics at the Jan Casimir University of Lvov from 1891 to 1900, and later dean of its faculty of theology and rector of the university.

Pope Leo XIII appointed Joseph as metropolitan archbishop of Lvov on 17 December 1900, and he was consecrated on 20 January 1901 in Lvov Cathedral. As archbishop he expressed the wish that his whole soul and all his strength should be devoted to the service of God and of his flock, in emulation of his great predecessor in the premier archbishopric, Bd Jakub Strzemie, who as the first archbishop of Lvov (1391–1409; beatified in 1790) laid the foundations of Christianity in Ukraine. Prayer and the Eucharist were the cornerstones of Joseph's spirituality and his pastoral approach, and he followed the teachings of Pope Pius X in encouraging frequent Communion and devotion to the Blessed Sacrament, as well as emphasizing the need for regular attendance at Sunday Mass and encouraging priests and parents to attach great importance to the preparation of children for their First Communion. During the First World War he proposed a revival of devotion to the Sacred Heart as a means of strengthening the faith of his flock during a period of turmoil, and invited all the families in the archdiocese to dedicate themselves to the Sacred Heart of Jesus.

From the start of his time as archbishop, Joseph was concerned with building new churches, conscious of the distance that many of his faithful had to travel to attend Mass. He used his own financial resources as a spur to stimulate clergy and laity into donating funds to build churches. His efforts produced 328 new churches and chapels in the archbishopric during his tenure. For these he needed more clergy, and so he asked that every family should pray at least one Our Father and one Hail Mary daily for vocations to the priesthood. The number of priests in the archdiocese rose from seventy-nine in 1900 to over 140 in 1923.

Joseph placed equal emphasis on the quality of his priests, requiring them to set a personal example of prayer, social concern, and courage in the face of opposition. Because the number of new churches and chapels far exceeded the increase in priests, he invited nuns to form pastoral centres near chapels and refuges, to catechize children and adults, care for the sick, lead worship, and prepare people for the sacraments. Established Orders opened new houses in the archdiocese, while Fr Zygmunt Gorazdowski (beatified in the same ceremony) established the Sisters of Mercy of St Joseph.

Archbishop Bilczewski laid especial stress on the importance of children, young people, and adults having a sound knowledge of the basics of the faith, which he saw as being inculcated by all lessons in school, not just religious education, and he encouraged mothers to teach their children daily prayer and the catechism. At the same time he was concerned for society on a wider scale, in the spirit of Pope Leo XIII's encyclical *Rerum Novarum*, which laid the basis of the Church's current social teaching, dealing with the problems of industrial and rural workers in a time of burgeoning capitalism.

Joseph died in Lvov on 3 March 1923 and was buried at his own request in the Janow cemetery there—a gesture of solidarity with the poor, as this was the city paupers' cemetery. Pope John Paul II in his homily at the beatification ceremony pointed up his significance for the religious and political future of the part of the world from which he himself comes and for which he has an abiding concern: at Archbishop Joseph's consecration, the bishop of Kraków was joined by the Latin-rite bishop of Przemysl and the Ukrainian Greek Catholic metropolitan Andrej Szeptyckyj (see The Martyrs of Ukraine; 7 Mar.), symbolizing the essential unity of a region long torn between East and West. (By coincidence, this entry was written on the day that seemed to portend the shift of at least western Ukraine "back" to the Christian West with the election as president of Viktor Yushenko in the re-run election of 26 December 2004, at least hinting at the prospect of the Pope's desired "communion that remains threatened by the memory of past experiences and by the prejudices stirred up by nationalism").

23

St Rebecca Ar-Rayès (1832–1914)

Rebecca, born Boutroussieh (or Butrusia) Ar-Rayès, came from a poor family of Maronite Christians living in the town of Himlaya. (The Maronites, named after St Maro, a friend of St John Chrysostom, originated around the seventh century when their local church disagreed with Rome over doctrine and they were excommunicated. They were brought back into communion after contact with the Crusaders in the twelfth century and have been in continuous communion ever since.) Her father's name was Mourad Saber Al-Chabaq (or Choboq) Al-Rayès, and her mother's Rafqa (Rebecca in English) El-Gemayel. Her mother died when she was seven years old, and in order to help the family financially Rebecca went as soon as she was old enough to work as a domestic servant for a Christian Lebanese family living in Damascus. Her father, who had remarried two years after her mother's death, summoned her home when she was fourteen, thinking it time she were married. She had no desire to marry and seems to have repulsed various suitors for some years until, when she was twenty-one, she fled after hearing her stepmother and aunt discussing who her husband should be.

Rebecca made her way to Our Lady of Deliverance, a convent of the Mariamette Sisters, a new teaching Order founded by the Jesuits for local women. On her way she met three other young women and persuaded two of them to come to the convent with her. The superior immediately accepted her but told the other two to come back another day. She then turned away Rebecca's parents when they arrived to take her home. She never saw them again.

She was clothed in 1855 and professed the following year in Ghazir as Sr Anissa (Agnes). She worked as cook in the convent for seven years, but also found time to study Arabic, writing, and arithmetic and was able to start teaching in 1860. That year the Druze, a fanatically anti-Christian Lebanese tribe, carried out a terrible massacre, killing some 8,000 Christians in twenty-two days. An Arab hid the Sisters in a stable, even though the Druze did not normally kill women. After the trouble was over, Sr Agnes spent ten more years teaching in various locations, first in Deir-el Qamar, then in Jbëil, then in Ma'ad, and finally in a village where a wealthy Christian benefactor named Antoun Issa had asked the Sisters for a teacher for the local school. She spent the last six years of the ten there, living with Issa and his wife.

In 1871 the Jesuits wanted to merge the Mariamette Sisters with the Daughters of the Sacred Heart (whose aims were very similar), and suppressed both Institutes when they could not agree on certain points. Many of the Sisters returned to secular life, but Agnes sought entry to a monastery. Antoun Issa recommended her to the archbishop and offered to pay any expenses involved in her move. The Maronite Order of Lebanon, founded in 1695, had split into two monastic Congregations in 1770, one of which was the Baladiya Order; and she was admitted to their monastery of St Sé'man El-Qarn, where she was professed in August 1873. This time she took her mother's name, Rebecca, in religion. The Baladiya Order was also known as the Order of St Antony the Great (of Egypt; 17 Jan.), and her choice was inspired by a dream of St Antony.

As a nun, now leading a more contemplative life, she was noted for her hard work, cheerfulness, and charity to all. She devoted herself without stint to comforting any nun who was sick or in distress, and even asked to share in the penance of any who had incurred a sanction from the superior. However, she felt that God was not with her in every way as he had not come to her in the suffering of illness. On Rosary Sunday in October 1885 she prayed to be made ill, and it seems that her prayer was immediately answered. She felt a violent pain in her head and her eyes. She gradually lost the sight of her right eye, which was then gouged out by a quack doctor, concentrating the pain in her left eye.

Rebecca was sent to the monastery of Saint Joseph at Jrabta (or Grabta), nearer sea level and so warmer, with no need for the wood fires that made the pain worse. But she soon lost the sight of her remaining eye, and the pain from what may have been a cancer of the bone became even worse. She became paralyzed except for her hands, with which she knitted socks for the community or said the rosary, and she spent seventeen years in this agony, never complaining but saying only that her sufferings were as nothing compared to the agony of Jesus: "My head is not crowned with thorns; there are no nails in my hands or in my feet. I have sins to expiate, but he, in his love for us, has borne an infinite degree of opprobrium and so much suffering, and we think so little of it." On one occasion some movement was mysteriously restored for a short time, enabling her to attend Mass on the feast of Corpus Christi, when she managed to drag herself along the floor from her bed to the church. Once the superior, Mother Ursula Doumit, asked if she had no special wish for herself, and she replied that she longed to see her Sisters; she found she could see them for an hour.

Rebecca dictated her autobiography at the request of Mother Ursula, who was the first person to be cured (possibly of throat cancer) after praying to Rebecca after she died, on 23 March 1914 at the age of eighty-two. Rebecca was beatified by John Paul II on 17 November 1985, after a cure of a Lebanese woman from cancer of the uterus was accepted in 1983 as due to her miraculous intervention, and canonized by him on 10 June 2001.

The ceremony was attended by the spiritual leader of the Maronites, Patriarch Sfeir, 150 Maronite clergy, many Lebanese civic dignitaries, and an enthusiastic crowd of some 10,000 Lebanese from all over the world. There was chanting from the scriptures in Arabic as a gesture to Arabic-speaking Christians in general and the Lebanese in particular, and St Peter's Piazza became a sea of waving Lebanese flags whenever her name was mentioned. The pope spoke of her "generous and passionate love for the redemption of her [fellow humans], counting on her union with the crucified Christ for the strength to accept voluntarily and love the suffering as an authentic path to sainthood." Whether all would agree that an apparently chosen life of suffering is the ideal example to present, especially to women of a time and place where suffering inflicted by others is so pervasive, is perhaps arguable. The pope's resolution of

91

any dilemma was to pray, "May the sick, the afflicted, the war refugees and all victims of hatred, yesterday and today, find in St Rafqa a companion on the road so that, through her intercession, they will continue to search in the night for reasons to hope again and to build peace." Patriarch Sfeir had previously called her "the saint of suffering and pain" and, as such, a "unique source of inspiration for Christians in the beleaguered country of Lebanon."

❖

Butler, March, pp. 223–6; *Bibl.SS.*, 11, 66–7; Joséph Mahfouz, *La bienheureuse Rafqa (Rebecca) de Himlaya* (2d edn, 1985). On the Maronites see P. Day, *A Dictionary of Christian Denominations* (2003), pp. 299–300; ODCC (1957), p. 861, with bibliography.

Bd Dominic Methodius Trcka, *Martyr* (1886–1959)

This Redemptorist priest worked with, suffered with, and was beatified with his fellow-Czechoslovakian, Bishop Paul Peter Gojdič (17 July).

He was born in Frydlant nad Ostravici, which was then in northern Moravia, and is now in the northernmost province of the Czech Republic, Severocesky Kraj, close to the present-day borders of both Germany and Poland. The date of his birth was 6 July 1886, and he joined the Redemptorists in 1902, began his novitiate in 1903, was professed in 1904, and was ordained priest in Prague on 17 July 1910.

The characteristic Redemptorist function was the preaching of parish missions, and Dominic devoted his early years as a priest to this. He cared for Croatian, Slovene, and Ruthenian refugees during the First World War, and then in 1919 asked to work with the Eastern Catholic Church. He was sent to Lvov, the principal city of western Ukraine (see The Martyrs of Ukraine, 7 Mar.), where he learned Ukrainian and worked among members of the Greek Catholic Church. He took the name Methodius after the great apostolic bishop St Methodius (815–884; 14 Feb., with St Cyril).

After two years in western Ukraine he was sent to Stropkov in eastern Slovakia, where he founded the first joint Latin and Byzantine-rite Redemptorist community, of which he became superior. He worked tirelessly preaching missions in the eparchies (dioceses) of Prešov (Bishop Gojdič's diocese), Uzhhorod (then in the Czechoslovak region of Ruthenia—see note below), and Križevci in Croatia. As superior he was responsible for establishing Greek Catholic Redemptorists in Michalovce in Slovakia.

In 1932, in need of a less stressful life, Methodius returned to parish work in Stropkov. In 1935 the Roman Congregation for the Oriental Churches appointed him apostolic visitor to the Basilian Sisters in the eparchies of Prešov and Uzhhorod. From 1936 to 1942 he served a second term as superior at

Michalovce; his activities there included building the church, setting up retreat houses, and founding an association for women domestic servants, whose spiritual welfare was seriously neglected.

During the Second World War Methodius and the Redemptorists were accused by the Slovak State of placing Ruthenian interests above those of Slovak nationalists; he resigned as superior in order to save the community from closure. At the end of the war (in 1945) the Redemptorists established a vice province in Michalovce, and the following year Methodius was appointed its vice provincial. In 1948 a Soviet-backed Communist regime took power in Czechoslovakia, bringing in anti-religious propaganda and then outright persecution. In 1949 the vice province was suppressed, and on 13 April 1950 its religious were all taken to concentration camps, where they were brutally interrogated and tortured.

A year later Methodius was accused of collaborating with Bishop Gojdič through disseminating his pastoral letters. His continuing reports to his superiors in Prague and through them to Rome brought charges of treason and a twelve-year prison sentence. In April 1958 he was transferred to Leopoldov (where the bishop was held in solitary confinement). When he sang a carol at Christmas he was placed in the "correction cell," where he caught pneumonia. When another prisoner, who was a doctor and could see how serious Methodius' condition was, asked that he should be moved to the prison hospital, the gaolers placed him in solitary confinement. Eventually moved back to his own cell, he died there on 23 March 1959. He was buried in the prison cemetery, but after the 1968 "Prague spring" his remains were allowed to be transferred to the Redemptorist church of the Holy Spirit in Michalovce. He was beatified as a martyr on 4 November 2001, having, as Pope John Paul II said in his homily, "passed his life in the service of the gospel and of the salvation of his brothers and sisters, even to the supreme sacrifice of his life."

❖

Ruthenia is one of those entities that render the history and politics of Eastern Europe virtually opaque to non-specialists. The term as applied here should more properly be "Sub-Carpathian Ruthenia" and refers to the area south-west of the Carpathian mountains, covering an area of 4,874 square miles, with a population of 725,000. Before the First World War it formed the north-eastern tip of Hungary. When Czechoslovakia was created by post-war treaty and the Austro-Hungarian Empire was dissolved, it was assigned to be a federated part of Czechoslovakia, with the fullest possible autonomy compatible with the unity of the Czechoslovak State. During the Second World War the area was re-occupied by Hungary, before being restored to Czechoslovakia at the end of the war in Europe. On 29 June 1945 the Czechoslovak government illegally ceded it to the Soviet Union. With the post-1989 formation of the Russian Federation, it became part of Ukraine, of which it is at the time of writing (Dec. 2004) the westernmost province, Zakarplats'ka Oblast (*Atlas*, plate 78, K2, L2). A web search for Ruthenia will produce far more information, much of it outdated, some of it slanted: www.carpatho-rusyn.org/fame/pod includes a map.)

28

St Joseph Sebastian Pelczar, *Bishop and Founder* (1842–1924)

Joseph (Jozef) was born into a traditionally pious family in the province of Rzeszów in south-eastern Poland. His parents recognized him as an unusually gifted child and sent him to a boarding school, the Academy, in the provincial capital after he had completed two years of elementary school in his birthplace, the small town of Korcyzna. After six years in the Academy he was convinced that only the priesthood could satisfy his ideal of a life lived for others, and he transferred to the diocesan minor seminary, before progressing to theological studies at the major seminary in Przemysl, a few miles from what is now the Poland–Ukraine border (then in the crown land of Galicia in the Austro-Hungarian Empire).

Joseph was ordained on 17 July 1864 and worked for a year and a half as curate in the parish of Sambor, before being sent to Rome to study for a doctorate in theology at the Gregorianum (then the Collegium Romanum). He followed this with a second doctorate, in canon law from the Lateran University (then the Institute of St Apollinaris). He also used his time in Rome to study the ascetical writings of the Church Fathers, and on a summer vacation in Gennazano wrote his first book, *Zycie duchowne* ("On the Spiritual Life"). Back in Poland, Joseph had another short spell as a curate and was then appointed professor at the major seminary of Przemysl, where he taught for eight years before being moved to the Jagellonian University in Kraków, first as a theological faculty member, then as professor. He was there for twenty-two years, becoming dean of the theology department and serving a year as rector of the university in 1882–83, a mark of the respect in which he was held by the whole institution.

Joseph was far from forgetting his ideal and, despite the pressure of academic work, involved himself in the charitable work of the St Vincent de Paul Society, besides serving as president of the Society for the Education of the People for sixteen years. He was responsible for opening hundreds of public libraries, delivered free lectures, was very active in devotional book publishing and distribution, opened a school for servants (it not being the time when churchmen were likely to ask why there have to be servants), and established the Fraternity of Our Lady Queen of Poland, a religious community dedicated to the care of the poor, orphans, apprentices and domestic servants, the sick, and those without work. In 1894 he founded the Congregation of Sister Servants of the Most Sacred Heart of Jesus, to provide vowed religious to care for young girls in danger, for the sick, and for the poor and disadvantaged of all sorts.

In 1899 Joseph returned to Przemysl as auxiliary to the ageing Bishop Solecki, and was consecrated diocesan bishop on the latter's death the following year. As bishop for twenty-four years, he led by example and was totally devoted to the needs of his flock. He made regular pastoral visits to the parishes and pursued the moral and intellectual formation of his clergy. He encouraged devotion to the Blessed Virgin, to the Sacred Heart, and to the Blessed Sacrament. He built new churches and chapels and saw to the restoration of many more. The region was poor, had little in the way of economic resources, and had been fought over for centuries, so the social needs were many and deep, with a large portion of the population seeking to emigrate. He established soup kitchens, nurseries, refuges for the homeless, and free schools for girls in rural areas. Inspired by the social teaching of the Church as recently articulated in *Rerum novarum* and other documents by Pope Leo XIII, he spoke out on behalf of workers treated unjustly by employers, forced to leave their homes to look for work, or unable to find work and so compelled to emigrate.

Joseph still found time to write, producing works of theology, history, and canon law, prayer books and school textbooks, besides a stream of pastoral letters, sermons, and conferences. He steered his diocese through the turmoil of the First World War and the re-establishment of Polish independence after the war. He died on 28 March 1924, having been both an outstanding scholar and an exceptional bishop. Pope John Paul II beatified him in Rzeszów on 2 June 1991 and canonized him in Rome, together with another Pole, Virginia Centurione Bracelli, on 18 May 2003. His remains are interred in Przemysl Cathedral.

❖

The Sister Servants of the Most Sacred Heart have convents in Poland, France, Italy, the U.S.A., Africa, and South America. They continue to care for young people in schools and beyond, for the poor, the aged, and the sick, in the spirit of St Francis and of their founder.

APRIL

1

Bd Ludovic Pavoni, *Founder* (1784–1849)

Ludovic (Lodovico) Pavoni might be described as a Don Bosco of an earlier generation. He devoted himself wholly to the education, training, and welfare of boys, doing much in the smaller northern Italian city of Brescia of what Don Bosco was to do in the much larger city of Turin. Whereas Don Bosco operated in a climate of religious oppression under anticlerical Italian governments, Fr Ludovic operated in a climate of political oppression, under the domination of the Austro-Hungarian Empire, which, while nominally Catholic, interfered endlessly in church affairs.

He was born into a wealthy and distinguished family of Brescia and revealed early talents that might have led into painting or architecture. Instead he chose to become a diocesan priest, and was ordained as such in 1807 after receiving his theological training from the Dominican Fr Carlo Ferrari, later to become bishop of Brescia. He concerned himself with the education and recreational activities of boys, particularly poor ones, who were usually left without schooling and as prey to every vice a city could place in their way. He founded an Oratory for their Christian formation.

In 1812 Ludovic became secretary to the bishop, Mgr Gabrio Nava, and six years later he founded an orphanage with an associated trade school, to provide orphan boys with a means of earning their living, on the principle that it was impossible to improve spiritual conditions without first improving social conditions. After three years this became the Institute of St Barnabas, which taught boys to become carpenters, silversmiths, blacksmiths, shoemakers, tool makers, dyers, farmers, and, above all, printers and publishers. In 1823 he started his own publishing house there, the Publishing House of the Institute of St Barnabas: it is still publishing as Editrice Ancora. For the first ten years of the Institute he had to operate out of a small corner of the building (which he called his rat hole), which was a former Augustinian monastery, as the Austrian army was using the rest for storage. In 1841 he managed to persuade them to hand over the whole monastery, which enabled him to expand his operations into a grammar school, a school of design, and a music school. He was also placed in charge of a local school for deaf-mute children, his remarkable educational abilities being increasingly appreciated. A cholera epidemic in 1836 led the city council to ask him to assume responsibility for the orphanage as well.

Ludovic's educational methods were enlightened for his time. He aimed to turn out "well-rounded" individuals who could make a contribution to society. He encouraged self-confidence through play-acting, while also insisting on good manners. He appreciated that poor children were often held back through malnutrition, and he personally supervised the kitchens to make sure they were well fed—even allowing them a modest measure of wine. Planning for the continuation of the school's work after his death, he brought together a group of priests and brothers, forming them into the Congregation of Mary Immaculate, in which he was one of the first members to make their profession, in 1847. Pope Gregory XVI had authorized it for Brescia four years earlier, but Austrian bureaucracy delayed its implementation, though the emperor, Ferdinand I, did show his appreciation of Ludovic's work by awarding him the knighthood of the Iron Crown: he would, he said, have been happier with a sack of flour to feed his boys.

In 1849 the region of Lombardy, in which Brescia was situated, rebelled against Austrian rule, and there was widespread fighting and destruction. Brescia went up in flames, and Ludovic was forced to take his pupils and flee to the village of Saianco, seven miles outside the city. The shock of seeing his whole Institute in flames broke his health, and he died shortly afterwards, on 1 April, which was Palm Sunday. Pope Pius XII declared him Venerable in 1947, and he was beatified by Pope John Paul II on 14 April 2002. It is possible to think that had he worked in a larger city and had politics not physically destroyed his work, he might have become as great a figure as Don Bosco, who certainly followed his methods to a large degree. As the Pope said in his homily at the beatification ceremony, "His activity branched out in many directions, from that of education to the publishing sector, with original apostolic intuitions and courageous innovations."

The fullest web source is R. MacNamara on www.stthomasirondequoit.com/SaintsAlive/id473 (though he confuses "Venerable" with "Blessed").

2

Bd Peter Calungsod (about 1655–1672)

Peter was a Philippine boy from Cebu in the Visayan Sea area (as his surname indicates in Tagalog). This is in the approximate middle of the archipelago, with the islands of Cebu and Negros on its southern side. He had been educated by the Jesuits, who gave him the name Pedro (Peter), and spoke Visayan, Spanish, and Chamorro. He was also adept at painting, singing, and carpentry, and was a trained catechist. He was only thirteen when in 1668 the Jesuit priest Diego Luis de San Vitores (beatified on 6 Oct. 1985), who had appointed him his personal assistant, took him on a mission to catechize the Chamorros of the Northern Mariana Islands (stretching north from Guam, then under the ecclesiastical jurisdiction of the diocese of Cebu).

All that is known of their mission and death comes from accounts of their last days provided by fellow missionaries. When they were evangelizing the natives of the village of Tumhom on San Juan (present-day Guam), a native chieftain who had earlier been converted turned against the Catholic faith and joined with a non-Christian native to attack Fr Diego. Peter rushed to his defence and was promptly speared through the chest and had his skull split with a machete (or *catana*). Fr Diego suffered the same fate. The date was 2 April 1672, making Peter either seventeen or eighteen years old.

The beatification process was started in 1994, and Peter was beatified in Rome by Pope John Paul II on 5 March 2000. More than 5,000 Filipinos, led by the president, José Estrada, and the first lady, Luisa Ejército Estrada, joined in the celebrations, as did a separate delegation from Guam. A statue of Peter had been unveiled in the cathedral of Cebu the previous month. At the ceremony, the pope held Peter up as an example and a challenge to young people today, especially those of the Philippines. The same ceremony, the first of the Jubilee Year, also saw the beatification of thirty martyrs in Brazil, one in Burma, eleven in Belarus, and the protomartyr of Vietnam, demonstrating Pope John Paul II's wish to universalize the Church's examples for the third millennium.

Cardinal Jaime Sin entrusted Fr Catalino Arevalo, SJ, with writing his story (in Tagalog, 1998) for the people of the diocese of Cebu. See *Atlas*, Plate 14, D6, for Cebu; Plate 3, map 1 for Guam.

3

St Aloysius Scrosoppi, *Founder* (1804–1884)

Luigi Scrosoppi was born in the city of Udine, in the Friuli region of northern Italy, on 4 August 1804. He came from a devout family, the youngest of three children born to Domenico Scrosoppi, a jeweller, and his wife, Antonia Lazzarini. His eldest brother, Carlo, was ordained when Luigi was six, and his other brother, Giovanni, a few years later. Conditions in this border region, which, following decades of war, was then struck by drought, famine, typhus, and smallpox, were desperate for many of the inhabitants. The number of orphans made a deep impression on Luigi as a boy, and he entered the diocesan junior seminary at the age of twelve. He was ordained on 31 March 1827, with his two priest brothers assisting at the ceremony.

With a group composed of other priests and some young teachers, Aloysius focused his charitable efforts on housing and educating poor and abandoned girls. Two priests had acquired a house for this purpose some ten years before his ordination; they were now elderly, and to carry on the work after their retirement Aloysius' half-brother, Fr Carlo Filaferro, took over the venture. Aloysius joined him in 1826 and was soon putting all his personal resources of time and money into the establishment. Despite the (non-financial) support of the city authorities, so much attention paid to young girls attracted some unfavourable comment, and the venture struggled. Aloysius toured the streets begging for funds and succeeding in raising sufficient to buy the building. After further begging for money and materials, they were able to enlarge the premises to accommodate nearly 100 boarders and a further 230 day pupils.

The work was completed in 1936, and the building was named "The House of the Destitute." He gathered a team of young women to teach sewing and embroidery, as well as the "three Rs". Nine of these women decided to mark their dedication in a more formal and permanent way, and on 1 February 1837, under the guidance of Aloysius, they formed themselves into the Congregation of the Sisters of Providence. More came to join them, women from wealthy and aristocratic backgrounds as well as poor and humble ones. Aloysius told them: "More than anything else, these daughters of the poor need to be educated in affection and to learn all that is needed to live an honest life." He drew up a Constitution for them, and the Congregation was to receive provisional and then final approval from Pope Pius IX (now Blessed; 7 Feb.) in 1862 and 1871.

Aloysius himself, drawn to the idea of total poverty, had been contemplating joining the Franciscans, but in 1846, at the mature age of forty-two, he decided instead to join the Congregation of the Oratory founded by St Philip Neri (26 May). The founder's spirit of joy and freedom combined with prayer and practical charity was something he could pass on to his Sisters of Providence, the first of whom had been clothed in 1845. He committed himself to opening twelve houses of the Congregation before he died, and so he did. In 1854 he was elected provincial of the Oratorians. Three years later he opened a home and school for deaf-mute girls, but this was forced to close after fifteen years. He also founded "Providence House" for former students who had been unable to find work.

The success of the campaign for Italian unity ushered in anticlerical governments in the 1860s, forcing many religious houses and Congregations to close, including the Oratory in 1866. Aloysius was unable to prevent the loss of all their property in Udine, but with the help of a sizeable inheritance he was able to carry on the houses of the Sisters of Providence, to save a convent of Poor Clares from ruin, and even to support a popular Catholic newspaper. He also established a foundation to give practical support to poor, sick, and elderly priests.

Aloysius' charitable works sprang from a deep attachment to the person of Jesus Christ and were carried out in full understanding of, "Just as you did it to one of the least of those who are my family, you did it to me" (Matt. 25:40). His preferred option was always for the poorest and most disadvantaged. He echoed Jesus' saying in the words: "The poor and the sick are our owners, and they represent the very person of Jesus Christ." He was an outstanding example of a life of contemplative prayer bearing fruit in an active apostolate. Every day—and night—of an extraordinarily busy life, he found time for meditation, visits to the Blessed Sacrament, making the Stations of the Cross and praying the rosary.

As his health declined, Aloysius handed over the running of the orphanages to the Sisters themselves, keeping in touch with them through a steady stream of letters. He told them not to fear for the future, because, "It was God who raised up your religious family and made it grow, and it is he who will see to its future." A long illness finally took its toll on 3 April 1884, not before virtually the whole of Udine had flocked to his bedside to beg a final blessing. Pope John Paul II beatified him on 4 October 1981. Then, in 1996, with the inexplicable cure of a terminal AIDS patient—a young catechist in Zambia named Peter Changu Shitima—attributed to his intervention, the way was cleared for his canonization. Changu, who had a great devotion to the then Blessed Fr Aloysius, was sent home from hospital by his doctors one day as there was nothing further they could do for him. That night he dreamed of Aloysius, and he "returned [the next day] brimming with health." He became a seminarian. Aloysius Scrosoppi was canonized on 10 June 2001.

Butler, April (1999), pp. 20–1; *Bibl.SS.*, 11, 753–4. New works issued at the time of his canonization include Ivo Valoppi, *"A riverderci in paradiso." La storia di san Luigi Scrosoppi* (2001); and Various, *San Luigi Scrosoppi, prete per i più poveri* (2001); Roberto Meroi, *Padrut* (a novel based on his life: 2001). See also "A Journey of Providence" at www.scrosoppi.it/en/index.

The Sisters of Providence he founded (there are several other Congregations with the same name) are still active in Italy, Brazil, and Paraguay.

5

St Mary Crescentia Höss (1682–1744)

Born the daughter of poor wool-weavers at Kaufbeuren in Bavaria, this "Cinderella among saints" was the seventh of eight children of Matthias Höss and his wife, born Lucia Hoermann. She was christened Anna. A devout child given to praying alone in the local Franciscan convent, she one day heard a voice there say, "This shall be your home." Her parents did not try to persuade her to stay at home to help support the family but encouraged her to join the convent. Her father took Anna there to ask the nuns to accept her as a postulant, but he was told that the house was so poor that it could not accept her unless she provided a dowry. Her family was at least as poor, and a dowry was out of the question.

Besides being poor (or mean, or both), the nuns also objected to the more rumbustious manifestations of working-class culture in the shape of a noisy tavern that disturbed the peace and quiet of the convent. They tried to buy it so that they could close it but could not raise the asking price. Eventually the town mayor, who was a Protestant, bought it and closed it. He knew Anna, then aged twenty-one, and was impressed by her holiness. He made her acceptance into the convent—with no dowry—a condition of buying and closing the inn. They accepted her as a tertiary Sister and made the early years of her religious life as miserable as they could. She was given the worst cell and then turned out of this when a wealthier postulant arrived, being obliged to beg floor-space from other nuns; she was given only the most menial tasks and reminded in every way of her humble origins. Through all of this, Sr Mary Crescentia, as she had become, behaved with perfect charity and restraint. She won the respect of some of the younger nuns, who protested on her behalf, but she would not add her own voice to the protests. She was eventually given a small, damp cell of her own and appointed doorkeeper, where she earned a reputation for kindness to the poor people who came to the convent door seeking help from the nuns (which must have been a fairly fruitless quest).

The tone of the convent changed for the better when a new mother superior was elected. She made Mary Crescentia a full member of the community and appointed her to the important post of novice-mistress, a post she held from 1726 to 1741. She was then elected mother superior, a promotion she did not seek or relish, but the duties of which she carried out conscientiously until her death three years later.

Mary Crescentia's prayer life, honed in the years of humiliation imposed on her by the older nuns, was intense, overflowing into physical manifestations. She experienced visions and ecstasies, and every Friday shared the sufferings of Christ's passion for its traditional six-hour span, from nine in the morning till three in the afternoon, with an intensity that often left her unconscious. As mother superior "She was generous to the poor, motherly with her sisters, and kind to all who needed a kind word" (homily at her canonization). Her reputation for holiness brought "simple men and women, princes and empresses, priests and religious, abbots and bishops" (*ibid.*) to the convent to seek her wise counsel.

She died of natural causes on Easter Day 1744, and her tomb rapidly became a place of pilgrimage. Her cause took a long time to reach the stage of beatification, however, and then another century to canonization: she was beatified by Pope Leo XIII in 1900, and for a further fifty years the next step languished, but the cause was reopened in the 1950s and she was eventually canonized by Pope John Paul II on 25 November 2001.

Butler, April, p. 35, citing the decree of beatification, in *Anal. Eccles.*, 8 (1900); *Bibl.SS.*, 7, 601–3; G. Gatz, *Leben der seligen Creszentia von Kaufbeuren* (2d edn, 1953).

7

Bd Josaphata Hordashevska (1869–1919)

The first member of the Sisters-Servants (or Handmaids) of Mary Immaculate was born in Lvov, the principal city of western Ukraine (see The Martyrs of Ukraine; 7 Mar.) in 1869 and christened Michaelina (Mykhailyna). By the age of eighteen she felt she had a vocation to the religious life, but was unsure which Order was best suited to her. Most women religious in the area at the time belonged to Latin-rite Congregations, whereas she wanted to keep to her Eastern rite, which left only the contemplative Basilian Sisters. Michaelina consulted her confessor, Fr Jeremiah Lomnytsky, OSBM (Order of St Basil Magnus, or the Basilian Order of St Josaphat, founded by St Basil the Great in the fourth century), who at the time was planning, together with Fr Cyril Seltsky, a new Congregation for women, which would have an active orientation. He asked her if she would become its first member, and she agreed. She entered the convent of Felician Sisters (Sisters of St Felix, founded in Warsaw in 1855 under the spiritual direction of Bd Honoratus Kosminski; 16 Dec.) in Zhovkva for her preparation in the religious life, in which she took the name Josaphata, in memory of the great Ukrainian bishop and martyr Josaphat (*c.*

1580–1632; 12 Nov.—the first Eastern-rite saint to have his cause processed by the Roman Congregation of Rites, canonized in 1867).

The new Congregation, the Sisters-Servants of Mary Immaculate, was to undertake various parish ministries, run schools, provide health care for the elderly, and instigate new missions. Seven young women were received as the first postulants in August 1892 in the church of Zhuzhel in western Ukraine, with Josaphata responsible for their formation. Like so many other pioneering women of the period she experienced opposition from clerical and other sources, and the remainder of her short life was difficult. She also developed tuberculosis of the bone, which led to her death in great pain on 7 April 1919.

Her cause was initiated by the diocese (eparchy) of Przemysl (one of the five eparchies of the Ukrainian Greek Catholic Church [UGCC] just over the border in Poland) in 1992. Josaphata was declared Venerable in April 1998 and beatified, with the Martyrs of Ukraine, by Pope John Paul II at Lvov racecourse on 27 June 2001. The Pope in his homily spoke of "her daily dedication to the gospel in an extraordinary way, in the service of children, the sick, the poor, the illiterate and the marginalized, often in difficult situations marked by suffering."

There is a biography available in English and Ukrainian: Sr Dominic Slawuta, SSMI, *Prayer and Service* (1996).

The Sisters-Servants received formal Vatican approval in 1932 and made a first foundation in the U.S.A. in 1935. During the Soviet occupation the Congregation was forced underground. The then superior general escaped to Rome and established the Generalate there, where it remains, and where Josaphata's remains were transferred in 1982. The Sisters work in UGCC parishes in their native lands and among emigrants in Argentina, Australia, Brazil, Canada, several European countries, and the U.S.A.: *Orders*, p. 274; see also pp. 30–2; 136–7.

24

St Benedict Menni, *Founder* (1841–1914)

This great pioneer in the treatment of psychiatric patients was born in Milan on 11 March 1841 and baptized with the names Angelo Ercole (Angel Hercules) on the same day in the parish church of Saint Mary at the Fountain. His parents, Luigi and Luisa Menni, were wealthy merchants distinguished by honesty in their social and commercial dealings, and they gave Angelo a solid Christian foundation, imbuing him with a keen sense of the Christian duty to help the poor and the sick.

His first job was as a clerk in a Milan bank, but he resigned after being asked to falsify records. In 1856 Italy went to war with Austria, and three years later Angelo volunteered to transport those wounded at the battle of Magenta (twelve miles outside Milan) from Milan railway station to the Araceli hospital, run by the Hospitallers of St John of God. This brought him into contact with the Order for the first time, and the encounter was to have a decisive effect on his life. Inspired by the Brothers' example, he entered their novitiate in 1860 and made his solemn profession in 1864, taking the name Benito (Benedict) in religion.

Benedict was ordained priest on 14 October 1866 and was almost immediately personally commissioned by Pope Pius IX (beatified in 2000; see 7 Feb.), on the advice of the prior general of the Order, Fr Juan María Alfieri, to go and restore the Order in Spain. Founded there in the sixteenth century by St John of God (8 Mar.), it had been banned by decrees of the First Minister, Mendizábal, in 1835 and 1836. Menni, aged only twenty-six, was astonished at the commission, but he went, into an anticlerical and revolutionary climate in Spain, then engaged in the second Carlist war. He spent some months in France on the way, studying how the Order there had been reconstituted after the French Revolution. By the end of 1867 he had opened the first children's hospital and refuge in Spain, in Barcelona.

The following year a revolutionary government deposed Queen Isabel II and reintroduced sanctions against religious Orders. In 1872 Menni was appointed superior of the Hospitallers in Spain, but his life was constantly in danger, as he was accused of helping the Carlists, and he was forced to leave the country. He and five Brothers joined the Red Cross in Marseilles, and as (neutral) members were able to move back into the Basque Provinces to aid the victims of the Carlist war. They tended the wounded at the front, acted as stretcher-bearers, and worked as doctors and nurses in the hospitals. Menni came to know the area well and to love the Basque people and appreciate their deep piety. In 1875 he was planning to open a hospital in Escoriaza, to cater for three classes of patient: "First, the demented, who are at present held in prisons in various towns, with no attention paid to their cure for lack of the necessary shelter; second, the war-wounded; third, male children who, on account of the war or through other misfortunes have been left deserted ..." The civic authorities of the province of Guipúzcoa welcomed the initiative, but it failed to prosper under the liberal government set up after the defeat of the Carlists in 1876, which equated religious with Carlist.

Menni went back to Barcelona to reorganize the children's hospital. He next moved to Madrid, reaching the capital "pale, emaciated, beset by hunger and without a cent," according to Sr Trinidad Isern, a novice in the lunatic asylum of Santa Isabel de Leganés. But Benedict was immediately active: he acquired a building and some land at Ciempozuelos, twenty miles outside the city, and on 23 February 1877 he was authorized to found a psychiatric hospital there. This was to serve as the motherhouse for the restoration of the Order and as the springboard for reform of the treatment of mentally disturbed patients in Spain. He soon realized that care of the mentally sick and of handicapped children required women's hands and mother's hearts, to be embodied in a female branch of the Order. His first recruits, after much searching, were María Josefa Recio and María Angustias Giménez, both from Granada. He clothed them and eight others with a new habit in May 1881, and the following year the cardinal archbishop of Toledo approved the Constitution for an initial period of five years. María Josefa was attacked by a mentally sick patient in 1883 and died from the injuries she received; María Angustias lived on to 1897. Pope Leo XIII formally recognized the Congregation in 1892 and gave final approval to its Constitution in 1908.

During his time with the Red Cross in the Basque Country, Menni had been in contact with many priests and nuns who had come from all over Spain to support the Carlist cause, and these now became a fruitful source of vocations to both branches of the Hospitallers. He devised norms of care for the sick based on moral principles and a holistic approach, absolutely forbidding any form of physical chastisement, still prevalent at the time. He chose postulants on the basis of "the persons' circumstances, aptitude, and decision of their will to deny themselves totally for love of God." Between 1875 and 1897, Menni founded eleven psychiatric hospitals (which were then the only resource for mentally sick patients) in Spain. Foundations were extended to Portugal and to Mexico, and in 1884 he received papal approval for a joint Spanish-American province of the Order. In 1885 his Brothers and Sisters were outstanding in tending those affected by a serious outbreak of cholera around Madrid; like Don Bosco's followers thirty years earlier in Turin, Menni's Hospitallers were often the only people in an affected area to have a basic understanding of hygiene.

The later years of his life were beset by difficulties within the Order and outside it. Although Benedict nominally acquired greater status—apostolic visitor of the Order in 1903 and superior general in 1911—he also made enemies. The general climate in Spain was anticlerical, and the press seized on an accusation of abuse of a mentally sick woman to portray him as a perverted beast. There was no substance in the accusation, which was dismissed for lack of evidence, but some mud always sticks. By 1912 he felt that he had lost the confidence of the Order and resigned as superior general. Some of its male members certainly felt that he had neglected them and paid too much attention to the female branch, and he had removed some whom he suspected of Modernism, but the campaign against him was still strangely intense. He had moved to the motherhouse in Rome on his appointment; as opposition to him mounted, he was first ordered to leave Rome and stay with the Sisters of the Order in Viterbo, then to leave Italy and live in France, but not in any of the

Sisters' houses there. He was finally deprived of a secretary, which cut him off from written communication as he had lost the use of his writing hand as the result of a stroke. He developed senile dementia and died of a second stroke, at Dinan in northern France, on 24 April 1914.

Benedict's body was taken by train to Madrid, but the train was delayed at Irún while the Spanish authorities refused to allow the body into Spain until it had been embalmed. When it eventually reached Madrid, a great gathering of Brothers and Sisters, municipal authorities, and ordinary people accompanied it to the funeral ceremony and burial in Ciempozuelos. In 1924 his remains were solemnly enshrined in the chapel of the motherhouse of the Sisters, next to those of his two co-founders, María Josefa and María Angustias—perhaps a deserved snub to the male members of the Order, perhaps simply recognition of the fact that, while he had revived the Brothers, he had actually founded the Sisters.

He was beatified on 23 June 1985 by Pope John Paul II, who canonized him on 21 November 1999. The Congregation of the Hospitaller Sisters of the Sacred Heart of Jesus spread to Africa and Asia and is now present in twenty-four countries, with over a hundred care centers. In October 2003 Benedict was declared patron of church volunteers in the diocese of Taytay in the Philippines. Cardinal Sin of Manila declared: "In his life we see divine inspiration and holiness, which leads others to sacrifice their lives to seve God and neighbor, especially the sick and the needy. We need a model to show us that the fullness of consecrated life consists in total trust in God for everything. And we see in St Benedict the genuine qualities which all volunteers should possess." His work stands as an example of total recognition of the presence of Jesus in the persons of the sick: "I was sick and you took care of me" (Matt. 25:36). He pioneered treatment of the whole person, not just of the symptoms of sickness, and brought a new dimension of humanity to the care of the mentally ill.

Butler, Apr., pp. 177–9. Letters to the Sisters in J. Gonzáles (ed.), *Cartas del Servo de Dios Benito Menni* ... (2d edn, 1975). There are biographies in Spanish by F. Bilbao (1939) and J. Alvárez Sierra (1968), and one in Italian with English translation: M. Soroldoni, *Sanctity Proved in Fire: the Chequered Life of Benedict Menni* (1985). The usual web sources are complemented by a lecture by Dr M. Martín Carrasco, "Benito Menni y la fundación de los hospitales de Santa Agueda (Arrasate–Mondragón)," 5 June 1997, delivered to inaugurate the centenary of the foundation: www.menni.org/historia/fundacion.

Bd Mary Elizabeth Hesselblad, *Founder* (1870–1957)

The tenth of thirteen children (of whom three died young) born to a devout Lutheran Swedish couple, Auguste Robert and Karin Hesselblad, Mary Elizabeth (Maria Elisabetta) was born on 4 June 1870 and baptized a few weeks later. Her birthplace was Faglavik, a village in the south-western Swedish province of Västra Götaland, where her parents ran a grocery store. This failed to prosper, and the family moved to Falun, a town in the Dalarana province of central Sweden. Again, they failed economically, and her father was declared bankrupt in 1886, forcing Elizabeth to take work as a housemaid and then, two years later, encouraging her to emigrate to the U.S.A.

She arrived in New York and was enrolled in the nursing school at Roosevelt Hospital in Manhattan. There she came into contact with Irish Catholics injured in the building of St Patrick's Cathedral. She had from childhood wondered why Christ's desire for "one fold and one shepherd" was not realized, and her first contact with Catholics and their constant invocation of the Mother of God and the saints tended to confirm her view that they were hardly Christian. An assignment to care for a nun in a convent, however, led her to study Catholicism more seriously.

Elizabeth returned to Sweden for a month's vacation in 1894 and on her return to New York was befriended by and went to live with a wealthy Catholic family named Cisneros. They took her with them to Sweden once more in 1900, where they visited Elizabeth's family. She and two Cisneros sisters then travelled on to Brussels, where they watched the Corpus Christi procession pass. Not wanting to kneel except to "you alone, Lord," she hung back in a church portal, but as the monstrance passed she heard an inner voice saying, "I am the one whom you seek." She fell to her knees and later told her friends of her experience. From then on she gradually overcame other doubts concerning the role of the Virgin Mary and the fact the Catholic Church seemed very obviously to be a Church of sinners as well as of saints. Then one of the Cisneros sisters decided to enter the Visitation Convent in Washington. Anguished at the thought of losing such a close friend, Elizabeth eventually saw that the Church could make such demands because it was the community in which Jesus' saying about giving up "home, brothers or sisters …" (Matt. 19:29) could be realized. On 12 August 1902 she went to see a priest, Fr John Hagen, and demanded to be admitted immediately. Surprised, he agreed to her suggestion that he question her on "any point of doctrine," as she had been studying and agonizing for twenty years. As a result, he agreed to admit her on the feast of the Assumption, three days later.

Elizabeth went on pilgrimage to Rome at the end of that year. There she was confirmed and visited the house on the corner of the Piazza Farnese where St Bridget, Sweden's great pre-reformation saint and founder (with her daughter St Catherine) of the Brigittine Order, had died in 1373. It was then a Carmelite convent. She returned there in 1904 and asked to be admitted. Her health, always precarious after a serious childhood illness, worsened to the point where she was given the last sacraments, but she recovered and was admitted as a postulant. Her dream was the re-conversion of Sweden to Catholicism, and the means she sought were a re-establishment of the Brigittines, by then reduced to four scattered and independent convents. In 1906 she was first admitted to the Carmelite novitiate and then, with special permission from Pope Pius X, clothed in the Brigittine habit, taking the Order's vows.

Elizabeth spent the years 1908–1911 touring the existing convents, learning about the Rule and history of the Order. She was often in severe pain and frequently faced discouragement, but in 1911 two postulants joined her, and she was able to open the first house of the new Brigittine Sisters in Rome, or Order of the Most Holy Saviour of St Bridget, in premises loaned by the Carmelites. She defined the new foundation's task as "Contemplation, adoration, and reparation." It was canonically approved, and in 1920 she became the first abbess.

In 1923 she went to Sweden for the 550th anniversary of St Bridget's death, with celebrations in Vadstena, where Bridget had founded her first monastery. Elizabeth wanted to found a house there but was dissuaded by the local bishop on the grounds that anti-Catholic prejudice would not tolerate a purely religious foundation. She amended the project to a "St Bridget Rest Home" in the suburbs of Stockholm, still run by Sisters in their habits but with a visibly social purpose, and so less provocative. She founded a house in Lugano in Switzerland, then another in England. In 1929 she was able to move into the house in the Piazza Farnese, vacated by the Carmelites. In 1935 she realized her longstanding ambition to open a convent in Vadstena, which was not entirely well received by the people. Two years later her first mission house was founded in southern India.

During the Second World War Elizabeth used the motherhouse in Rome to offer refuge to Jews and others threatened by the Nazis. She managed to import necessary supplies from neutral Sweden and used them to dispense charity to Italian partisans, Germans, and Poles. Underlying all her efforts was a passionate longing for Christian unity in the "one fold," and she was influential in the conversion of a Baptist minister who had written a biography of St Bridget, and of the Chief Rabbi of Rome. Numbers of Catholics increased marginally in Sweden, but the country as a whole remained staunchly Lutheran, although relations between the two faiths improved markedly in later decades. After the war she was pleased to offer the Rome house as the first headquarters of the Unitas Association founded by Fr Charles Boyer, SJ.

Elizabeth's later years were marked by chronic sickness, and eventually a weakening of her heart led to her death on 24 April 1957. Pope John Paul II beatified her on 9 April 2000, praising her as a pioneer of Catholic ecumenism.

✤

R. F. McNamara in Saints Alive Index; A. Marie, OSB, in *Letter of St Joseph's Abbey*, Clairval, 23 July 2001. For St Bridget see *Butler*, July, pp. 180–6. The house in Piazza Farnese has subsequently been restored to the Brigittine Sisters, who currently have thirty-seven houses: sixteen in Europe (of which two are in Sweden); thirteen in India; three in the Philippines; four in Mexico; and one in the U.S.A.

25

St Peter of St Joseph Betancurt (?1626–1667)

Peter was born on 16 May 1617 (according to one Vatican source; 19 March or 18 September 1626 according to others) at Chasna de Villaflor, on Tenerife in the Canary Islands. His un-Spanish family name probably comes from Jean de Béthencourt, a Norman conqueror of the Islands. His family was poor and devout, and he worked as a shepherd until he decided to seek a more rewarding life in the New World—spiritually rather than materially rewarding, as he was inspired to help improve the lot of the people of "the Indies."

In 1650 (so aged either thirty-one or twenty-three) he sailed to the West Indies, aiming for Guatemala, where a relative was secretary to the governor general. The ship docked at Havana, where his funds ran out, so he had to work his passage onward, sailing to Honduras and then walking to Guatemala City, a journey of at least 200 miles. Peter arrived there literally as a beggar, dependent on the Franciscan friars for his food. One, Friar Fernando Espinoso, befriended him, found him work in a textile factory, and became a valued counsellor for the rest of his life. Peter's ambition was to be accepted at the Jesuit College of San Borgia in order to study for the priesthood, but his lack of education forced him to abandon this course shortly after his enrolment, as he was unable to keep up with the plan of studies.

Friar Fernando invited him to become a Franciscan lay brother, but Peter preferred to remain in the world. He did, however, make private vows and become a Franciscan Tertiary in 1655, taking the name Peter of St Joseph (Pedro de San José). He dedicated the rest of his life to alleviating the suffering of those at the bottom of the heap of an extremely brutal and unequal society: slaves from Africa, Indians forced into inhuman conditions of work, immigrants without means, and abandoned children. He was to become known as "the St Francis of the Americas."

In 1658 Peter was given a hut, and he turned this into a hospice for the sick poor who had been discharged from the city hospital but still needed somewhere to convalesce. He called this "Our Lady of Bethlehem" (the Child Jesus at Bethlehem was the principal object of his own meditations throughout his life). Both the civil and religious authorities aided him, and he was able to open a hostel for the homeless, a school for poor and abandoned children, and an oratory. He arranged for Masses to be said in the very early morning, so that Indians and others could attend them before setting out for work, and he had chapels built in the poorest *barrios*, where the children of the poor could receive instruction. He started the custom of singing the Seven Joys of the Franciscan Rosary on 18 August each year, a tradition that is still continued in Guatemala today. He is also credited with originating the procession held on Christmas Eve, known as lodgings (*"posadas"*), in which people acting as Mary and Joseph beg a night's lodging from their neighbours. This later spread to other Central American countries and to Mexico. He toured the wealthier quarters ringing a bell and inviting the inhabitants to repent and to contribute to his ventures among the poor.

Others came to join Peter, becoming the foundation of the Bethlehemite Congregation (also known as Belemites, Brothers of Bethlehem, or Hospitallers of Bethlehem). They made simple vows originally, but were authorized to make solemn vows according to the Augustinian formula by Pope Innocent XI in 1687. A similar foundation for women was started the year after Peter's death, but it met with various difficulties and became defunct. The Rule embraced both an active life caring for the sick and all classes of unfortunate and a deep interior life involving prayer, fasting, and penance.

Peter died in Guatemala City on 25 April 1667, so at either forty-eight or forty-one years of age. His tomb became a place of pilgrimage, where it was said that petitioners for his intercession need only tap lightly on the tomb to have their prayers answered. His cause progressed only slowly, despite his local fame: he was declared Venerable in 1771, but then over 200 years elapsed before his beatification by Pope John Paul II—determined to find examples of holiness from all over the world—on 22 June 1980. In July 2001 a miracle was recognized that cleared the way for his canonization. At the ceremony of promulgation, Cardinal José Saraiva Martins, prefect of the Congregation for the Causes of Saints, described him as "a tireless missionary, an intense and genial educator, who invented his own teaching method, using songs, games, and dance." His canonization took place in Guatemala City before vast and enthusiastic crowds on 30 July 2002, the day before the aged and ailing pope, who had just attended the World Youth Congress in Toronto, flew on to Mexico City to canonize Juan Diego. Pope John Paul II ended his homily by declaring, "Guatemala, I carry you in my heart."

Vatican news services and Patron Saints Index, with different dates for his birth; *Butler*, April, p. 186, citing *Bibl.SS.*, 3, 142–3; *A.A.S.*, 73, pt 1 (1981), pp. 253–8; Day, *Orders*, p. 50.

MAY

2

St José María Rubio y Peralta (1864–1929)

The Jesuit priest who became known as the "apostle of Madrid" was born in the town of Dalías, twenty miles west of Almería in south-eastern Spain, on 22 July 1864. He was the eldest of twelve children born into a farming family, six of whom died young. His parents were devout and used to pray the rosary with the children every evening. After elementary school in Dalías and just one year of secondary school in Almería, he decided that he wanted to become a priest, and at the age of twelve he entered the diocesan junior seminary. He moved on to the major seminary in Granada in 1878, studied philosophy, theology, and canon law, and was ordained on 24 September 1887.

José María's ambition was to become a Jesuit, but it seems that his father objected to this, and there was a practical obstacle in the form of an elderly priest committed to his care, who lived for a further nineteen years. He became assistant priest in Chinchón, about thirty miles south east of Madrid, and then parish priest in Estremera, a little farther east. In 1890 Rubio was summoned to Madrid by the bishop, who appointed him a synodal examiner and teacher of metaphysics, Latin, and pastoral theology at the diocesan major seminary, as well as chaplain to the nuns of the Bernardine convent. He earned a reputation as an excellent confessor and retreat director. His father died in 1905, removing one obstacle to his becoming a Jesuit. He went on pilgrimage to the Holy Land the following year, which proved a deep spiritual experience, and then entered the Jesuit novitiate in Granada, making his profession on 12 October 1908.

He moved to the Jesuit house in Madrid in 1911 and exercised his ministry from there for the rest of his life. During the international eucharistic congress held in Madrid in 1911 he was given the task of organizing the "Honour Guard of the Sacred Heart," whose members attended regular extra services, prayed novenas, and carried out charitable works. Another task was to organize "Marys of the tabernacles," who would keep vigil in sanctuaries deserted by local Catholics (this seems to have been a common problem in Spain at the time). They had to lead strictly virtuous lives, forbearing from wearing fashionable clothes, dancing, and reading novels. He organized Holy Hours and generally re-inspired devotion to Christ in the Blessed Sacrament. He became a much sought-after confessor, hearing Confessions and giving spiritual direction from early in the morning, and his preaching was noted for its apparent simplicity, which drew crowds and moved many to repentance.

He was adept at mobilizing lay people to carry out works of charity, guiding from the background and letting them take responsibility. Groups of lay people opened free schools in which children could study academic subjects as well as learning trades. He organized popular missions in the poorest districts of the city, calling people back to the practice of their faith with direct preaching with plenty of emphasis on hell, but always treating his audience as deserving of respect. The source of his own inspiration was hours of prayer before the Blessed Sacrament, and he was able to pass this spirit of prayer on to his lay collaborators.

The title "apostle of Madrid" came first from the bishop and soon became generally used. A strange incident—or story told of him—toward the end of his life helped to win Rubio fame as a miracle-worker. One day an old woman asked him to come to a certain address to hear the Confession of a man who was about to die. He went and found a young man playing the piano, who answered to the name he had been given. Fr José María recognized the woman from a photo on the wall, which the young man said was of his mother, dead for some years. The young musician made his confession and was found dead in his bed the following morning.

Fr José María died in Aranjuez (the site of an eighteenth-century royal palace with magnificent gardens) on 2 May 1929, in the novitiate house of the Jesuit province of Toledo, to which he belonged. He had been sent there by his superior for a rest, suffering from exhaustion and diagnosed with cardiac angina. The news of his death was widely reported in the national as well as the religious press. One national notice read, "during the eighteen years of his stay in Madrid he won universal affection. He succeeded in becoming a popular, humble and modest priest, so that his mere presence, both attractive and good-natured, had the hallmark of a saint." He was beatified by Pope John Paul II on 6 October 1985, when the Pope called him "an authentic other Christ," and canonized by him on 4 May 2003.

Butler, May, p. 15, citing biographies by C. M. Staehlin (1953) and T. Ruiz del Rey (1957). There are also entries in *Bibl.SS.*, 11, 452–3 and J. N. Tylenda, *Jesuit Saints and Martyrs* (1983). Web sources include a somewhat fulsome account from Saint Joseph's Abbey Newsletter, March 1999, which has a full notice of the inexplicable cure of a small girl apparently dying of meningitis after her mother found a relic of Fr Rubio and pressed it to the child's body. This was accepted as the miracle that cleared the way for his beatification.

5

Bd Catherine Cittadini, *Founder* (1801–1857)

Caterina was born in Bergamo (north-east of Milan) on 28 September 1801 and baptized two days later in the parish church of St Alessandro in Colonna. Her mother died when she was seven, and her father abandoned her and a younger sister, Giuditta, who were taken in by the orphanage of the Conventino in Bergamo, founded in the sixteenth century by St Jerome Emiliani (8 Feb.), to whom Catherine developed a deep devotion. There they received a thorough formation in the faith and a strong sense of social responsibility. Catherine was also able to study for an elementary teacher's diploma.

In 1823 the sisters left the orphanage and went to live with two cousins who were priests, Giovanni and Antonio Cittadini, at Calolzio, a parish in the diocese of Bergamo. Catherine was taken on as first a temporary and then a permanent teacher in the school for girls in nearby Somasca, where St Jerome Emiliani's Congregation, the Clerks Regular of Somasca (Somaschi) had first been established. Both sisters felt a call to the religious life and were advised by their confessor that their vocation was to establish a new religious family in Somasca. They moved there in 1826 and by October had been able to buy and furnish a building, which was to function as a boarding school for girls and the motherhouse of the future Institute. The school, where Catherine pioneered an "oratory" style of education, with orphaned and other disadvantaged children living in the house, was a great success, and she started two more, a private school in 1832 and a boarding school for girls from farther afield in 1836. Giuditta was placed in charge of these, but she died suddenly in 1840. Her death was closely followed by that of Fr Antonio and then by that of her spiritual director from the orphanage. Catherine was devastated by this triple blow and fell gravely ill, recovering apparently through prayers to St Jerome Emiliani.

In 1845 Catherine gave up teaching to devote herself full time to the administration of the boarding school, to care for orphans, and to forming her companions into a religious Institute. She wrote a first draft of a Rule, and then a second, based on that of the Ursulines of Milan, but neither was accepted by the bishop of Bergamo. A third version was provisionally accepted in September 1854, under the name of Ursuline Sisters of Somasca. There was still no official, permanent, acceptance, however, and the strain of waiting and hoping took an increasing toll on Catherine's health. She died on 5 May 1857, and the bishop's approval was given six months later, followed in 1927 by pontifical approval.

Catherine's cause was introduced in 1967, the diocesan process was completed in 1978, and the decree on her heroic virtues was issued on 17 December 1996. A miracle of healing through her intercession was accepted on 20 December 1999, and her beatification took place on 29 April 2001 in St Peter's Piazza. Her life and achievements were very similar to those of another Catherine beatified in the same ceremony, Catherine Volpicelli (2 Jan.). Pope John Paul II in his homily stressed her devotion to the Eucharist and the way in which she had turned her own experience of being orphaned into a deep love of orphans and others in need, ending with the comment: "How very timely is her spiritual legacy for those who are called to be teachers of the faith and want to pass on the values of Christian culture to the new generations in this time of great social change!"

From the beginning of the twentieth century the work of the Institute spread to other parts of Italy and elsewhere. Today they teach and care for orphans among Italian immigrants to Switzerland, in Belgium, and among the poor in Bolivia, Brazil, India, and the Philippines.

6

St Anna Rosa Gattorno, *Founder* (1831–1900)

The second of the six children of Francesco Benedetta and Adelaide Campanella Benedetta, she was born on 14 October 1831 in Genoa and christened Rosa Maria the following day. Her parents were wealthy and pious and, as was the custom at the time, had their children educated at home. Confirmed at the age of twelve by the cardinal archbishop of Genoa, she grew up speaking several languages, adept in music, drawing, and dancing, and well-versed in the running of a large household. Genoa had ceased to enjoy its status as a free republic with Napoleon's invasion, and after his defeat had become part of the kingdom of Sardinia, torn by political and religious rivalries. Rosa Maria grew up in a turbulent time in European politics, being seventeen in the "year of revolutions" of 1848 and well aware of the issues involved, affecting the Church as well as the State—which spread into her family, as her paternal grandfather was fervently anticlerical.

With Rosa Maria's position in society and her talents she was not short of distinguished suitors. Her father favoured the wealthy and brilliant young lawyer Tito Orsini, but she preferred her less glittering but seemingly steadier distant cousin Gerolamo Custo, and they were married in November 1852. They moved west along the coast to Marseilles, but failed to prosper financially there and were forced to return to Genoa. Other misfortunes rapidly followed: their eldest child was left deaf and dumb following a serious illness; Gerolamo died in 1858, leaving Rosa Maria a widow with three young children; then the youngest died a few months later. While some might have railed against God for this torrent of misfortune, Rosa Maria decided that her experience of suffering equipped her to work for those who had also suffered pain, poverty, and loss. She underwent what she referred to as a "conversion" to love of Our Lord and to her neighbours. She became a daily communicant—most unusual at the time—and in 1858 made a private vow of chastity and obedience; three years later she made a vow of poverty and became a Franciscan tertiary. Throughout this process she continued to care for her children with loving tenderness.

Rosa Maria's sphere of apostolic work widened: as she wrote in her memoirs, "I dedicated myself with greater zeal to pious works and to visiting hospitals and the poor sick at home, helping them by meeting their needs as much as I could and serving them in all things." This zeal did not go unnoticed in active Catholic circles in Genoa, and various associations competed for her time and service. She was made president of the Pious Union of the New Ursulines, Daughters of Mary Immaculate, and entrusted by the archbishop with revising their Rule. This, however, led to the inspiration to devise a Rule for a new religious foundation of her own. She prayed and asked for advice, fearing that such a venture would separate her from care of her children, but was encouraged by her confessor and the archbishop. Still unconvinced, she appealed to Pope Pius IX (now Blessed; see 7 Feb.), who told her in an audience that it was God's will that she should proceed with the foundation immediately and that God would look after her children. She made the new foundation in Piacenza (disappointing various associations and the archbishop in Genoa) and named it Daughters of St Anne, Mother of Mary Immaculate. She herself made her profession in the new Institute, with twelve other Sisters, on 8 April 1870, taking the name Anna Rosa. Her choice of religious name and that of the Institute's name reflected her own status as a mother, and the purpose was to seek out and alleviate any form of suffering and poverty. The Sisters cared for elderly persons, for the lonely and abandoned, for street children, and for girls at risk of being forced into prostitution through poverty. She told them to be "Servants of the poor and ministers of mercy," and they were soon widely appreciated as such in civil society as well as in Church circles. The Institute was officially approved in 1879, though its Rule was not confirmed until 1892.

Anna Rosa had a special interest in deaf-mutes on account of her elder daughter, and she worked with Bishop John-Baptist Scalabrini (beatified in 1997; see 1 June), who had been appointed bishop of Piacenza in 1875, in his foundation of a special institute for them. She built a motherhouse for her Institute in Rome in 1873 and started schools, nursery schools, and refuges there. She was passionately devoted to the missionary objectives of her work, wanting to be "Jesus' voice" to the whole world, and the Institute grew and spread rapidly. In 1878 Anna Rosa sent the first Sisters outside Italy, to distant Bolivia, then to Brazil, Chile and Peru in South America, where Italians were emigrating in large numbers, as well as to France, Spain, and Eritrea. By the time of her death there were 3,500 Sisters working in 368 houses.

Like other nineteenth-century founders who bequeathed great works to the Church and the world, Anna Rosa drew her energy and inspiration from a continuous consciousness of the presence of God: "Although I am in the midst of such a torrent of things to do, I am never without the union with my God." Also like others, she too had the envy and deviousness of certain members of her Institute added to the more than ample sufferings she endured in life.

Anna Rosa caught a virulent form of influenza in February 1900, from which, weakened as she was by severe penances and the exhausting tempo of her life, she never recovered, dying in the motherhouse on 6 May. The informative diocesan process of inquiry into her holiness was begun in 1912 and finished in 1927. The study of the *Positio super virtutibus* was completed in 1991, a cure attributed to her intercession in the same year was accepted as miraculous in 1998, and she was declared Venerable. Pope John Paul II, in his address to the pilgrims who came to Rome for her beatification ceremony on 9 April 2000, said of her: "She makes a strong appeal to us all to love, defend, and promote life, showing us the depth and tenderness of God's love for every creature."

Further branches of the Institute are still active in many parts of the world: the Contemplative Order of the Daughters of St Anne; the Sons of St Anne, a religious association of priests; the Secular Institute of Daughters of St Anne; and the lay Movement of Hope. The archdiocese of Genoa, where Sisters are still active, joyfully and generously celebrated the thirty-five years she had lived there: www.paginecattolice.it/BeataAnnaRosaGattorno. For Bd J.-B. Scalabrini see *Butler*, December Supp., pp. 275–7.

7

St Augustine Roscelli, *Founder* (1818–1902)

Augustine (Agostino) Roscelli was born in Bargone de Casarza, in Liguria, northern Italy, on 27 July 1818 and baptized the same day because of fears for his health. His parents, Domenico Roscelli and Maria Gianelli, were poor peasant farmers, and as a child Augustine helped mind the sheep. He was clearly intelligent, and his parents sent him to the parish priest, Fr Andrea Garibaldi, to acquire a basic education. When he was seventeen he attended a parish retreat given by Antonio Maria Guanelli, parish priest of Chiavari (and later bishop of Bobbio), which convinced him that he had a vocation to the priesthood. Despite his poverty, he went to Genoa to study, which he was able to do with the help of several benefactors (including Guanelli, who found him a post as sacristan and guardian of the church of a girls' school), and he was ordained on 19 September 1846.

Augustine was appointed to a working-class parish, San Martino d'Albaro and, as parish priest, soon made an impression by his obvious zeal and the austerity of his life. He spent long hours in the confessional, which developed his concern with young people, especially girls, who had less access to education than boys and were forced to seek menial work in the city, where they were liable to be seduced or enticed into prostitution. He gathered a group of young women and with them founded a "sewing workshop," in which girls could receive practical and professional training as well as Christian instruction. Not neglecting the boys, he started a similar "young craftsmen" institute for them in 1858. In 1872 Augustine began a ministry to prisoners, and two years later he was appointed warden of the new provincial orphanage of Monte dei Fieschine, where, over a period of twenty-two years, he was to baptize over 8,000 children, as well as providing care for young single mothers, not condemning them but seeing them as simple souls led astray on account of lack of rewarding work.

Augustine lived in an atmosphere of intense prayer, with which he inspired his helpers. The women who ran the sewing workshop, known as "Roscelli's Collaborators," decided that their apostolate would be helped if they were to consecrate themselves to Christ in a more formal way. Augustine was reluctant to start another religious Congregation, but he was encouraged to consult Pope Pius IX, who said, "May God bless you and your good works," and so he went ahead. The Sisters of the Immaculate Conception came into being on 15 October 1876, and Augustine clothed the first of them a week later. He acted as their spiritual director and oversaw the early growth of the Congregation beyond Genoa and then outside Italy. He continued to refer to himself as a "poor priest" until his death on 7 May 1902.

He was beatified by Pope John Paul II in Rome on 7 May 1995 and canonized by him on 10 June 2001. The pope said of him that "he embodied the image of the Good Shepherd who takes care of the flock entrusted to him, who goes in search of the lost sheep and sacrifices his own life for the good of all … The indivisible love of God and of other people was the basic direction that characterized his spirituality, in which contemplation and action were fused."

Oss.Rom. 20 (1995), pp. 2–3; 24 (2001), pp. 1–4; 25 (2001), pp. 4–5; *Doc.cath.* 11 (1995), p. 564; abbaye-saint-benoit.ch/hagiographie/r/roscelli.htm.

10

Bd Ivan Merz (1896–1928)

Ivan was born in Banja Luka, now (since the Dayton Accord of 1996) in the Republika Srpska section of the Bosnia-Herzegovina Federation, of which it is the largest city after the capital, Sarajevo. Its long recorded history goes back to Roman times, when it was part of the province of Illyria, and includes nearly three centuries of Turkish rule, from 1582. Ivan was born on 16 December 1896, eighteen years after Bosnia-Herzegovina had been assigned to Austro-Hungary at the Congress of Berlin, which re-aligned many European boundaries after the Russo-Turkish war of 1877–1878. Under the empire the city flourished, with the Franciscans at the monastery of Trapisti leading development of arts and crafts. It became better integrated into central Europe with the opening of rail links to Vienna and Budapest in 1891, and the city's first grammar school was opened in 1895. Ivan's education reflected this situation: after primary and secondary school in Banja Luka he briefly went to the military academy of Wiener Noustadt and then enrolled in Vienna University in 1915. His ambition was to become a teacher, but his studies were interrupted by the First World War, when he was conscripted and spent almost two horrific years on the Italian front from early 1917.

The experience changed his outlook on life: already a committed Catholic, Ivan now determined to put all his trust in God and to strive for perfection. "It would be terrible if this war had no meaning for me!" he wrote in his diary in February 1918, "I must begin a life regenerated in the spirit of this new understanding of Catholicism. The Lord alone can help me, as man can do nothing on his own." He reinforced his commitment with a private vow of perpetual chastity, though he decided to remain a layman.

After the war Ivan returned to his studies in Vienna from 1919 to 1920, followed by two years at the university of Paris, with a further year to obtain a PhD with a thesis on "The Influence of the Liturgy on French Authors." After the war and the break-up of the Austro-Hungarian empire, the Banja Luka district became part of the kingdom of Serbs, Croats, and Slovenes. This was a fragile construct, but under it the city expanded rapidly and also became a focus of anti-fascist activity.

Ivan returned there and taught French language and literature, spending all his spare time on Church-related activities, studying philosophy and theology and becoming actively involved in work for young people. He helped to establish Catholic Action in Croatia, and under its umbrella he started the League of Young Croatian Catholics and the Croatian League of Eagles. Their aim was to be the vanguard of apostolic activity, and this included liturgical renewal, which he was one of the first to promote in Croatia. Through his writings and the meetings he organized he became a major influence, drawing young people and adults alike into greater commitment to their faith. People who knew Ivan characterized him as having "his mind and heart immersed in the supernatural," while he described his vocation simply as "the Catholic faith."

Ivan's promise was cut short tragically early as he died at the age of thirty-two, in Zagreb, the capital of Croatia, on 10 May 1928. He was originally buried in the cemetery, but as his cause made progress his remains were transferred in 1977 to the Shrine of the Sacred Heart. Between his death and his beatification his homeland went through a number of traumas: Croatia allied itself with the Axis during the Second World War, under the Fascist Ustashi regime; when the Russians invaded in April 1945 Banja Luka was virtually destroyed; it was re-built and then destroyed again in an earthquake in October 1969. It lived under Communist rule until the break-up of the former Yugoslavia; it was not bombarded or occupied during the Bosnian conflict in the 1990s, but the whole area was affected by "ethnic cleansing," and today about one-third of its population is made up of refugees or displaced persons.

Beatifying Ivan Merz in Banja Luka on 22 June 2003, during an apostolic visit to Bosnia-Herzegovina designed to re-build trust, especially between Catholic and Orthodox Churches, the Pope sent "fraternal greetings" to the Patriarch and Synod members of the Serbian Orthodox Church, and greetings also to the Jewish and Islamic communities. He told the civil authorities that "the Pope ... constantly brings before the Lord in prayer the sufferings that still burden your journey and shares with you in hope the expectation of better days." He presented Ivan Merz as "the just man" who shed the light of God's presence on those with whom he came in contact. Just as he had been an inspiration "for an entire generation of young Catholics," the Pope appealed to the present generation "not to step back, not to yield to the temptation to become discouraged, but to multiply initiatives that will make Bosnia-Herzegovina once more a land of reconciliation, encounter, and peace."

17

Bd Julia Salzano, *Founder* (1846–1929)

Julia (Giulia) was the daughter of Diego Salzano, a captain of Lancers in the army of Ferdinand II of Naples (r. 1830–1859), and Adelaida Valentino. She was born on 13 October 1846 in the village of Santa Maria Capua Vetere in the province of Caserta, fifteen miles north of Naples. Her father died when she was four years old, and she was sent to be raised by the Sisters of Charity in their

Royal Orphanage of San Nicola la Strada. She made her first Communion on 8 December 1854, the day of the proclamation of the dogma of the Immaculate Conception. She stayed in the orphanage until she was fifteen, then studied for a teaching diploma and taught in the school in Casoria, on the northern outskirts of Naples, where her family moved in 1865.

Julia worked with her friend Catherine Volpicelli (beatified in 2001; see 2 Jan.) to spread teaching of the catechism and to encourage devotion to Our Lady and the Sacred Heart, adopting the motto *Ad maiorem Cordis Jesu gloriam* ("To the greater glory of the Heart of Jesus"). She and Catherine were influenced by the Franciscan Louis (Ludovico) of Casoria (1814–1885, beatified in 1993; 29 Mar.), founder of the *Frati Bigi* ("Grey Friars," from the colour of their habits) and *Suore Bigie* ("Grey Sisters"), whom they met in 1854. Julia had to give her catechism classes in the afternoons after school had closed for the day, partly through talks given in the church of Mount Carmel, to which men, women, and children flocked. The diocese of Naples was enjoying a strong revival of catechetics and devotions, and Julia became a prominent part of this movement. She used visual displays of scenes from the Old and New Testaments to aid understanding, and taught with untiring patience. Eventually she decided that an organization was needed to spread her work, and in 1905 she founded the Congregation of the Catechist Sisters of the Sacred Heart. The Sisters were to reach out to the poorest members of society and instruct by example, putting "life before words:" "These truths must be lived, not explained; if you do not live them, your presence is irrelevant," she told them.

Julia guided the Congregation until her death on 17 May 1929, known everywhere as Donna Giulietta and already famous for her holiness by the time of her death. The diocesan cause for her canonization was started only eight years after she died, in 1937. A large dossier on her life and virtues was presented to the Congregation for the Causes of Saints in 1994, and Pope Paul II decreed her "heroic virtues" in April 2002, recognizing a miracle attributed to her intercession in December 2002 and beatifying her on 27 April 2003. In his homily he called her "an apostle of the new evangelization, in which she combined apostolic activity with prayer, offered ceaselessly, especially for the conversion of the 'indifferent.'"

20

Bd Arcangelo Tadini, *Founder* (1846–1912)

A priest of the diocese of Brescia for all his working life, Fr Tadini was one of many Italian priests forced by the anticlericalism of the post-1870 Italian State and the appalling conditions of workers in a newly industrialized society to find fresh ways of responding to pressing social problems. He did so from the heart of his vocation: a conviction that a healthy society was one gathered into a parish as a eucharistic community. He was a social reformer—somewhat despite his conservative instincts—because he was a dedicated priest. He was also by upbringing a fervent nationalist, inspired by stories in particular of the "ten days of Brescia,"in March of the year in which he was born, 1846, when the inhabitants had risen up against the occupying Austrian forces, fighting against superior forces for ten days and earning Brescia the title"lioness of Italy."

Arcangelo was born into a moderately well-to-do (some sources say minor nobility) family in Verolanuova on 12 October 1846. His father, Pietro Tadini, was secretary of the commune. With his first wife, Giulia Gadola, Pietro had seven children, but she then died in childbirth. He married her younger sister, and they produced four more children, of whom Arcangelo was the youngest. His health was delicate, and his parents looked after him devotedly. After attending the local elementary school, he followed his elder brothers to the *gymnasium* (high school) in Lovere and then entered the diocesan seminary of Brescia (where his brother Giulio was already a student). At the seminary he had an accident that left him with a stiff leg and a limp for the rest of his life. He was ordained in 1870, when Italy was finally unified with the annexation of the Papal States, but had to spend his first year as a priest at home with a serious illness.

In 1873 Arcangelo was appointed curate in the mountain village of Lodrino. From there he moved to be chaplain at the sanctuary of Santa Maria della Noce, near Brescia. He taught at the elementary schools in both places. When a flood left many of his parishioners homeless, he organized a soup kitchen in the priest's house, serving 300 meals a day. In 1885 he was appointed curate at Botticino Sera, and he became parish priest two years later, in which post he was to remain for twenty-five years. A totally dedicated parish priest, he formed a choir and a music group, as well as introducing various confraternities; he reformed liturgical observance, and devised catechetical courses suitable for all ages. He was a vigorous preacher, always capable of making the word of God apposite to his congregation, and he spent long hours in the confessional.

The first wave of industrialization was sweeping over Italy, in the form of a primitive capitalism that paid little heed to the conditions of the workforce. The Church, anxious for its flock but at the same time suspicious of the "working class" as a hotbed of socialism, cast about for a role, finding it usually at local level in the foundation of a host of movements, societies, and religious associations, before finally finding a wider voice in 1891, with the publication of Pope Leo XIII's *Rerum novarum*. Arcangelo started a Workers' Mutual Aid Association, which assured workers of some assistance or pension in sickness, unemployment, and old age. His most pressing concern, however, was the fate of girls and young women forced to travel ten miles to find work in a spinning mill. This meant their spending six days of the week away from their families, exploited—"squeezed like lemons," as he put it—and prey to every sort of moral danger, from "new doctrines" to prostitution. Inspired by *Rerum novarum*, Arcangelo sank the whole of his family's savings, donations from generous friends, and a bank loan into the construction of a mill in Botticino Sera where local girls could work without leaving their family and parish community (there were already two mills in the town, but they did not provide enough work places and also refused to collaborate with him). Four years later this was finished: like Don Bosco's (30 Jan.) printing works, it was no amateur clerical endeavour but fully equipped with the latest machinery.

Arcangelo found that some of the workers were orphaned or abandoned, or came from outside the town, so he acquired an adjacent property and turned it into a boarding house. He then needed someone to educate and look after the girls, and found young women willing to join a community for this purpose. This developed (though not formally until after his death) into the Sisters Workers of the Holy House of Nazareth. They were called "Sisters Workers" because Tadini had the insight to see that they had to influence the girls by example, earning their keep at the loom or workbench beside them; "of Nazareth" because the supreme example was the Holy Family, in which Jesus for many years worked with carpenter's tools, not ashamed of having calloused hands and a forehead running with sweat. The aim was to provide a workplace in which work could be seen as a calling worthy of Christian human beings, and a sharing in Christ's work of redemption of the world, not just a curse imposed by an unjust society.

The Institute had still not received official approval by the time of Arcangelo's death, but he had an absolutely clear vision of its purpose. In a letter to the Congregation for Religious dated 2 November 1910, he wrote: "[The Institute] wishes to call itself Sisters Workers of the Holy House of Nazareth: to go into factories and industrial establishments, not so much to direct and supervise, as to work together with the workers, becoming workers themselves." The Vatican, constitutionally averse to women religious "gadding about," took some convincing. An eminent Jesuit, Fr Chiaudano, for example, had attacked any form of women's emancipation in a pamphlet that was taken up by the archbishop of Turin and by Cardinal Merry del Val, with the result that Chiaudano was appointed editor of the influential Jesuit review *La Civiltà Cattolica* (which now sings to a different tune) by Pope Pius X in 1913. Women, in the view of influential churchmen, should not work in schools, factories, or offices and should seek no other advancement in society beyond "a more perfect application of Christian principles." As Tadini's biographer, Luigi Fossati, has pointed out, the Brescia daily *Il Cittadino*, sympathetic to the prevailing Vatican climate, published a eulogy of Arcangelo the day after his death without making any mention of his social work. He may have seen it as stemming from his priesthood; others thought otherwise.

Despite his fragile health and gammy leg, Arcangelo found the strength to carry all this through while spending long hours in church—saying Mass, in the confessional, or standing in front of the Blessed Sacrament (which may have looked penitential but was enjoined by his leg, which prevented him from kneeling). He carried a rosary wherever he went and undoubtedly drew his strength from an intense inner life of prayer. This, as much as his outward attention to their needs, was apparent to his flock, who saw him as a living saint. Totally devoted to others and to the glory of God, he was in many ways the perfect spiritual leader in the mould cast by the Council of Trent. He was at the same time a reader of the "signs of the times" in a way that anticipated Pope John XXIII and the Second Vatican Council. In his homily at the beatification ceremony on 3 October 1999, Pope John Paul II said of him:

> "Precisely because he was a person totally given to God, he could also be a priest totally dedicated to others. The needs arising then in the working world spurred his pastor's heart to search for new ways to proclaim and bear witness to the gospel. His ideal of life and the solidarity he practised toward the weakest groups in society continue today in the commitment of the religious congregation he founded, the Worker Sisters of the Holy House of Nazareth."

L. Fossati, *Don Arcangelo Tadini e la sua Opera Sociale* (1977); *Oss. Rom.*, 3 Oct. 1999, with a perceptive series of linked articles, available at www.pagine-cattoliche.it/Beato_Arcangelo_Tadini, on which the above mainly depends. For the "ten days of Brescia" see S. Onger (ed.), *Brescia 1849: il popolo in rivolta ...* (2002). The Sisters Workers now organize retreats, arrange youth activities and summer camps, and work in factories, schools, surgeries, and holiday houses in Italy and in England, as well as in dispensaries and schools and generally on behalf of women in Africa: *Orders*, p. 396. They also have an extensive and informative website.

25

St Christopher Magallanes and Companions, *Martyrs* (from 1915 to 1937)

The twenty-two Mexican priests and three laymen commemorated here were killed during the decades of religious persecution in the early twentieth century, the first in 1915, the last in 1937, and the remainder in the period of the *Cristero* uprising between 1926 and 1929. They were beatified on 22 November 1992 and canonized on 21 May 2000.

During the mid-nineteenth century the Church had seen its position undermined by liberal governments, culminating in the expulsion of the religious Orders in 1876. Under the dictatorship of Porfirio Díaz, which lasted until he was deposed after the 1910 revolution, the hierarchy re-established its position.

The Virgin of Guadalupe was solemnly crowned in 1895; new seminaries were opened and dioceses formed; and an influx of European religious Orders spear-headed education, evangelization, and the organization of the Church according to the Roman model embodied in the First Vatican Council of 1870. For the first three years of the revolutionary government that deposed Díaz, under Francisco Madero, the Church was able to go on developing the civic and social action movements promoted by Leo XIII. But Madero was murdered in 1913, and the hierarchy gave its support to his assassin and successor, Victoriano Huerta. His seizure of power produced the peasant revolts led by Pancho Villa and Emiliano Zapata, which (though in some ways representing traditional rural Catholicism) contained anticlerical elements. These were codified in the 1917 Constitution devised by Venustiano Carranza (president from 1917 to 1924), described as Masonic by the Church and later denounced in a 1937 encyclical by Pope Pius XI. This Constitution denied the Church any legal status, severely curtailing its right to hold property, and removing the political and civil rights of clergy, with the overall aim of denying the Church "any role within the Mexican society produced by the revolution" (De Solis). This Constitution was not fully implemented until 1926, when its articles became law during the presidency of Plutarco Elías Calles (1924–1928). This led to widespread outbreaks of religious persecution, in response to which the hierarchy declared the suspension of all public worship.

The bishops ordered all rural priests to go into hiding in the cities for their own safety, and Catholic peasants from various parts of the country rose in revolt against the government, using the slogan, "Long live Christ the King and the Virgin of Guadalupe." This was the start of the *Cristero* movement, which all the government forces were unable to subdue for three years. The official Church did not support armed uprising, but at most levels there was Church involvement in the wider movement that formed around it, under the heading of League for the Defence of Religious Freedom. The acute phase of the revolt was finally brought to an end with an agreement between the government and the hierarchy that while the "Calles law" would not be abrogated it would not be applied rigorously; but sporadic conflict smouldered in several States for a further decade.

Many priests remained in rural areas, dedicated to providing the sacraments to their people—and involved in the *Cristero* movement to some degree, though all those now canonized as martyrs were overtly opposed to violence. These twenty-five were (in chronological order of their date of death):

David Galván Bermúdez, born in 1881. He studied at the diocesan seminary of Guadalajara, but left after some years to pursue a life of dissipation. Repenting, he returned and was ordained in 1909. He taught at the seminary, was arrested as a priest during Carranza's 1914 uprising, then released. On 30 January 1915, while on his way to aid the victims of a confrontation in Guadalajara between Carranza's supporters and those of Pancho Villa, he was seized by a group of soldiers. Warned that he might be killed, he replied, "What greater glory is there than to die saving a soul?" He was executed by firing squad.

Luis Batiz, and the three laymen **David Roldán Lara**, **Salvador Lara Puente**, and **Manuel Morales**, all accused of fomenting rebellion through the League for the Defence of Religious Freedom, and killed on 15 August 1926 at Chachihuites, Zacatecas.

Luis, born in 1870 and ordained in 1894, was the spiritual director of the seminary of Durango and chaplain to ACJM ("Catholic Action of Mexican Youth") a militant movement that was part of the League. He was also parish priest of Chachihuites, where he built a workshop and a school and catechized both adults and children. After telling a meeting of the League that the banning of public worship had been decreed by the hierarchy, not the government, and so should be respected, he took refuge in a private house. Soldiers found him there and arrested him. The local authorities decided that he should be taken to Zacatecas, and a two-car convoy set out the next day, but the soldiers decided to take the law into their own hands, stopped the car on the way, took him out and shot him.

The three laymen were members of ACJM and officers of the League: Manuel Morales was its president. Born in 1898, he had studied for a time at the seminary of Durango but had been forced to leave in order to work to support his family. Arrested after he remonstrated at Luis' arrest, he was in the front car with him. Luis asked the soldiers to spare him as he was married with three children, but he told the soldiers, "I am dying for God, and God will take care of my children." He raised his hat as the soldiers fired. David Roldán had likewise been a seminarian who was forced to leave to support his family. He became president of ACJM in 1925 and then vice president of the League. Salvador Lara was yet another ex-seminarian forced to leave on account of his family's poverty. He had become secretary of the League and local president of Catholic Action. He tried to organize Luis' release but instead shared his fate. The four had been offered their freedom if they recognized the legitimacy of President Calles' anti-religious laws, but all of them had refused. He and David were pulled out of the second car, which stopped behind the first. They died crying out "*Viva Cristo Rey! Viva la Vírgen de Guadalupe!*"

A further eight martyrs were put to death between January and May of 1927.

On 17 January **Jenaro Sánchez**, born in 1886 and ordained in 1911, a pastor in Tecolotlán in the State of Jalisco and known as a devoted parish priest with a gift for preaching, was arrested and hanged from a mesquite tree. When the soldiers put the rope around his neck, he said, "My countrymen, you are going to hang me, but I pardon you, and my Father God also pardons you, and long live Christ the King!" He had previously been so savagely beaten that it was some time before his body was recognized and taken away for burial.

As a young priest **Mateo Correa**, born in 1866, had been parish priest in several parishes, including Concepción del Oro, where he became a close friend of the family of Miguel Pro (Nov. 23), and gave Mexico's most famous martyr his First Communion. In 1926 he was arrested and accused of being in league with the *Cristeros*, but was released. The following year, frail and elderly, he was taking the *viaticum* to a sick parishioner near Valparaíso when he was arrested again. The local army commander, General Ortiz, who had ordered his first arrest and been furious at his release, ordered him to be taken to Durango, to hear the Confessions of some *Cristeros* awaiting execution. When Ortiz demanded to know what they had said, Mateo refused to answer, and he was shot on 6 February.

Julio Alvarez Mendoza, also born in 1866, who was ordained in 1894, and pastor of Mechoacanejo in Jalisco, refused to go into hiding. He was arrested when on his way to say Mass on a ranch, tied to the saddle of a horse, and led away to León. On hearing his sentence, he said, "I know that you have to kill me because you are ordered to do so, but I am going to die innocent because I have done nothing wrong. My crime is to be a minister of God. I pardon you." He crossed his arms, and the soldiers fired; then they threw his body on to a rubbish heap near the church, where a memorial to him now stands. The date was 30 March 1927.

David Uribe, born in 1888, was ordained in 1913 and then worked with the bishop of Tabasco. He was forced into hiding several times but had gone back to his people when he was arrested. While in prison in Cuernavaca he wrote, "I declare that I am innocent of the things of which I am accused ... I pardon all my enemies and I beg pardon from any that I have offended." On 12 April he was shot in the back of the head near San José Vidal, Morelia.

Sabás Reyes Salazar, born in 1879, studied at the seminary of Guadalajara, was ordained in 1911, and in 1927 had for some years been parish priest of Totolán in Jalisco. He was returning from administering a baptism when troops attacked the village. He hid in a house for several days but on 11 April was discovered. He was beaten and tortured; his hands and feet were burned; he was starved, left in the sun, and given nothing to drink. A number of his bones were broken and his skull was fractured. On 13 April he was taken to the cemetery and shot.

Román Adame Rosales, born in 1859, had been another seminary student at Guadalajara, ordained in 1890. The founder of the Association of Daughters of Mary, he was parish priest of Nochistlan, Zacatecas, and had been forced into hiding in private houses and on ranches when he was denounced and arrested on 18 April 1927. Aged sixty-eight, he was forced to walk barefoot from

Mexticacán to Yahualica, until a soldier offered his horse when he realized the elderly priest could not walk another step. For three days he was kept tied to the columns in front of his jail without food or water. A ransom was paid, but he was taken to the cemetery on 21 April and shot. One of the members of the firing squad refused to fire and was himself shot as a punishment.

Christopher (Cristóbal) Magallanes Jara, who gives his name to this group of martyrs, was born in 1869 to a poor family and worked on the land until he entered the Guadalupe seminary at the age of nineteen. He was ordained in 1899 and in 1910 was appointed parish priest of Totalice. There he helped to found schools and catechetical centres for young people and adults. He started a newspaper and built carpentry shops and an electric plant to power the local mills. From 1914 to his death he pioneered the re-evangelization of the Huichole Indians, who had effectively lost contact with the Church since the expulsion of the Jesuits in the late eighteenth century. When the diocesan seminaries were closed by government decree, he gathered displaced seminarians together and started his own seminary. This was quickly suppressed, but twice more he started new ones, and when these were closed he arranged classes in private houses. Despite the fact that he wrote and preached against violence, he was accused of fomenting the *Cristero* revolt. On 21 May 1927 he was on his way to say Mass on a ranch when he was caught up in a battle between government troops and rebels. He was arrested and shot four days later, without a trial. He declared, "I am innocent and I die innocent. I forgive with all my heart those responsible for my death, and I ask God that the shedding of my blood may serve to bring peace to divided Mexicans."

Agustín Caloca, born in 1898 and ordained 1923, was Fr Christopher's curate at Totalice and also head of the auxiliary seminary he had founded, responsible for ministering to the outlying ranches. He was arrested while arranging for the seminary students to disperse to private houses and shot together with Fr Christopher on 25 May at Colotitlán, Jalisco.

Between June 1927 and the end of the year, a further six of this group of martyrs were put to death:

José Isabel Flores, born in 1866, had been a distinguished student at Guadalajara and was ordained in 1896. He founded several Associations, including the Daughters of Mary, and was known as a devoted priest of several parishes. His last post was at Zapotlanejo in the State of Jalisco, where he was denounced, arrested, and starved for three days. He was then offered his freedom if he would subscribe to the Calles law, which he refused to do. On 21 June he was taken to the cemetery and tortured by being hanged from a branch of a tree, then pulled up and suddenly lowered three or four times. Finally he told his tormentors: "This is not the way you are going to kill me, my children

... But just let me say, if you received the sacraments from me, don't cripple the hands that served you." One of the soldiers present, whom Fr Flores had baptized, then refused to take part in the execution; he was immediately shot, but then the guns of the remaining soldiers failed to fire, and the commanding office slit Fr Flores' throat with his sword.

José María Robles, born in 1888, another bright student from Guadalajara, was ordained in 1913. He had a deep devotion to the Sacred Heart and founded the Congregation of Sisters known as the *Hermanas del Corazón de Jesus Sacramentado* ("Sisters of the Eucharistic Heart of Jesus"). He was pastor of Tecolotlán in Guadalajara when he was forced into hiding. In response to suggestions that he should leave his parish to avoid persecution, he said, "The shepherd can never abandon his sheep." He was arrested on his way to say Mass in a private house and, despite a legal stay of execution, he was taken on horseback to an oak tree out in the country, from which he was hanged after he had prayed briefly, blessed the members of his parish, then pardoned and blessed his murderers, kissed the rope, and put it around his neck. The date was 26 June.

Miguel de la Mora, born in 1875 into a peasant family, had worked on their land before deciding he had a vocation to the priesthood. He was ordained in 1906 and worked as a parish priest in the diocese of Colima. Arrested when the persecution began but then released, he was on a trip with friends and stopped for breakfast on a ranch when a woman asked him if he was a priest and, if so, if he would officiate at her daughter's wedding. Some government officials overheard the conversation and arrested the group, taking them back to Colima. Told he had been sentenced to death, Fr Miguel calmly recited his rosary. He was shot in a stable at Cardona on 7 August, the first martyr from the diocese of Colima.

Rodrigo Aguilar Alemán, born in 1875, studied at the auxiliary seminary of Guzmán, where he showed great literary talent. Ordained in 1905, he worked in various parishes. He was acting parish priest in Unión de Tula, Jalisco, when he was denounced and forced to hide on a ranch. He was betrayed and discovered there by government soldiers and taken, on 28 October, to the main square of Ejutla, to be hanged from a mango tree. One of the soldiers arrogantly asked, "Who lives?" telling him he would be spared if he would answer: "Long live the supreme government." Instead, in a firm voice, he replied, "Christ the King and Our Lady of Guadalupe." The soldier pulled on the rope to suspend him in mid-air, then he lowered him and again asked, "Who lives?," only to receive the same answer. After the third time, the soldier left him to hang until he was dead.

Margarito Flores, born in 1899, worked on his peasant family's land until he entered the seminary of Chilapa, where he was ordained in 1924 and soon appointed professor and vicar. During the height of the persecution he took refuge in Mexico City, teaching in a school there. He was arrested but then released. When he heard that the bishop of Chilapa could not find a priest willing to go to the parish of Atenango del Rio, because the municipal governor had threatened to shoot any priest found there, Margarito volunteered at once. On the way there, however, he was arrested and forced to walk to Tulimán in the blazing sun, half naked and barefoot. After calmly sharing his last meal with his captors he was taken behind the church, where he blessed the soldiers and prayed before being shot. This took place on 12 November.

Pedro Esqueda Ramírez, born in 1887, studied at Guadalajara until the seminary was closed in 1914. He then returned to his native town of San Juan de los Lagos, Jalisco, where he worked as a deacon until 1916, when he was ordained and served as assistant priest. When advised to leave the parish for his safety, he replied, "God put me here; He knows where I am." He worked underground until, on 18 November, he was captured by government troops at a private house, where he had hidden the sacred vessels in a hole in the floor. Dragged out, he was brutally tortured for four days but suffered in silence. On 22 November he was taken to Teolcaltitlán, led to a mesquite tree, and ordered to climb it. Although he attempted this, he could not because his arm was broken. He was tortured again, then shot.

A further five of this group were martyred in 1928:

Jesús Méndez Montoya, born in 1880, studied at the seminary of Michoacán and was ordained in 1906. When persecution broke out he was the parish priest of Valtierilla, a dedicated priest noted for his devotion to the Eucharist, long hours spent hearing Confessions, and concern for parish Associations. On 5 February 1928 he had just celebrated Mass secretly when he heard fighting outside the house in which he was staying. He left by a back window, hiding a ciborium full of consecrated hosts under a *tilma*, but was stopped by a soldier who thought he was carrying arms. He managed to consume the hosts before admitting he was a priest. He was taken to the town plaza, where he was made to sit on the trunk of a fallen tree while the commanding officer shot at him. On the first attempt the officer's pistol misfired, so he ordered his soldiers to shoot. Not a single shot hit him, possibly because no one wanted to kill him. Finally he was made to stand, the soldiers removed his medals and cross, and at their third attempt they succeeded at least in wounding him; one of the soldiers then gave him the *coup de grâce*. His body was thrown on railroad tracks to be cut to pieces by a train, but the wives of the town officials took it away for a proper wake and burial.

Toribio Romo González, born in 1900, studied at Guadalajara, where he was prominent in the social ministry of Catholic Action. Ordained in 1922, he served as assistant priest in several parishes and was noted for his powerful preaching. During the persecution he lived a nomadic life, hiding and establishing an oratory in a disused factory in the city of Tequila and emerging at night to minister to its inhabitants. In the early morning of 25 February 1928, government troops forced the local mailman to show them where the secret Masses were celebrated. They surprised Fr Toribio and shot him in his bed, stripped his body of clothing, and threw the naked corpse in front of the city hall.

Justino Orona Madrigal, born in 1877, came from an extremely poor but devout family. He studied at Guadalajara, returning home frequently to help his family. Ordained in 1904, he served as parish priest in four different parishes in urban areas, contending with a general climate of anticlericalism and indifference. As parish priest at Cuquío, Jalisco, in 1928, he wrote to a friend, "Those of us who walk the road of sorrows with fidelity can leave for heaven with a feeling of security." He wanted to stay with his people but was forced into hiding on a ranch belonging to friends. There at dawn on 1 July he was seized by soldiers who broke into the house where he was sleeping; he was shot forthwith.

With Fr Orona was his young assistant, **Atiliano Cruz Alvarado**, who was of indigenous descent, born in 1901. He had spent his childhood working the land until his family took him to Teocaltiche so that he could learn to read and write. He entered the local seminary in 1918 and moved on to Guadalajara two years later. Ordained in 1927, he had been sent to the ranch just the day before. With Orona he had recited the rosary and planned their hidden ministry. When asked if he was afraid of the soldiers, the younger priest replied that he would greet them with the words, *"Viva Cristo Rey."* When the soldiers burst in, he did just this, in a strong clear voice. Orona died immediately; Cruz was mortally wounded and died soon after. Their bodies were thrown in the town plaza, but parishioners came and took them, burying them the same day.

Tranquilino Ubiarco, also of Indian descent, was born in 1899 into an extremely poor family. He somehow studied for the priesthood, despite continual interruptions to his studies due to sporadic persecution. Ordained in 1923, he started catechetical study centres and a journal of Christian doctrine. He had been parish priest of Tepatitlán, working from hiding in private houses, for fifteen months when he was arrested on 5 October, while officiating at a wedding in a private home. He was allowed to hear the Confessions of those arrested with him. As he was being led to his execution, he asked who was commissioned to kill him. When all the soldiers remained silent, he said, "All of this is God's will; the man who is made to kill me is not responsible." One of the soldiers then confessed that he was the one who had been chosen, but he now felt that he could not carry out the assignment. Calmly, Father Ubiarco blessed all the soldiers. They hanged him from the branch of a eucalyptus tree before firing at him and the others. Once again, the soldier in charge of the execution refused to carry out the order, so he was shot.

✤

The last of this group of martyrs, **Pedro de Jesús Maldonado**, born in Sacramento in 1892, also had his studies for the priesthood, at the seminary of Chihuahua, interrupted by the revolution. After some time spent learning music instead, he was ordained in El Paso, Texas, in 1918. Returning home, he became parish priest of Santa Isabel, Chihuahua. His ministry concentrated on children's catechism, night adoration of the Blessed Sacrament, and the formation of Marian Associations. He survived the period of intense persecution from 1926 to 1929, but this broke out again in 1931, when the churches were again closed. He was arrested, maltreated, and released in 1932 and again in 1934, when he was sent back to safety in Texas. He begged to be allowed to return and did so, but in 1937 a fire broke out in the public school in the village where he was staying, and the authorities blamed him. A group of armed and drunken men seized him at his house and made him walk barefoot to Santa Isabel. He recited his rosary along the way. He was beaten and hit on the head so hard that his left eye popped out. He had prayed for the grace of receiving final Communion. He had a consecrated host with him in a pyx, and when his murderers found it, one of them forced him to eat it saying, "Eat this, this is your last Communion!" He was beaten unconscious, then taken to the hospital in Chihuahua, where he died on 11 February.

Butler, Dec., Supp., pp. 270–5. Additional details of deaths from Catholicmatch. com. There is an extensive bibliography, titled "Persecution of Mexican Catholics during the Mexican Revolution," at www.holycross.edu/departments/history/ vlapomar/persec/mex. Photographs in Ann Ball, *Faces of Holiness* (1998) and on Vatican websites. For Miguel Pro see *Butler*, Nov., pp. 194–6.

29

St Ursula Ledóchowska, *Founder* (1865–1939)

The founder of the "Grey Ursulines" was born in eastern Austria, at Loorsdorf, forty miles west of Vienna, on 17 April 1865 and christened Julia. Her father was a Polish noble, Count Antoni Ledóchowski, and her mother, Josephine Salis-Zizers, came from a prominent Swiss family. Both sides of her family had produced eminent statesmen and politicians, distinguished soldiers, and high-ranking ecclesiastics (an uncle was a cardinal), as well as religious. Their five children were all expected to take their religion seriously and actively, including visiting the sick and the poor. The first three all entered religious life, and indeed Julia's elder sister, Maria Theresia, who founded the Sodality of St

Peter Claver, was beatified in 1975 (6 July), while her younger brother Vladimir ("Wlodzimierz" in Polish) became provincial superior of the Jesuits in Poland.

Count Antoni suffered financial reverses, moved the family to Lipnica Murowana, near Krakow in southern Poland, in 1883, and then died of smallpox in 1885, whereupon his brother Cardinal Lebo Ledóchowski assumed financial responsibility for the family. Julia entered the Ursuline convent in Krakow the following year and spent the next twenty-one years there, taking the name Ursula (with the standard prefix of Mary) in religion. She was responsible for establishing the first university hall of residence in Poland when women were permitted to study at universities. The Ursulines ran schools for girls in the area and also farther afield, in Galicia (western Ukraine) and Russia.

In 1907, at the request of Pope St Pius X (21 Aug.), Sister Ursula and two others went to St Petersburg to take over the running of a boarding school for girls, near the Polish St Catherine's High School. They had to live clandestinely, as Roman Catholic religious Orders were not allowed to operate in Orthodox Russia, but their numbers grew and they became an autonomous house, with Ursula—now Mother Ursula—as superior and even a secret novitiate.

From there she started another house on the Gulf of Finland, incorporating a convent and a boarding school. She became deeply involved in what she saw as the plight of the Churches in Finland—Protestant as well as Catholic—seeing them as "troubled and abandoned like sheep without a Shepherd"(Matt. 9:36). Making herself their shepherd, Ursula prepared and published a Finnish catechism and an inter-denominational prayerbook and hymnal, and held ecumenical services in the convent chapel, as well as organizing joint Bible study groups.

The outbreak of the First World War in 1914 forced Ursula to leave St Petersburg. She moved to Stockholm and then to Denmark, gradually bringing the other Sisters from St Petersburg and starting a school for Scandinavian girls. She also became involved with the organization set up in Switzerland by Henryk Sienkiewicz to help war victims.

Before the war, Poland had been partitioned between Prussia and Russia and officially wiped off the political map. Ursula was a passionate Polish patriot, and she began to argue publicly for its independence in a post-war settlement, travelling widely and addressing kings, ambassadors, and politicians. When her desire became fact after the war, she moved her Sisters to Poland, establishing a motherhouse at Pniewy, west of Poznań. They brought back a large number of children of Polish emigrants orphaned by the war.

In 1920 the community was approved by the Holy See as a Separate Congregation within the Ursuline family, the Ursulines of the Agonizing Heart of Jesus (popularly known as Grey Ursulines from the colour of their habit). It was to keep to the spirit of Ursuline spirituality and continue their commitment to education, as well as reaching out to meet current social needs, especially those of the poor. She told them: "It is not enough to pray, 'Thy Kingdom come,' but to work, so that the Kingdom of God will exist among us today."

The venture flourished, with several new houses opening in Poland, extending to Italy in 1928 and to France in 1930, where Sisters went with young women seeking work. She continually associated lay people with the work, and invited young women to give a year or two of their lives to work in the very poor border regions of eastern Poland, with their complicated and shifting national and religious allegiances. She also brought the Eucharistic Crusaders (now the Eucharistic Youth Movement) and the Marian Sodality to Poland, both intended to encourage young people to take an active charitable role in the Church and in society. Ursula backed up her educational drive by publishing magazines for children and young people, as well as herself writing books for them. She became a distinguished figure in the religious, cultural, and social life of the country, and both Church and State in Poland bestowed several major awards on her.

In 1928 Ursula established the Generalate of the Congregation in Rome, together with a free boarding school intended to bring poor children into contact with the heart of the Catholic Church and with Western civilization. Besides teaching, her Sisters also went to work among the poor of Rome. She died there on 29 May 1939, already widely regarded as a saint. Pope John Paul II beatified her in Poznań—the first beatification to take place in Poland—on 20 June 1983. In 1989 her body was exhumed and found to be incorrupt; it was then transferred to the chapel of the motherhouse in Pniewy, where it still rests. In 2002 a miracle brought about through her intercession was accepted, and she was canonized in Rome on 18 May 2003, in the same ceremony as two Italian women, one religious and one lay—Maria de Mattias (20 Aug.) and Virginia Centurione Bracelli (15. Dec.)—and a Polish bishop, Joseph Sebastian Pelczar (28 Mar.). In his homily Pope John Paul II praised her in terms that express the aims she set out in her conferences:

> "She addressed to all the language of love, borne out by her work. With the message of God's love she crossed Russia, the Scandinavian countries, France and Italy. In her day she was an apostle of the new evangelization, demonstrating a constant timeliness, creativity, and the effectiveness of gospel love by her life and action ... We can all learn from her how to build with Christ an ever more human world—a world in which values such as justice, freedom, solidarity [a term that first gained currency in Poland] and peace will be more and more fully achieved. From her we can learn how to put into practice every day the 'new' commandment of love."

The Patron Saints Index site has errors of date and place, but there is a chronological summary (available in English) and much more (in Italian), including a selection from her conferences and letters and other works, at www.orsoline. it/orsola (or /julia_engl for English version). See also catholicyouth.freeservers. com/saints/bl_ursula for an account concentrating more on her spirituality. On Mary Teresa see *Butler*, July, pp. 46–7; on the Sodality (or Missionary Sisters) of St Peter Claver see *Orders*, pp. 329–30.

The Grey Ursulines, numbering 900 Sisters in 100 communities, still work in Poland and the neighbouring nations to the east, Belarus and Ukraine; also in Finland, where they returned in 1976, France, and Germany; in the New World they are in Argentina, Brazil, and Canada; and in Africa in Tanzania. A clematis, *Matka Urszula Ledóchowska*, bred by Br Stefan Franczak in 1980, is named after her.

30

St Joseph Marello, *Bishop and Founder* (1844–1895)

Joseph (Giuseppe) Morello was born to Vincenzo and Anna Maria Marello in Turin on 26 December 1844. After his mother had died, while he was still very young, his father moved the family to Santo Martino Alfieri, near Asti, thirty miles east of Turin. Joseph entered the junior seminary in Asti at the age of twelve. He had a great devotion to Our Lady and, when he contracted typhus at the age of nineteen, promised her that, if he recovered, he would continue with his studies for the priesthood. He did recover, and he was ordained on 19 September 1868.

He worked in diocesan adminstration, first for thirteen years as secretary to Bishop Carlo Savio in which capacity he attended the First Vatican Council in 1869–1870, where the future Pope Leo XIII appreciated his obvious talents. He was then appointed diocesan chancellor, which meant taking charge of the diocesan curia. One of his actions was to save a retirement home from bankruptcy by purchasing it for the diocese. There was also an intensely spiritual side to his priestly activities: he heard Confessions assiduously, acted as a spiritual director, and took a particular interest in the moral welfare of young people.

Joseph contemplated leaving the active ministry and becoming a Carthusian, but Bishop Savio persuaded him to channel his spiritual energies into a new Congregation. In 1878 he founded the Oblates of St Joseph, with the objectives of caring for the poor, educating young people, and providing whatever assistance bishops might need at any given juncture. After a series of anticlerical government measures, there were no other male religious in Asti at the time. Their guide and inspiration was to be St Joseph on account of his "life of hidden service, joined with deep interior life" (homily at canonization ceremony), but Joseph Marello had not lost his attraction to the contemplative life and exhorted his oblates to be "Carthusians inside your house and apostles outside." The Congregation received papal approbation in 1909.

On 17 February 1889 Joseph was consecrated bishop of Acqui. He was an active and approachable bishop, making regular visitations to all the parishes in his diocese and writing six pastoral letters encouraging study of the catechism, parish missions, and closer contact between clergy and laity. In 1895, after six years as bishop, his health was failing, but he insisted on going to Savona to take part in the celebrations for the third centennial of St Philip Neri (26 May). He died there of a stroke on 30 May, leaving a powerful memory of his six years as bishop, which grew with time and led to a local cult.

The cause for his canonization began in 1948, the "decree of heroic virtue" was approved in 1978, and Joseph was beatified by Pope John Paul II in Asti on 26 September 1993. In 2000 the inexplicable cure of two children from broncho-pulmonitis was declared a miracle attributable to his intercession, and he was canonized on 25 November 2001. The pope referred in his homily to his formation in "the golden period of holiness in the Piedmont area, when, in the midst of numerous forms of hostility against the Church and the Catholic faith, the champions of the spirit and of charity flourished" (referring to SS John Bosco, Joseph Cottolengo, Joseph Cafasso, and others, now joined by Joseph Marello).

M. A. Verna and G. Citera, OSJ, *Bd Joseph Marello, A Life for God and Neighbour* (n.d.); Oblates of St Joseph, *Holiness in the Ordinary* (n.d.); a contemporary biography by Giovanni Sisto is translated into English as *I, the Undersigned Poor Sinner* (n.d.). See also Siro Dal Degan, OSJ, *OSJ. History of the Congregation 1878–1993* (bound MS, 1994); *Oss.Rom.*, 25 Nov. 2001; and other usual Vatican sources.

The Oblates of St Joseph are active in the U.S.A., with a seminary at Pittston, Pennsylvania, and another, with a house of studies, in California. It conducts missions in India, the Philippines, Poland, Romania, Slovakia, and several countries in South America: *Orders*, p. 239.

31

Bd Mariano of Roccacasale (1778–1866)

Roccacasale lies on the slopes on Monte Morrone in the Abruzzo region of Italy, towards the Adriatic coast east of Rome. Archaeological remains date its origins to pre-history. Mariano (baptized Domenico) was born there on 14 June 1778, the younger son of Gabriele di Nicolantonio and Santa di Arcangelo, who were peasant farmers and shepherds, poor and devoutly Catholic. Domenico stayed at home to mind the sheep after his elder siblings had married and left home. A "prodigy" related of him in this period in some measure anticipates that of Lourdes some half century later. Hot, tired, and thirsty but unable to find any water on the hillside, he lay down and fell into a deep sleep. In a dream, he saw a Franciscan friar, who told him to wake up, when he would find water running over his head. He woke up and moved a large stone on which he had placed his cape. Water began to flow from the ground and has been flowing ever since.

In September 1802 Domenico was clothed with the Franciscan habit at the convent of Arisquia, taking the name Mariano of Roccacasale in religion. A year later he made his solemn profession. He stayed there for twelve years, dividing his time between prayer and manual work as carpenter, kitchen gardener, cook, and doorkeeper, but he did not feel that the convent provided the spiritual atmosphere he sought. This was due mainly to the obstacles placed in the way of conventual life by the turmoil of the Napoleonic wars, which began to recede only with the return of Pius VII from imprisonment in France in 1814. At that time Mariano heard of the hermitage at Bellegra, with its austerity and fame of many holy friars since the times of its founder, Thomas of Cori (canonized in Nov. 1999; see 11 Jan). His superiors at Arisquia acceded to his request to be allowed to make a pilgrimage there. Once there, he left his community and stayed. He was then thirty-seven years old.

Mariano was soon appointed doorkeeper and continued in this office for over forty years. It became his mission and his path to holiness. It was his duty to welcome pilgrims, travellers, and the poor to the hermitage, and to offer them what traditional Franciscan hospitality could provide for them: the greeting "Peace and good!"; praying with them and offering them simple instruction; washing their feet; lighting a fire if the weather was cold; and providing them with hot soup, again using this as an opportunity for offering instruction and advice. He had a smile for everyone, as Bd Diego Oddi (beatified with him; 3 June) discovered in 1864, two years before Mariano's death. He devoted as much as possible of the time he was not on duty to prayer.

Mariano died on 31 May 1866, which was the feast of Corpus Christi that year. In his homily at the beatification ceremony on 3 October 1999, Pope John Paul II said of him:

> "Regarding the life and spirituality of Blessed Mariano of Roccacasale, Franciscan religious, we can say that they sum up in emblematic fashion St Paul's affirmation to the Christian community in Philippi, 'The God of peace will be with you' (Phil. 4:9). His life of poverty and humility, following in the footsteps of St Francis and St Clare of Assisi, was constantly directed toward his neighbours, in the desire to listen to and share the troubles of every one of them, in order to present them later to the Lord in his long hours of prayer before the Eucharist."

Oss.Rom., weekly edn, 3 Oct. 1999. The Franciscan Province of Rome has provided accounts of his life and death and the "prodigy" on the hillside: *Relazione della preziosa morte del servo di Dio Fra Mariano da Roccacasale* (1872); *Il segreto di una chiave: Il venerabile Fra Mariano da R.* (1963); and *Incontrò Dio nel silenzio della montagna—Fra M. da R.* (1999).

JUNE

3

Bd Diego Oddi (1839–1919)

Giuseppe Oddi was born on 6 June 1839 in Vallinfreda, in the diocese of Tivoli, twenty miles to the east of Rome. His parents, Vicenzo Oddi and Bernardina Pasquali, were poor peasants and devout Catholics. With little formal education, he nevertheless learned as much about the faith as he could. When he was twenty, he felt a strong call to the religious life, reinforced by the evening visits he made to the local church to "converse" with Jesus and Mary.

Despite his parents' strong objections, he went on pilgrimage to the Franciscan hermitage at Bellegra (see St Thomas of Cori; 11 Jan), where the place and the lives of the Franciscans made an indelible impression on him. But, obedient to his parents, he returned to work on the family land for a further four years. He went again to Bellegra in the spring of 1864, when the door was opened to him by an elderly friar who had been the porter there for forty years. This was Mariano of Roccacasale (also beatified on 3 Oct. 1999; 31 May). Giuseppe knew of his reputation for holiness and asked him for a word of advice. "Be good! Be good, my son!" was the reply, which remained with him on the journey back to Vallinfreda, where he worked for a further seven years.

His parents finally relented in 1872 (by which time Giuseppe was thirty-three), and he joined the monastery at Bellegra, initially as an "oblate tertiary." In 1877, with an anticlerical government passing laws dispossessing religious Orders, the friars were expelled from the hermitage and forced to live with supporters in the town. They managed to retain the convent garden by nominally making it over to a friend, and Giuseppe was able to continue working this. The following year the friars were allowed back. The novitiate was re-opened in 1884, and Giuseppe was admitted as a postulant, taking the name Diego in religion. He made his first profession in 1886 and took his final vows on 16 May 1899. This marked the start of a new life for him: Diego was to spend the next forty years walking the roads of Subiaco and the surrounding districts begging for alms. His illiteracy proved no barrier to talking to people, and his begging turned into an iterant preaching mission, as he found words of counsel and comfort for all who came into contact with him. He often spent the night in prayer in churches in villages where he had been begging during the day, telling the local sacristan that he would ring the evening Angelus and close the church for the night.

Diego lived a life of strict personal penance and austerity, but was careful to conceal this. The fame of his holiness spread during his lifetime. Pope John XXIII was an admirer and visited Bellegra to visit his tomb and see mementoes of him in 1959, later dying on the same day of the year, 3 June, in 1963 (Diego died on 3 June 1919). In his address to the pilgrims in Rome for his beatification, Pope John Paul II called him "an angel of peace and good for all those who met him."

❖

Oss.Rom., weekly edn, 3 October 1999.

Bd John XXIII, *Pope* (1881–1963)

Regarded as *un papa di passaggio*, a "transitional" (in the sense of "stop-gap") pope, when he was elected at the age of seventy-seven in 1958, John proved transitional in quite an unexpected way. Through his calling of the Second Vatican Council, he steered—or pushed—the Church through transition from what Karl Rahner called its "second age," the European Church begun by St Paul's mission to the gentiles, into its "third age," that of being a truly "universal Church." Like other great figures of the modern age—Archbishop Romero falls into the same category—there was apparently little in his earlier life to suggest what was to come.

Angelo Giuseppe Roncalli was born at Sotto il Monte, a village in the Piedmont ("foothills") in the province of Bergamo in northern Italy, on 25 November 1881. His parents, Battista Roncalli, who died in 1935, and Marianna Mazzola, who died in 1939, were peasant farmers, and he was the fourth of their fourteen children: he was to describe his family as "so poor that the children had no wine." He was baptized on the day of his birth by the parish priest, Fr Rebuzzini. Angelo attended the village school and was then sponsored, in view of his obvious intelligence, to enter the diocesan minor and major seminaries, after which he progressed to the San Apollinare Institute in Rome, where he studied from 1901 to 1905 (including a year of military service, which he described as "a real pugatory"). He was awarded a doctorate in theology on 13 July 1904 and ordained priest on 10 August. After completing his studies the following year he went on pilgrimage to the Holy Land.

The next year the new and reforming bishop of Bergamo, Giacomo Maria Radini-Tadeschi, appointed Angelo as his secretary and took him back to Bergamo. He supported the bishop's pro-union stance and became inseparable from him for ten years. He also taught Church history, patristics, and apologetics at the diocesan seminary and edited the diocesan journal, *La vita diocesana*.

He began what was to prove almost a lifelong task, editing the "visitation documents" of St Charles Borromeo (4 Nov.), his accounts of his application of the reforms of the Council of Trent in the diocese of Bergamo: the last part (of five) was to appear in 1957. In August 1914 the bishop was told he had cancer and had not long to live. By the end of the year he was dead, but Angelo carried on teaching in the seminary and continued several pastoral functions. He also wrote a biography of Radini-Tadeschi.

A new pope, Benedict XV, was elected to succeed Pius X (canonized in 1954; 21 Aug.), and in 1915 Italy entered the First World War. Angelo was called up for military service in the medical corps, with the rank of sergeant. He acted as chaplain to wounded soldiers and grew an impressive handlebar mustache. After the war he opened a Student House to care for the spiritual needs of young theologians returning from active service. In 1919 he was made spiritual director of the Bergamo seminary, then in 1921 he was summoned to Rome to become Italian president of the Society for the Propagation of the Faith. He also taught a course on the Fathers of the Church at the Lateran seminary in Rome, where he acquired a reputation for rambling somewhat in his lectures and advancing some fairly revolutionary (for the time) ideas, such as that mixed marriages might sometimes be admissible. These seem to have brought a promising academic career to an abrupt close, as he was relieved of his post after three months. (After his election as pope he consulted his file at the Holy Office and found he was "suspected of Modernism.") He nevertheless continued his researches into the life of Borromeo at the library of the Ambrosianum in Rome, where the librarian was Cardinal Ratti, who became pope as Pius XI in 1922.

As pope, Ratti appointed Angelo titular bishop of Areopolis and sent him as apostolic visitor to Bulgaria in 1925. Bulgaria had only a small minority of Catholics (some 50,000) and was not considered important. Angelo found that he had very little to do, which did not suit his active temperament. He complained of "acute inner sufferings"—brought about not by the country or its people, but by "the central organs of ecclesiastical administration," which he found deeply hurtful. He earned the gratitude of the people for his care of survivors of an earthquake in 1928. After ten frustrating years in Bulgaria Angelo was given the titular archbishopric of Mesembria, appointed apostolic delegate to Turkey and Greece, and moved in 1934 to Turkey—another remote outpost of Vatican diplomacy, though as administrator of the apostolic vicariate of Istanbul he at least had more pastoral duties to perform. He was in Greece at the outbreak of the Second World War in 1939 and set up a network for aiding refugees from the Nazis, epecially Jews (for which he was later to be awarded the title of "saviour" by the Raoul Wallenberg International Foundation). Ironically, his efforts were funded by the German ambassador to Turkey, Franz von Papen, an anti-Nazi who desired Germany's defeat in the war.

Pius XII appointed him papal nuncio to France on 22 December 1944, which certainly rescued his career from obscurity—though his previous obscurity was an advantage, as he brought no political "baggage" from the war years with him. General de Gaulle had demanded a new nuncio to replace Valerio Valeri, who had collaborated with the Vichy government during the war. So had many other bishops, and Angelo handled the post-war recriminations with tact and skill, persuading De Gaulle that they should not all be dismissed. Robert Schuman, the French prime minister (himself a candidate for beatification), called him "the only man in Paris in whose company one feels the physical sensation of peace." He progressively endeared himself to the French over nine years, visiting the great shrines and taking part in manifestations of popular piety. He was rewarded by being made a cardinal in 1953 and being appointed patriarch of Venice three days later. (There has recently been controversy, starting in the *Corriere della Sera*, over whether he refused to hand French Jewish children who had been baptized back to their parents, but Vatican documents subsequently released seem to have exonerated him.)

He devoted himself to the people of his patriarchate for five years, rejoicing in the opportunity to exercise direct pastoral care of a diocese for the first time. He found time to travel and made pilgrimages to the great Marian shrines, including Lourdes, Fatima and Czestochowa. Angelo had thus had long experience of the world outside the Vatican by the time Pius XII died on 9 October 1958. Though he had been in the service of the Curia, he never saw himself as a "curialist" and made clear that his prime task was to be a "good shepherd." The conclave to elect a successor began two weeks later and he was elected pope on the twelfth ballot—the "stop-gap" who would occupy the throne of Peter for a few years, until Giovanni Battista Montini of Milan, who was not then a cardinal, was thought ready to succeed (as he did, as Paul VI). Angelo was aghast at his election: "*Horrefactus sum,*" was his reaction, quoting from the Book of Job. He could see that the Church, though well preserved by recent popes as a "perfect society" (meaning one "sufficient unto itself" rather than "perfect" in the usual sense), was inward- rather than outward-looking. His "horrifying" task would be "to love the world in a special way, to minister to it, and to serve it" (R. B. Kaiser). He had to make the message of the Church acceptable to the whole world, to take it to a world in need of Christ. The vision of the Church as above the world, dominant throughout the nineteenth century and the first half of the twentieth, had to be replaced by something more positive and more biblical. Significantly, Angelo chose the name John.

He refused to change his easy-going ways to the aloof manners expected of popes and was soon hugely popular in Rome, where he walked about freely, saying to people in the poor suburbs, "I am one of you" (recalling his humble origins), and visited the sick and prisoners—telling these that two of his cousins had been in prison and survived. The wider world gradually realized that something rather remarkable was happening to the papacy. His conventionally pious spiritual writings were published as *Il Giornale dell'anima* (*Journal of a Soul*) and became a worldwide bestseller. But he still felt imprisoned by the narrow, traditional world of the Vatican government, the Roman Curia—as he famously remarked to Cardinal Richard Cushing: "*Sono nel sacco qui*" ("I'm in a bag here"). The way out, for himself and for the Church, came to him, at the instigation of the Holy Spirit, he claimed, when he was receiving reports on the problems of the Church around the world and on the state of the world itself from Cardinal Tardini, his pro-Secretary of State: "A council." Tardini is variously reported as accepting the idea enthusiastically and as telling curial officials that John would soon forget about it.

John did not forget and told the curial cardinals of it after celebrating the stational Mass at the basilica of the apostle to the Gentiles, St Paul's Outside the Walls, on 25 January 1959, announcing both a Roman diocesan synod and an ecumenical council. The idea of the latter was first received with some incredulity within the Church and largely with incomprehension outside, but it gradually came to be seen as a serious attempt to respond to a world in crisis. John had proclaimed an "ecumenical" council, a word understood differently by Reformed and Orthodox Churches and hardly known in Roman Catholic circles. It suggested that the council would have to address the historic splits in Christianity between East and West, between Catholic and Reformed traditions. This indeed was John's intention: "Let us come together. Let us make an end of our divisions." The Catholic press generally interpreted this as proposing a "return" to the "one true fold," in the manner suggested by Pope Pius IX (7 Feb.) before the first Vatican Council: but this was not what John had said. At a press conference on 30 October 1959, Cardinal Tardini, clarified the pope's intentions, which fell short of inviting representatives of other Churches to participate, by unveiling the plan to invite them as "observers."

Despite obstruction and the slow ways of the Curia, preparations went ahead, the media gradually became better informed about what was proposed, and worldwide interest in Pope John's project grew. In March 1960 John took a major step forward when he approved the establishment of a Vatican Secretariat for Promoting Christian Unity, proposed to him by the scholarly Jesuit cardinal Augustin Bea. Also in 1960, he openly refused to countenance any sort of "crusade" against Communism; in November of that year Nikita Khruschev sent him a birthday greeting, calling him a "man of peace." The following year he revolutionized the Church in Africa by calling for the immediate consecration of thirteen indigenous bishops. He set his face against centuries of anti-Semitism by asking Cardinal Bea to prepare an outline document that would remove the age-old charge of "deicide people" against the Jews. His encyclical letter *Mater et Magistra* ("Mother and Teacher," 1961) dealing with the Church and social issues, was accused in Franco's Spain of fomenting strikes. His next encyclical, *Pacem in Terris* ("Peace on Earth," 1963) again avoided condemnation of any political system. In every sphere, Pope John was reaching out to the whole world, breaking down barriers, trying to show the relevance of Christ to the world as it was.

In the Vatican, the Central Commission formed to digest all the suggestions sent in from bishops and others all over the world was trying to do the opposite: but this story and that of the reaction of the Council Fathers at the first session belong now to general history. John himself broadcast his vision in a radio message "to the world," delivered on 11 September 1962. It began, "The world indeed has need of Christ, and it is the Church that must bring Christ to the world," and it ended by recalling Jesus' wish "that they all may be one" in John 17. Pope John lived to see only the first of the council's four sessions completed. When it closed on 8 December 1962 he described it as "an introduction, slow and solemn, to the great work of the Council." He saw the difficulties but remained hopeful, trusting in the Holy Spirit. He was suffering from stomach cancer and had a massive intestinal hemorrhage on 27 November 1962 (which the Vatican press office, not yet accustomed to openness, described as a "heavy cold," while rumours that he was actually dead sped around Rome). He rallied, but his health declined during the first half of 1963, and he died on 3 June. He had gathered his Roman cardinals on the last day of May, told them that he was "on the point of leaving," and expressed his final wish: "that the great work will be crowned with success." He left as his own testament the encyclical on peace, *Pacem in terris*, dated 11 April 1963.

Many of the Council Fathers wanted him canonized by acclamation, as was done locally before the process was reserved to the Holy See. Cardinal Suenens of Malines-Brussels and other bishops circulated a document claiming that to do so would show the world that "we see him as a true Christian, indeed a saintly one, a man filled with love for the world and for all mankind." The Congregation for the Causes of Saints, however, clung to its prerogatives and insisted on the four-centuries-old process of investigation being followed. Conservative quarters suspected that the proposal to canonize John by acclamation was more "political" than pastoral, aimed at contrasting him with his predecessor, Pius XII. Pope Paul VI solved this dispute by announcing that the cause of Pius XII would proceed at the same time as that of John XXIII (and thus seeming to indicate that all modern popes would eventually be candidates for sainthood). In the event, John's cause has proceeded faster, despite two postulators dying before the assembly of the necessary documents to complete the *positio* could be completed: he was beatified by Pope John Paul II (who took the two names to express his desire to carry on the work of "good Pope John" and of his successor) on 3 September 2000. His "pope companion" in beatification was to be not Pius XII but the equally controversial Pius IX, whose reign from 1846 to 1878 is still the longest in history. At the beatification ceremony Pope John Paul II recalled the familiar image of "Pope John's smiling face and two outstretched arms embracing the whole world" and said, "The Council was a truly prophetic insight of this elderly Pontiff who, even amid many difficulties, opened a season of hope for Christians and for humanity."

John's body was exhumed early in 2001, to be moved from the grotto under St Peter's to an altar in the basilica itself. It had been injected with formaldehyde, to enable the faithful to venerate it after his death, but not embalmed, and it was found to be perfectly preserved. The preservation of his face "intact and smiling" was described by the Vatican Secretary of State as "a gift from God," but great care was taken not to claim anything miraculous about the body's incorrupt state, which could naturally be attributed to the formaldehyde and the traditional triple coffins.

❖

The official documents of his papacy are in *AAS* 50 (1958)–55 (1963). His biography of Radini-Tedeschi was originally published in 1916 and was reissued after his death (1963). His study of the visitation documents of St Charles Borromeo was published in 1936 and 1957, and that of Cardinal Baronius in 1961. *Il Giornale dell'Anima*, ed. L. Capovilla (1964) appeared in English translation by D. White, *Journal of a Soul*, in 1965. His homilies and other speeches appear most completely, as edited for *Oss. Rom.*, in Giovanni XXIII, *Discorsi, messaggi, colloqui del Santo Padre*, 5 vols. (1960–63). Other writings include *Souvenirs d'un Nonce* (1963); *Pensieri dal Diario* (1964).

The many biographical studies that appeared during his lifetime or shortly after his death include L. Algisi, *Giovanni XXIII* (1961), trans. P. Ryde, *John XXIII* (1963); E. Balducci, *Papa Giovanni* (1964), trans. D. White, *John "The Transitional Pope"* (1965); N. Fabretti, *Papa Giovanni* (1966); A. L'Arco, *Il segreto di Papa Giovanni* (1967); and D. Aqasso, *Il Papa delle grande speranzi* (1967). Among more recent biographies are L. Elliott, *I Will Be Called John* (1974); P. Johnson, *Pope John XXIII* (U.S. 1974; U.K. 1975); P. Hebblethwaite, *John XXIII, Pope of the Council* (1984); T. Cahill, *Pope John XXIII* (2002).

Studies of the Second Vatican Council (in English) include R. B. Kaiser, *Inside the Council* (1963); G. Bull, *Vatican Politics at the Second Vatican Council, 1962–65* (1966); L. M. Redmond. *The Council Reconsidered* (1966); G. McCoin, *What Happened at Rome? The Council and Its Implications for the Modern World* (1966); and J. Moorman, *Vatican Observed. An Anglican Impression of Vatican II* (1967). For further bibliography see H. Jedin (ed.), History of the Church, Vol. 10: *The Church in the Modern World*, pp. 814–17.

For his efforts in rescuing Jews in the Second World War see S. Shaw, *Turkey and the Holocaust: Turkey's role in rescuing Turkish and European Jews from Nazi persecution, 1933–45* (1992); P. Hoffmann, "Roncalli in the Second World war," *J.E.H.* XL (1989), 74–99; V. U. Righi, *Papa Giovanni sulle rive del Bosforo* (1971); and R. M. della Roca, "Roncalli Diplomatici in Turchia e Grecia 1935–44," *Cristianesimo nella Storia* VIII/2 (1987), 33–72. On the progress of his cause see D. O'Grady, "Almost a Saint," *St Anthony Messenger*, November 1996, at www.americancatholic.org/Messenger/Nov1996/feature1.asp.

Probably the most striking portrait is the pencil study by Pietro Annigoni (June 1962), which appeared on the cover of *Time* magazine (reproduced as frontispiece in Kaiser, *op.cit.*). There is an impressive bronze relief on the Jubilee door of St Peter's Basilica.

8

Bd Mariam Thresia Chiramel Mankidiyan, *Founder*
(1867–1926)

Thresia, as she was baptized, was born in a village named Puthenchira in the Trichur District of the Indian State of Kerala on 26 April 1867. Her parents, Thoma and Thanda Chiramel Mankidiyan, suffered the effects of Thoma's father having to pay dowries to marry seven daughters. Thresia was the third of five children, with two brothers and two sisters. Her father and one of her brothers took to drink to try to forget the family's worsening circumstances, but Thresia was more influenced by her devout mother and described herself, in a short autobiographical document written later under obedience, as always wanting to serve God. She fasted and denied herself sleep, practices that her mother urged her to moderate.

Her mother died when she was twelve, when she also had to leave school. Thresia dreamt of leaving home and living a life of prayer and penance in a hermitage in the woods, but was forced to be more realistic. With three companions, she performed services such as cleaning for her local church, and she began to visit the sick, the old, and the lonely of the parish, not recoiling from the most disfiguring cases of leprosy. When sick women died, she took care of their children. She and her companions were breaking with custom in travelling the roads unaccompanied by men and were fiercely criticized, including by some clerics, for "taking to the streets" (something the Church has for centuries been unwilling to countenance: "gadding about" was the accusation levelled at Mary Ward's IBVM nuns in the sixteenth century). Thresia declared that she was safe through her trust in the Holy Family.

She reputedly began to see frequent visions, of Jesus and Mary in particular, which guided her to pray, fast, and work for the conversion of sinners. She reverted to, or continued with, the extreme penitential practices of her childhood. She was subject to some of the most troubling physical manifes-tations of mysticism, such as being witnessed by many people hanging high up on the wall of her room on Fridays with her arms spread to form a cross. She was subjected to frequent exorcisms by her parish priest, on the orders of the local bishop, between 1902 and 1905, but the manifestations continued. Though the exorcisms made some people presume that she must be a sinner and possessed by evil spirits, the priest, Fr Vithayathil, never doubted her good faith and holiness; he acted as her spiritual director for the rest of her life.

Thresia had asked in 1903 for the bishop's permission to build a house of prayer, but this had been refused, as he thought she should try her vocation with existing Orders, which she did not consider suitable for her. In 1904 she added Mariam to her baptismal name, claiming she was doing so in response to a direct command from Mary. In 1913 the bishop finally relented and allowed her to build her house of prayer, and she moved in, soon followed by her three faithful companions. From there they continued to visit the sick and the needy, while living austere lives of prayer and penance. The bishop saw this as a new form of religious life and in 1914 gave it canonical status with the name of the Congregation of the Holy Family. Mariam took perpetual vows and was appointed first superior, while her companions became postulants, and Fr Vithayathil was appointed chaplain. The bishop adapted the Constitution of the Holy Family Sisters of Bordeaux, who had a house in Sri Lanka (then Ceylon) for them. Numbers grew throughout the years of the First World War and after, and within twelve years there were three more convents, two schools, two hostels, and an orphanage, with education of girls Mariam's first concern.

She suffered from diabetes, which prevented a wound to her leg from healing and led to her death on 8 June 1926. Fr Vithayathil continued to oversee the Congregation until he died in 1964. The fame of Mariam Thresia's holiness grew, with many miracles claimed through her intercession. The diocesan process for her beatification presented its findings in 1983 and she was declared Venerable in 1999. The cure that enabled her cause to proceed to beatification was that of a boy with two club feet, scarcely able to walk until both were cured successively after his family had offered two month-long vigils of prayer and fasting to Mariam Thresia. Born in 1956, this boy, Mathew Pellissery, was present as an adult at her beatification in St Peter's Piazza on 9 April 2000.

Fifty-five of Mariam Thresia's letters are extant, all but two addressed to her spiritual director. Her Congregation now has over 1,500 Sisters working in Kerala, in provinces in northern India, and also in Germany, Italy, and Ghana.

Bd Nicholas of Gesturi (1882–1958)

This future Capuchin friar was born to Giovanni Messa Serra and Priama Gogoni Zedda at Gesturi, in the province of Cagliari in southern Sardinia, on 5 August 1882. He was baptized the following day and given the names Giovanni Angelo Salvatore. He was confirmed, according to the custom of the time and place, long before making his First Communion, at the early age of not quite four. This was shortly before the death of both his parents. He was their sixth child, and by this time an elder sister was already married to a wealthy local man. She took him into their household, and he worked on their farm. He made his First Communion at the age of fourteen and from then on began to spend his time in prayer and develop an antipathy for all "worldly" attractions.

Giovanni attended early morning Mass daily, as well as eucharistic devotions each evening, while continuing to work conscientiously for his brother-in-law, for whom he developed a great admiration, but who did not seem to be prepared to pay for him to study for the priesthood. At the age of twenty-nine he was cured of a painful rheumatic fever, and this moved him to fulfil his ambition to become a religious. He entered the Capuchin friary in Cagliari, where he was accepted as a third order oblate on the strength of a warm recommendation from his parish priest. He was clothed on 30 October 1913, taking the name Nicholas in religion. He made his solemn profession in February 1916, after which he worked, mainly as cook, in three other friaries over a period of eight years.

At the provincial Capuchin chapter held in Cagliari in 1924, Nicholas was assigned the office of questor ("seeker after alms") in the Cagliari friary. For the next thirty-four years he tramped the streets, soon never openly asking for alms as his humble and modest demeanour seemed to make people want to give him something spontaneously. He became known as "Nicholas the silent," speaking only a few words of thanks to those who gave to him, using the Capuchin silence as a mode of prayer for those he encountered, and perhaps as a reproach to those who gave nothing when they could have given something. Silence in him became an eloquent mode of expression. People turned to him more and more for help, at first just asking for a prayer or a word of advice, then calling him to visit the sick in hospitals or in their homes, which led to many remarkable cures being reported. He gave people an impression of the presence of God and became an inspiration to peace in a divided—particularly during the fascist period and the Second World War—and often violent society.

An illness requiring surgery told Nicholas that the end of his life was approaching, and he died in the provincial infirmary on 8 June 1958. He was seventy-six years old and had spent the last forty-five of them as a Capuchin. The news of his death, carried by the newspapers the following morning, spread throughout the city and beyond, and huge crowds besieged the infirmary in quest of a relic. Two days later, some 60,000 people lined the route of his funeral procession, throwing flowers on to his coffin. The people continued to bring flowers to his grave over the years, and this popular cult encouraged the archbishop of Cagliari to open the diocesan process for his beatification in 1966. In 1996 the survival of a tiny baby born ten years earlier at twenty-three weeks was accepted as a miraculous result of his intercession, and Pope John Paul II beatified him on 3 October 1999. Speaking to the Capuchins and other pilgrims, especially those from Sardinia, the pope pointed out that through his silence, Nicholas had "closely followed the example of St Francis, who loved to invite everyone on to the path of good with his example rather than with his words, and wished his friars to do likewise."

❖

Beato Nicola da Gesturi: Frate Cappuccino 1882–1958 (pamphlet prepared by C. Mellon OFM Cap. for the cause of his beatification); *Beatificazione Piazza San Pietro, 3 Ottobre 1999* (pamphlet prepared for the ceremony), both translated H. de Maria, OFM Cap. and ed. John Cooper, OFM Cap. Summarized by Australian Capuchin friars at www.capuchinfriars.org.au/saints/nicholas, with photographs of him in the streets. Pope John Paul II was citing *Vita Seconda di Tommaso da Celano*, CLVII.

10

Bd Edward Poppe (1890–1924)

Edward (Eduard) was born into the family of a baker of modest means, Désiré Poppe, in the small town of Temse, close to Ghent in Belgium, on 18 December 1890. His mother, Josefa, was a woman of strong character, and intensely devout. She needed to be: his father, though hardworking, seems to have been rather more inclined to take life as it came—which it did in abundance, in the form of eleven children. Of these, three died in infancy, the two boys became priests, five daughters became nuns, and just one was left to stay at home to care for her parents.

As a boy, Edward was cheerful, exuberant, and somewhat clumsy, seemingly given to overeating (easily indulged in a bakery) and signs of hyperactivity. He made his First Communion and received Confirmation together, as was the general practice at the time, at the age of twelve, after which he was apparently somewhat calmer in his behaviour. Two years later, his father expressed the hope that he would take an apprenticeship in bakery with a view to helping him expand the business—but Edward had already set his heart on becoming a priest, and his father acquiesced in what he saw as God's will. In autumn 1904 Edward went to Sint Niklaas minor seminary in Waas, and less than three years later his father was dead of exhaustion. His mother told him that she had promised to let him continue his studies, which he did.

Edward had to break off to do his military service (to which seminarians were liable) in 1910, called up into a university battalion that was nevertheless rough and rude, especially to a budding priest. He hated his first few months but gradually came to see that much of his companions' vulgarity overlaid a need for friendship, and found that he was actually able to offer them spiritual counsel. It was during his military service that he came across St Thérèse of Lisieux' (1 Oct.) *Story of a Soul*, which immediately struck a deep chord with its simple, practical contemplative method, making prayer an integral part of everyday life. "In it," he was to write, "I have learned things that years of study could not have shown me."

Freed from military service after two years, he entered the senior seminary at Louvain. There his initial enthusiasm was all but destroyed by the pessimistic attitude of many of his fellow students. A sympathetic confessor, however, advised Edward simply to cast himself on Christ when downcast, and gradually his spirits lifted once more. The following year he moved to the seminary at Ghent, but after a year of theology there he was drafted to serve as a nurse on the outbreak of the First World War in the summer of 1914. He was engaged in the battle of Namur, which left him half dead with exhaustion. He was taken by ambulance to the village of Bourles, where the parish priest looked after him for five months, teaching him to pray to St Joseph in emergencies—which he did with some seemingly miraculous results. Early in 1914 Cardinal Mercier, archbishop of Malines–Brussels, managed to secure his exemption from further service, and he returned to the seminary in April 1915. He was ordained on 1 May the following year.

Edward's first appointment was as curate in the working-class parish of Saint Colette in Ghent. This was a recently-formed parish, with a somewhat rigid parish priest and a very low level of observance. He gradually succeeded in making himself known to the people and then loved by them, overcoming the instinctive anticlericalism characteristic of so much of industrialized working-class life at the time. His work was hindered by the parish priest, who ordered him to concentrate on "the faithful," among whom he was at least allowed to include the sick and dying. He devoted his first summer, of 1917, to organizing camps for working-class children, somehow inspiring them with the notion that those who attended both 7 a.m. Mass and Benediction in the evening were the bravest. He founded a League of Communion for children, to encourage them to set one another a good example, and through this won many working-class families back to the notion of their children making their First Communion.

His health became precarious after a summer of such intense activity, and he was ordered a month's complete rest. On his return the parish priest, no doubt from sincere motives of concern, forbade him any contact with the Communion League, youth clubs, or catechism lessons. Edward saw his work falling apart, but obeyed in deference to the example of Jesus, obedient even to death on a cross. The following summer he was weaker, and he asked the bishop for a transfer. The bishop sent him as rector to the convent of Sisters of St Vincent de Paul in the village of Moerzeke, where he was joined by his mother and two sisters, who came to live in the village, and by a companion from the seminary, with whom he instituted evening devotion to the Blessed Sacrament, in which the residents came to share.

Edward suffered a heart attack on 11 May 1919. He was not expected to recover and received the sacrament of Extreme Unction, but he survived and from his bed carried on his ministry to numerous visitors. He had another attack a month later and again survived, though precariously. He spent his time in study and contemplation, managing to write to his brother priests on what he saw as the major threats of the age: Marxism, socialism, secularism, and materialism. He was deeply influenced by the works of Bd Antony Chévrier (1826–1879; 2 Oct.), who had had a revelation of the meaning of divine poverty that led him "to follow Jesus Christ as closely as possible," working principally with abandoned children and the poor. Edward proposed that all priests should embark on a crusade of re-evangelization, making the Eucharist the focus of renewal, first of themselves and then of others. His sickbed became the source of a mission radiating out to priests, politicians, and social workers; he preached inner renewal, social regeneration, and the resurgence of Flanders from its war-torn state. He survived for four years in this way, spending about half the time in bed. In September 1920 he was well enough to travel to Lisieux and visit the grave of Thérèse, where, he said, he received "the biggest grace of my life."

In October 1922 Edward was considered fit enough to be appointed spiritual director of students for the priesthood doing military service at the camp at Leopoldsburg. He spent fifteen months there, delighted to be instructing the priests of the future. A heart attack on 1 January 1924 sent him back to his sick bed at Moerzke; a more serious one followed a month later. He hovered between life and death for another five months, still receiving visitors when he was strong enough, but died of a stroke on 10 June, only thirty-three years old. He had become the best-known and best-loved priest in Flanders, and his legacy survived in several pamphlets, 284 articles in journals, and over a thousand letters. His spirituality appears now as a mixture between the most extreme Marian and Church-focused piety of his time and an anticipation of the Second Vatican Council in its recognition of the priority of conscience and the autonomy of secular values.

Edward was beatified on 3 October 1999. Welcoming pilgrims from Belgium the following day, Pope John Paul II said of him: "In prayer and in the Eucharist he found the strength for his daily life and for his pastoral mission. By loving Christ totally, he dedicated himself to imitating him in all things, in doing the will of our heavenly Father and in welcoming all people. In his intimate relationship with the Lord of the harvest, Fr Poppe offered the world to God so that he could offer God to the world."

Soon after his death, Cardinal Mercier commissioned a biography by his close friend Mgr Odilon Jacobs. On the web there is a long and exceedingly pious Monthly Letter to the friends of the Abbey of Saint-Joseph de Clairval, 13 May 2001; also an examination of his priestly spirituality (based on Jacobs), by Paolo Risso, "Don Edward Poppe: il sacerdote è per il sacrificio eucaristico," with a good photograph, at www.collevalenza.it/riv0300/Riv0300_11.

11

Bd Ignatius Maloyan, *Bishop and Martyr* (1869–1915)

Archbishop Maloyan was a bishop of the Armenian Catholic Church, one of the smaller eastern Churches in communion with Rome. Armenia has the proud title of the first nation to embrace Christianity as its official religion, in 301. Its history since then has been an almost continuous story of wars and persecutions, culminating in the genocidal attempt to exterminate all Armenians, and all Christians of every denomination living on Turkish territory, during the First World War (in which Turkey sided with Germany and Austria against Britain, France, and Russia).

The fourth of eight children born to Melkon and Farida Maloyan, Ignatius was born in Mardin in south-eastern Turkey, then in the prefecture of Vilayet in the province of Diyarbakir, and christened Shoukr Allah (or Chukrallah, or Shokr Allah) on 20 April 1869. Mardin, a few miles over the border from the north-eastern tip of Syria, was ruled by an Ottoman Sultan and was unusual in having 22,000 Christians out of its total population of some 50,000. It had an Armenian Catholic community led by Bishop Melkon Nazarian, a Syrian Catholic community with its own bishop, Capuchin friars, Franciscan nuns, and Protestant missionaries. Ignatius was a notably pious boy as well as an excellent student in general and linguist in particular, and he attracted the attention of the bishop, who sent him at the age of fourteen to the convent of the Virgin of Sorrows at Bzommar, the Catholic Armenian motherhouse since 1749, to begin studies for the priesthood.

He spent five years there, during which he learned French and Italian (to add to his Turkish, Arabic, and Armenian) and studied classical Hebrew. His health then collapsed, perhaps affected by his harsh regime, and he returned to Mardin for medical treatment. After three years he returned to Bzommar. He moved to the study of philosophy and theology and was ordained priest on 6 August 1896, taking the name Ignatius in memory of St Ignatius of Antioch (17 Oct.). In November that year he was sent to Egypt to assist the Armenian patriarch. In Alexandria he met the papal nuncio and the French consul and prominent Armenian citizens, but he found the clergy spiritually lazy and personally ambitious; he set a quite different example, devoting himself to the sick and the poor. He also made contact with the larger Coptic community and engaged in theological debate aimed at greater understanding. He became an excellent speaker, in demand for conferences, retreats, and lectures. The Jesuits invited him to lecture in Arabic in Cairo.

In 1898 Ignatius had to have an operation to remove a cyst near his right eye, and this left him with permanent problems. The following year there was a severe outbreak of "Indian fever;" the patriarch transferred him to Cairo, where he was bedridden for ten days and left with bronchial troubles that became progressively more severe during the rest of his life. He was secretary to the Armenian Catholic bishop of Cairo as well running a parish and trying to open an Armenian school; all this placed too great a strain on his health, and he was transferred back to Alexandria, where he resumed his parish ministry but was ordered to rest from intellectual pursuits. Patriarch Boghos Bedros XII of Constantinople then appointed Ignatius his secretary, and he moved there, but after a short time his health again worsened and he returned to Egypt to consult the doctors who knew him, giving rise to talk of a rift between him and the patriarch, which he struggled to refute. He had a major operation on his throat in Egypt and the patriarch then asked him to return to Mardin as his vicar.

Ignatius found a diocese in chaos, with an aged and sick bishop who had retired to Bzommar to die. He arrived to a tumultuous welcome on Palm Sunday 1905, secured the bishop's resignation, and set about restoring the diocese with the help of well-trained priests brought in from elsewhere—though many were reluctant to come, in view of the bad reputation of the diocese. In addition to ecclesiastical troubles, there was widespread poverty, exacerbated by a severe famine in 1911. The obvious candidate to succeed as bishop, he was consecrated in Rome on 21 October 1911, returning to Mardin by way of Bzommar, where he stayed for several months. He struggled with lack of priests, lack of financial resources, increasing political pressure from the Turkish government, and his own health. In 1913 he needed an operation on his nose, which, he was told, could be carried out only in Padua, where he spent a month convalescing. The following year he was suffering severely from asthma and rheumatism.

On 3 August 1914 Turkey entered the war on the German and Austrian side against the Allied powers of Britain, France, and Russia. Conscription was introduced for all males between the ages of twenty and forty-five. Many, including Christians, sought to avoid it, and recruitment methods became increasingly brutal. Ignatius tried to intervene, telling the authorities that the priests would find genuine deserters, so that there was no need to ransack family homes and even convents. By February 1915 planning for the extermination of "internal enemies" was under way. That Easter saw a contradictory signal, when the Sultan awarded the archbishop an imperial honour. He, however, knew that persecution of Christians was being systematically increased, using local Muslims to foment hatred against them. Christian shops were burned; churches desecrated; Christian soldiers disarmed; Kurds and tribesmen incited against Christians; and Muslims too old for the army were being armed as militias: for those who read the signs, genocide was being prepared. Maloyan wrote his will in the form of a pastoral to his people telling them to be strong but prepared for the worst, and setting out arrangements for the administration of the diocese were he to disappear. By May 1915, selected assassinations were following arrests and torture of Armenians. The archbishop was urged to flee across the mountains to a tribal homeland where refugees were still welcomed; he refused.

Mass arrests of Armenian men followed; they were then divided into groups of fifty or a hundred, marched into remote areas, killed, and their bodies dumped in deep caves or wells. In Mardin a militia known as the Khasmine was secretly formed under the brutal police commissioner Mamdouh Bey. Despite the secrecy, Maloyan was informed of this, and that arrests would take place under the pretext of searching for hidden arms. On the evening of the feast of Corpus Christi, 3 June 1915, he was summoned to the governor's residence, locked up, and kept in solitary confinement. The following day 662 Christians were arrested, followed by another 200 the next day. Maloyan was taken before a tribunal and accused of hoarding arms and plotting against the government. He told them: "Your accusation is all made up. I never opposed the government in anything. On the contrary, I have defended its rights ... for I am its citizen, and in its kindness it has conferred upon me an imperial decoration and a Turkish title." In response, Mamdouh hit him with his belt, declaring, "Today, the sword replaces the government."

Maloyan was tortured horribly over the next four days, then all the prisoners, some 1,600 in all, were divided up into three convoys and marched out of the town on different days. Christians were told that if they came out of their houses to help them in any way they would be shot. The only eyewitnesses who returned to tell what happened next were Kurds and militiamen, who told slightly varying versions to a Dominican and a Syrian priest who somehow avoided arrest and death. The prisoners were told to choose between converting to Islam and death; they unanimously replied that they chose death. They were marched for six hours, those who could not keep up being killed immediately. Maloyan, who had been made to lead the first convoy, on 10 June, managed to give absolution and improvise a last Mass—during which, according to the witnesses, "a bright cloud covered them." A hundred were thrown into deep caves called the Caves of Sheikhan. Their bodies were never found. A hundred more were marched farther on, to Kalaa Zerzewan, where they were either stabbed or bludgeoned to death and their bodies thrown down wells. The rest were left another night and marched on the next day, which was the feast of the Sacred Heart, and killed in open country. The archbishop alone was taken on horseback a further hour's journey towards Diyarbakir, to a place named Farkabro. Mamdouh asked him if he would finally save his life by converting to Islam, to which he replied, "I am surprised by your question. I have told you I shall live and die for the sake of my faith and religion. I take pride in the cross of my God and Lord." Furious, Mamdouh drew his pistol and shot him in the neck. A militiaman boasted that he had then stabbed the body three times in the throat and chest. Mamdouh sent soldiers on to Diyarbakir to obtain a death certificate stating that he had died of a heart attack on the way. Some eyewitnesses reported that his body radiated light for three days after his death.

In all, 1,500,000 Armenians died in the first great genocide of the twentieth century, which has been largely forgotten by the rest of the world, subsumed in the mass slaughter of the First World War and then the horrors of Stalin's purges and the Holocaust. The Apostolic Armenian Church has declared the other 416 victims of 11 July 1915 martyrs, and its Synod of Bishops sent the documents concerning Ignatius Maloyan to Rome, resulting in his official beatification by the Catholic Church on 7 October 2001 (which does not exclude the later beatification of the others).

S. Rezkallah, translated P. Desbleds, *Monsignor Ignatius Maloyan, Archbishop and Martyr, 1869–1945* (n.d.): www.armcathpat.org/english/news/monsignor-maloyan/maloyaneng; there are biographies in Armenian, French, Arabic, Spanish and Portuguese: information from Notre Dame de Bzommar Convent, 5081 Bzommar, Lebanon. Other accounts give the date of his death as 10 June or even 11 April, but 11 June is the date selected for his memorial.

26

Bd Andrew Hyacinth Longhin, *Bishop* (1863–1936)

The long-serving bishop of Treviso, who became known as the "bishop of catechism," was the only son of poor tenant farmers, Matteo and Judit Longhin. He was born on 22 November 1863 in the village of Fiumicello di Campodarsego, in the province and diocese of Padua, in the Veneto region, twenty miles inland from Venice, and was baptized Giacinto (Hyacinth) Bonaventura. His family was devout, but his father opposed his decision to enter the Capuchin novitiate, which he did nonetheless in Venice on 27 August 1879, aged only sixteen, taking the name Andrew (Andrea) di Campodarsego in religion. He studied at Padua and Venice and was ordained on 19 June 1886.

For the next eighteen years Andrew held various offices within the Order: teacher at the seminary of Udine, director of teachers at Padua in 1889, director of theology students in Venice in 1891, and provincial minister of Venice in 1902. In 1893 Giuseppe Melchior Sarto (the future Pope St Pius X, from 1903 to 1914; 21 Aug.) was appointed cardinal patriarch of Venice, and he came to have a great admiration for Andrew. The year following his election as pope he appointed him bishop of Treviso (a see to which he himself had been appointed in 1875), and Andrew was consecrated in Rome by Cardinal Merry del Val on 17 April 1904, moving into his diocese, where he was to remain for thirty-two years, on 6 August.

Before arriving, he had already issued two pastoral letters outlining his plans for the diocese. He embarked on a pastoral visitation of all its parishes, which took five years to complete—Treviso was the largest and most populous diocese in the Veneto region. At the end of this he summoned a diocesan Synod, which was entrusted with carrying out all the reforms initiated by Pius X. These and the new bishop's zeal were not always welcomed by his clergy, but he was determined to be close to them whether they would or not. He reformed the course of studies in the diocesan seminary, and made the clergy go on spiritual retreats. He laid down precise guidelines for the actions he required his priests to carry out, and monitored the results during two more pastoral visitations, from 1912 to 1918 and 1926 to 1934. He also drew lay associations into his efforts, particularly in the field of social action, where his views were progressive, encouraging the formation of trade unions. He brought in many religious Congregations to help in specialized aspects of his work, increasing the number of male institutes active in the diocese from seven to twelve and female ones from ten to twenty-four. He himself set an example of personal austerity and carried out an extensive preaching and catechizing mission to children and adults. He held two diocesan catechetical congresses, in 1922 and 1923, which led to the appellation "bishop of catechism."

When Italy was drawn into the First World War in 1915, Treviso was subjected to terrible air and ground attacks by the Axis forces. Much of the city, and forty-seven parish churches in the diocese, were reduced to rubble. The civil authorities fled, but the bishop stayed and encouraged his clergy to do the same, becoming the focus of religious and civil affairs in a time of turmoil when reactions to the war varied greatly from one political group in Italy to another. Some accused Andrew of defeatism for taking an impartially charitable stand, and some of his priests were even tried and imprisoned. After the war he resumed his interrupted second pastoral visitation and oversaw the rebuilding of the churches. His efforts during the war were eventually appreciated and acknowledged with the award of the Cross of Merit.

The post-war period saw the start of the rise of fascism, which attracted many Catholics but which he opposed, insisting that Catholicism should mean social justice, which had to be sought by non-violent means. He openly supported the *Leghe Bianche* (White League), a Christian union movement. Fascist groups targeted Catholic lay associations working in the social field, and Bishop Andrew told his flock that the Church militant had to be prepared for martyrdom. Other dioceses also suffered divisions between their bishop and their clergy, and Pope Pius XI (1922–39), who also had a great respect for Andrew, appointed him visitator and apostolic administrator of the dioceses of Padua and Udine successively to resolve the situation.

In 1935 his mental faculties began to deteriorate with the onset of what was probably Alzheimer's disease, and he died in Treviso on 26 June 1936. His body was interred in the cathedral, and devotion to him quickly spread through the dioceses of Treviso and Padua and within the Capuchin Order. His beatification process was initiated in 1964, and in that year a boy named Dino Stella recovered from diffused peritonitis after his family had invoked Andrew's intercession. This was accepted as a miracle in 2002, and he was beatified with five others on World Mission Sunday, 20 October 2002. Pope John Paul II in his homily called him "a simple, poor, humble, generous pastor always available for his neighbour, in accordance with the genuine tradition of the Capuchins," and continued: "In an age that was noted for tragic and painful events, he was outstanding as a father for his priests and a zealous pastor of the people, always close to his people, especially in moments of difficulty and danger."

St Josemaría Escrivá de Balaguer, *Founder* (1902–1975)

The founder of *Opus Dei* ("the Work of God," usually referred to by its members simply as "the Work") was born on 9 January 1902 in Barbastro in the region of Aragon in north-eastern Spain, a town in the province of Huesca, forty-five miles north east of Zaragoza, the regional capital that was to pay an important part in his life. (Barbastro was to suffer some of the worst violence at the outbreak of the Spanish civil war in July 1936: 88 per cent of its diocesan clergy, including the bishop, were killed, as were all the staff and students at the Claretian house of studies.) His parents, José Escribá, a textile merchant of some prosperity, and Dolores Albas, had six children, of whom José María Julián Marino, as he was christened on 13 January, was the second. They were a devout couple, if—as a joint portrait indicates—proud of their middle-class status. José María was seriously ill when he was two and was not expected to live; he made an overnight recovery, which his mother attributed to their prayers to Our Lady, and which certainly surprised the local doctor.

They formed an affectionate and happy family, but misfortune struck them between 1910 and 1914, when the three youngest girls all died—Rosario at nine months, Lolita aged five, Chon aged eight—and José's business collapsed owing to the machinations of one of his partners. He moved the family to the larger town of Logroño, over to the west in the province of La Rioja, where he had found a job as a sales clerk in a textile business similar to the one he had previously part-owned. José María made his First Communion on 23 April 1912. When he was just sixteen the sight of bare footprints in the snow, which he realized must have been made by one of the Carmelite friars, inspired him with the idea of a life of self-sacrifice for God. He told his father that he wanted to be a priest; his father was distressed but did not oppose the decision, advising him only to study a useful career—law—alongside his seminary commitment. He spent a year as a day student at the diocesan seminary in Logroño and then moved to the seminary of San Carlos in Zaragoza. There he developed a great devotion to the ancient Virgin of the Pillar. He was ordained on 28 March 1925, while still in mourning for his father, who had died suddenly the previous

November. He said his first Mass in the basilica of the Virgin of the Pillar, in memory of his father.

José María was sent three days later to supply for a priest in the village of Pedreguera, near Zaragoza. He found the church filthy and observance neglected, so set about cleaning the former and reorganizing the latter. He introduced sung Mass, Benediction, Confessions, and catechism classes, and was still remembered there with affection and respect at the time of his death fifty years later. Returning to Zaragoza once his emergency stint was over, he finished his law degree and then, with the bishop's permission, enrolled in the Central University in Madrid, the only institution in Spain that offered a doctorate in law. In Madrid he lodged in a house sponsored by the *Damas Apostólicas* ("Congregation of Apostolic Ladies of the Sacred Heart of Jesus") and was soon aware of the social deprivation of thousands living in shanty towns on the periphery of the capital, drawn in from the countryside by the hope of work. He threw himself into the apostolate, working among the sick and poor wherever the Apostolic Ladies indicated a particular need.

His mother and surviving brother and sister moved to Madrid in late 1927, living in poverty, and he helped them to survive by giving private tuition and teaching college courses in law while still working for his doctorate. On 2 October 1928 José María was on the annual retreat for diocesan clergy given by the Vincentian Fathers. That night he experienced some sort of vision that showed him what he was to be called to do: to enable ordinary people living in the world to become apostles and saints in the world. He gave this task the name of "the Work of God," and *Opus Dei* dates its foundation to this vision. Enquiries showed him that there was no church organization doing precisely this, which convinced him further that the call came from God.

He began discussing the message with students, professional men, and priests—all men at first: but then in 1930 another vision or inspiration told him that women should be included so that the Work could be carried on through the sanctification of family life. A priest, a woman, and a layman committed themselves to working with him. By 1933 he had gathered a group of students with whom he discussed the project and who helped him in the apostolic work he was still doing in the slums of Madrid. This developed into classes in Christian formation given in an apartment known as the "DYA Academy" from the supplementary classes in *Arquitectura y Derecho* (Architecture and Law) given there. His mother then received an inheritance and was able to buy a larger house in the Calle de Ferraz, where the first resident followers were able to lodge. Also in 1934, José María gathered a series of "points" or brief spiritual meditations into a book titled *Consideracions espirituales*, re-issued in revised form five years later as *El Camino* ("The Way"), which became the foundational text of *Opus Dei*.

In July 1935 an engineering student, Alvaro del Portillo, asked to join the group. He was to become the founder's closest collaborator and to succeed him as leader. A year later, General Franco led his Nationalist uprising against the Republican government and Spain was engulfed in civil war, with Catholic and nationalist virtually synonymous. Republican militias rounded up priests in Madrid and elsewhere, and most of those they found were shot. José María and two companions had a very narrow escape from arrest, and for some months he moved from one "safe house" to another before finding a longer refuge in a psychiatric hospital, where the director helped by certifying him as mad. He then took refuge in the embassy of Honduras, which, like others, was packed with refugees. By September 1937 battle lines had become more or less established across Spain, with the Nationalist headquarters in Burgos, in northern Castile. But there was no way to cross the front between Madrid and Burgos, and to get there required crossing the Pyrenees into France and then back into Spain via the Basque Country. With improvised documentation he reached Barcelona, from where convoys of refugees were smuggled over the mountains. He joined one of these and by 2 December had reached Andorra, from where he could cross safely into France. He turned west, paused to give thanks to Our Lady in Lourdes, and crossed back into Spain at Hendaye, from where he could make his way to Burgos.

In the temporary Nationalist capital, crammed with churchmen, politicians, and professional people waiting to get back to Madrid and other cities, José María set about re-establishing old contacts and making new ones. He returned to Madrid with the first military convoy on 28 March 1939. The city was largely in ruins, as was the DYA Academy, but he found another residence and began re-building his group. He moved his mother and sister, who had survived the war in Madrid, there to manage the household for his students, and "to this is owed, in good part, the family tone that can be found to this day in all the centres of Opus Dei" (as a biographical website states without a hint of irony). By the summer he was preaching a retreat for students in "liberated" Valencia; *El Camino* was published in September; and recruits began to join in increasing numbers, though the outbreak of the Second World War put a stop to any thoughts of international expansion.

In the early 1940s his reputation in Spain grew, and several Spanish bishops asked him to give retreats to their clergy. His brand of "National Catholicism" was well attuned to Franco's "crusade" to build Spanish Catholicism into a bastion against communism and involved tacit, if not overt, support for Hitler as defender of Western values against the Slav threat from the East. His mother died in 1941: he had left her, apparently not seriously ill, to preach a retreat to priests.

Despite steady expansion and the support of some bishops, especially Mgr Leopoldo Eijo y Garay of Madrid, the organization began to have its critics, described in its literature as "a full-blown campaign of rumours and even calumnies." The critics came from within church ranks as well as outside, and José María responded by seemingly turning the movement further in on itself by providing its own priests from within its ranks. The first three, all previously engineers, were ordained by the bishop of Madrid on 25 June 1945. They were designated members of the Priestly Society of the Holy Cross. By 1950 a further step toward clerical incorporation into what had originally been a lay movement had been taken, when it was decided (quite by whom is a little unclear) that diocesan priests could also become members of the Priestly Society without— at least in theory—abandoning their obedience to their diocesan bishops. However, as they were not obliged even to tell their bishops that they had become members, a certain tension was inevitable. (How this is resolved is still a matter of debate: see, e.g., letters in *The Tablet* of 22 Jan. 2005).

The end of the Second World War made expansion beyond Spain a possibility once more, and José María decided that the movement's headquarters had to be in Rome. One object of the mission was to determine what status the movement could have within the official Church, and this could only be decided by the pope. Alvaro del Portillo had previously made overtures, but Pius XII had indicated that he would decide the matter only with the founder. So in June 1946 José María (at the time seriously ill with diabetes) travelled to Rome, a journey that in immediate post-war conditions involved a steamship—which was caught in a major storm—from Barcelona to Genoa. In Barcelona he preached to his faithful but was also made aware of strong opposition, largely brought about by the secrecy surrounding membership, which led to some extreme claims, such as that they were a Jewish sect allied to the Freemasons. He arrived in Rome after an arduous car journey over ruined roads from Genoa, and soon declared to friends that the pope was his third love, after Jesus and Mary. Pope Pius XII received him in audience after a few weeks. In 1947 he promulgated the Apostolic Constitution *Provida Mater Ecclesia*, which established a canonical framework for Secular Institutes, an "ecclesial reality" beginning to grow in preference to traditional religious Orders. Opus Dei was the first such to be recognized, and thus received the official status whose lack had been at the root of much criticism. Branches were established in Portugal, Italy, and Great Britain in 1946, then in France and Ireland in 1947, Mexico and the U.S.A. in 1949, Chile and Argentina in 1950, Colombia and Venezuela in 1951, and Germany in 1952. A college was founded in Rome in 1948—the Roman College of the Holy Cross—to provide training courses for men, many of whom went on to become priests, followed by another for women, the Roman College of Holy Mary, five years later.

Jose María made friends in high places, including the future Popes John XXIII (beatified in 2000; see 3 June) and Paul VI, as well the latter's predecessor as archbishop of Milan, Cardinal Schuster (who had hailed Italy's military support for the Nationalist side in the Spanish civil war: beatified in 1996; 30 Aug.). It was Schuster who warned him that powerful figures in the Curia were out to destroy the new Institute—though who these were is not clear: perhaps the Jesuits, who certainly mistrusted the movement, and who themselves had in the past been suppressed for a seeming excess of power?—and advised him to take firm action. He got a letter to the pope via Cardinal Tedeschini, and "the plan"—apparently an attempt to separate the founder from the movement, as had happened to St Alphonsus Liguori (1 Aug.) among others—was "stopped dead in its tracks" (official website), though José María seems to have led a more secluded life for some years. Opus Dei acquired a new headquarters in Rome in the former Hungarian embassy, which became known as Villa Tevere, with virtually no funds according to its own sources, although with substantial help from Duchess Virginia Sforza Cesarini according to others.

In April 1954 the diabetes from which José María had suffered for over ten years mysteriously disappeared after he underwent an anaphylactic shock, perhaps as a result of too high a dose of insulin, and seemingly nearly died. He began to lose the excess weight he had gained from the diabetes. Expansion went on throughout the 1950s, and José María made several journeys to visit new foundations, including short summer breaks in England, where he admired the universities but worried about "the Christianity of the City." In 1952 he had founded a university owned and run by Opus Dei, the University of Navarre, in Pamplona, through which the movement contributed greatly to developing Spanish intellectual life—or increased its grip on it, depending on one's point of view. By the early 1960s, Opus Dei members occupied important posts in Franco's "technocrat government," which certainly did much to end Spain's post-war isolation and to begin to modernize its industry. Unfortunately they too were heavily involved in the "Matesa affair," a scandal involving export licences on a huge scale, which ended many promising careers. A second Opus Dei university was founded in Piura in Peru in 1969, followed by many other educational institutions in Latin America and around the world.

José María—by then Monsignor, having been appointed a domestic prelate to the pope—welcomed the opening of the Second Vatican Council in 1962 and regarded its decrees as confirming his views on the Church, the priesthood, and the apostolate of the laity. In November 1965 Pope Paul VI opened the "Centre ELIS" in the Tiburtino district of Rome, established by Opus Dei to educate working-class children. During the post-conciliar years José María and his organization became increasingly concerned about the direction in which the Church seemed to be moving and were to become protagonists of the Vatican "restoration" process led by Cardinal Ratzinger. Insider sources talk about "arbitrary and questionable interpretations" of the Council's texts, and he declared in 1970 that, "We are living in a time of madness. Millions of souls are confused." There are no overt references to the main cause of his pessimism, but the widespread rejection of Pope Paul VI's 1968 encyclical *Humanae vitae* and its teaching on contraception was certainly what he saw as the "attack [on] the authority of the Roman Pontiff, which cannot be limited by anyone except God." The Latin American bishops' conference at Medellín in Colombia in the same year, which effectively launched liberation theology and the "option for the poor," was another cause of grave concern.

159

The year 1968 was also when José María petitioned for and was granted the defunct title of marquess of Peralta—an episode seemingly glossed over in "insider" accounts of his life. By then he had taken to writing his Christian names as one word—Josemaría (there is a debate about whether or not he also dropped the accent). Typically, he embarked on a tour of Marian shrines as a way to counter rebellion in church ranks: Fatima in Portugal, Guadalupe in Mexico, and Torreciudad in northern Spain, where he had commissioned a new sanctuary to commemorate his "miraculous" cure at the age of two. Wherever he went, he organized "catechetical" meetings with groups of the faithful, many of which were recorded on film. In 1973 he assured Pope Paul that, whatever the rest of the world might think, there were thousands of Opus Dei members and hundreds of its priests around the world entirely faithful to his teaching. In 1974 he toured Latin America, preaching, meeting people, urging fidelity to the pope and the *magisterium,* conversion, and frequent Confession.

He celebrated the fiftieth anniversary of his ordination quietly on Good Friday, 28 March 1975, having publicly the day before given thanks for the worldwide spread of Opus Dei: "You Lord, have done it all … you have spread the Work all over the world. People are thanking you all over Europe, and in places in Asia and Africa, and in the whole of America and Australia. Everywhere they are giving you thanks." In May he went back to contemplate the progress of the reredos he had commissioned in Torreciudad. On 26 June he visited "his daughters" in the Roman College of Saint Mary at Castelgandolfo, and on his return he suddenly collapsed and died.

His body lay in an open coffin in the chapel at Villa Tevere while a stream of mourners, including cardinals and bishops, filed past. Stories of graces received through his intercession poured into Rome from around the world, and petitions for the cause of his canonization to be opened apparently had the support of over 1,300 bishops. The decree introducing the cause was promulgated in 1981; Pope John Paul II declared the heroicity of his virtues in 1990; a miracle was sanctioned in 1991, and he was beatified in Rome (with the somewhat unlikely companion of the slave girl Bd Josephine Bakhita; 8 Feb.) on 17 May 1992. There was (though played down by Opus Dei) widespread disquiet at the speed with which the process had been completed, unusual in modern times with the exhaustive scrutiny process required—though this speed has since been overtaken by the mere six years between Mother Teresa's death and her beatification (see 5 Sept.). The prefect and secretary of the Congregation for the Causes of Saints even took the unusual step of publishing a lengthy statement in the *Osservatore Romano,* in which they said they were aware of "discordant voices" in the Church opposing the process and gave an assurance that the proper procedures had been "carefully followed." A second miracle, the complete recovery made by a Spanish surgeon, Manuel Nevado, from cancerous and incurable radiodermatitis in 1992 after he had prayed for José María's intercession, was recognized in 2001, and he was canonized on 6 October 2002, an occasion that provoked far less controversy.

His life and views, as Kathleen Jones observes (*Butler*, June, p. 207), need to be understood in the context of the times in which he lived, particularly his undoubtedly traumatic experiences in the Spanish civil war. He was hardly alone among prominent churchmen in regarding communism as a greater threat to the institutional Church than Nazism. A particular difficulty in assessing his life, however, is posed (as Michael Walsh has recently pointed out in connection with a new part biography) by the tendency of "inside" accounts to adopt "the style of a medieval saint's *vita*," in which everything is attributed to heavenly intercession, there is virtually no analysis of human motives, and anything remotely inconvenient (such as the gentrification of his name—besides the single-word spelling of his Christian names, he progressively changed the spelling of his paternal surname from Escribá to Escrivá and used its additional "de Balaguer", as well as adding his mother's surname, Albas—and his acquisition of the title) is simply omitted.

Opus Dei itself continues to divide Catholics (and others) as no other Secular Institute or other organization does. Its financial arrangements—with at least those in its highest echelons, the "numeraries," contributing their incomes to the organization and having a reasonable portion allotted back—cause many to regard it as a sect rather than as part of the Church, as it appears to have itself rather than the whole Church (let alone the world) as the main recipient of its "Work." The secrecy with which membership has been surrounded (now lessened) has been another ground for the "sect" accusations. Its status within the Church is further complicated by the "personal prelature" status of its leader, originally sought by José María in 1962 and eventually granted to his successor by Pope John Paul II in 1978, which effectively removes the organization from any diocesan control. In addition, it has allied itself squarely, particularly in Latin America, with repressive and corrupt regimes: most obviously, perhaps, with that of President Fujimori in Peru. Members and supporters would doubtless argue that "God's work" has to be carried out in all social conditions.

Butler, June, pp. 202–7. On the massacre in Barbastro in July 1936 see *Butler*, July, pp. 171–2. Lives written from within Opus Dei include, in Spanish, those by L. Carandell (1975); S. Bernal (1977); A. Vasquez de Prada (1983); and in English, W. Keenan (1990). The most authoritative is P. Berglar, *Opus Dei: Life and work of its founder, Josemaría Escrivá* (1993: English translation of *Opus Dei: Leben und Werk des Gründers, Josemaría Escrivá*). There are many accounts of life inside Opus Dei by those who have left it: the best known is M. del Carmen Tapia, *Beyond the Threshold* (1996): the author spent five years working with José María. Michael Walsh has been a consistent critic since his *The Secret World*

of Opus Dei (1989), to which W. Connor, *Opus Dei: An Open Door* (1992), is a riposte. The source of the quote from Walsh above is his review of W. Keegan, *St Josemaría Escrivá and the Origins of Opus Dei*, in *The Tablet*, 22 Jan. 2005. The "exposure" of its activities in Dan Brown's *The Da Vinci Code* (2004) seems to have produced a sensible reaction in using the information revealed about locations and the like as a PR opportunity, with the London headquarters at least becoming a tourist attraction. Another indication of diminishing secrecy is the public admission by Ruth Kelly, appointed education minister in the British government in January 2005, that she is a member, though she accompanied this with the statement that her faith is "spiritual and private" and will not affect her exercise of her job, which once more raises the question of for whom, or what Opus Dei is meant. Opposition websites, numerous if not distinguished for literacy, are easily found.

The principal works of Mgr Escrivá published in English (with worldwide diffusion and languages) are: *The Way* (1939), the "basic text," 999 short meditations, 4,500,000 in forty-four languages; *Furrow* (1950), 1,000 "points," 500,000 in nineteen languages; *Christ is Passing By* (1973), sermons 1951–1971, 500,000 in fourteen languages; *Friends of God* (1977), homilies 1941–1968, 400,000 in thirteen languages; *The Rosary* (1981), written in 1931, 500,000 in nineteen languages; and *The Forge* (1987), 1,055 "points," 400,000 in fourteen languages. Also *In Love with the Church* (1985), homilies 1972–1973, also published as *In God's Household*, with one extra 1972 homily and an epilogue by Alvaro del Portillo; *Conversations with Josemaría Escrivá* (1968), newspaper interviews following the Second Vatican Council, also includes the 1972 homily "Passion for the World," given at the opening of the university of Navarre—to which it would be difficult to take exception.

JULY

1

Bd Ignatius Falzon (1813–1865)

The second, in date order, of the three Maltese beatified together (see also 25 Feb. and 26 July), Ignatius (Ignazio, shortened to Nazju in Maltese), was born on 1 July 1813 in Valletta and baptized the next day, receiving the names Rocco Angelo Sebastiano Vincente Ignazio Rosario. His father, Giuseppe Francesco Falzon, was a judge, and his mother, Maria Teresa Debono, the daughter of a judge. With such a background, it is not surprising that he and all three of his brothers became lawyers. Two brothers, Calcedonio and Francesco, went on to become priests and to achieve relatively high ecclesiastical posts. Ignatius, a pious child who became known as "the little saint," took minor orders while still in his teens and studied theology, but he then decided he was not worthy to proceed to ordination.

He graduated as a doctor of law in 1833 but had studied for his degree merely to follow the family tradition, without intending to earn his living (which he did not need to do) as a lawyer. Ignatius dedicated himself to helping the poor, at a time when there was no form of social assistance. He used his own money from rents on family properties, and when this ran out, he begged. His time was spent partly in private prayer in the family chapel, daily Mass (or Masses), and other devotions, including the Way of the Cross and the rosary. He was seen to levitate on frequent occasions. In the afternoons he gave catechism classes to children and adults. There were already four Institutes giving religious instruction in Valletta, but Ignatius was a pioneer in that he gave instruction to poor families. He also taught Latin and English (in which he had made himself fluent) to poor children in his own house. Love of the Eucharist was the wellspring of his spirituality, and he used to help the family maid with her housework to enable her to attend Mass.

A major part of his mission was to British soldiers and sailors stationed in Valletta. Many of these were Irish Catholics, and he used to invite them to his house for evening rosary and discussion. They invited Protestant friends, and the group had to move to the Jesuit church, where confessors and other catechists were available. They prayed the rosary for the conversion of England, and several servicemen went on to study for the priesthood. By the time of the

Crimean War (1853–1856), there were up to 20,000 troops stationed in Malta, and over time some 600 Protestants became Catholics—though Ignatius, with a respect unusual in his time, did not make special efforts to convert them (as the pope was to stress at the beatification ceremony). He helped many combat alcoholism and made friends for life, who corresponded with him after their return home. He imported religious works from England, distributed rosaries, prayer cards, and scapulars, and wrote a book of prayers, *The Comfort of the Christian Soul*.

His heart had always given him problems, and his health declined in his later years. On 29 June 1865 he was obviously dying; he recited the Pentecost hymn to the Holy Spirit, and as he reached the line "With thy sevenfold gifts descend,"those present claimed to see a globe of fire with seven tongues appear on his head. Ignatius died an early death two days later, on his fifty-second birthday, 1 July 1865. His funeral service in the Ta'Giezu Church in Valletta was attended by thousands, and he was buried in the family vault in the chapel of the Immaculate Conception. The diocesan process in his cause was heard from 1892 to 1899, with the apostolic inquiry held from 1906 to 1908 and then lapsing until 1930–1931. His remains were enshrined near the altar of the Immaculate Conception chapel in 1952, but it was not until May 1987 that the decree on his heroic virtue was issued. The cure of a 64-year-old man from cancer in 1981 was accepted as a miracle due to his intercession, and Pope John Paul II beatified him and the two other Maltese Venerables in the Floriana Granaries (the largest square in Valletta, so called because grain silos had formerly stood there) on 9 May 2001. In his homily, the Pope said,"He renounced the worldly success for which his background had prepared him, in order to serve the spiritual good of others, including the many British soldiers and sailors stationed in Malta at the time. In his approach to them, few of whom were Catholic, he anticipated the ecumenical spirit of respect and dialogue, which is familiar to us today but which was not always prevalent at that time."

Short biography by Dr J. Sammut in *Franciscan News*, Malta, 24 April 2001.

7

Bd María Romero Meneses (1902–1977)

The Nicaraguan woman who was to become known as the female Don Bosco and the social apostle of Costa Rica came from a wealthy, upper-class family of Granada, south-east of Managua on the shore of Lake Nicaragua. Born on 13

January 1902, she was one of eight children, and her father was a government minister. She received a thorough education at the hands of her parents, some aunts, and the local Salesian school, becoming proficient in drawing and painting as well as playing the violin and piano. She had a setback at the age of twelve when she spent a year severely ill with rheumatic fever. She made an apparently miraculous and sudden recovery after praying to Mary, Help of Christians (the patron of the Salesian Sisters), but was left with permanent damage to her heart—which did not prevent her from living a very full and relatively long life.

She joined the Salesian Sisters in 1920, at the age of eighteen. Her spiritual director told her: "Even though difficult moments will come and you will feel torn to pieces, be faithful and strong in your vocation." Her full training took nine years, and she made her final profession in Nicaragua in 1929. This was the period when General Augusto César Sandino was waging guerrilla war against the occupation of the country by U.S. marines, who were ostensibly providing conditions of stability for a coalition government, but which led to the appointment of General Anastasio Somoza García as director of the National Guard: a military dictatorship by him and then his son that lasted until the Sandinista (FSLN) victory of 1979.

María was transferred to more peaceful and relatively more prosperous Costa Rica in 1931 and was to spend the remainder of her life there. The Salesian Sisters ran a fee-paying school for the daughters of wealthy families and devoted surplus income to the provision of free education and training for the daughters of the poor in the *barrios*. María was active in both "camps" and worked to form her wealthy pupils into *misioneritas* ("little missionaries"), who would help her in materially aiding and catechizing poor and excluded children. This was to become the main focus of her life's work—inspiring those who had plenty in a very unequal society to help those who had little or nothing.

In 1945 she opened recreation centres (very much on the model of what Don Bosco had done for the poor and abandoned children of Turin); in 1953 centres for the distribution of food; and in 1961 her own school to educate poor girls without charging fees. This was followed in 1966 by a clinic, where she attracted the services of able doctors on a voluntary basis, as well as donations of the necessary drugs (echoing the achievements of the Salesian Brother Artemide Zatti in Argentina: see 15 Mar.). In 1973 she began the nucleus of what was to be a village providing decent homes for poor people, Centro San José, with seven houses on a piece of land outside the capital. She was later able to add a farm, a market, and a centre for catechesis and training for jobs, as well as a church dedicated to Our Lady, Help of Christians. She had proved herself to be an able fundraiser, but of course there was never enough money to do all the things she wanted.

As old age crept up on her, María had to abandon full-time teaching, but she never ceased catechizing young people and adults. The Salesians were not social revolutionaries, but she had followed their tradition of spreading a social gospel in the areas directly under her influence and helping its ripples to spread. In Costa Rica she was also fortunate to find a local Church, under Archbishop Víctor Sanabria Martínez (1899–1952), which appreciated the importance of the social apostolate: in a 1938 pastoral letter Mgr Sanabria wrote; "The *social question*! A word of transcendental value today! What has the Church done to resolve it and what can it do today in this direction?" He even supported a populist government against the oligarchy and permitted Catholics to join a new "PopularVanguard"derived partly from the communist party. In Nicaragua, on the other hand, the Church led by the archbishop of Managua attributed the 1931 earthquake to God punishing the sins of the people, supported the dictator Somoza García, and officially mourned him when he was assassinated in 1957.

María was sent back to Nicaragua for a long rest at the Salesian house of Las Peñitas in León but died there of a heart attack on 7 July 1977. Her remains were transferred back to San José and interred in the Salesian chapel there. She was declared Venerable on 18 December 2000 and beatified on 14 April 2002, together with Artemide Zatti, whose work so much resembled hers. The Pope in his homily described her as "an exemplary religious, apostle and mother of the poor people, who were her real favourites."

On the Daughters of Mary, Help of Christians, see *Butler*, St John Bosco, January, pp. 226–30; St Mary Mazzarello, May, pp. 80–1; *Orders*, p. 272. "Nicaragua History" and "Costa Rica History" produce informative sites. *Atlas*, Plate 110, P & Q 11 & 12 for the setting. Comment on the relative stances of the Church in Costa Rica and Nicaragua from E. Dussel (ed.), *The Church in Latin America, 1492–1992* (1992), pp. 148–9; see also R. Cardenal, "The Church in Central America," in *ibid.*, pp. 243–70, with chronological table and bibliography.

9

St Augustine Zhao Rong (d. 1815) and 119 Companions, *Martyrs* (from 1648 to 1930)

This mass canonization, held on 1 October 2000, bestowed the rank of saint on 120 martyrs in China, previously beatified in groups during the twentieth century, the latest two in 1983. The occasion itself in some way illustrated the historic misunderstanding between China and Christianity that has persisted in varying forms for centuries. For the Vatican, the date chosen was the feast of St Thérèse of Lisieux, proclaimed a principal patron of all missionaries in 1927; for the Chinese government, it was the anniversary of the triumph of the Communist revolution in 1948. The previous week, Cardinal Roger Etchegaray had visited China, and relations had seemed on the brink of improving. Then came the accusation over the date chosen, which prompted an outburst from the Chinese Foreign Ministry spokesman Sun Yuxi in which he claimed that "Most [of the new saints] were executed for violating Chinese law during the invasion of China by imperialists and colonialists," while others "were killed for bullying the Chinese people ... The sanctification of such people distorts truth and history, beautifies imperialism and slanders the peace-loving Chinese people" (*BBC News* report). Pope John Paul insisted that this was not the moment to discuss the historical record and that by creating the first Chinese saints the Church was merely honouring the Chinese people. A year later he did address the historical dimension, speaking to a group of Chinese and Western scholars gathered in Rome for a symposium to mark the 400th anniversary of the arrival of the Jesuit Matteo Ricci in Beijing:

> History ... reminds us of the unfortunate fact that the work of members of the Church in China was not always without error, the bitter fruit of their personal limitations and of the limits of their actions. Moreover, their action was often conditioned by difficult situations connected with complex historical events and conflicting political interests ... I feel deep sadness for these errors and limits of the past, and I regret that in many people these failings may have given the impression of a lack of respect and esteem for the Chinese people on the part of the Catholic Church ... For all of this I ask the forgiveness and understanding of those who may have felt hurt in some way by such actions on the part of Christians.

This was an extraordinarily handsome apology on the part of an institution that normally prefers to let the past bury the past.

The 120 canonized on this occasion comprise eighty-seven Chinese-born and thirty-three foreign missionaries, mostly priests and women belonging to religious Orders. Augustine Zhao Rong gives his name to the whole group as the first Chinese diocesan priest to be executed: "Having first been one of the soldiers who had escorted Bishop Dufresse [d. 1815, see below] from Chengdu to Beijing [in summer 1815], he was moved by his patience and had then asked to be numbered among the neophytes. Once baptized, he was sent to the seminary and then ordained a priest. Arrested, he had to suffer the most cruel tortures and then died in 1815" (Vatican News Service: his ordination seems to have taken place with extreme speed). The Chinese ranged in age from nine to seventy-two at the time of their deaths; many were trained as catechists, and four of them had been ordained diocesan priests. Most died during the Boxer Rebellion in 1900, and it was a proclamation by the provincial governor of Shangtu province on behalf of "the Boxers" (from the Chinese *Hi*

Yo Chuan, meaning "Righteous Harmony Boxers," or "Fists") that provided the Church with its argument that those killed were persecuted for religious and not political reasons—and so could justifiably be claimed as martyrs: "The European religion is wicked and cruel; it despises the spirit and oppresses peoples. All [Chinese] Christians who do not sincerely repudiate it will be executed ... Christians, hear and tremble! Give up this perverse religion! Let all Christians hear and obey: the Boxers will not hurt persons—it is this religion they hate."

A historical account of missions and martyrdoms in China is given in *Butler* for 17 February, with a supplementary notice of the last two missionaries killed (in 1930) under 25 February. Here only dates, names, and basic details are given.

1648	Francis Fernández de Capillas	Spanish Dominican priest, recognized as the protomartyr of China
1747	Peter Sans i Yordà	Catalan bishop
1748	Francis Serrano	Spanish Dominican priest
	Joachim Royo	Spanish Dominican priest
	John Alcober	Spanish Dominican priest
	Francis Diaz	Spanish Dominican priest
1814	Peter Wu	Chinese lay catechist
	Joseph Zhang Dapeng	Chinese lay catechist
1815	John Gabriel Taurin Dufresse	Bishop of Paris Foreign Missions (MEP)
	Augustine Zhao Rong	Chinese diocesan priest
1816	Blessed John da Triora	Italian Franciscan priest
1817	Joseph Yuan	Chinese diocesan priest
1820	Francis Regis Clet	French Vincentian priest
1823	Thaddeus Liu	Chinese diocesan priest
1834	Peter Liu	Chinese lay catechist
1839	Joachim Ho	Chinese lay catechist
1856	Augustus Chapdelaine	French MEP priest
	Laurence Bai Xiaoman	Chinese layman
	Agnes Cao Guiying	Chinese widow
1858	Jerome Lu Tingmei	Chinese catechist
	Laurence Wang Bing	Chinese catechist
	Agatha Lin Zao	Chinese catechist
1861	Joseph Zhang Wenlan	Chinese seminarian
	Paul Chen Changpin	Chinese seminarian
	John Baptist Luo Tingying	Chinese layman
	Martha Wang Luo Mande	Chinese laywoman

1862	John Peter Néel	French MEP priest
	Martin Wu Xuesheng	Lay catechist
	John Zhang Tianshen	Lay catechist
	John Chen Xianheng	Lay catechist
	Lucy Yi Zhenmei	Lay catechist

1900	(*Beatified in 1946*)	
	Gregory Grassi	Italian Franciscan bishop
	Francis Fogolla	Italian Franciscan bishop
	Elias Facchini	Italian Franciscan priest
	Theodoric Balat	Italian Franciscan priest
	Andrew Bauer	Alsatian Franciscan lay brother
	Anthony Fantosati	Italian Franciscan bishop
	Joseph Mary Gambaro	Italian Franciscan priest
	Cesidio Giacomantonio	Italian Franciscan priest
	Mary Hermina of Jesus (Irma Grivot)	French Franciscan Missionary of Mary
	Mary of Peace (Mary Ann Giuliani)	Italian Franciscan Missionary of Mary
	Mary Clare (Clelia Nanetti)	Italian Franciscan Missionary of Mary
	Mary of the Holy Birth (Joan Mary Kerguin)	French Franciscan Missionary of Mary
	Mary of Saint Justus (Ann Moreau)	French Franciscan Missionary of Mary
	Mary Adolfine (Ann Dierk)	Dutch Franciscan Missionary of Mary
	Mary Amandina (Paula Jeuris)	Belgian Franciscan Missionary of Mary
	John Zhang Huan	Chinese Franciscan seminarian
	Patrick Dong Bodi	Chinese Franciscan seminarian
	John Wang Rui	Chinese Franciscan seminarian
	Philip Zhang Zhihe	Chinese Franciscan seminarian
	John Zhang Jingguang	Chinese Franciscan seminarian
	Thomas Shen Jihe	Chinese layman
	Simon Qin Cunfu	Chinese lay catechist
	Peter Wu Anbang	Chinese Franciscan tertiary
	Francis Zhang Rong	Chinese Franciscan tertiary
	Matthew Feng De	Chinese Franciscan tertiary
	Peter Zhang Banniu	Chinese Franciscan tertiary
	James Yan Guodong	Chinese layman
	James Zhao Quanxin	Chinese layman
	Peter Wang Erman	Chinese layman

| 1900 | (*Beatified in 1955*) | |
| | Leo Ignatius Mangin | French Jesuit priest |

Paul Denn	French Jesuit priest
Rémy Isoré	French Jesuit priest
Modeste Andlauer	French Jesuit priest
Mary Zhu (born Wu), aged about 50	Lay Chinese
Peter Zhu Rixin, 19	Lay Chinese
John Baptist Zhu Wurui, 17	Lay Chinese
Mary Fu Guilin, 37	Lay Chinese
Barbara Cui (born Lian), 51	Lay Chinese
Joseph Ma Taishun, 60	Lay Chinese
Lucy Wang Cheng, 18	Lay Chinese
Mary Fan Kun, 16	Lay Chinese
Mary Chi Yu, 15	Lay Chinese
Mary Zheng Xu, 11	Lay Chinese
Mary Du (born Zhao), 51	Lay Chinese
Magdalene Du Fengju, 19	Lay Chinese
Mary Du (born Tian), 42	Lay Chinese
Paul Wu Anjyu, 62	Lay Chinese
John Baptist Wu Mantang, 17	Lay Chinese
Paul Wu Wanshu, 16	Lay Chinese
Raymond Li Quanzhen, 59	Lay Chinese
Peter Li Quanhui, 63	Lay Chinese
Peter Zhao Mingzhen, 61	Lay Chinese
John Baptist Zhao Mingxi, 56	Lay Chinese
Teresa Chen Tinjieh, 25	Lay Chinese
Rose Chen Aijieh, 22	Lay Chinese
Peter Wang Zuolung, 58	Lay Chinese
Mary Guo (born Li), 65	Lay Chinese
Joan Wu Wenyin, 50	Lay Chinese
Zhang Huailu, 57	Lay Chinese
Mark Ki-T'ien-Siang, 66	Lay Chinese
Ann An (born Xin), 72	Lay Chinese
Mary An (born Guo), 64	Lay Chinese
Ann An (born Jiao), 26	Lay Chinese
Mary An Linghua, 29	Lay Chinese
Paul Liu Jinde, 79	Lay Chinese
Joseph Wang Kuiju, 37	Lay Chinese
John Wang Kuixin, 25	Lay Chinese
Teresa Zhang (born He), 36	Lay Chinese
Lang (born Yang), 29	Lay Chinese
Paul Lang Fu, 9	Lay Chinese
Elizabeth Qin (born Bian), 54	Lay Chinese
Simon Qin Cunfu, 14	Lay Chinese

Peter Liu Zeyu, 57	Lay Chinese
Ann Wang, 14	Lay Chinese
Joseph Wang Yumei, 68	Lay Chinese
Lucy Wang, 31	Lay Chinese
Andrew Wang Tianqing, 9	Lay Chinese
Mary Wang (born Li), 49	Lay Chinese
Chi Zhuze, 18	Lay Chinese
Mary Zhao (born Guo), 60	Lay Chinese
Rose Zhao, 22	Lay Chinese
Mary Zhao, 17	Lay Chinese
Joseph Yuan Gengyin, 47	Lay Chinese
Paul Ge Tingzhu, 61	Lay Chinese
Rose Fan Hui, 45	Lay Chinese

1900 *(Beatified separately in 1951)*
      Alberic Crescitelli   Italian priest of the Pontifical Institute
                                          of Foreign Missions of Milan

1930 *(Beatified in 1983)*
      Louis Versiglia   Italian Salesian bishop
      Callistus Caravario   Italian Salesian priest

Missionary activity continued and increased during the first half of the twentieth century. Numbers of Chinese priests, religious Sisters, and lay helpers grew faster than the number of foreign missionaries, so that there was a strong indigenous Christian presence by the time the Communists expelled all foreign missionaries. The Catholic Church split into an "official" Church, loyal to the regime and not recognizing or recognized by the Vatican, which counts four million adherents, while the Vatican claims eight million Catholics (many in Taiwan and Hong Kong) as part of the Roman Catholic Church. The bishops from Taiwan and one from Hong Kong attended the canonization ceremony, but none was allowed to travel from mainland China. Protestantism has grown faster in recent decades, after suffering perhaps as many martyrs as Catholicism during the Boxer uprising, and now probably has some fourteen million adherents.

Butler, February (1998), pp. 175–184, 248–51, with bibliography. The Vatican *Zenit* news service for 1 October 2000 gives brief biographies and a simpler historical account than *Butler*. Additional material on the canonization from BBC World Service, 26 September and 1 October 2000.

St Pauline of the Suffering Heart of Jesus, *Founder*
(1865–1942)

Mother Pauline is yet another example of the remarkable nineteenth-century pioneering women whose lives have found official recognition in recent years, and who had to contend with opposition from within the Church in their day. She was born on 16 December 1865 in Vigolo Vattaro, in what is now the province of Trent in northern Italy (at the time part of South Tyrol and under the rule of the Austrian Empire). Her name was Amabile Lucia Wisenteiner, and her parents were Antonio Napoleone Wisenteiner and Anna Pianezzer.

In the latter part of the nineteenth century the area where Amabile was born was desperately poor, and emigration to seek a better life in the New World was taking place on a large scale. Her parents, together with about a fifth of the population of her home town, emigrated to the State of Santa Catarina in southern Brazil, where the Brazilian government was providing land for immigrant settlers. These families, with many others from the Trentino, established the town of Vigolo near the coast (now part of Nova Trento). Amabile made her First Communion at the age of twelve and began to take an active part in parish life. She taught the catechism to younger girls and visited the sick, while having to work hard on the land to help her parents support a large family.

The local Jesuit missionaries encouraged her to think about a religious vocation. The idea came to fruition in 1890 when Amabile and a close friend, Virginia Rosa Nicolodi, were caring for a woman suffering from cancer. They had left home to do so and were living together in a cottage near the chapel of St George in Vigolo. Their life dedicated to caring for the sick was formalized in a religious Congregation, the Little Sisters of the Immaculate Conception, approved by the bishop of Curitiba in December 1890 when the two friends, together with a third, Teresa Anna Maule, made their religious professions. Amabile took the (very typical late nineteenth-century, when devotion to the Sacred Heart had reached a peak) name of Pauline of the Suffering Heart of Jesus (*Paulina do Coraçao Agonizante de Jesus* in Portuguese, but "agonizing" has a somewhat different sense in English) in religion. The Congregation, the first to be formed in southern Brazil, grew quickly, and in 1903 Mother Pauline was elected superior general "for life." In the same year she left Nova Trento and followed her Jesuit spiritual director north to the city of São Paulo, where there were huge social problems attendant on rapid growth, with thousands of orphans, children of slaves, and old former slaves dying with no support. (Brazil, which received up to 1.5 million slaves, by far the largest number of any South American country, had been the last to abolish slavery, in 1888, largely under British and American pressure.)

A misunderstanding with the archbishop of São Paulo (or a series of disputes within the Congregation: or perhaps both) in 1909 led to Pauline being removed from her "for life" position as mother superior and sent to work with the sick and aged at the Hospice of St Vincent de Paul at Bragança Paulista. She accepted the suffering with humility, even the archbishop's declaration that "she should live and die as an underling," and continued to work and pray for the wellbeing of the Congregation. Her period of "exile" came to an end in 1918, when the mother superior recalled her to the motherhouse in Ipiranga, where she was to remain until her death twenty-four years later, living a hidden life of prayer and care for Sisters who were sick. She suffered from diabetes, which began to cause severe complications in 1938, when her right arm had to be amputated.

On 19 May 1933 the Holy See granted a "Decree of Praise" to the Little Sisters, in which she was acknowledged as "Venerable Mother Foundress." In 1940 she wrote her spiritual testament, but her eyesight was failing and she spent the last two years of her life blind. By the time Pauline died, on 9 July 1942, there were forty-five houses of her Congregation in Brazil. She was beatified by Pope John Paul II on 18 October 1991, at Florianópolis on the coast of Santa Catarina, and canonized by him in Rome on 19 May 2002. She had been known locally as "nurse," implying a life lived for others; the pope called her "a manifestation of the Holy Spirit." She had written, poignantly in view of her setbacks, "Be humble. Trust always and a great deal in divine Providence; never, never must you let yourselves be discouraged, despite contrary winds. I say it again: trust in God and Mary Immaculate; be faithful and forge ahead!" Mother Pauline was the first Brazilian to be canonized.

❖

Fuller than normal Vatican sources; *Butler*, July, pp. 69–70, citing two biographies in Portuguese: J. L. da Costa Aguilar, *Madre Paulina do Coraçao Agonizante de Jesus* (1962); F. Dalcin Barbosa, *A Coloninha* (1981).

There are currently some 600 houses of the Little Sisters of the Immaculate Conception, and its members work in Argentina, Brazil, Chad, Chile, Italy, Mozambique, Nicaragua, and Zambia. On the Congregation see *Diz. Inst. Perf.*, 6, 1638; on the Brazilian background E. Dussel (ed.), *The Church in Latin America, 1492–1992* (1992), pp. 123, 135–6, 185–200.

Bd Marija Petković, *Founder* (1892–1966)

Her name in religion translates as Mary of Jesus Crucified, but as that is also the name taken by Mariam Baouardy (beatified in 1983; 26 Aug.), she is referred to here by her baptismal name to avoid confusion. Marija (Mary) was born in Blato, a small town on the island of Korčula, off the coast of southern Croatia, on 10 December 1892. Her parents, Antun Petković-Kovać and Marija Marinović, had thirteen children, of whom Marija was the sixth.

She attended elementary school and the then new municipal school in Blato, started by the Servants of Charity (a new Congregation founded in Italy by Bd Louis Guanella), who had recently arrived from Italy. After the prescribed three years of schooling she moved on to the school of domestic science, also run by the Sisters. In 1906 she joined the Association of Daughters of Mary (for young lay women), of which she was to be president from 1909 to 1919. This had 300 members, divided into subsidiary groups, and she started as one of twenty "Good Shepherds," who visited the sick, prepared children for their first Communion, and prayed to the Sacred Heart to make reparation for the sins of the world, according to the current spirituality of her time and place.

Marija's father died in 1911, and she had to help her mother care for the younger children and provide for their education. The First World War affected the area severely, bringing ravaged agricultural land, disease, many deaths, and a perpetuation of social injustice. Marija's response was to increase her involvement in a number of Catholic organizations. With the guidance of Bishop Josip Marcelic of Dubrovnik, she started the Society of Catholic Mothers in 1915; in 1917 she was given the guidance of the local Franciscan Tertiaries; and in 1918 she made a formal promise to the citizens of Blato that she would remain there and help the poor, living among them.

In 1919 she and a friend, Marija Telenta, entered the local convent of the Servants of Charity, but they found themselves virtually the only inhabitants when the mother superior died two months after they had joined and all the other Sisters except two decamped back to Italy for what were described as "political reasons." Marija asked the other Croatian Sisters whether they wanted to leave or stay; both decided to stay, and Bishop Josip watched over the small remnant, giving them the rule of the Third Order of St Francis for the time being. He appointed Marija Petković superior, warning her that this meant being "the last among the Sisters, and if necessary [going] barefoot while the Sisters wore shoes, she hungry and the Sisters full, following the example of the crucified Jesus." In the winter of 1919–1920 she opened a day recovery centre, a child-care nursery, and an orphanage in Blato.

The religious status of the group was uncertain, and Marija decided to form them into a new Congregation, writing its Constitutions in 1920 and calling it Daughters of Mercy. This was to be an independent Franciscan Congregation, and it was formally inaugurated by the bishop on 4 October, the feast of St Francis. Marija took the name *Marija od Propetoga Isusa* (Mary of Jesus Crucified) and became the first superior. Their mission was to spread knowledge of the love and mercy of God through the exercise of works of mercy. This cost money, and the small group's funds were soon exhausted. Marija travelled abroad to beg for funds, which were forthcoming, including a donation from Pope Pius XI. She expanded the mission, opening a children's home in Subotica (in northern Serbia), followed by many others in the Balkans. During her lifetime she opened forty-six new communities. In 1936 she spread the work to Latin America, living in Argentina from 1940 to 1952. The Sisters' social work extended to working in nursing homes, hospitals and nursery schools, besides helping in parishes and seminaries. In Latin America they taught nursing, hygiene, home economics, sewing and tailoring, knitting, and typing.

In 1952 Marija purchased a building in Rome to serve as the Congregation's headquarters. In 1954 she had a stroke, which left her partially but permanently paralyzed. She continued to run the Congregation until 1961, when she decided that she could best serve it through a ministry of prayer and suffering, and resigned after forty years as mother superior. She lived on to see the beginning of momentous changes in religious life ushered in by the Second Vatican Council, in which she took a keen interest. She died aged seventy-four, on 9 July 1966, leaving her Sisters a last testament: "Love infinitely the most sweet Lord Jesus Christ; do everything for him alone and spend your life in works of mercy and of love." She was buried in the Campo Verano cemetery in Rome, but her remains were transferred to Blato in 1998 and buried in the chapel of the monastery of Christ the King.

The miracle claimed as coming about through her intercession that cleared the way for her beatification was somewhat different from the usual inexplicable cures, and derives from her activities in Latin America. On 26 August 1988 a Russian trawler operating in the south Pacific rammed and sank a Peruvian submarine. Lieutenant Roger Cotrina Alvarado prayed for Marija's help as the submarine sank, and found himself able to lift the hatch against the pressure of thousands of pounds of water, enabling the crew of twenty-two to escape. A report of this was sent to the Congregation for the Causes of Saints in February 1989, and in May 1998 Pope John Paul II accepted its initial report confirming the miraculous nature of the incident and decreed that her heroic virtues be recognized, making her Venerable. The miracle was formally ruled to be such in December 2002, and Marija was beatified in the harbour square of Dubrovnik on 6 June 2003. In his homily the Pope referred to the sufferings of Croatia, especially of its women, in the conflict with Serbia in the 1990s and prayed: "May your Christian community grow and be strengthened in mutual forgiveness, charity, and peace."

On the Servants of Charity see *Orders*, p. 80; *Butler*, October, pp. 172–4.

13

Bd Ferdinand Mary Baccillieri (1821–1893)

Born in Campodoso, near Módena in the Emilia Romagna region of northern Italy, between Bologna and Ferrara, on 14 May 1821, Ferdinand (Fernando) was educated first by the Barnabite Fathers (founded by St Antony Zaccariah; 5 July) at their school in Bologna, and then by the Jesuits in Ferrara. With an excellent education behind him, he entered the Jesuit novitiate in Rome, but his health was too poor for the Order to accept him, and he returned to live with his family for a time, after which he went to Ferrara to study theology. He was ordained priest in 1844.

Ferdinand preached Lenten and other missions throughout the archdiocese of Bologna, as well as teaching Italian and Latin to students in the seminary at Finale Emilia. Four years after his ordination he began studies at the Pontifical University of Bologna for a doctorate in civil and canon law. The archbishop, Cardinal Oppizzoni, however, had other plans for him and asked him to take charge of a troubled parish, Santa Maria, in the small town of Galeazza. He improved conditions in the parish to such an extent that the local people and other priests persuaded the cardinal to appoint him parish priest. He was thirty-one years old at the time of his appointment, and he served his parish faithfully for the next forty-one years, refusing the other more prestigious posts for which he was regularly proposed on the strength of his doctorate.

In 1867, fifteen years into his ministry, which depended largely on his powerful preaching, he lost his voice and was forced to pay others to deliver his sermons for him, while he concentrated on aspects of his work that were less taxing on his voice, such as spiritual direction. Like the Curé d'Ars (St John Vianney; 4 Aug.), who in the immediately preceding decades had transformed his parish largely through his ministry in the confessional, Ferdinand spent up to sixteen hours a day hearing confessions.

Also, like the Curé d'Ars, he found he needed helpers. Fr Vianney had started *La Providence* as a free school and a shelter for orphans and other homeless children, and Fr Bacillieri, who was a member of the Third Order of Servants of Mary, or Servites, started a group that became the Confraternity of the Sorrowful Mother for much the same purpose, to provide a free education for poor girls in the parish. They were soon helped by other women, who in 1866 were clothed as *Mantellate*, taking the Rule of the Sisters of the Third Order of Servites founded in Rome by St Juliana Falconieri (19 June), niece of one the seven founders of the Order. This was in effect a new foundation, to which Fernando gave the name of Sisters Servants of Mary of Galeazza, and required official approval, which was delayed until after his death, being approved by the archdiocese of Bologna in 1899 and by the Holy See in 1919. They spread to other places in Italy, and to Germany, the Czech Republic, Brazil, and South Korea.

Fernando died, largely from exhaustion, on 13 July 1893. He was beatified on 3 October 1999. The following day Pope John Paul II, greeting the Sisters who had come for the beatifcation ceremony, expressed the wish:

> "May the spiritual daughters of this new Blessed and all who invoke him as their protector welcome his invitation to reflect constantly on the Christian message and to foster a tender devotion to Our Lady of Sorrows. It is important to understand that following Christ necessarily involves that serious revision of one's life to which he exhorted everyone, especially on the occasion of parish missions. May the desire to offer each one the clear teaching of the gospel grow in those who, in following his example, continue his apostolic action to reach families and individual faithful."

On the origins of the Servite Order, see *Butler*, February, pp. 167–9. The Order was largely responsible for spreading the devotion known as the Seven Sorrows of the BVM.

Bd Mariano de Jesús Euse Hoyos (1845–1926)

"Padre Marianito," Colombia's first non-martyr Blessed (seven Colombian priests killed in Spain during the civil war have been beatified), was a rural parish priest in the province of Antioquia, north of Medellín in the Andean north-west of Colombia, for most of his life. He was the eldest of six children, born to Pedro Euse (a French surname: his grandfather had emigrated from Normandy) and Rosalía de Hoyos, in Yarumal, in the diocese of Antioquia, on 14 October 1845. He grew up at a time when the liberal-led Republic was engaged in trying to reduce the privileges of the Catholic Church, a process that reached its height in the 1850s with the expulsion of the Jesuits and some bishops and the expropriation of church property. The pendulum later swung back, with Conservative Party support for the Church leading to a Concordat with the Vatican in 1887 that set the tone for almost a century of Church–Conservative alliance.

Mariano's parents were devout and refused to send him to the local school, where the atmosphere was very hostile to religion, preferring to educate their eldest son personally at home. They gave him such a sound basic education that he was soon teaching children from less fortunate families, although he never lost his rural simplicity, which was to stand him in good stead in his later ministry. When he was sixteen he declared that he wanted to become a priest—not an easy thing to do publicly at the time, so his parents sent him to stay with his maternal uncle, Fr Fermín Hoyos, parish priest of Giradota (later of San Pedro), and known for his virtue and learning. Mariano spent eight years with Fr Fermín, learning and helping. By 1869 conditions had improved and a new seminary opened in Medellín. Mariano was admitted and ordained three years later, on 18 July 1872.

He began his priestly ministry as curate to his uncle at San Pedro, at the latter's request, but Fr Fermín died in 1875, and Mariano was sent, still as curate, first to his birthplace, Yarumal, and then in 1878 to Angostura, in the same diocese, where the death of the elderly incumbent, Fr Rudesindo Correa, soon left him in sole charge. He set about tackling a multitude of problems with a simple energy that soon endeared him to his flock. He completed the half-built parish church, somehow finding the funds and despite often having to hide in the mountains or in caves from roving bands of anticlericals. He later completed the bell tower, two hermitages, and the cemetery. He was formally appointed parish priest, and the fame of his holiness began to spread. His peasant background enabled him to empathize with the poorest of his people: he preached in language they could understand; his own devotion to the Eucharist, the Virgin Mary, and the Sacred Heart was inspirational; and he was never too busy to visit the sick and the old, or to supervise the formation of young people. He brought his flock back to the practice of attending Mass on Sundays and feast-days, as well as encouraging family rosary and various associations.

Despite great personal austerity, Mariano's health held out for over forty-five years of unremitting work for and devotion to his parish. In 1926, however, he succumbed to a urinary tract infection, inflammation of the prostate, and finally enteritis. He was so poor that the parishioners who looked after him had to beg for a change of bedclothes. On 12 July he declared that he had lived long enough and wanted only to be with Jesus. He died the following day, the forty-sixth anniversary of his ordination, and was buried in the chapel of Our Lady of Mount Carmel, which he had built.

Those who knew him considered him a saint in his lifetime. In 1936 his body was exhumed and found to be incorrupt, and popular devotion grew, with a rapidly expanding list of spiritual favors, cures, and other miracles, as well as exorcisms, attributed to him. By 1990 the Vatican had to ask for a guard to be placed over his tomb to prevent it from being looted for relics. Always slower than the people, the official process for his beatification was begun in 1980 but had to wait for the confirmation of the inexplicable cure of a priest pronounced terminally ill in 1987 but healthy ten years later as a miracle attributable to Mariano's intercession. This was pronounced in April 1998, and Pope John Paul II beatified him in St Peter's Piazza on 9 April 2000, expressing the hope that the occasion would "mark a new phase in which all Colombians will build a new Colombia together, one based on peace, social justice, respect for human rights, and brotherly love among children of the same homeland"—a hope that remains just that. Meanwhile, stories of cures worked through Fr Marianito's intercession are still told almost daily to his surviving relatives.

Besides the usual Vatican sources, there is an account of popular devotion (and cures attributed) to him in *El Tiempo* of Medellín, 9 Apr.il 2000.

Bd Carlos Manuel Rodríguez Santiago (1918–1963)

The first blessed from Puerto Rico was a layman and has the unique distinction of having had his cause introduced by laypeople. He was born in Caguas in Puerto Rico on 22 November 1918, the second of five children of Manuel Baudilio Rodríguez and Herminia Santiago, and was generally known as Charlie. When he was six years old, his family's house and the store they ran were burned to the ground, and they were forced to move in with his mother's parents, where his grandmother, Alejandrina Esteras, was a strong influence on his piety and that of his siblings: a younger brother went on to become a Benedictine monk and the first Puerto Rican abbot, and a sister became a Carmelite nun.

Carlos was a brilliant student at school, but at thirteen he began to suffer from ulcerative colitis, which was to blight his career and eventually lead to his early death. His health prevented him from attending the University of Puerto Rico, and he worked as an office clerk till 1946. He was keen on hiking and also taught himself to play the piano and the organ. He then earned his living as a translator (from English into Spanish). Liturgy was an abiding interest and he founded a Liturgy Circle at Caguas, as well as using his modest salary to publish two magazines, titled *Liturgy* and *Christian Culture*. He also started a choir, known as *Te Deum laudamus*.

Carlos then moved on to the Catholic University Center at Río Piedras, where he taught catechism classes to the students—evangelizing the teachers at the same time. He organized another liturgy circle, the "Christian Culture Circle," and published another journal to help students appreciate the liturgical seasons. He worked to help both clergy and laity develop a love of the liturgy, advocating lay participation and the use of the vernacular well before the reforms of the Second Vatican Council. His spirituality focused on the resurrection, and he made the Easter Vigil a major part of his devotion, encouraging others to see it in the same light.

His health deteriorated with the onset of rectal cancer, which necessitated aggressive surgery. He suffered a "dark night of the soul" and told his Benedictine brother that he was not ready to die, but before the end he recovered his faith and his enthusiasm and became reconciled to his fate. He died from his cancer on 13 July 1963. In 1981 a women suffering from lung cancer recovered her health after praying to him, and this was accepted as a miracle paving the way for beatification. Pope John Paul II declared his heroic virtue in 1997 and beatified him on 29 April 2001. In his homily he stressed Carlos' emphasis on the importance of the Easter Vigil: "The new blessed, illumined by faith in the resurrection, shared with everyone the profound meaning of the paschal mystery, repeating frequently, 'We live for this night,' the Easter Vigil. His fruitful and generous apostolate chiefly consisted in the effort to help the Church in Puerto Rico to attain an awareness of this important event of our salvation."

❖

Círculo Carlos M. Rodríguez, *Vida de Carlos Manuel Rodríguez, primer puertor-riqueño en ser beatificado* (1997, based on the *Informatio super Virtutibus*); *ibid.*, *¿Un santo puertorriqueño?, Carlos M. Rodríguez* (4th edn, 2001; English translation *Carlos M. Rodríguez. A Puerto Rican Saint?*, 2003). Further information from Abadía San Antonio Abad; abadiasanantonioab8@hotmail.com; Círculo Carlos M. Rodríguez, Centro Universitario Católico, Mariana Bracetti 10, Río Piedras, PR 00925.

In June 2004 the Blessed Carlos Manuel Hispanic Center was opened in the diocese of Venice, Florida, as a focus for a new parish to cater for the increasing numbers of Spanish-speaking Catholics.

16

Bd Bartholomew dos Mártires, *Bishop* (1514–1590)

Bartholomew (Bartolomeu) was born in Lisbon on 3 May 1514. He was baptized in the Church of Nossa Senhora dos Mártires ("Our Lady of the Martyrs") on the same day, and "of the Martyrs" replaced the family name Vale. He received the Dominican habit on 11 November 1528, entering the novitiate in Lisbon and making his solemn profession on 20 November 1529. He was a brilliant student and completed his courses in philosophy and theology in 1538, after which he spent twenty years teaching philosophy, first at the College of St Dominic in Lisbon, then in the priory at Batalha (north of Lisbon in the coastal province of Leiria), and finally at Évora (capital of the province of the same name, east of Lisbon). There he was named royal tutor and preacher.

In 1558 Queen Catherine of Portugal, then regent for her infant grandson Sebastian I (the successor of John III, who died two weeks before his son's birth), nominated Bartholomew for the archbishopric of Braga, a provincial capital in north-western Portugal. He was reluctant to accept, but did so out of obedience to his prior provincial, the great spiritual writer Fray Luis de Granada (now Venerable)—who had himself been the queen's first choice but had urged her to put Bartholomew's name forward instead. His appointment was confirmed by Pope Paul IV in the Bull *Gratiae divinae praemium*, dated 27 January 1559, and he was consecrated in St Dominic's Priory in Lisbon on 3 September.

The archdiocese covered a vast area and there was much to be done. Bartholomew used the pastoral visitation, which he introduced, as his main contact with his clergy, and preached a clear gospel message to his people, backing this with his example of charity, giving virtually all the money he had to the poorest among them. When reproached for doing so, he replied, "You will not see me ever so foolish as to spend with the leisured classes what I can use to keep the poor alive." He also established several schools of moral theology, for the moral and cultural formation of the clergy, in various parts of the archdiocese. Of them, he said, "It is evident that if your zeal corresponded to your office ... the flock of Christ would not stray so far away from the road to heaven." He never changed his austere way of life, and this earned him respect. He elaborated his teaching in a *Catechism of Christian Doctrine and Spiritual Practices*, which was still being reprinted in the 1960s. This was just one of thirty-two published works, another being the *Stimulus pastorum*, which was still considered sufficiently valid in the nineteenth and twentieth centuries for copies to be presented to the Fathers of the First and Second Vatican Councils.

Bartholomew played an active part in the Council of Trent from 1561 to 1563: a leading advocate of reform, he presented no fewer than 268 petitions, which had a considerable impact on the decrees passed and influenced the teaching of both Pope Pius IV and St Charles Borromeo (on whose memorial day, 4 Nov., he was to be beatified). He implemented the reform measures in his own diocese by establishing a diocesan synod in 1564, followed by the Provincial Council of Braga two years later. In 1571 he began building the diocesan seminary in Campo Vinha, where priests could be formed in accordance with the teaching of the council.

Seeing his principles put into effect, he tried several times to stand down as archbishop. His petition was finally accepted in 1582, and he retired to the Dominican priory of the Holy Cross in Viana do Castelo (on the coast to the north-west of Braga), which he had built as a study house for priests and where he died on 16 July 1590. He was buried in the church there. The people of his archdiocese, who revered him for reasons other than his administrative reforms, accorded him the title, "Holy archbishop, father of the poor and the sick." He was declared Venerable by Pope Gregory XVI in 1845, and after the recognition of a miracle attributed to his intercession was beatified by Pope John Paul II on 4 November 2001. The Pope said in his homily that he, "with great vigilance and apostolic zeal, gave himself to safeguarding and renewing the Church in her living stones, without looking down on the provisional structures that are her inert stones."

International Dominican Information 395 (Sept. 2001), pp. 178–9.

Bd André de Soveral, Ambrósio Francisco Ferro, and Companions, *Martyrs* (1645)

On Christmas Day 1597 an expedition of Portuguese colonists reached what is now Natal (Portuguese for "birth" or "nativity") in the State of Rio Grande do Norte, in north-eastern Brazil. At the time it was in the Portuguese colony of Maranhão, the northern part of what became present-day Brazil with the achievement of independence in 1822. As was the custom, missionaries accompanied the colonizers in order to "evangelize" the indigenous people they found. This expedition was accompanied by two Jesuits and two Franciscans. The religious Orders, especially the Jesuits, soon came to see the inherent contradiction in a Christianity based on the "Great House" of the coastal sugar plantations, and the use of slave or domesticated Indian labour. These martyrs were in any case not victims of those they were trying to evangelize but of divisions within the Western Christendom that was claiming to bring the truth to the native population.

The Portuguese/Catholic occupation continued for some decades, but the area was then invaded by Dutch Calvinists, who gradually assumed control and set about persecuting the Catholics, turning many of the natives against them. On Sunday 16 July 1645 Fr André de Soveral was celebrating Mass in the Chapel of Our Lady of the Candles in Uruaçu. At the moment of the elevation, a group of Dutch soldiers, supported by armed Indians, burst into the chapel and killed Fr André and many of the sixty-nine faithful attending Mass. Then, on 3 October the same year, some 200 armed Indians, led by some Flemish soldiers under the command of a fanatical Calvinist convert, set out to slaughter Catholics. Many, including the parish priest of Cunhaú, Fr Ambrósio Francisco Ferro, were hacked to death. One layman, Mateus Moreiras, had his heart torn out through his back.

The two priests and their lay parishioners, men and women whose names are mostly unknown, were beatified as André de Soveral, Ambrósio Francisco Ferro, and twenty-eight companions, in Rome on 5 March 2000, the protomartyrs of Brazil and the first to be beatified in the twenty-first century.

For a somewhat polemical summary of the Church in Brazil, see E. Hoonaert in E. Dussel (ed.), *The Church in Latin America, 1492–1992* (1992), pp. 185–200, with further bibliography.

17

Bd Paul Peter Gojdić, *Bishop and Martyr* (1888–1960)

Peter Gojdić (pronounced *Goydich)* was born near Prešov, the capital of the
Prešovsky *Kraj* (province) in what is now eastern Slovakia, sixty miles from the
border with western Ukraine. His father, Štefan Gojdić, was a Greek Catholic
priest, and his mother was named Anna Gerbeyová. He went to school in nearby
Cigelka and Bardejov, then in Prešov itself, followed by studying theology there
and then at the Central Seminary in Budapest, where outstanding students
were sent. He was ordained as a celibate priest soon after completing his
studies in late August 1911. He had a brief spell as assistant priest to his father
and was then appointed prefect of the eparchial (diocesan) boarding school
for boys, The Alumneum, teaching religion in a higher secondary school at
the same time. Posts as head of protocol and archivist in the diocesan curia
followed, combined with assistant parish priest in Sabinov. He was appointed
diocesan chancellor in 1919.

Instead of steadily ascending the ecclesiastical ladder, in 1922 Peter decided
to become a Basilian monk, entering the monastery of St Nicholas on Černecia
(Mount) Hora near Mukacheve (then in Slovakia, now in the western-most
province of Ukraine) and taking the name Paul (Pavol) in religion. His desire for
a quiet and ascetic life was not to be fulfilled, however, as on 14 September 1926
he was appointed apostolic administrator of the eparchy of Prešov. He tried to
resist on the grounds that he had not yet made his monastic profession, but was
told to do so as soon as possible and return prepared to become a bishop.

Paul's first act was to issue an apostolic letter on the eleven hundredth
anniversary of the birth of St Cyril, apostle to the Slavs (14 Feb. in the Western
Church; 11 May in the Eastern), indicating his desire to follow in the footsteps
of the founder of Slavonic liturgy, who always remained faithful to Rome. He
was nominated titular bishop of Harpaš (in Asia Minor) early in 1927 and
consecrated in San Clemente in Rome on 25 March. He was received in private
audience by Pope Pius XI, who gave him a gold cross and told him, "This cross is
only a faint symbol of the crosses that God will send you, my son, in your work
as bishop."

As bishop, which gave him responsibility for Greek Catholics over a very
large area, Paul worked tirelessly: he developed the spiritual life of clergy and
laity, insisted on proper celebration of the liturgy, erected new parishes, set up
an orphanage in Prešov, and founded a Greek Catholic school there, as well as
supporting two journals, *Messenger of the Gospel* and *Thy Kingdom Come.* He
drew on strong personal devotion to Christ in the Eucharist and to the Sacred

Heart, spending long hours in private prayer. He was appointed apostolic administrator of Muckacheve on 13 April 1939. By this time Hitler had invaded Czechoslovakia, and Paul found himself at odds with the civil administration. He offered to stand down, but Pope Pius XII refused to accept his resignation and instead appointed him residential bishop of Prešov, where he was solemnly enthroned on 8 August 1940. In 1946 his jurisdiction over Greek Catholics throughout Czechoslovakia was confirmed.

In 1948 Communists took power and made the Greek Catholic Church their principal ideological target in Slovakia, trying, as they did in Ukraine, to force its leaders and members to assimilate to the Russian Orthodox Church. Many submitted, but Paul resisted all pressure to break with Rome. On 28 April 1950 the Greek Catholic Church was formally outlawed, and he was arrested. He was charged with treason and, at a show trial in January 1951, was sentenced to life imprisonment. For the next two years he was moved from one prison to another, kept in solitary confinement, and always forced to do the most humiliating and degrading tasks. He never protested, prayed in silence, and managed to celebrate the Eucharist in secret. He was accused of "hating and betraying" the people, yet large groups of these people managed to find out where he was being kept and congregated outside the prison walls to pray and sing hymns.

Paul's health eventually broke after he had suffered severe pain for some months without complaining, and he was transferred to the prison hospital; doctors failed to discover the cause and he was moved out of hospital, then in again, several times. The authorities (who really did not want a martyr) then sent him to a clinic in Brno, where the doctors diagnosed terminal cancer. He was moved to a prison hospital in Leopoldov and was allowed a priest to keep him company in his final days, hear his Confession, and give him Communion. A nurse who looked after him testified that he

> "cherished an immense love for his clergy and people. He often spoke of Greek Catholic customs and ceremonies and, with great enthusiasm, used to explain why his people must remain united with the Apostolic See. He told us how, during his long interrogations, they used to torture him and how they tried, with all sorts of promises, to sway him to accept Orthodoxy. They even promised to make him a patriarch ... There is no doubt in my mind that Bishop Gojdić was a martyr for his faith" (cited in Byzantine Leaflet Series, No. 40).

Paul had expressed a hope that he might die on his birthday, and did so on 17 July 1960, his seventy-second. His remains were buried in the prison yard, marked only with the number 681. After the "Prague Spring" of 1968 they were transferred to Prešov on 29 October. During the "Velvet Revolution" of 1989 he was legally rehabilitated and posthumously awarded two high State decorations, the Order of T. G. Masaryk and the Cross of Pribina. His remains were then re-interred in the chapel of the Greek Catholic cathedral of Prešov on 15 May 1990. He was beatified with seven others in St Peter's Piazza on 4

November 2001, when Pope John Paul II spoke of his "long calvary of suffering, mistreatment, and humiliation, which brought about his death on account of his fidelity to Christ and his love for the Church and the pope."

❖

J. A. Mikus, *Three Slovak Bishops* (1953); J. Vojtassak, *The Trial of the Slovak Bishops* (1951); T. J. Zubek, "Slovak Bishops—Martyrs for Christ," *The Jurist*, Oct. 1955. Further bibliography on www.cross.edu/departments/history/ vlapomar/persecut. Byzantine Leaflet Series issued by Byzantine Seminary Press, Pittsburgh, PA 15214, on www.carpatho-rusyn.prg/spirit/gojdich. On the Basilian monks (Order of St Basil the Great) see *Orders*, pp. 31–3.

23

Bd Vasil' Hopko, *Bishop and Martyr* (1904–1976)

Vasil' was born in the east of Slovakia, the eastern part of the former Czechoslovakia, in the village of Hrabské, on 21 April 1904. His father died when he was just a year old, and he spent three years in the care of his mother; she then emigrated to the U.S.A. in search of work, leaving him with his grand-father. When he was seven he went to live with an uncle, a Greek-Catholic priest named Demeter Petrenko, who inspired him to become a priest. In 1923 he entered the Greek-Catholic seminary of Prešov (now the provincial capital of the north-eastern region of Slovakia). He was ordained on 3 February 1929 and sent to Prague as pastor to the Greek-Catholic community there. He worked with young people (starting a Movement of Greek-Catholic Students and the Greek-Catholic Youth Union) and with the elderly, the unemployed, and orphans. He helped to build a church for the community, making it into a parish, of which he became parish priest. His mother returned from America, and they were reunited after twenty-two years.

Vasil' returned to the seminary in Prešov in 1936, in the post of spiritual director. In 1941, with the country under German occupation, he became secretary to the Episcopal curia, and two years later he was appointed professor of moral and pastoral theology at the university. He founded and edited a magazine, *Blahovistnik* ("Gospel Messenger"), and found time to write several books. The end of the war left Czechoslovakia under Russian occupation. As the process of Stalinization increased, the bishop of Prešov, Mgr Gojdić, asked for an auxiliary to be appointed to help him defend the Greek-Catholic Church against what he saw as inevitable attack. The Holy See appointed Vasil', who took office on 11 May 1947. The Communist coup of 1948, which brought about the death of Jan Masaryk, the foreign minister, and the resignation of President Edvard Beneš, led to intensified pressure, and on 28 April 1950 the Communist Party held the "Council of Prešov," to which the bishops were not invited, and declared the Greek-Catholic Church no longer in existence, with all its priests, faithful, and churches transferred to the Orthodox Church. The bishop and his auxiliary were placed under arrest.

Vasil'was brutally interrogated and tortured, to prepare him to admit to various false accusations at a show trial. This lasted more than a year, during which he refused to deny his faith in any way. He was placed on trial on 24 October 1951 and condemned to fifteen years' imprisonment. In prison he was not only tortured further but given regular small doses of arsenic to undermine his health. He was released in May 1964, physically weak and subject to bouts of depression but still able to contribute to the resurgence of the Greek-Catholic Church. After the "Prague Spring" of 1968, this was re-established and active persecution ceased—even though the Russians sent tanks to crush the reform movement.

Vasil' returned to Prešov, and in December Pope Paul VI confirmed him as auxiliary bishop to all Greek-Catholics in Czechoslovakia. He was able to exercise pastoral care of his flock until he died in Prešov on 23 July 1976. Analysis of his bones proved the presence of arsenic, so that it was considered he had died as a result of his mistreatment in prison and could be regarded as a martyr. He was beatified by Pope John Paul II during his apostolic visit to Slovakia, at a ceremony held on the Petrčalka Esplanade in Bratislava, capital of the Slovak Republic, on 14 September 2003. The Pope congratulated the Slovak people on keeping the faith throughout times of trouble, exhorted them to cling to the gospel as their most precious possession, and held up Vasil' and Sister Zdenka Schelingová, beatified with him (see 31 July), as "radiant examples of faithfulness in times of harsh and ruthless religious persecution."

26

Bd Andrew of Phú Yên, *Martyr* (1625–1644)

Andrew, known as Andrew the Catechist, is the protomartyr of Vietnam, though he was far from the first to be beatified: a group of 117, of whom ninety-six were Vietnamese, were canonized in 1988 as Andrew Dung-Lac and Companions. They suffered in various persecutions, mainly between 1745 and 1862.

The present territory of Vietnam was first evangelized in the sixteenth century, but it was not until the arrival of the French Jesuit Fr Alexandre de Rhodes in 1623 that Christianity began to take root. In that time the country was divided between the Trinh lords in the north (Tonkin) and the Nguyen in the south (Annam and Cochin China). De Rhodes devised the *quoc ngu* system of writing

Vietnamese in Roman rather that Chinese characters, which is still in use. He and his fellow missionaries trained native catechists, who became quite capable of working independently.

Andrew (Anrê Phú Yên, or Anreâ Phuù Yeân, in Vietnamese) was one of these catechists. Born in Ran Ran, he was baptized by Fr de Rhodes in 1641, when he was about fifteen, together with his widowed mother and his brothers and sisters. He joined the Maison Dieu community of catechists, led by another European Jesuit, Fr Ignatius (Inhaxiô), the following year. Its members were vowed to celibacy and took a public vow to spend their lives spreading the gospel and helping priests. From the point of view of the local rulers, however, Christianity was the work of foreigners intent on alienating their subjects.

Andrew's community was in a province of the kingdom of Annam, and in July 1644 its royal representative, Mandarin Ong Nghe Bo, was ordered by the king to stop the spread of Christianity. Unaware of this, Fr de Rhodes had paid the mandarin a courtesy visit, but he was told that he had to leave the country and that any of the king's subjects embracing Christianity would receive severe penalties. The mandarin sent soldiers to arrest Fr Ignatius, who happened to be away from the community on a mission. Andrew offered himself in his place. He was seized, beaten, bound, and taken to the governor's palace.

On 25 July he was brought before the mandarin, who tried to make him "desist from that foolish opinion of his and give up the faith." Andrew replied that he was willing to undergo any suffering rather than abandon his faith, adding, "I wish I had a thousand lives to offer to God in thanksgiving for what he has done for me," for which he was taken away to prison. Many people came to visit him there to ask for his prayers, but he asked them to pray for him, that he might find the grace to be faithful to the end. The following day he was taken in public audience before the governor, who condemned him to death. He was led in procession to a field outside the city, followed by Fr de Rhodes, Portuguese and Vietnamese Christians, and many unconverted Vietnamese. He was repeatedly stabbed with a sharpened bamboo and finally beheaded with a scimitar. He was nineteen years old.

The news of Andrew's martyrdom spread rapidly, and his body was ceremoniously taken to Macao, the base for the evangelization of Vietnam. On the way, the ship was attacked by pirates and driven onto rocks, which tore a hole in its side. But, apparently miraculously, a large stone blocked the hole and it was able to proceed to Macao. The process for his beatification was begun just five months after his death but then made no progress until the Second Vatican Council (1962–1965), when the Vietnamese bishops asked Pope Paul VI to reopen it. Perhaps the concept of one native martyr, before any European missionaries had suffered in that country for their faith, was alien to Roman thinking, and his actual beatification had to wait for Pope John Paul II's declared intent to broaden the ethnic and geographical base of official sainthood. Andrew was finally beatified on 5 March 2000, one of the first group to be beatified in the twenty-first century. His biographer declared, "Andrew is our first martyr, and this is a great honour for all our catechists. The Holy See has recognized the good seed that led future generations to follow this good example." The bishop of My Tho, Bui van Doc, commented, "We have been waiting for his beatification for a long time; now, at last, we can celebrate him."

There is a biography by the Vietnamese Catholic poet and journalist Pham Dinh Khiem, *The First Witness* (Saigon, 1959). See *Butler*, February, pp. 22–8, for a general account of the Martyrs of Vietnam, with bibliography; *Oss.Rom.*, weekly English edn, 5 Mar. 2000. There are several entries on the web for the occasion of his beatification, some in Vietnamese, with English summary: www. vietcatholic.net. The Vatican news service (from which the above quotes are taken) attributes the delay in the process of his beatification to "historical and political reasons."

Bd George Preca, *Founder* (1880–1962)

This remarkable Maltese proponent of the apostolate of the laity was born in Valletta, the capital of Malta, on 12 February 1880, and baptized five days later, receiving the names George Paul Pius John Emmanuel. His father, Vincent Preca, was a businessman who later became a public health inspector; his mother, Nathalie Ceravolo, was a teacher. He was confirmed on 2 August 1888 in Hamrun, about five miles inland from Valletta, to where his family had moved, and went on to study at the Lyceum, the best public secondary school on Malta. From there he progressed to the major seminary, where he excelled in his studies, especially in Latin. After being ordained deacon, he collapsed, with only one lung functioning. An eminent doctor told his father not to bother with buying him vestments or a missal as he was bound to die soon. After praying to St Joseph, he made a sudden recovery.

George was ordained priest just before Christmas 1906 in the co-cathedral of St John. By then he had befriended a group of young men (whom he found loitering on the waterfront or in the city squares) and developed the idea of a Society made up of permanent deacons, young men chosen and instructed by him so that they in turn could go out and teach others. In March 1907 he rented a small house in Hamrun and began to put the concept into practice, having first received the approval of his confessor, Mgr Louis Attard. After resisting a temptation to become a Jesuit he began serious instruction of his young men, many of whom knew absolutely nothing about their supposed faith. He banished all married men and widowers from the group, which caused some offence, but he stuck to his decision. He initially called his Society the *Societas Papidum*, meaning "the pope's spiritual children," and under this name its members took part in the International Eucharistic Congress held in Malta in 1913. He called members "apostles," and they were soon spreading the word in their places of work. In his talks to them, which could last up to three hours, he dwelt on the Four Last Things and the imitation of Christ, drawing his inspiration mainly from the Bible (phrases from which he translated into Maltese, as no vernacular version existed) and Thomas à Kempis.

The idea of instructing the working classes was revolutionary at the time and soon drew the attention of the ecclesiastical authorities: this was before the days of Catholic Action, inaugurated under Pope Pius XI (1922–39), and fifty years before the Second Vatican Council. The vicar general, Mgr Vincent Grech, listened to various calumnies and eventually asked George to close down all his centres. He humbly accepted the verdict, but his parish priest persuaded Mgr Grech to rescind the decision, and the work went on. They adopted the acronym MUSEUM as their popular name, as precious things are found in museums. George devised a Latin motto to fit: *Magister, utinam sequator evangelium universus mundus* ("Master, that the whole world would follow the gospel!"). Secularism was making considerable inroads in Malta, taking advantage of an ignorant though nominally Catholic population. George's lay teachers became the best defence against this new ideology. They were often mocked, but they persevered.

Further ecclesiastical trials came in the person of a new bishop of Malta, Dom Maurus Caruana OSB, a monk of Fort Augustus, who again took note of gossip and summoned George to explain himself, appointing a commission to examine the activities of the Society in spring 1916. After a priest sent to one meeting had been so impressed by one of the members, who had been asked to speak on any topic he chose, the inquisition ceased. Mgr Enrico Bonnici, a close friend of George, eventually won round the recalcitrant bishop, who asked Bonnici to tell George to draw up a set of Rules. These were approved in 1932, and the bishop and the Society, officially called the Society of Christian Doctrine, together sang a solemn *Te Deum* in the cathedral to celebrate.

Centres were opened in nearly all the parishes of Malta. George began writing a series of spiritual works to impart a more solid formation to his members, several of which have subsequently been translated into English. He was never superior of the Society, never sought the limelight, never asked for statistics that might prove its success, and never wanted to be photographed: as he was fond of saying, in Italian, "*Il bene non fa chiasso e il chiasso no fa bene*" ("Good makes no noise and noise does no good"). But his teaching, in homilies and now books, remained the central inspiration. He spread cards bearing the words *Verbum Dei caro factum est*, believed to be a powerful talisman against temptation, all over Malta, and he began to acquire a reputation as a healer. He encouraged devotion to the Holy Trinity and to Mary, especially as Our Lady of Mount Carmel, becoming a Carmelite tertiary himself. He wrote endless letters of spiritual direction and became a much-sought-after confessor.

The early years of the Second World War saw Malta subjected to ferocious air raids, and the Society's activities were inevitably somewhat curtailed. By late 1942 conditions had improved; the Society's *Rule Book* was printed for the first time, and the first centre for boys was opened on the neighbouring island of Gozo. In 1952 the Church authorities, earlier so mistrustful of his work, appointed George a private chaplain to the pope, with the rank of Monsignor, to his considerable embarrassment. He continued to live in extremely simple and poor conditions—one of the members came to install electric light, which he had not bothered with, as late as 1958. In 1952 the Society began to expand overseas, in the wake of widespread emigration from Malta, with five members going to Australia.

As he grew older, George's strength visibly declined, but he continued to give open-air conferences. His condition worsened, and he received extreme unction on 21 July 1962. He was still reading the Gospels on 25 July, but died in the evening of the following day. Despite his desire for a simple burial, he was given a magnificent funeral, seemingly attended by most of the population of Malta, and his body was buried in a zinc-lined casket in the crypt of the motherhouse of the Society.

Initial proceedings in his cause began the following year, with the formal diocesan proceedings started in 1976 and completed in 1988. Pope John Paul II decreed him Venerable in June 1999 and beatified him, together with two other Maltese, Ignatius Falzon and Maria Adeodata Pisani, at the Floriana Granaries in Malta on 9 May 2001. In his homily, using the Maltese for "Fr George," *Dun Gorg*, the Pope compared his message to that of the Beatitudes and his example to that of Christ on the cross, forgiving everyone, and asked, "Is not this message of mutual respect and forgiveness especially needed today in Malta and in the world?" He also asked, "Was it not Dun Gorg's ability to communicate the freshness of the Christian message that made him the great apostle that he was?"

The above is based on a short biography posted on the web in English translation by Margaret Mortimer, OBE, *George Preca, His Life and Vision for the Laity* (1998), from the Maltese original published by the Society of Christian Doctrine (1965): www.geocities.com/dungorg.

28

St Pedro Poveda Castroverde, *Founder and Martyr*
(1874–1936)

The founder of the Teresian Association (as distinct from the Association of St Teresa started by María de las Maravillas, canonized with him; see 11 Dec.) was born in Linares, in the province of Jaén in south-eastern Spain, on 3 December 1874, into a solidly Christian family of modest means. He felt a call to become a priest at an early age and entered the diocesan seminary in Jaén in 1889, at the age of fifteen. Seminaries were fee-paying establishments, and when his father became ill and was forced to stop working, Pedro had to leave. The bishop of Guadix, in the province of Granada to the south, offered him a scholarship, and he moved to its seminary and was ordained on 17 April 1897.

He taught in the seminary for a while, then went to Seville for further studies, where he obtained a licentiate in theology in 1900, after which he returned to exercise a special ministry among the desperately poor cave-dwellers of Guadix, a town whose outskirts consist largely of caves cut out of clay hillocks. In three years of exhausting work Pedro built two schools for the children, and workshops where adults could acquire the skills needed if they were to secure employment, while at the same time concentrating on their Christian formation. This social and educational apostolate, at which he was evidently successful and in which he believed deeply, made him very popular among the cave-dwellers and earned the approval of the town council, who named a street after him. However, it outraged some of the more traditional Catholic lay people and clergy, who conspired to have him dismissed (glossed over as "being misunderstood" in the *Osservatore Romano* biography published on the occasion of his beatification).

Pedro left Guadix so as not to be a cause of further dissension, and was for a time unattached to any diocese. He was then "promoted" to the prestigious post of canon of the basilica at the shrine of the Virgin Mary, known as *La Santina*, in Covadonga, hidden away on the northern slopes of the Cantabrian Mountains of Asturias in the north-west, about as far from Guadix and his social apostolate there as it is possible to go in Spain. Most of the canons were old and retired, whereas he was thirty-two and very energetic. Covadonga had developed as a shrine and pilgrimage centre on the basis of being the place where the re-conquest of Spain from the Moors had originated, and Fr Poveda made it the springboard for a new sort of apostolate. His main area of concern was the type and quality of education available in Spain, and he began publishing a series of articles and pamphlets on the professional formation of teachers. In 1911 he opened a student residence in Oviedo, named the St Teresa of Avila Academy. Staffed with like-minded teachers concerned for the active presence of Christians in society, this became the starting point for the Teresian Association, dedicated to the spiritual and pastoral formation of teachers.

Education (or the lack of it) was a burning issue in Spain at the time. At the end of the nineteenth century 68 per cent of men and 79 per cent of women were illiterate—a striking illustration of failure by both providers, State and Church. The national mood of despair prompted by the loss of Spain's last colony, Cuba, in the 1898 war with the U.S.A. led the group of intellectuals known as the Generation of '98 to look to the provision of free, secular education as the mainspring of national regeneration. This movement gathered around the *Instituto Libre de Enseñanza* ("Free Institute of Teaching") founded by Francisco Giner de los Ríos, designed to be an antidote to the (fee-paying) schools run by the religious Orders, which were seen as both reactionary and ineffective. The Church did provide free basic schools for working-class children, but these were paid for by selling the products of their workshops, so they came to be seen as a threat by working people. Pedro sought to provide teachers trained to the same professional standards as those from the Free Institute, but committed to Catholic principles and to working in the State system. His Catholic principles included the promulgation of social justice as set out in Leo XIII's *Rerum Novarum*, for which his experiences in Guadix had shown him the need.

The early members of the Teresian Association were women involved in all levels of education, from elementary to the provision of higher education for women—this a daring innovation in Catholic circles at a time when "piety, duty, and domesticity remained the female cardinal virtues" (Lannon, p. 56). In 1912 Pedro joined the Apostolic Union of Secular Priests and began opening new teacher-training colleges and launching periodicals in the field of education. In the first of these, which bore the significant title *La Enseñanza moderna* ("Modern Teaching"), setting out his stand in the first editorial, he wrote: "What moves us, then? Love of culture. Where are we going? To awaken this in the people." He proposed the foundation of a Catholic Institute of Teaching to counter the Free Institute, but never managed to get this established.

In 1913 Pedro was appointed canon of Jaén Cathedral, with additional duties of teaching in the seminary and the teacher-training college, as well as becoming spiritual director of *Los operarios* (The workmen's) Catechetical Centre. In May 1914 he opened an *academia* (a hall of residence) for women graduates, where they could also receive help with their studies and religious formation, in Madrid. This was the first such institution in Spain and was soon replicated in other university cities. In 1921 he moved permanently to Madrid as royal chaplain. The following year he was made a member of the national board to combat illiteracy, and he was involved in all major educational discussions and initiatives throughout the 1920s.

The Teresian Association continued to grow and to spread its influence, and Pedro continued to devote as much time as could to it. He resigned as director but as founder still worked to consolidate its work, which spread to Chile and later to Italy. It received papal approval in 1924 and was granted the status of a Secular Institute in 1951.

Although his liberal-minded approach hardly made him an enemy of the people, Pedro was seen as such (on account of his prominent involvement in Catholic education) by revolutionary elements at the outbreak of the civil war in July 1936. Madrid was a Republican stronghold but, despite warnings from friends, he refused to move away from it. He was seized by militiamen just as he finished saying Mass in the chapel of the Teresian house on the morning of 27 July. He was taken for interrogation before a series of military tribunals throughout the day, and then vanished from sight. His body was found near the boundary wall of the East Cemetery the following morning. Apparently, when asked to identify himself, he had replied, "I am a priest of Christ." The scapular he was wearing shows the hole made by the bullet through the heart that killed him.

Pedro was beatified, together with a teacher member of the Teresian Association, Victoria Diez y Bustos de Molina, who was shot near Seville on 12 August 1936, on 10 October 1993. Pope John Paul II canonized him, with four other Spanish priests and religious, in Madrid's Plaza de Colón on 4 May 2003. In his homily, the Pope said of him that, "grasping the importance of the role of education in society, [he] undertook an important humanitarian and educational task among the marginalized and the needy ... convinced that Christians must bring essential values and commitment to building a world that is more just and mutually supportive."

Butler, July, pp. 230–3, with an account of Victoria Diez, who still awaits canonization, although there is little doubt of the reality of her martyrdom. Spanish sources are abundant, including "Pedro Poveda—una pedagogía para nuestro tiempo" in *Textos pedagógicos hispanoamericanos* (1986; cited in F. Lannon, *Privilege, Persecution and Prophecy: the Catholic Church in Spain 1875–1975*, p. 56); N. San Martín, *Historia de un hombre incómodo: Pedro Poveda* (n.d.); M.-D. Gómez Molleda, *Pedro Poveda, educador de educadores* (English translation *Pedro Poveda: A Biographical Essay*, 1993). His spiritual writings are published in Spanish: *Escritos espirituales* (1968); English selection in *Staunch Friends of God* (1997, Eng. trans. of Gómez Molleda, ed., *Amigos fuertes de Dios*); also Teresian Association, *A Christian Challenge: Extracts from the Writings of Pedro Poveda* (1985).

30

St Mary of Jesus Venegas de la Torre, *Founder* (1868–1959)

María Navidad Venegas de la Torre was born in a small village in the munici-
pality of Zapotlaneljo in the Mexican State of Jalisco. Her mother died when she
was still in her infancy and her father when she was nineteen, leaving her in the
care of one of his sisters. She felt strongly drawn to the religious life and as a
first step joined the Association of Daughters of Mary in 1898. In 1905 she was
advised by her spiritual director to follow a course of spiritual exercises in the
city of Guadalajara, and this inspired her to join a community of young women
dedicated to the care of the sick in the Hospital of the Sacred Heart.

María worked devotedly as a nurse, distinguished by her humility, charity, and
the cheerfulness with which she dealt with patients, co-workers, and the public
at large. She was appointed superior general of the community in 1921; she re-
named it the Sisters of the Sacred Heart of Jesus and wrote Constitutions. These
were approved in 1930 and it became an Institute recognized by the diocesan
Church. Maria made her solemn profession, taking the name Mary of Jesus in
the Sacrament (*María de Jesús Sacramentado*) in religion.

Her life continued without apparent outward incident, a steady progress of
service to the needy in the persons of the sick. She died peacefully on 30 July
1959, and the diocesan process for her beatification soon began. Pope John
Paul II beatified her in St Peter's Piazza on 22 November 1992 and canonized
her, after accepting the recovery of a man who had stopped breathing for ten
minutes under anaesthetic prior to an operation as a miracle due to her intercession, with Christopher Magallanes and other Mexican martyrs, on 21 May
2000.

31

Bd Zdenka Cecilia Schelingová, *Martyr* (1916–1955)

Cecilia was born in the village of Krivá, in the district of Orava in the Tatra
Mountains region of northern Slovakia, just a few miles from the Polish border.
Her parents, Pavol Schelingová and Zuzana Pániková, had ten children and
gave them all a sound Christian upbringing. She went to the local school
from the ages of six to fourteen and in 1929 came into contact with the Sisters
of Mercy of the Holy Cross, who established a house in the parish. She was

attracted to the discipline and devotion of their way of life, dedicated mainly to helping the sick, and in 1931 she and her mother went to the motherhouse of the Congregation to ask if she could join. They sent her first to nursing school, then on a specialist course in radiology, and allowed her to join their novitiate in 1936. She made her first vows on 30 January 1937, taking the name Zdenka in religion.

Zdenka proved a totally selfless and devoted religious, loving and compassionate to all, especially the hospital patients placed in her care at Humenné, in eastern Slovakia, her first hospital posting. In 1942 she was moved to the hospital in Bratislava, the capital, in the south-west of the region, and she worked there throughout the war and its aftermath of Russian occupation. She wrote:"From the altar of God I go to my work. I take up my duties in the ward. I am not afraid of anything; I seek to begin everything with joy. I can proclaim the Lord's message better by my example than by my words, just as we have to recognize Christ himself in the way he lived his life" (quoted on the Holy Cross Sisters website). The Communist coup of 1948 deprived the Catholic Church of all its rights and began systematic persecution. Those arrested who became sick were, however, treated in hospital, including priests. Zdenka learned that a certain priest, accused of being a Vatican spy (a fairly standard accusation needing no basis in fact), was due to be shipped to the *gulag* in Siberia, where he was certain to die. She put sleeping pills in his guard's tea and so enabled him to escape.

Becoming perhaps over-bold, she tried to help three more priests and three seminarians to escape but was discovered and arrested on 29 February 1952. She was interrogated and brutally tortured, suffering severe damage to her right breast from kicking by the police. Sentenced to twelve years' imprisonment, she was moved from one prison to another over the next three years. She developed a malignant tumour in the breast that had been damaged by the police, and the president of the Republic ordered her release so that she would not die in prison and be regarded as a martyr to the regime's brutality. But the Sisters at the Congregation's motherhouse in Bratislava refused to take her back, afraid of police surveillance and the possible consequence. Nor would the hospital where she had worked so devotedly admit her as a patient, again on account of police harassment. Finally a friend in Trnava (thirty-five miles north-east of Bratislava) took Zdenka to lodge with her and she was eventually admitted to hospital there.

She died on 31 July 1955, from breast cancer, but because the origin of this was at least associated with her treatment at the hands of the Communist regime and because she was not properly treated for the disease, she is regarded as a martyr. Interestingly, in 1970 the regional court in Bratislava, still nominally part of a repressive Communist regime but perhaps demonstrating nationalist resistance to the Russian occupation that followed the crushing of the"Prague Spring"of 1968 (or perhaps equally not wanting a martyr), reversed the sentence of high treason passed on her in 1952, declaring that the State police had manipulated the facts and had brought a false accusation, whereas she had acted from humanitarian motives. She was beatified in Bratislava on 14 September 2003, with Bishop Vasil' Hopko (see 23 July).

The Sisters of Mercy of the Holy Cross (or Holy Cross Sisters, or Ingenbohl Sisters) were founded in 1856 in Switzerland. They have expanded their original nursing mission to include teacher-training colleges and both boarding and free schools. They work in several European countries, the Far East, Africa, and the U.S.A., with headquarters at Merrill, Wisconsin: *Orders*, p. 286.

The photograph issued by the Vatican—evidently genuine and informal, unlike so many somewhat forbidding representations painted from photographs—shows a young woman with dark eyes, a retroussé nose, and a delightful, wide, slightly gap-toothed smile. It is easy to imagine her saying the words cited above.

AUGUST

1

Bd Maria Stella Mardosewicz and Ten Companions, *Martyrs* (1943)

These Sisters, also known collectively as the Martyrs of Nowogródek, were members of the Congregation of the Sisters of the Holy Family of Nazareth, founded in 1875 by Bd Frances (Franciszka) Siedliska, Mother Mary of Jesus the Good Shepherd in religion (beatified on 23 April 1989). She was Polish but made her first foundation in Rome—perhaps because Poland at the time was divided among Russia, Prussia, and Austria—with a first Polish foundation at Kraków in 1881. In 1885 half the Sisters there (eleven) were sent to the U.S.A. and founded a house in Chicago. In 1929 further Sisters from the foundation were invited by Bishop Zygmunt Kosiński to the small town of Nowogródek, then in north-eastern Poland, now in western Belarus (diocese of Hrodna, or Grodno), to start a small convent and school. The local people were mainly Protestants or Jews and tended to view the Sisters with some suspicion. From very humble beginnings, however, their mission prospered, and the convent grew to twelve Sisters, who gradually earned the respect and indeed affection of the locals, becoming known as "the Kneelers" from their attendance at the local Church of the Transfiguration.

When Nazi Germany invaded Poland on 1 September 1939, the Soviet Union retaliated by invading from the east, and Russian troops had occupied Nowogródek by the middle of the month. The Sisters were forced to disband (abandoning their convent and school), to wear secular clothing, and to depend for their needs on the kindness of the villagers, while continuing to perform what acts of charity they could as individuals. Two years later, the Nazis drove the Russians out and began rounding up and executing Jews and Communist sympathizers, although they allowed the Sisters back into their convent. Special Gestapo units were then based in nearby Baranowice and began more intense persecution, starting with Jews and Poles, especially priests. Sixty people were shot in July 1942. In spring 1943 the Sisters intensified their religious and charitable activities. Mass was said every morning in the Church of the Transfiguration, known as the "White Church," by the one priest the Gestapo seemed to have overlooked in the area, with exposition of the Blessed Sacrament and rosary every evening.

On 18 July a new wave of arrests threatened 120 factory workers with execution, and members of their families begged the Sisters to intercede. They prayed together and resolved to offer their own lives, asking that those with dependants might be spared. Sister Maria Stella declared, in the presence of the parish priest: "My God, if lives must be sacrificed, it is better that they should shoot us rather than those who have families. We pray that God may accept our offer." Their prayer was unexpectedly answered when most of the factory workers were transported to work camps in Germany instead of being shot, and some were even released. But the priest's life was still in danger, and the Sisters repeated their offer. On 31 July 1943 they were told to report to the Nazi commissariat at 7.30 in the evening. Unknown to them, the Gestapo had decided to kill all priests and religious figures without trial or warning. They were herded into a truck and taken out of the town to be shot. But the place they were being taken to could be seen by shepherds bringing in their flocks, and the Sisters were taken back and kept in a basement at Gestapo headquarters for the night. Very early in the morning eleven Sisters (the oldest, Sister Maria Malgorzata Banas, having been left behind) were taken to a place in the woods where a large grave had already been dug. They were ordered to kneel alongside it and were shot one by one, their bodies falling forward into the grave.

The eleven were:

Adelaide Mardosewicz, born on 14 December 1888 in present-day Belarus, professed in the Congregation in 1910, taking the name Maria Stella of the Most Holy Sacrament in religion. A teacher by training, she moved to Nowogródek in 1936 and acted as superior to the community during the war.

Jadwiga Karolina Zak, born on 29 December 1892 in Oświęim in the district of Auschwitz, professed in 1911 as Maria Imelda of Jesus of the Host. She worked as sacristan at the Church of the Transfiguration.

Anna Kukolowicz, born on 24 August 1892 near Vilnius in Lithuania, professed in 1918 as Maria Raimunda of Jesus and Mary, who joined the community in 1934. She seems to have been a simple soul and to have suffered badly from arthritis.

Eleonora Aniela Jóswik, born on 25 January 1895 in Poizdów in Poland, professed in 1920 as Maria Daniela of Jesus and Mary Immaculate, who went to Nowogródek in 1932. Also uneducated, she immersed herself in prayer and domestic service and was much loved by the schoolchildren.

Józefa Chrobot, born on 22 May 1896 at Raczyn, near Czêstochowa, professed in 1921 as Maria Kanuta of Jesus in the Garden of Gethsemane, after apparently being warned off marriage to her fiancé, Stanislaw, in a dream. She was the first to be sent to Nowogródek, in 1931, and worked in the convent kitchen.

Julia Rapiej, born on 18 August 1900 at Rogozyn, professed in 1922 as Maria Sergia of Our Lady of Sorrows. After her novitiate she was sent to Philadelphia, where the Order had a house and helped Polish immigrants. She returned to Europe despite warnings of a coming war, and went to Nowogródek in 1932, asking to do manual work, which she combined with a rich interior life.

Helena Cierpka, born on 11 April 1900 in Granowiec, professed in 1927 as Maria Gwidona of the Divine Mercy. She was sent to Nowogródek in 1936, after taking her final vows, and worked on the Sisters' farm. The locals remembered her as "a titan in work and prayer."

Paulina Borowik, born on 30 August 1905 at Rodno in the Lublin region, professed in 1932 as Maria Felicita. She was sent to Nowogródek after taking her first vows in 1935. Described as "shy as a sparrow," she was much loved by the other Sisters, but little is known of her.

Leokadia Matuszewska, born on 8 February 1906 at Stara Huta in the district of Wieck, professed in 1933 as Maria Heliodora, who also went to Nowogródek after taking her first vows in 1935. Described as always smiling, she carried out various functions and was adored by the schoolchildren.

Eugenia Mackiewicz, born on 27 September 1903 at Suwaski in the diocese of Komja, professed in 1933 (after having worked as a teacher) as Maria Kanizja. She went on teaching after taking her first vows in 1936, first in Kalisz and from 1938 in Nowogródek. For her, "The soul of a child has to be the most important thing." Even though she was nicknamed "Sister discipline," she was admired and respected by her pupils.

Weronika Narmontovicz, born on 18 December 1916 at Wiercieliszki in the region and diocese of Hrodna (Belarus), professed in 1936 as Maria Boromea, and sent to Nowogródek in August 1935. Uneducated, she was made to do the cleaning in the school after the Russians took it over; she then went back home at her parents' request, but wanted to "go back to the Sisters," which she soon did.

✤

Four of the eleven had taken temporary vows only, three of them being prevented by the war and occupation from taking permanent vows, while the youngest, Sister Maria Boromea, had taken her first vows only a month before the outbreak of war. As soon as she dared, Sister Maria Malgorzata found the grave, and after the war she was able to secure the bodies' re-burial in the graveyard of the Church of the Transfiguration, where they remain. The bishop of Hrodna has described their beatification as "the foundation stones on which the Church in Hrodna will rise up from spiritual ruin," referring to the decades after the Second World War when Belarus was part of the Soviet Union.

✤

Articles by T. Górska and Bishop A. Kaszkiewicz in *Oss.Rom.* 5 March 2000. The Sisters of the Holy Family of Nazareth opened a house in London in 1895, after the foundress had tried to start a Polish mission there the previous year. On 13 September 1994, the centenary of this attempt was marked by the proclamation of Bd Frances Siedliska as patron of Catholic Missions in England and Wales. There are currently some 1,600 Sisters working in thirteen countries.

8

Bd Bonifacia Rodríguez Castro, *Founder* (1837–1905)

One of many redoubtable women from Spain of this period who sought to offer a religious response to a particular social problem and were misunderstood and even persecuted for doing so, Bonifacia was the eldest of six children born to Juan Rodríguez and his wife Natalia Castro. She was born in Salamanca, the beautiful old university town 120 miles north-west of Madrid, on 6 June 1837. Her father was a tailor, and she grew up in an atmosphere combining home with work.

Bonifacia went to primary school and then learned cord-making, by which she was contributing to the family income by the time she was fifteen, when her father died; and so at an early age she came to know the long hours and low pay that characterized work done by women. In time she was able to start her own shop, selling cord-work, embroidery and dress accessories. She was fervently attached to two popular devotions of her time: to Mary Immaculate (following the declaration of the dogma of the Immaculate Conception in 1854) and to St Joseph (proclaimed patron of the universal Church in 1870), and she aimed to make the spirit of her workshop that of the Holy Family at Nazareth, as described in the Gospels of Matthew and Luke.

Four of her five siblings died young, and in 1865 the only surviving one, Agustina, married. Bonifacia and her mother intensified the piety of their lives, with daily visits to the nearby Jesuit church, the *Clerecía*. Their house-cum-shop and way of life attracted a number of young women who began to meet there regularly, and this group developed into the Association of the Immaculate and St Joseph, later called the Josephine Association, which formed an antidote to the attractions of street and city life. Bonifacia herself felt increasingly drawn to the religious life and planned to enter the Dominican convent of Santa María de Dueñas in Salamanca. But in 1870 a Catalan Jesuit, Fr Francisco Javier Butiña y Hospital, came to the Jesuit house in Salamanca. He was deeply concerned with the plight of manual workers and preached the sanctification of work. His views chimed deeply with Bonifacia, and she asked him to become her spiritual director. He steered her away from the idea of joining the Dominicans (old rivalries dying hard, perhaps), and proposed that she join him in founding a new Congregation for women, whose purpose would be the provision of work for women and the protection of women in the workplace. They would call it *Siervas de San José* ("Servants of St Joseph"). Six women, including Bonifacia's mother, began living in community in her house.

The bishop of Salamanca, another Catalan, Don Joaquín Lluch y Garriga, was immediately sympathetic to the project and signed the decree giving the community the status of a religious Institute on 7 January 1874. The idea of a religious community living in an actual place of work was a daring one at the time, and was bound to arouse opposition. The more traditional of the Salamanca clergy began to plot its downfall. Their opportunity came when the political upheavals in Spain following the Second Carlist War (with five short-lived presidents of the First Republic in 1873–1874, leading to the restoration of the monarchy with Alfonso XII, recalled from exile in 1874), produced an anticlerical swing and the exiling of the Jesuits, including Fr Butiña. The sympathetic bishop was also transferred to Barcleona, and Bonifacia found herself effectively in sole charge of the community. The new bishop appointed secular priests as directors, and they took it upon themselves to make the Sisters doubt the wisdom of their working way of life and of sheltering other women in their house. Bonifacia stuck to the original project and would not allow changes.

Fr Butiña returned from exile to Catalonia and founded other houses of the Servants of St Joseph there. Bonifacia went to visit these in 1882, and the clerical directors took advantage of her absence to remove her as superior. She accepted this with Christ-like humility and suggested that a solution might be found if she were to start a new house in Zamora, thirty miles to the north. The bishop agreed, and in July 1883 Bonifacia and her mother moved to Zamora to re-create the "House of Nazareth" pattern of life there, while the rest of the community began to turn the original foundation into something clerical, conventional, and alien to the founding spirit. The directors modified the Constitutions, sending the new version to Rome for papal approval; this resulted in Pope Leo XIII (presumably more misled than malicious) granting this approval with the specific exclusion of the house in Zamora. Bonifacia tried to get an explanation from the bishop of Salamanca and, when none was forthcoming, journeyed there to talk to her Sisters, only to receive the response that they had been told not to receive her. Humiliated, she returned to Zamora vowing never to set foot in Salamanca again, but she told no one, and the facts of what had happened emerged only after her death. She said to the Sisters in Zamora that unity would be established only after her death, as proved to be the case. She died in Zamora on 8 August 1905, and the house there was re-incorporated into the Congregation on 23 January 1907.

Bonifacia was beatified on 9 November 2003. Pope John Paul II in his homily made no mention of her treatment at the hands of senior clergy, from the pope of the time down, but praised her for questioning the values of a market-driven society and setting protection of "the person beginning with his or her social condition or work" above the temptation to "turn everything into commodity and profit." "In the simple and protected life of the Holy Family of Nazareth," he continued, "she discovered a model of the spirituality of work that gives the human person dignity and makes every activity, however little it may seem, an offering to God and a means of sanctification." All of which is true, but seems to leave out of account other things she was obliged to "offer up."

13

Bd Mark of Aviano (1631–1699)

Carlo Domenico Cristofori was born in the town of Aviano in what is now the Friuli-Venezia Giulia region of north-eastern Italy. He was initially educated at home and then sent to the Jesuit school in Gorizia (to the east, now on the border with Slovenia). When he was sixteen he decided he wanted to be a martyr in the war between Venice and the Ottoman Turks and set off on foot, intending to reach the island of Crete. After a few days march down the eastern coast of the Adriatic he was taken in by the Capuchin friars in Capodistria, who let him rest, fed him, and advised him to return home.

The deep impression the friars left on him inspired Carlo to seek entry to the Order, and he became a novice at Conegliano Veneto in 1648, making his formal vows a year later, when he took the name Mark in religion, to which the friars added the town of his birth. He was ordained in Chiogga (at the southern end of the Venice Lagoon) in 1655 and lived a cloistered life until he was called to preach missions in 1664. He spent eight years travelling all over Italy. He was then elected superior, at Belluno (in the foothills of the Alps, due north of Venice) in 1672 and Oderzo (to the south-east, half-way to the coast) in 1674. He suddenly became famous when, while preaching a mission in Padua, he prayed over a nun who had been bed-ridden for thirteen years, Sister Vincenza Francesconi, who made an immediate recovery. From then on, those who listened to his preaching also sought miracles of healing. From being regarded as something of a peasant Mark became a celebrity acceptable to everyone: judged unworthy to preach to the "polite and cultured citizens of a city such as Udine" when he began a mission there, he left these same polite and cultured people demolishing the pulpit from which he had spoken for relics when he had finished.

Mark was appointed papal legate and apostolic nuncio to Austria and became the trusted counsellor on both religious and political affairs to the Holy Roman emperor, Leopold I (1640–1705; emperor from 1658 to his death). In 1683 the Ottoman Turks, who occupied the Balkans and large parts of central

Europe, were threatening to take Vienna itself. One hundred thousand troops under the command of the grand vizier Kara Mustafà had besieged the city from July to September, while Pope Innocent XI tried to persuade European monarchs to unite in a new Crusade—undermined by Louis XIV of France and quarrels over who should assume supreme command. Mark supported the Polish king John Sobieski (1629–1696; commander-in-chief of the Polish-Lithuanian armies from 1668, elected king in 1674), and his spiritual authority carried the day. He blessed the army at a morning Mass on 12 September, and by evening the Turkish army had been routed by a force half its size. Two days later Mark intoned a solemn *Te Deum* in St Stephen's Cathedral, while Sobieski sent a message back to the pope: "*Veni, vidi, Deus vincit*" ("I came, I saw, God conquered")—infuriating Leopold. Mark continued to cajole and inspire the pious but irresolute Leopold, becoming the chief architect of the Holy League (the Empire, Poland-Lithuania, and Venice, later joined by Russia) against the Turks and negotiating the liberation of Buda in September 1686 and of Belgrade two years later. He achieved this by acting as a peacemaker among the Catholic powers of Europe. The treaty of Karlowitz in 1699 between the League and the Turks secured the freedom of Austria, Hungary, Transylvania, Slovenia, Croatia, and parts of Serbia and Vallacchia from Ottoman occupation.

Shortly after this seal on his diplomatic efforts, the pope recalled Mark to Vienna to preach yet another mission, even though he was by now in poor health. He died there of cancer on 13 August 1699, with the emperor, who owed him so much, at his bedside. In many ways Mark had seemed the monarch and statesman and Leopold, educated for the priesthood, the religious: but Mark was always conscious of being simply an instrument in God's hands and never sought any glory for himself, continually pointing out that even the cures hailed as miracles in fact sprang from the patient's deep repentance. His involvement in public affairs came about through his unquestioning obedience to the Holy See, and he preached repentance to monarchs as the way to victory (because the advance of the Turks was generally seen as a result of the sins of Christian nations). Convinced of the righteousness of the "crusade" against the Muslim Turks, he nevertheless counselled rigorous self-discipline on the part of Christian soldiers, extending to humane treatment of prisoners of war.

The instructive process for Mark's beatification was begun in 1891, but it was to be a further 112 years before it took place. When it did, on 27 April 2003, a month after the American-led occupation of Iraq, it was perhaps inevitable that some politicians (notably of the Northern League in Italy) should seize on him as an anti-Muslim champion, but the timing in relation to the invasion can only have been a coincidence. (Although Pope John Paul II appeared to lend some support to this view by quoting Sobieski's "I came, I saw, God conquered" to Poles attending the beatification ceremony—Poland being the only Catholic European country in which the majority of Catholics supported the war.) Nevertheless the question of why he was beatified then—the "odd one out" in a group of mainly nineteenth-century "social" pioneers—can legitimately be asked. A more likely context is the Vatican's desire to see "Europe's Christian roots" enshrined in the new European Constitution then under discussion in draft form, a policy many saw (and see) as a cover for a desire to exclude Turkey from eventual accession to the European Union. The Pope effectively said as much in his homily at the beatification ceremony: "Blessed Mark of Aviano reminds the European continent, opening up in these years to new prospects of cooperation, that its unity will be sounder if it is based on its common Christian roots" (the last clause italicized in the Vatican version).

A thorough biography by M. Heyret, German original with Italian translation, produced for the "instruction" of the cause of his beatification, argues the supremacy of "the man of God" over the brilliant strategist or "thaumaturge of the century" in his character. E. Feigl, *Mezzaluna e croce. Marco d'Aviano e la salvezza d'Europa* (Ital. trans. of German original) provides a more right-wing political view. There are reflections on this and other aspects of the beatification in a series of articles from the *Messaggero Veneto* at www.friulicrea.it/itstories/story. Encyclopedia articles on John Sobieski, Leopold I, and Innocent XI are readily accessible.

It is said that when the Turks fled from Vienna they left behind ample supplies of strong, bitter Turkish coffee. The Christians made this palatable to their taste by adding honey and milk and called the resulting brown beverage after the Capuchin habit worn by Mark of Aviano, thus instituting *cappuccino*.

20

St Maria de Mattias, *Founder* (1805–1866)

Maria was born on 4 February 1805 and baptized the same day. Her birthplace was a small town named Vallecorsa, then at the southernmost extreme of the Papal States, in a mountainous region about half-way between Rome and Naples. The setting and its recent history had a considerable influence on her life. She was the second surviving child of Giovanni de Mattias and his second wife, Ottavia de Angelis, who had seven children, of whom the three preceding Maria died in childhood, leaving her with a sister, Vincenza, eleven years older, and two younger brothers, Michele and Antonio. The family were relatively wealthy and cultured, but in the region and the period it was not considered suitable for girls to receive a formal education. Maria learned her faith and much about the scriptures from her father talking and reading to her. She was confirmed at the age of ten and made her First Communion a year later.

Maria grew up in a period of turmoil following Napoleon's seizure of the Papal States, deportation of Pope Pius VII, and harsh measures against the Italian clergy, who were forced to sign an oath of allegiance to Napoleon and abjure their allegiance to the Holy See. Combined with the continual warring between the various States that made up Italy—Vallecorsa was virtually on the border of the Papal States and the Kingdom of the Two Sicilies—law, order, and organized religion virtually collapsed from 1810 to 1825. Maria's surroundings were bandit country, with young men from defeated armies or hiding from conscription joining others driven to kidnapping and extortion by lack of work in the plentiful caves, and preying on the local population. Girls from wealthy families were not safe, and Maria was largely confined to the house. She developed—not surprisingly—into a bored and self-absorbed adolescent, much given to admiring herself in the mirror.

One day, when she was about sixteen, Maria looked from the mirror to an image of the Virgin nearby and heard a voice say, "Come to me." Her outlook changed, and she began to pray and also taught herself to read, devouring works of spirituality. But she was still alone and realized that she remained as focused on her own piety as she had previously been on her looks.

She found the guidance she was inwardly seeking when a "Precious Blood Mission" was preached in Vallecorsa in Lent 1822, lasting three weeks. Missions were proving the most successful way of re-evangelizing Italy, and several religious Orders were making them their speciality. The Society of the Precious Blood was one of these, founded in Rome by Gaspare del Bufalo (canonized in 1954; 28 Dec.), a priest who had been exiled from Rome and imprisoned in various Italian towns during the four years of Napoleon's rule. With a friend, Fr Francesco Albertini (now Venerable), who had started a Confraternity dedicated to the Precious Blood, Gaspare used his time in prison to plan how he would help to restore the Church after his release. He returned to Rome after Napoleon's downfall and asked the restored Pius VII what he should do. Pius told him to preach missions aimed at restoring religion and morality, and Gaspare opened the first mission house in 1815. He himself led the mission to Vallecorsa, with which Maria became totally involved. Missions usually employed terror tactics first, with sermons on sin, judgment, hell, and the need for repentance, followed by reassurance of God's love and mercy, Mary's compassion, and heaven. Maria was duly first terrified into sleepless nights and then comforted and inspired to help spread the message of conversion and salvation.

The townspeople, in the flush of enthusiasm resulting from the mission, wanted to establish a permanent house for Precious Blood missioners in the town, but there were all sorts of problems connected with the ongoing political instability, and outright opposition from anticlericals and Freemasons. When Maria's father was deposed as mayor and imprisoned, the way forward became even more difficult. Gaspare del Bufalo returned to preach part of the Lent mission the following year, and in 1824 he sent a dynamic young priest, Giovanni Merlini, to preach the mission, establish a series of associations, and finally set about establishing a house. Maria felt attracted by him—worrying that this might be for the wrong reasons—and eventually approached him, found that she could relate easily to him, and became involved in the association for girls, the Daughters of Mary, of which Merlini soon put her in charge. She began to gather young women to her family house on Sunday afternoons; they would pray together and carry out devotions, then she found she could speak to them directly and instruct them. Merlini began to see her as someone who could lead the projected female branch of the Society of the Precious Blood, which del Bufalo and Albertini had planned in some detail when imprisoned together in 1811.

Conditions in Vallecorsa, however, remained too disturbed for a settled community to be possible. Another Congregation, the *Maestre Pie* ("Pious Teachers"), did manage to open a school for girls there in 1827, and Merlini suggested that Maria might join them for a time. She lived with them in community for three years. Then plans were made to send her to start a Precious Blood house in Norcia (St Benedict's Nursia), where the bishop was one of the missioners and had been one of del Bufalo's earliest collaborators. But this too came to nothing, and Maria began to wonder if she should abandon the idea and join an established enclosed community. Del Bufalo dissuaded her, telling her that she could find holiness anywhere and that convent prayers were not the only means of saving souls. Toward the end of 1833, Bishop Giuseppe Maria Lais of Agnani invited her to start a school in Acuto, thirty miles north-west of Vallecorsa.

Armed with the plans made by del Bufalo and Albertini (embodied in a document they had drawn up and called the "Fundamental Articles"), Maria planned much more than a school. This would be a mission house run by women for women; it would have a boarding school at its core to train future teachers (and to bring in revenue) but would also be a retreat house and provide educational and devotional opportunities for older women. She opened the school and founded the Institute, named the Sisters Adorers of the Precious Blood, on 4 March 1834. The community way of life was to combine adoration with apostleship: she daringly encouraged her Sisters to receive Communion daily, and began and ended the day with periods of meditation. They had not taken any formal vows or taken the missioners' oath of fidelity, and twenty years elapsed before they finally decided what sort of religious community they should be. In the meantime, the inhabitants of Acuto flocked to instruction and devotions, and the initiative became famous throughout the region.

Mayors of towns and bishops asked Maria to send them teachers, and as girls left the school in Acuto they spread into other areas and formed new communities. In many villages there was no resident priest and so her Sisters became the only source of instruction and devotional life for the people. Maria travelled as much as her health and duties in Acuto and Rome allowed her: she taught crowds of hundreds from balconies and standing on tables in town squares. She found herself rather enjoying the praise and popularity and expressed scruples about this to Merlini, who continued to be her spiritual adviser, but he told that her that the joy she felt was part of God's will for her.

Despite poor health, with recurrent fevers and asthma attacks, Maria expanded the Institute steadily for the next thirty years, contending with permanent shortage of funds, anticlericalism in some areas of society, and envious rivalry from some women who sought to join her or emulate her—not to mention being called a "would-be priest" by the archpriest of Acuto and having Paul's ban on women teaching (1 Tim. 2:12) thrown at her by at least one bishop. She finally wrote the Rule and Constitutions for the Congregation in 1857.

She died in Rome on 20 August 1866, at the age of sixty-one, by which time there were over fifty Precious Blood schools in Italy, including two in Rome opened at the specific request of Pope Pius IX (beatified in 2000; see 7 Feb.), and foundations in Austria, England, and Germany. The Society petitioned Pius for permission to inter her body in their mother church of Santa Maria in Trevio, but there was a ban on burials inside churches for reasons of hygiene, and Pius refused. Instead, he himself purchased a tomb for her in the Verano cemetery and commissioned a bas-relief to be carved on it, depicting the vision of Ezekiel: "Dry bones, hear the word of the Lord," as she had brought the word to the deprived areas of central Italy.

The process for Maria's beatification began in the 1890s, and Pope Pius XII beatified her on 1 October 1950. Pope John Paul II canonized her with three others on 18 May 2003. She had in several ways anticipated the Church of the Second Vatican Council: she fostered lay auxiliaries and invited them to pray with the Sisters; she saw women's potential as spreaders of the word (despite St Paul and the bishop); and her devotion to the "precious blood" stressed an element now available to all in Eucharistic Communion, although not in her time. In her 1857 Constitutions she called on her community to be "patterned and shaped into a living image of that divine charity with which this divine blood was shed and of which it is the sign, expression, measure, and pledge."

The above is based largely on the Eternal Word Television Network account at www.ewtn.com/library/MARY/MATTIAS, which gives details of studies, conference papers, and translation of her letters, as well as prayers and readings for her feast day, liturgically observed on the anniversary of her birth, 4 Feb. Fr Merlini (now Venerable, who outlived her) wrote a "Compendium" of her life. *Butler*, August, p. 204, citing the official life by M. E. Pietromarchi produced at the time of her beatification (1950). On the Sisters Adorers and Society of the Precious Blood see *Orders*, pp. 340–1; on St Gaspar(e) del Bufalo, *Butler*, December, pp. 221–3, with bibliography.

25

Bd María del Tránsito Cabanillas, *Founder* (1821–1885)

The daughter of a wealthy family living on a large estate in the province of Córdoba in central Argentina, María del Tránsito (referring to the "transit" or "passing"—she is also called María del Paso—of the Virgin into heaven, and so the Assumption, the feast of which was her birthday) Eugenia de los Dolores (to complete her baptismal names) was the third of eleven children, of whom three died in infancy, three became nuns, four married, and one became a priest. Her father, Felipe Cabanillas Toranzo, came from a family that had emigrated from Valencia in the seventeenth century and amassed a fortune in the New World. Her mother was born Francisca Antonia Luján Sánchez, the family names also indicating distinguished Spanish forebears. The family managed to combine its wealth with deep piety.

She received her early schooling at home and was then sent to Córdoba, capital of the central Argentine province, a city with a university founded by Franciscans in the seventeenth century. She combined her studies with looking after her younger brother, who was at the seminary of Our Lady of Loreto there, until he was ordained in 1853. By then her father had died (in 1850) and her mother with the rest of the family had moved into Córdoba. María lived in the family home, near the church of San Roque, helping her mother with the care of the younger children (as well as five orphaned cousins who had moved in with the family) and also working as a catechist and, with her cousin Rosario, visiting the poor and sick of the city.

María's mother died in 1858 and she was guided by her confessor, the Franciscan Fr Buenaventura Rizo Patrón, to become a Franciscan Tertiary. Her wish was to progress further towards total dedication of her life to God, so she took a private vow of virginity and contemplated founding a religious Institute to care for poor and abandoned children. A meeting with a certain Sra Isidora Ponce de León, however, steered her in another direction, as this lady was involved in establishing a Carmelite convent in Buenos Aires. This was inaugurated in March 1873, and Isidora and María entered as its first postulants. The arduous Carmelite routine proved too much for her health, and she had to leave the convent the following year. After six months of recuperation, María entered the convent of the Visitandine Sisters (founded by St Jane Frances de Chantal; 12 Dec.), but this again proved too hard for her and she had to leave.

Accepting these reversals with resignation, she returned to her concept of an

Institute to provide a religious education for poor children. She was encouraged by several Franciscans, one of whom gave her a house in which to start the venture. She obtained ecclesiastical approval for the foundation and on 8 December 1878, with two companions, Teresa Fronteras and Brigida Moyano, she became one of the first members of the Franciscan Tertiary Missionaries of Argentina, which was dedicated to helping poor, orphaned, and abandoned children. María asked a Franciscan priest, Fr Ciríaco Porreca, to be its spiritual director. The three women made their religious profession in February 1879 (when María added "de Jesús Sacramentado"—"of Jesus in the Sacrament"—to her already lengthy name), and in 1880 the Congregation was accepted by the minister general as part of the Franciscan family. It flourished from the start, and within five years had opened schools in three other provinces. María guided it wisely in its early years, but the work placed an increasing physical strain on her, and she died on 25 August 1885.

She was declared Venerable by Pope John Paul II on 28 June 1999 and beatified by him on 14 April 2002, together with her compatriot Artemide Zatti and the "social apostle of Costa Rica," María Romero Meneses. She was the first Argentinian woman to be beatified. The Pope said of her in his homily: "The flame that burned in her heart brought María del Tránsito to seek intimacy with Christ in the contemplative life ... The Franciscan ideal then appeared as the true way God wanted for her, and ... she undertook a life of poverty, humility, patience and charity, giving rise to a new religious family."

The *Terciarias Misioneras Franciscanas de Argentina* are members of ICF–TOR, the International Franciscan Conference–Third Order Regular. They may be contacted at tercmisfcanas@hotmail.com. Their current (2004) provincial superior, Sr Isabel Gonzales Alonso, demonstrated the Congregation's continued commitment to the poor by signing an "Interfaith letter" from hundreds of national and local religious leaders delivered to the G8 summit on 8 June 2004, pressing for the cancellation of Third World debt. On the background see E. Dussel, "The Church and Emergent Nation States" and M. Salinas, "The Church in the Southern Cone," in E. Dussel (ed.), *The Church in Latin America; 1492–1992* (1992), pp. 117–38, 295–309.

27

Bd María Pilar Izquierdo Albero, *Founder* (1906–1945)

Born into a poor family in Zaragoza, capital of the province of the same name in the region of Aragón in north-eastern Spain, she was named after the famous Virgin of the Pillar, whose shrine is near Zaragoza. (The devotion is based on a legend that St James—the Greater, patron saint of Spain and inspiration of the Reconquest from the Moors; 25 July—saw a vision of Mary carrying the infant Christ while angels came behind carrying a pillar. Mary asked for a church to be built on the site.) Her health was poor as a child, obliging her to spend four years in a clinic, after which she worked in a shoe factory in Zaragoza to contribute to the family income.

When María was twenty she fell off a tram on her return journey from work one day and fractured her pelvis. The following year she suffered an outbreak of cysts that paralysed her and rendered her blind. She accepted all this as bringing her closer to the sufferings of Jesus. For nearly ten years she had to divide her time between hospital and home. Visitors found her inspiring and a source of good counsel.

The Spanish civil war broke out in July 1936, and she began to speak of "work of Jesus" aimed at reproducing his active life on earth "through works of mercy." Just after the end of the war, on the feast of the Immaculate Conception, 8 December 1939, she had an inexplicable remission of her paralysis and blindness. This enabled her to seek to put her vision of a new "work of mercy" into effect. She gathered a group of young people and went to Madrid to establish an apostolate to the poor. She initially called the group "Missionaries of Jesus and Mary" and received the official approval of the bishop of Madrid. She then—like virtually all women founders—encountered major difficulties, which led the bishop to withdraw his approval and ask for the venture to be discontinued, forbidding her from carrying out any sort of apostolate for a period of years. In 1942, when the ban was lifted, she renewed the work in a different form, under the name of Pious Union of Missionaries of Jesus, Mary, and Joseph. This was once again canonically approved by the bishop. The group carried out a fruitful apostolate in the poor quarters on the outskirts of Madrid for two years, but María then fell ill. She also suffered the usual jealousies and calumnies from some of her Sisters and was forced to withdraw from her own Congregation. Nine of the Sisters followed her.

María died in San Sebastián (on the Basque north coast of Spain) on 27 August 1945, at the age of thirty-nine. Three years after her death the Congregation re-formed for a third time under the name of *Obra misionera de*

Jesús y María ("Missionary Work of Jesus and Mary") and received a third and final form of canonical approval. They still carry on an apostolate to the poor in Spain. María Pilar was beatified with seven others on 4 November 2002. In his homily the Pope spoke of her suffering, "constant and not just physical … as she was busy doing all for the love of Him who first loved us and suffered for our salvation." He defined "love for God, for the cross of Jesus, for her neighbour in need" as "the great concerns of [her] life."

❖

A photograph on www.newsaints.faithweb.com/year/1945 shows a strong, pleasant, squarish face with no trace of any damage from the cysts that caused her blindness. Further information from Obra misionera de Jesús y María, Avda de la Paz 100, 26004 Logroño, Spain.

29

Bd Santia Szymkowiak (1910–1942)

Born on 11 July 1910 in the village of Mozdzanów near Ostrów Wielkopolski in the province of Kalisz in south-central Poland, the youngest of five children of Augustine Szymkowiak and Mary Duchalska was christened Giannina. The family was both devout and wealthy, and she, the only girl, received a good education, with high school followed by a degree course in foreign languages and literature at the university of Poznan, the regional capital, some seventy miles to the north-west of Ostrów Wielkopolski. As a pupil at school she had joined the Sodality of Mary and was noted for her outgoing nature and charity to the poor.

Giannina felt a call to the religious life from an early age, and on a pilgrimage to Lourdes in the summer of 1934 she privately dedicated her life to total service to the Blessed Virgin. She spent a year in the convent of the Oblate Sisters of the Sacred Heart at Montluçon, and on her return to Poland she joined the Congregation of the Daughters of Our Lady of Sorrows, or "Seraphic Sisters," taking the names Mary Santia (Sancja). She was determined to become a saint: "Jesus wants me to be a holy religious, and He will not be happy with me until I use all my strength for Him and become a saint … I have to become a saint at all costs. This is my constant preoccupation," she wrote in her diary, with youthful enthusiasm and self-confidence.

Maria Santia made her first vows on 30 July 1938 and worked in a nursery school in Poznan for a year, also beginning a course of pharmacology. War broke out in September 1939, and Poznan was in the path of the immediate Nazi invasion. The Sisters were placed under house arrest and obliged to look after a

German garrison of some hundred soldiers as well as, later, English and French prisoners of war. Her foreign language studies made her a useful interpreter for these prisoners, who came to call her "Saint Santia" and an "angel of goodness." She was offered a chance to return to her family when religious persecution intensified in February 1940, but saw it as God's will that she should stay in the convent and minister to Sisters, soldiers, and prisoners alike.

The constant hard work took its toll of her health, and she developed tuberculosis. She was able to make her solemn vows on 6 July 1942 but died on 29 August, aged thirty-two. At her beatification ceremony on 18 August 2002 in Kraków, which she shared with a Polish archbishop and two priests, Pope John Paul II, who made mercy the common theme linking the four, said of her that, "having embraced the religious life, she devoted herself to the service of others with greater fervour. She accepted the difficult times of the Nazi occupation as an occasion to give herself completely to the needy."

SEPTEMBER

5

Bd Teresa of Calcutta, *Founder* (1910–1997)

The diminutive nun known to the world as Mother Teresa was Albanian by birth, born in the city of Skopje: fought over down the centuries, this was part of Serbia at the time she was born and is now in the Former Yugoslav Republic of Macedonia. Born on 26 August 1910, she was the youngest of three children of Nikola and Drane Bojaxhiu and christened Agnes (though known in the family by her nickname, Gonxha). The family was prosperous; her father travelled extensively selling luxury goods, and brought back lavish presents for the children. She made her First Communion before she was six and was confirmed a year later. Her father died suddenly when she was eight, leaving her mother to bring up the children in straitened financial circumstances. The parish in which they lived was run by Jesuits and dedicated to the Sacred Heart, both of which had an effect on Gonxha's religious evolution.

At the age of eighteen she felt called to be a missionary and left her native country to join the Irish branch of the Institute of the Blessed Virgin Mary, or Loreto Sisters (founded in 1822 to provide higher education for girls in Ireland). She took the name Mary Teresa, after St Thérèse of Lisieux (1 Oct.), who had been canonized in 1925 and in 1927 been proclaimed a principal patron of all missionaries. (All IBVM Sisters take Mary as a first name but are generally known by the second name they add to this, so from then on she was Sr Teresa.) She was sent on the Indian mission in December 1928, arriving in Calcutta on 6 January 1929 and travelling by train to the convent at Darjeeling (in the extreme north of West Bengal, near the eastern end of Nepal—a long and sometimes hair-raising journey, finally involving a narrow-gauge railway looping back over itself to make the ascent). Teresa made her first profession there in May 1931, after which she joined the Loreto community at Entally in Calcutta and taught at St Mary's School for Girls. She made her final profession on 24 May 1937, becoming Mother Teresa. In 1944 she was appointed principal of St Mary's, in which role she was noted for her hard work and organizational ability, coupled with obvious love for the other Sisters and for her students.

Her twenty years with the Loreto Sisters were happy and productive, but Teresa then felt called to something different. She first felt this on 10 September

1946, when she was again travelling by train from Calcutta to Darjeeling to make her annual retreat. She received—directly from Jesus, she said, though in a way she could never explain—what she described as "a call within a call," an effective summons to dedicate her life to the poorest of the poor, at that time beyond the reach of Christian evangelization in India and, owing to the Indian caste system, beyond the concern of anyone else. The next few months brought Teresa a series of more detailed "instructions" from Jesus, including the foundation of a new religious Congregation to be called Missionaries of Charity. She spent two years seeking approval for the new foundation: there was lengthy ecclesiastical debate over whether she had to be "secularized" to leave the Loreto Sisters, in which case she would no longer be a religious subject to vows, or whether she could merely be dispensed from her vow of enclosure, as she wished. A decision for the latter course came in August 1948, when she left the Loreto Sisters and donned the white sari with blue borders that was to make her Sisters recognizable everywhere.

She studied medical care on a short course with the American Medical Mission Sisters at Patna (on the Ganges in the north-eastern State of Bihar) and then returned to Calcutta, where she lodged temporarily with the Little Sisters of the Poor in their convent on Lower Circular Road. She began tending the sick and destitute in the slum area of Motijil on 21 December 1948, starting a daily routine of ministering on the spot to those she found in most need, in the streets or in their houses, seeking out "the unwanted, the unloved, the uncared for," starting a small school under a tree (the school continues, though the tree has gone), and collecting surplus food from wealthy families at the end of the day to give to poor ones. Gradually, starting on the feast of St Joseph in 1949, numbers of her former students from St Mary's came to join her, and her family of Missionaries of Charity started its phenomenal growth.

Teresa asked the city authorities for a building that would serve as a hospice for the dying destitute and was given a former pilgrim hostel for the nearby shrine of Kali. She named it Nirmal Hriday, meaning "Place of the Pure Heart." She also opened a home for children, named Shishu Bavan. The Congregation of Missionaries of Charity was first officially established in the archdiocese of Calcutta in October 1950. By the early 1960s it had spread to other parts of India. In February 1965 it received provisional Vatican approval in the shape of a "Decree of Praise" from Pope Paul VI, which encouraged Mother Teresa to open her first house outside India, in Venezuela. The next foundations were in Rome and Tanzania, and then the Sisters spread to every continent.

Teresa decided that there were needs that could best be met by men and so founded the Missionaries of Charity Brothers in 1963. Then she felt that the active missionaries should be backed by powerhouses of prayer, leading to a contemplative branch of the Sisters in 1976 and of the Brothers in 1979. This was followed by the addition of a Congregation of priests, the Missionaries of Charity Fathers. (These last three initiatives never in fact involved large numbers.) From there she spread the net to embrace non-consecrated lay people, with the Co-Workers of Mother Teresa and the Sick and Suffering Co-Workers. These reached beyond the Catholic Church and beyond Christianity itself, forming a network of prayer and practical support in the form of collection of goods and money, stretching virtually around the globe. Lay people who wished to dedicate themselves more formally could join a sort of Third Order, the Lay Missionaries of Charity, and then in 1981 the Corpus Christi movement enabled priests who wished to share in the spirit of her movement but were committed to other Orders or their dioceses to do so.

In purely organizational terms it was a considerable achievement; in wider terms it can perhaps be seen as a significant contribution to the re-evangelizing of the secularized West by the developing world. Seen in a different light, the whole endeavour can look like a new and expanded version of the myriad charitable foundations made by so many other "strong women," and not a few men, in the nineteenth century (to which so many entries in this work bear witness). Teresa certainly made use of the rapid travel and communications media of the second half of the twentieth century, being photographed with monarchs, presidents, and other heads of State, everywhere and continually, besides, of course, Church leaders, particularly Pope John Paul II, whose "ideal woman" she represented and whom she visited for the last time during the last few weeks of her life. Her diminutive figure and strong aquiline features are likely to remain one the most iconic images of an image-conscious century. Prince Charles visited her in Calcutta in 1980; Presidents Reagan and Bush, Sr, both received her at the White House; Senator Edward Kennedy went to see her in Bangladesh; Queen Elizabeth II presented her with an honorary Order of Merit in 1982; Pope John Paul II visited Nirmal Hriday in 1986; Princess Diana visited her in Rome in 1992, when she was recovering from a serious bout of pneumonia. Her work was recognized by the world community in the awards of a number of prestigious prizes, including the first Templeton Prize for Progress in Religion, presented by Prince Philip in the London Guildhall in 1973, and culminating in the Nobel Peace Prize in 1979.

In other ways Teresa turned her back on the spirit of the times (which may have contributed to her vast popularity), and she has certainly been criticized, by liberation theologians and others, for not using her undoubted prestige and influence to address the fundamental wrongs of society—"Tough on poverty but not on the causes of poverty," in current (British) political jargon—and for refusing to provide medical care but simply assuring people "a Catholic death." That was the verdict passed on her by Professor Germaine Greer, writing in the British *Independent* newspaper (22 Sept. 1990), who called her a "religious imperialist" and went on: "Mother Teresa epitomises for me the blinkered charitableness on which we pride ourselves and for which we expect reward in this world and the next." She had earlier made a very different impression on the once-sceptical journalist Malcolm Muggeridge, who interviewed her for a television film in 1969 and commented: "It will be for posterity to decide whether she is a saint. I can only say that in a dark time she is a burning and a shining light; in a cruel time, a living embodiment of Christ's gospel of love; in a Godless time, the Word dwelling among us, full of grace and truth." The most sustained attack on her was made by the journalist, author, and commentator Christopher Hitchens (who declares himself atheist and hostile to religion), in a book and a film for TV (the latter never shown in the U.S.A.), who pointed out that she had a long history of supporting some of the most evil dictators of the time, from Enver Hoxha of Albania to "Baby Doc" Duvalier of Haiti; that her stated motive for her work was proselytization for the most extremely conservative interpretation of Catholic doctrine; that she deliberately lent her support to anti-reform campaigns, such as the "No" side in the referendum on legalizing divorce in Ireland; and that her Congregation was a bottomless pit into which millions of dollars poured continually from around the world with no accountability and very little to show except the building of more and more convents.

It was not until after her death that her writings revealed that she had spent most of fifty years in an endless "dark night of the soul," feeling separated from and even rejected by God from the time she began her work for the poor with such confidence that she was acting virtually on a direct command from God.

Her health declined as she moved into her eighties, and in March 1997 Teresa finally relinquished her direct control of her worldwide family and resigned as superior general of the Missionaries of Charity, blessing her successor, Sr Nirmala Joshi, a convert from Hinduism. But her last weeks were still spent receiving visitors and issuing instructions to her Sisters. She died on 5 September 1997 and was accorded a State funeral by the Indian government. She was buried in the motherhouse in Calcutta, which rapidly became a place of pilgrimage for people of all nations, all classes, and all faiths. It was hardly surprising that the cause for her canonization started in the shortest time since the usually lengthy modern process was introduced. Miracles attributed to her intercession were widely reported: one—the cure of an Indian woman, Monika Besra, of an abdominal tumour—was decreed on 20 December 2000, and she was beatified by her great friend and admirer Pope John Paul II on 20 October 2003, World Mission Sunday.

The crowd at the ceremony numbered 300,000, including 500 Missionaries of Charity, over a hundred cardinals, and representatives of the Orthodox Church and Muslim communities from Albania. The front rows were reserved for a selected 3,500 poor people, who were given lunch afterwards in the Paul VI Hall, served by representatives of the U.N. Food and Agricultural Association from around the world. There were Indian songs and dances, and a procession of young Indian women in white saris bore a relic in procession to the altar. The Pope recalled her as someone "I have always felt near to me" and in his homily (read for him by Archbishop Sandri of the Secretariat of State and Cardinal

Ivan Dias, archbishop of Bombay) called her "an icon of the Good Samaritan, [going] everywhere to serve Christ in the poorest of the poor." "Her life," he continued, "is a testimony to the dignity and the privilege of humble service. She had chosen to be not just the least but to be the servant of the least. As a real mother to the poor, she bent down to those suffering various forms of poverty. Her greatness lies in her ability to give without counting the cost, to give 'until it hurts.' Her life was a radical living and a bold proclamation of the gospel." In Calcutta celebrations of her beatification lasted almost four weeks, ending with an inter-religious ceremony at which the Hindu mayor expressed his "gratitude to the Catholic Church" for providing Calcutta with such a figure as Mother Teresa.

In Rome the papal household preacher, Fr Raniero Cantalamessa, devoted three Advent meditations to consideration of her spirituality. Referring to the "darkness" of her spirit revealed by her letters and diaries, he said that while this placed her in the classical tradition of mysticism in the vein of St John of the Cross, it could also be seen as a "means of protection invented by God for today's saints who live and work constantly under the spotlight of the media," the modern equivalent of St Paul's "thorn in the flesh" (2 Cor. 12:7), preserving her from letting the world's adulation go to her head. She herself wrote at the time she received the Nobel Peace Prize: "The interior pain that I feel is so great that I don't feel anything from all the publicity and people's talking." At a deeper level, her "dark night of the spirit" was a sharing in the sense of abandonment felt by Jesus in the Garden of Gethsemane and echo of his cry from the cross, "My God, my God, why have you abandoned me?" Nevertheless, "the joy and serenity that emanated from Mother Teresa's face was not a mask but the reflection of the profound union with God in which her soul lived. It was she who deceived herself about her story, not the people."

Fr Cantalamessa's meditations (7, 14, and 21 Dec. 2003) are available through Zenit, as are reflections by several people who knew her, made in the wake of her beatification. Relatively early studies include G. Gorvee and J. Barvier, *For the Love of God* (1974); D. Doig, *Mother Teresa: Her People and Her Work* (1976); M. Muggeridge, *Something Beautiful for God* (1977, from which the above quotation is taken); D. Porter, *Mother Teresa: The Early Years* (1977); R. Royle and G. Woods, *Mother Teresa: A Life in Pictures* (1992). Selected prayers and sayings are collected in Missionaries of Charity (ed.), *A Fruitful Branch on the Vine, Jesus* (2000) and in numerous similar works. The sisters Eileen and Kathleen Egan became great friends of Mother Teresa and produced several works: E. Egan, *Such a Vision of the Street: Mother Teresa* (1986), the authorized biography; *idem., Blessed Are You: Mother Teresa and the Beatitudes* (1992); *ead.* and J. Bauer, *At Prayer with Mother Teresa* (1999); E. and K. Egan, *Prayertimes with Mother Teresa: A New Adventure in Prayer involving Scripture, Mother Teresa and You* (1989). Christopher Hitchens' critique is published as *The Missionary Position: Mother Teresa in Theory and Practice* (1995); his film, for the BBC "60 Minute" series, was shown as *Hell's Angel* (he had wanted to call it *Sacred Cow*). An interview with him, from *Free Inquiry* magazine, is at www. secularhumanism.org/library/fi/hitchens.

By the time of Mother Teresa's death the Missionaries of Charity numbered about 4,000 (now 4,500), based in 610 houses in 123 countries (now 710 in 132), providing social, physical, and spiritual aid to the poor across the world through "soup kitchens, shelters, nursing homes, prison ministries, hospices for the dying, and a very extensive foreign mission commitment": *Orders*, p. 80. They consistently refuse to leave countries where their safety is threatened by ongoing conflicts: Sri Lanka, Rwanda, Burundi, Colombia, Israel, and, most recently, Iraq. The Brothers Missionaries number about 400, caring mainly for drug addicts, AIDS sufferers, alcoholics, and former prisoners. The women contemplatives (founded in the Bronx in 1976 with St Nirmala as co-founder), number around 100, and in fact divide their time between community prayer and practical works of charity. The men contemplatives, numbering only about thirty, work in prisons, hospitals, and for the homeless. The priests, numbering twenty-five, work on city streets and in slum areas. The lay helpers are numbered in many thousands.

The saris that are the trademark of the Sisters everywhere are made by cured lepers in a workshop dedicated to Mahatma Gandhi in Titaghar, north of Calcutta.

7

Bd Eugenia Picco (1867–1921)

Born in the Crescenzago district of Milan on 8 November 1867, Anna Eugenia had a far from conventionally pious upbringing. Her father, Giuseppe Picco, was a famous musician, a violinist with La Scala opera of Milan. Blind from a childhood accident, he was inevitably partly dependent on others, and eventually on his wife, Adelaide Del Corno, who had married him more for the glamour and wealth attached to his position than out of love. He spent more and more of his time on tour, taking Adelaide with him and leaving their daughter to be raised mainly by her grandparents. The tours extended from Europe to the U.S.A., from where Adelaide returned without Giuseppe, telling Anna he was dead, which may not have been the case. He vanished without trace, even a police search failing to find him. Adelaide set up home with Basilio Recalcati, with whom she had three more children. When Anna was seven, her mother seized her from her grandparents and kept her with her new "family," which plunged her into what the Vatican biography describes as "an irreligious and morally corrupt environment."

She seems to have adapted to the new situation and, an attractive and lively girl, learned to love the theatre and the society life of Milan. She nevertheless clung on to her faith, or came back to it, praying every day in the basilica of St Ambrose in Milan, and by the age of twenty was convinced she had a vocation to the religious life, an idea that certainly did not appeal to her mother. Anna conveyed this to the Ursuline Sisters, who were in close contact with Don Agostino Chieppe (1830–1891; now Venerable), who in 1865 had founded the Little Daughters of the Sacred Hearts of Jesus and Mary, and told him about Anna's situation. She ran away from home and was immediately accepted into the Congregation. Her mother tried to grab her back but then resigned herself to her loss. Anna began her novitiate in Parma in 1888 and made her first profession in 1891, and her solemn profession in 1894. She progressed steadily, serving as novice-mistress, archivist, general secretary, council member, and finally superior general from 1911 until her death ten years later.

During the First World War she concerned herself in every possible way with those whose lives were disrupted, impoverished, or otherwise affected by the conflict, combining ceaseless works of charity with her administrative tasks as superior general, finding strength and energy in her central devotion to Christ in the Eucharist. She also found time to write a biography of Don Agostino. She accomplished all she did despite a degenerative bone condition, which sapped her strength and in 1919 forced her to have her lower right leg amputated, which she accepted in a spirit of cheerful self-sacrifice.

Anna died on 7 September 1921, regarded by all around her as a saint. Her cause was initiated by the diocese of Parma in 1945, and her heroic virtue was decreed in 1989. In 1999 a father of four living in Zaire, Camille Kingambe Talubingi, was taken to hospital suffering from a tropical disease of the spleen plus suspected liver cancer. An operation led to a violent hemorrhage, and hope for his life was abandoned, except by two Sisters of Eugenia's Congregation, who were nursing him. Declaring that, "Now only you, Eugenia, can help," they prayed to her and placed an image of her on his body. Within an hour he was standing up and asking for food, and a few weeks later he was discharged from hospital, apparently completely cured. This was accepted as a miracle brought about by her intervention on 1 December 1999 and cleared the way for her beatification on 7 October 2001.

Apart from the usual Vatican sources, the *Piccole Figlie* ("Little Daughters") have an informative, if fussy, website in Italian with more information about her parents: www.pfiglie.org/Eugenia.

9

Bd Pierre Bonhomme, *Founder* (1803–1861)

Pierre, the son of a cutler, was born on 4 July 1803 in Gramat, a small town in the Haut Quercy region of the *département* of the Lot, twenty-five miles north-east of Cahors. Feeling an early call to the priesthood, he entered the minor seminary in Montfaucon at the age of fifteen, in November 1818, moving on to higher education at the Collège Royal in Cahors and then to the major seminary there, where he was ordained on 23 December 1827.

The Church in the region, as in all of France, was suffering the after-effects of the French Revolution. There had been years without vocations to the priesthood, and the clergy was aging. Pierre was to be a dynamic example of a new generation of priests who tackled the apostolic needs of the time with verve and enthusiasm. After first being sent to teach catechism classes at the cathedral in Cahors he returned to Gramat, where he opened a school for boys. The following year he opened another at Prayssac, on the flood plain of the Lot, west of Cahors. After being assistant to both parish priests of Gramat, he had to take the place of one, who was sick, and proved to be an inspiring preacher. He started a group of Children of Mary to help attend to the pressing social needs of the town. One of the most urgent was the building of a hospice to serve the elderly and dying, many of whom were confined to their houses without medical or spiritual care. He achieved this in collaboration with the welfare services of the town and then looked for a Congregation to staff it. Failing to find one, he decided to start a new one.

Pierre appealed to the Children of Mary in 1833, and four of the older girls volunteered—two pairs of sisters: Hortense and Adèle Pradel, and Cora and Mathilde Roussot. He took them on retreat to the sanctuary of Our Lady of Rocamadour, and on their return they took a vow of virginity and "to consecrate themselves to God in the religious life for the service of the poor and the education of children." The Congregation took the name Sisters of Our Lady of Calvary, as its inspiration was the figure of Mary at the foot of Jesus' cross. It received diocesan approval the following year, establishing its motherhouse at Gramat. Five years later it opened another house, in the big city of Limoges, about eighty miles north of Gramat.

Meanwhile Pierre, known as "the missionary of Quercy," was preaching missions all around the area—over seventy in ten years. He preached in the local dialect, in the extreme heat of summer and the intense cold of winter, and with a power that began to threaten his voice, forcing him to seek the curative waters of the spa at Eaux-Bonnes. (He is also supposed to have recovered his voice miraculously through praying to Our Lady of Rocamadour after losing it completely during a retreat.) The new bishop of Cahors relieved him of preaching missions. He restored pilgrimages to the old Marian shrines: Rocamadour, Our Lady of Livron, and Our Lady of the Snows at Gourdon.

In 1836 Pierre had made a retreat at the Trappist monastery of Mortagne and felt an urge to become a Carmelite, but the bishop had dissuaded him and asked him to continue with his missions. In 1848, however, he again lost his voice completely when preaching a retreat in the Lot district. A disease of the larynx was diagnosed and he had to give up public speaking altogether. His activities on behalf of the Congregation continued unabated: between 1856 and 1861 he established houses in other parts of France, with a school for deaf children in Mayrinhac-Lentour in the Lot, another in Bourg-la-Reine, and one for those who had recovered from mental illness in Paris. His inability to speak made him especially sensitive to the plight of deaf-mutes. He opened several new houses in his native Quercy region and one in Toulouse, the provincial capital fifty miles south.

Pierre's final years were devoted to writing a Rule for his Sisters, caring for their spiritual wellbeing, and finding fresh charitable work for them to undertake. He saw their numbers grow to over sixty, most working for the neediest in poor rural parishes. He died in Gramat on 9 September 1861, already widely regarded as a saint. His reputation for holiness grew after his death; the diocesan process in his cause opened in 1952, with the Roman process following in 1955. He was declared Venerable in 1987, a miracle attributed to his intercession was recognized in 2002, and he was beatified on 23 March 2003, the first priest from the diocese of Cahors to be declared Blessed.

In addition to Vatican sources, see Quercy.net/hommes/pbonhomme and catholique-cahors.cef.fr (linked from Patron Saints Index.)

After his death the Sisters of Our Lady of Calvary spread to Argentina, Brazil, Guinea, Ivory Coast, Paraguay, and the Philippines. Pierre had said that he wanted his Sisters "to be open to all the needs afflicting humanity, even to the ends of the earth." They have about 250 members.

Bd Maria Euthymia Üffing (1914–1955)

She was born in Halverde, in north-west Germany, on 8 April 1914. This was a small town, where her parents, August Üffing and Maria Schmidt, brought up eleven children in a pious environment. Christened Emma, she developed rickets at the age of eighteen months, which was to leave her with stunted growth and permanently weak health. Despite this, she worked on the family farm. When she was fourteen she decided she wanted to enter religious life, but from seventeen to nineteen she was apprenticed in household management at the hospital of St Ann in nearby Hopsten.

There Emma came into contact with the Sisters of Charity of Münster (or Clemens Sisters). The superior, Sister Euthymia Linnekämper, was impressed by her hard work and willingness. Emma returned home for a while to care for her father before his death in 1932, and then in 1934 asked to be admitted to the Sisters of Charity. After some hesitation on account of her physical condition, they accepted her and in July she joined the motherhouse in Münster as one of forty-seven postulants. She took the names Mary Euthymia in religion, the second in memory of the superior at St Ann's.

She took her simple vows in October 1936 and in the same month was sent to St Vincent's Hospital in Dinslaken, just north of Düsseldorf, where she studied for a nursing diploma, which she gained with distinction just at the outbreak of the Second World War, 3 September 1939. Euthymia nursed the sick through the difficult war years and in 1943 was placed in charge of prisoners of war and conscripted foreign workers with infectious diseases. These included British, French, Poles, Russians, and Ukrainians. A French priest who spent several years in the hospital as a prisoner of war, Fr Emile Esche, testified that she was "full of a charity and kindness that came from her heart ... She knew that sick prisoners do not have to contend with physical sufferings alone. Through her warm sympathy and closeness, she instilled in them a feeling of being safe and at home ... Sr Euthymia's life was a canticle of hope in the midst of war." She became known to her patients as "Mamma Euthymia." After the war she was placed in charge of the laundry room, which may seem something of a waste of her talent for dealing with people, but she accepted the move cheerfully, as she did a "promotion" to the larger laundry at the motherhouse and its attached clinic.

She spent most of the time when she was not working praying in front of the tabernacle but still managed to remain available to everyone—as she said: "The Lord can use me like a ray of sun to brighten the day." Her reputation for holiness grew in her lifetime to the point where people would ask her to intercede for them in her prayers. She contracted a virulent form of cancer and died on 9 September 1955 after weeks of painful illness.

Euthymia was beatified with six others on 7 October 2001. Pope John Paul II described her as living "the word of the gospel: 'We are worthless slaves; we have done only what we ought to have done' (Luke 17:10). In her faith in small things lies her greatness."

16

BB Juan Bautista and Jacinto de los Angeles, *Martyrs* (1660–1700)

Pope John Paul beatified these two Mexican lay martyrs in Mexico City on the day following the canonization of Juan Diego (see 9 Dec.). They were both born in 1660 in San Francisco Cajonos, in the State of Oaxaca in southern Mexico, and were martyred there together.

Both came from the Zapoteca tribe, indigenous to Oaxaca, and Jacinto was descended from an important tribal chief: both, however, were not only Christians but exercised a function entrusted to them by Dominican missionaries, that of "attorneys general," which meant that they held a watching brief over any Indian attempts to revert to "idolatry," which they had to report to the church authorities. Oaxaca was a newly evangelized area, and attachment to the old beliefs was still strong.

On 14 September 1700 they learned that an idolatrous rite was to be held at the house of a local Indian named José Flores. They informed the two Dominicans in charge of the parish, Fr Alonso de Vargas and Fr Gaspar de los Reyes, and went with them to surprise those taking part in the ceremony, who quickly blew out their candles and ran away before they could be identified. The following day they threatened retaliation, and the two attorneys were forced to seek refuge in the Dominican convent. By evening the "idolaters" had reached the convent, their identities masked, and they threatened to kill all those inside unless Juan and Jacinto were handed over to them. At first the Dominicans refused, but when the Indians broke the doors down, seized back the instruments used in their rite, and set fire to Juan Bautista's house nearby, the two were turned over to the mob.

Jacinto asked one of the Dominican priests to hear his Confession and give him Communion. After they had been effectively sacrificed by their fellow-Christians they were taken away, severely beaten, then taken to the local prison (which surely would have been under Catholic control?) for the night. The next day they were taken to the top of a steep hill and thrown down it; at the foot their battered bodies were clubbed and finally cut open so their hearts could be removed and thrown to dogs. Their bodies were thrown into an open pit but were gathered up by local faithful and taken for proper burial in the church at Villa Alta. In 1889 their remains were given to the bishop of Oaxaca, and they have been venerated in the cathedral ever since.

They were beatified by Pope John Paul II in Mexico City on 1 August 2002. It is of course impossible to judge events that happened in particular circumstances 300 years ago, but it is difficult to see that anyone, not even the vigilante martyrs themselves and certainly not the Dominicans, emerges with any credit from this horrible story. The pope in his homily praised Oaxaca's "rich mixture of cultures" and invoked "the sweet face of Our Lady of Guadalupe" (in front of whose image the ceremony took place), but there must remain a question over how reporting on and breaking up a traditional ceremony held by some Zapoteca Indians resistant to this phase of evangelization really accords with her message.

17

Bd Sigmund Felínski, *Bishop* (1822–1895)

Archbishop of Warsaw for a mere sixteen months, Sigmund (Zygmunt) spent most of his life as a "Polish shepherd-in-exile" in territory belonging to the Russian Empire. His birthplace, Wojutyn, is now in Volhynia (Volynska 'Oblast'), the most north-westerly province of Ukraine, but at the time it belonged to Russia. He was born the third of six children of Gerard Felínski and Eva Wendorff, on 1 November 1822. Two of his siblings died in infancy, and when Sigmund was eleven his father died. The region in which the family lived had previously been part of the Polish-Lithuanian Confederation (see the summary history under The Martyrs of Ukraine; 7 Mar.) but in the nineteenth century Poland was variously partitioned among the Prussian, Austrian, and Russian powers. Sigmund's mother was a passionate Polish nationalist, concerned above all for the social and economic conditions of farmers, and this earned her arrest by the Russians in 1838 and twelve years' exile in Siberia.

This did not prevent Sigmund from receiving a first-class education, studying mathematics at Moscow University from 1840 to 1844 and moving on in 1847 to Paris, where he studied French literature at both the Sorbonne and the Collège de France. In Paris in the "year of revolutions," 1848, he became involved with a group of Polish émigrés plotting the Poznan Revolt against Prussian occupation in the Grand Duchy of Poznan (roughly equidistant from both Berlin and Warsaw, and now in west-central Poland). The rising failed, partly due to differing aims among its protagonists, but Sigmund appears not to have suffered any adverse consequences from his involvement. From 1848 to 1850 he was tutor to the sons of the Brzozowski family in Munich and Paris.

In 1851 Sigmund decided to pursue a vocation to the priesthood, returned to Poland, then entered the diocesan seminary of Zhytomyr, in northern Ukraine and so in Russian territory, from where he progressed to the Catholic Academy in Saint Petersburg. He was ordained by Archbishop Ignacy Holowinski of Mohilev (Mahilyow in Belarus) on 8 September 1855, and posted to the Dominican-run parish of Saint Catherine in Saint Petersburg. He spent two years there and was then appointed spiritual director and professor of philosophy at the Ecclesiastical Academy. He started a charitable organization named "Recovery for the Poor" in 1856, and the following year brought the Sisters of the Blessed Virgin Mary of Mercy (a branch of the Mercedarian family) to Warsaw, where they opened an orphanage, which he supported.

In January 1862 Pope Pius IX appointed Sigmund archbishop of Warsaw. He arrived there in February, when the city was under siege by the Russian army, which had suppressed a Polish uprising the previous year, to which the ecclesiastical authorities responded by closing all the city's churches for four months. Within days Sigmund had re-consecrated the cathedral (desecrated by the Russians on 15 October 1861) and reopened all the churches, despite the fact that there were ongoing clashes between Russian forces and Polish nationalist fighters. He was archbishop for sixteen months only, during which he suffered from a Russian propaganda campaign to make the inhabitants and even some of the clergy believe that he was in fact working for the Russian government. This was despite all his activities, which indicated that he was doing precisely the opposite: he systematically opposed government interference in the internal affairs of the diocese; he made regular visits to its parishes and charitable foundations; he reformed the studies at the Ecclesiastical Academy to give priests a more solid intellectual formation; he did all he could to have imprisoned priests set free; and he encouraged his clergy to be bolder in proclaiming the gospel and setting moral standards, especially to the younger generation by opening parish schools.

Sigmund tried to intervene in the political situation by urging restraint in order to save lives, but when the Russians brutally repressed a revolt in January 1863, he resigned from the Council of State and wrote in protest to Tsar Alexander II, urging him to show mercy and stop the violence. He also protested against the handing of the chaplain, the Capuchin Friar Agrypin Konarski, to the rebels. The Tsar's response was to order his exile to Siberia. On 14 June 1863 Sigmund was deported to Jaroslavl and for the next twenty years he was cut off from any contact with Warsaw. In his place of exile he ministered to his fellow-prisoners and eventually even managed to build a church. He became know to the locals as "the holy Polish bishop." After diplomatic negotiations between the Holy See and the Tsar he was set free in 1883 and allowed to live in the Krakow region of southern Poland, assigned the titular see of Tarsus by Pope Leo XIII. He settled in the village of Dzwiniaczka, ministered to Polish and Ukrainian peasants, served as chaplain to two counts and built a school and kindergarten out of his own funds and a church and convent for the Sisters of Mercy. He also had time to prepare several volumes of spiritual and pastoral writings written during his Siberian exile for publication.

Sigmund died in Kraków on 17 September 1895 and was originally buried there, but his remains were moved to Dzwiniaczka on 10 October. They were transferred to Warsaw in 1920 and solemnly interred in the cathedral crypt on 14 April 1921. He was beatified in Krakow, together with John Balicki (15 Mar.), John Beyzym (2 Oct.), and Santia Szymkowiak (29 Aug.) by Pope John Paul II— who had been archbishop of Krakow—on 18 August 2002. In his homily the Pope said that the common strand uniting the four was their "devotion to the cause of mercy." It was Archbishop Felínski's "spirit of mercy toward his brothers and sisters" that earned him exile in Siberia and should inspire today's bishops to "create and carry out a pastoral program of mercy. May this program be the extension of your commitment, primarily in the life of the Church and then, as fitting and necessary, in the social and political life of the nation, of Europe, and of the world."

❖

The titles of his published works translate as: *Conferences on Vocations; Faith and Atheism in the Search for Happiness; Memories* (or *Recollections*, 3 vols); *Social Commitments in the View of Christian Wisdom and of Atheism; Spiritual Conferences; Under the Guidance of Providence.*

19

St Alphonsus de Orozco (1500–1591)

Alphonsus (Alonso) was born at Oropesa in the province of Toledo in Spain on 17 October 1500. His father, who was governor of the castle of Oropesa, sent him to study at Talavera de la Reina, after which he spent three years as a choirboy in Toledo cathedral. This gave him a love of music that was to remain with him all his life. He then moved, at the age of fourteen, to the study of law at the university of Salamanca, the foremost seat of learning in Spain at the time. An elder brother, Francisco, was already studying there.

At Salamanca he heard St Thomas of Villanova (22 Sept.) preach, and he was inspired to enter the Augustinian Order. He joined the novitiate, together with his brother, on 8 June 1522. Francisco died during his period of novitiate, which was a devastating blow to Alphonsus, but he persevered and was professed the following year, making his vows to Thomas of Villanova. He was ordained in 1527 and appointed to a preaching ministry. He also wrote, becoming perhaps the most prolific and widely read Spanish spiritual writer of his day. His writing was inspired by an appearance of the Virgin Mary to him in a dream when he was at the Augustinian monastery in Seville in 1542: she spoke just the one word, "Write!," and he was to obey the command for almost fifty years. His health was far from robust, and he was prevented from going as a missionary to Mexico by a severe bout of arthritis, which led to doctors forbidding him to travel on from the Canary Islands, the first staging post on the voyage.

In 1551 Alphonsus was appointed prior of the Order's house in Valladolid, then the capital of Spain. Three years later he was made "royal preacher" and chaplain to the court of Charles V (Holy Roman Emperor from 1519 to 1556, when he retired to the monastery of Yuste, leaving the Spanish part of his inheritance to his son, who reigned as Philip II). Philip moved the capital to Madrid in 1561, and Alphonsus went with the court, somewhat against his will. Despite his status, which carried a stipend and placed him outside the jurisdiction of his Order, he lived extremely austerely in a cell in the monastery of San Felipe el Real. He slept only three hours a night, on a wooden table with vine branches for a pillow. He had asked for a cell near the door, so that he could attend quickly to the poor people who came asking for help. He visited the sick in hospitals, prisoners, and the poor in their homes, all without neglecting his duties as preacher, his participation in the daily office, or his writing.

Alphonsus became known as "the saint of San Felipe" (St Philip's) during his lifetime, and he was as popular with the aristocracy as he was with the poor. He made no distinction of persons, treating everyone with the same gentleness and sensitivity. He founded three convents for contemplative Augustinian nuns and a college for the education of candidates to the Order, to which he had a deep devotion. He wrote about its history and spirituality and was instrumental in the development of a "recollect" movement within it. In obedience to his vision, he produced a fresh devotional work on Our Lady every year, finally, and only under obedience, telling the story of the vision in his *Confessions*, written near the end of his long life. Other spiritual works, some written in Latin and some in Spanish, included *Rule for a Christian Life* (1542); *Garden of Prayer and the Mount of Contemplation* (1544); *Spiritual Treasury* (1551); *The Art of Loving God and Neighbour* (1567); and *The Book of the Gentleness of God* (1576; "gentleness" used in the same sense as in "gentleman," with much the same meaning as Julian of Norwich's "courtesy"). When he was close to eighty years old he asked to be relieved of his court duties, but the king, supported by the court, refused to allow him to retire. He was to continue for a further ten years.

Alphonsus fell ill in August 1591 but continued to say a daily Mass, remarking that "God does no harm to anybody." King Philip II and his elder son both visited him and asked for his blessing, as did the cardinal archbishop of Toledo. He died on 19 September in the College of the Incarnation (now home to the Spanish parliament). His remains were taken to Valladolid and later placed in an altar in the new Augustinian church there. In 1978 they were transferred to the chapel of the contemplative Augustinian nuns in Talavera de la Reina. The poet, novelist, and politician Francisco de Quevedo testified that the people of Madrid broke down the doors of the convent in quest of a relic of "the saint of St Philip's." Quevedo and the playwright Lope de Vega were among those who led the initial stages of the process for his canonization, but this failed to make headway in Rome—perhaps the memory of Spanish troops sacking the city in 1527 lingered on. In the event he was not beatified till 15 January 1882, by Pope Leo XIII. He was canonized by Pope John Paul II on 19 May 2002. In his homily the pope stated that, "his pastoral dedication to the service of the poorest in hospitals and prisons makes him a model for those who, impelled by the Spirit, base all their existence on the love of God and neighbour."

❖

Bibl.SS., 9, 1241; *Butler*, September, pp. 186–7; www.vatican.va/news_services/liturgy/2002; www.osa-west.org/blessedalonsodeorozco. For his life and writings see T. Camara, *Vida y Escritos* (1882); for his teaching on prayer, J. A. Farina, *Doctrina de Oración del B. Alfonso* (1927).

20

St Joseph Mary de Yermo y Parres, *Founder* (1851–1904)

José María (Joseph Mary) was born in the *hacienda* of Jalmolonga on 10 November 1851, the son of Manuel de Yermo y Soviñas and María Josefa Parres. At the age of sixteen he left his family home to enter the Congregation of the Mission in Mexico City. After suffering critical doubts about his vocation he left the Congregation. He was ordained as a diocesan priest in the diocese of León on 24 August 1879.

His early years of priesthood were filled with activity and apostolic zeal. He was an eloquent orator, enthusiastically promoted the catechesis of young people, and efficiently discharged important responsibilities in the diocesan curia, which he was forced to give up because of illness. A new bishop placed him in charge of two small churches located on the outskirts of the city: El Calvario and Santo Niño. He saw this as demotion, and the appointment was a blow to his pride, though he had no choice but to accept the post.

One day José María chanced upon a horrible scene—some pigs devouring two abandoned newborn babies. The shock inspired him to start a home for the poor and abandoned, particularly to try to prevent young women being forced into prostitution through poverty. He sought and received the bishop's authorization, and by 13 December 1885 he had gathered four young women prepared to dedicate themselves to this work, enabling him to open the Sacred Heart Shelter on the summit of El Calvario. This was the effective foundation of the Servants of the Sacred Heart of Jesus and of the Poor (SSHJP).

The Congregation grew steadily, although it was not without its opponents. He founded schools, hospitals, nursing homes, orphanages, and a home for rehabilitating women. Shortly before his death on 20 September 1904 in Puebla de los Angeles, he embarked on the difficult mission among the Tarahumara Indians in northern Mexico. His fame of sanctity spread rapidly among the people, with widespread demands for his intercession. He was beatified by Pope John Paul II on 22 November 1992 and canonized by him, together with Mary of Jesus Venegas and the Mexican martyrs known as Christopher Magallanes and Companions, on 21 May 2000.

The SSHJP spread to the U.S.A. in 1907, three years after his death. It is concerned with education from kindergarten to high school, children's homes, clinics, and dispensaries. It is now also active in Central America, Colombia, Italy, and Kenya. The mission to the Tarahumara Indians continues with a school for girls in Ceracahui, in the Copper Canyon area of the northern State of Chihuahua, with seventy-five boarders and 180 day girls. The motherhouse is in Mexico City and there are over twenty other foundations in the country.

22

St Ignatius of Santhia (1686–1770)

This long-lived Italian Capuchin friar was born in Santhia in the diocese of Vercelli on 5 June 1686. The son of Pierpaolo Belvisotti and Maria Eisabetta Balocco, he was christened Lorenzo Maurizio. He was still very young when his father died, and little else is known about his childhood, except that his mother entrusted his education to a local priest, and Lorenzo decided that he had a vocation to the priesthood. He was ordained in 1710 and made a canon of the collegiate church in Santhia, followed by appointment as a parish priest. He seemed set for a promising ecclesiastical career but turned his back on that sort of advancement and joined the Friars Minor Capuchin.

Lorenzo was professed in Turin on 24 May 1717, taking the name Ignatius in religion, and placed under the tutelage of a novice about half his age for instruction in Capuchin life, which he took this with good grace. He was sent to the convent at Saluzzo, where he served as sacristan, followed by appointmeny as assistant novice-master in Chieri, then sacristan once more at the much larger Convento del Monte in Turin, which was a busy office, serving 87 priests all saying an individual Mass every day. In 1731 he became novice-master at Mondovi where he stayed for thirteen years, having to abandon the post in 1744 owing to a serious eye infection. He recovered from this and was, at the age of nearly sixty, appointed senior chaplain to the Piedmonese forces, who were resisting invasion by a combined Franco-Spanish army. He served with distinction and great charity for six years, regularly visiting the wounded in military hospitals, after which he returned to Del Monte.

There he became chaplain and confessor to the lay brothers, earning their love and trust because he as not above sharing in the manual and lowly tasks, such as "questing" (begging for alms) that they were required to carry out for the benefit of the ordained friars. He had already acquired a reputation as a wise and sympathetic spiritual director, and this increased as he advanced in age. He led many retreats for religious, and his preparations for these were collected into a book. His reputation for holiness grew, and thousands flocked to the convent to receive a blessing or a word of advice from him. He died on 22 September 1770, aged eighty-four, and his cause as introduced in 1782. It look a long time to process, but he was eventually beatified by Pope Paul VI on 17 April 1966. A miracle attributed to his intercession was decreed on 21 December 2001, and he was canonized by Pope John Paul II on 19 May 2002.

Butler, Sept., p. 210, citing Lives by P. da Castiglione d'Asti (1790); C. F. Poirino (1889); V. da Loano (1913); A. da Bra (1945); C. de Chaux de Fonds (1950). His retreat courses were published as "Meditazione per un corso di esercizi spirituali" in 1912.

Bd José Aparicio Sanz and 232 Companions, *Martyrs*
(died 1936)

These Spanish priests, religious, and lay people all died at the hands of Republican militias in the early days of the Spanish civil war, most in the city and region of Valencia. This mass beatification was the largest in the history of the Church, exceeding that of 206 martyrs of Japan by Pope Pius IX in 1867. It continued a process which could lead to the number of beatified martyrs of the Spanish civil war exceeding all those regarded as martyrs in all the previous Christian centuries. The figures are certainly horrific: 6,832 priests and religious, including thirteen bishops, were killed, as well as many lay people regarded as prominent Catholics—or who were just in the wrong place at the wrong time. In areas that did not fall quickly to the Nationalist uprising in July 1936, the people were armed by the local authorities, and it was these undisciplined militias who were responsible for the greater part of the deaths, with the diocesan clergy bearing the brunt of their fury, as the local focus of Catholicism, equated with privileged position under earlier repressive regimes and with Franco's declared Nationalist Catholicism.

In Valencia, 327 diocesan priests were put to death, representing 27 per cent of the total number. The figures were comparable in Barcelona and the Madrid area. The group beatified today included "men and women of all ages and states: diocesan priests, men and women religious, the fathers and mothers of families, young lay people. They were killed for being Christians, for their faith in Christ, for being active members of the Church" (homily by John Paul II at the ceremony). In more detail, there were:

> thirty-eight priests from the archdiocese of Valencia, with a large group of men and women, members of Catholic Action, also from Valencia; four Friars Minor and six Friars Minor Conventual; twelve Friars Minor Capuchin with five Capuchin women religious and a Discalced Augustinian; eleven Jesuits, with a young layman; thirty Salesians and two Daughters of Mary Help of Christians; nineteen Third Order Capuchins of Our Lady of Sorrows, with a laywoman co-worker; one Priest of the Sacred heart of Jesus (Dehoninan); the chaplain of La Salle College of Bonanova, Barcelona, with five Brothers of the Christian Schools; twenty-four Carmelite Sisters of Charity; one Servite Sister; six Sisters of the Pious Schools with two laywomen co-workers from Uruguay, who are the first blessed of this Latin American country; two Little Sisters of the Abandoned Elderly; three Third Order Capuchins of the Holy Family; a Claretian Missionary Sister; and, lastly, Francisco Castelló y Aleu, a young member of Catholic Action in Lleida. (*ibid.*)

As he had done at all ceremonies involving martyrs of the Spanish civil war, the pope stressed that these people were killed out of religious hatred, not because of any political involvement: "The new blesseds being raised to the altars today were not involved in political or ideological struggles, nor did they want to be concerned with them. This is well known to many of you who are their relatives and are taking part in this beatification today with great joy. They died solely for religious motives" (*ibid.*).

For a general account of the Martyrs of the Spanish civil war see *Butler*, July, pp. 169–79; for the first to be canonized see St Cyril Bertrand Sanz Tejedor and Companions in this volume (9 Oct.). Books dealing specifically with the religious persecution include F. Lannon, *Privilege, Persecution and Prophecy: the Catholic Church in Spain 1875–1975* (1987); A. Montero Moreno, *Historia de la persecución religiosa en España 1936–9* (1961); V. Cárcel, *Mártires españoles del siglo XX* (1966); R. Royal, *Catholic Martyrs of the Twentieth Century: A Comprehensive Global History* (2000; extracts at www.catholicherald.com/royal). For a full list of the names, states and ages of today's martyrs see "September 22—today's saints" at www.greenspun.com, also Patron Saints Index under martyrs of Valencia; for an extensive bibliography, compiled in memory of the Jesuit martyrs of the war, see www.holycross.edu/departments/history/vlapomar/persecut/spain (these and other sites via Google search: Martyrs

Spanish civil war). For the wider question of who should be regarded as martyrs in the twentieth century see Concilium 2003/1, *Rethinking Martyrdom*.

23

Bd Emily Tavernier (1800–1851)

Emily (Emilie) was the youngest of fifteen children, born on 19 February 1800 to Antoine Tavernier and Marie-Joseph Maurice, in Montreal, Canada. Her parents both died by the time she was four, and she was brought up by a paternal aunt, who sent her to school with the Sisters of the Congregation of Notre Dame, situated in Jean-Baptiste Street. This was the Congregation founded in Canada in 1653 by St Marguerite Bourgeoys (1620–1700; 12 Jan.). From an early age she was drawn to help the poor and disadvantaged: one of her brothers was widowed when she was eighteen, and she moved in to help him, laying down the one condition that their table should always be open to any hungry persons who came to the door.

On 4 June 1823 Emily married Jean-Baptiste Gamelin, a wealthy apple farmer, as concerned as she was with the plight of the poor. Misfortune soon struck them, as the three children they had all died young. After just four years of marriage, her husband died too. She turned to Mary, Mother of Sorrows, as a guide and comforter in her distress and sought a new family in the poor and needy. Beginning with a mentally handicapped child and his elderly mother, she turned her own house into a refuge for orphans, abandoned children, mentally sick people, immigrants, and any other class of unfortunate who came to her. It became known as "House of Providence," and she said that her challenge in life was to be "the human face of Providence." She was soon using the inheritance from her husband to find other houses to meet the ever-growing demand. She brought in members of her own family and friends to help, leading always by example, though some were inevitably suspicious of her motives. She carried on in this way for fifteen years.

The second bishop of Montreal, Mgr Ignace Bourget, was supportive and, on a visit to Paris in 1841, asked the Daughters of St Vincent de Paul to send Sisters to help her. They agreed, and on his return he began building a new house to accommodate them: but then they were somehow unable to leave, and this plan had to be abandoned. He appealed to the women faithful of the diocese of Montreal, and more helpers arrived. In 1843 he decided that they should form a new Congregation, and so the Sisters of Providence came into being. Emily was one of the novices who professed their first vows on 29 March 1844, and she became the first mother superior.

The city was growing fast and suffered the twin scourges of nineteenth-century cities before the arrival of sewerage systems and clean drinking water: cholera and typhus. As the numbers of sick increased, so did the numbers of the Sisters, but their early years were not without problems. Emily (as noted in this work of so many heroic nineteenth-century women) aroused envy in some less able and committed, and one such Sister gained the ear of Bishop Bourget, turning him against her for a while, although he eventually recognized her virtues and indeed heroism. This was a trial almost equal to that of the loss of her children and husband, and again she turned to the Mother of Sorrows for spiritual help. The Congregation had been in existence for eight years only, with its numbers grown to fifty, when Emily herself caught cholera in the epidemic of 1851, dying of it on 23 September.

Her cause initially made slow progress, but Pope John Paul II decreed her heroic virtue on 23 December 1993, and in December 2000 the cure of a fatally ill thirteen-year-old boy was attributed to her miraculous intervention, and she was beatified on 7 October 2001. The Pope in his homily described her as "a model for the men and women of today," continuing: "Blessed Emily's spiritual life gave her strength for her charitable mission; she emptied herself of all things and found the energy to comfort everyone. Taking her as your model, I urge you to put yourselves at the service of the poor and of society's most underprivileged, who are God's beloved, to alleviate their sufferings and thus make their dignity shine out."

❖

On the Congregation of Notre Dame see *Orders*, pp. 300–1; on the Sisters of Providence, *ibid.*, p. 345. The Sisters have a website that includes a pilgrimage in Emily's footsteps around Montreal; www.providenceintl.org/english/Actuality/ emilie.

The Sisters, of whom there have been over 6,000, still carry out their mission to the sick and needy of all sorts, with a speciality in teaching English as a second language to immigrants. The motherhouse is in Montreal, and they have spread to Chile (1853), U.S.A. (1856), Argentina, Cameroon, Egypt, Haiti, and, most recently, the Philippines (1989) and El Salvador (1995).

Bd Louis Tezza, *Founder* (1841–1923)

Louis (Luigi) Tezza was born in Conegliano in the Treviso province of the Venice region on 1 November 1841, and was baptized with the names Arturo Luigi Carlo Alessandro on 6 November. He was an Austrian citizen, as the whole of the Veneto region and other parts of what is now northern Italy belonged to the Austro-Hungarian Empire at the time. His father, Augusto, was a doctor in the hospital of SS John and Paul in Venice. His mother, Caroline Nedweidt, came from a wealthy family in Moravia (now a province of the Czech Republic) and had considered a religious vocation before marrying. Augusto then moved the family to Dolo, where he was appointed district health officer, but he died in January 1850, when Louis was nine. His widow moved to Padua and devoted herself totally to the education of her only son, and when he decided he had a vocation to the religious life and entered the novitiate of the Camillian Order (founded in 1582 by St Camillus de Lellis; 14 July) in Verona, she became a Visitation nun (founded in 1610 by St Jane Frances de Chantal; 12 Dec.) in Padua. He was able to see her before she died some years later, and they were able to bid each other a fond *"arrivederci* in heaven."

Louis was professed on 8 December 1858, declaring that he intended "to become a saint." At the end of his novitiate he was pronounced "most eminent in science and virtue," and he was ordained on 21 May 1864. In 1866 the battle of Custoza sul Minicio between the Austro-Hungarian army of occupation and Piedmontese resistance fighters filled the hospitals of Verona with wounded men, to whom Louis ministered with the devotion that was the hallmark of his Order.

Veneto was annexed to the new kingdom of Italy, whose parliament promptly decreed the suppression of religious houses. Louis was evicted from the Verona house in July 1867 and forced to seek shelter in a friendly country house. At this time Fr Daniel Comboni (now Saint, see 10 Oct.) was founding his Institute for Missions to Black People, or Verona Fathers, and he and Bishop Canossa of Verona tried to take advantage of the scattering of religious to recruit priests for the African missions. This was a project dear to Louis' heart, but the bishop wanted Camillians to go as diocesan priests, not members of the Order. Louis objected, and the bishop took the unwise course of agreeing and saying they could go in secret as religious. Louis' superiors discovered this and forbade him to go. He chose obedience in the Order over his desire to be a missionary in Africa: "Obedience, obedience, and always obedience to my superiors, and that's it," he wrote.

In 1869 his superiors sent Louis to Rome as vice novice-master. He again found himself caring for war wounded when the last of the Papal States, including Rome, fell to Victor Emmanuel's forces in 1870. The following year he was sent to France, initially as novice-master in the Camillians' new foundation at Cuisery (in the Saône et Loir department of east-central France). He worked there so successfully that there were soon several houses forming a new province of the Order, of which he became superior. He also opened convalescent homes in which he pioneered health care methods that came to be used throughout the Order. In 1880 all foreign religious were expelled from France. Louis left but returned in secret three months later and managed to re-establish the province, keeping always one step ahead of those seeking to arrest him. In 1889 he was elected vicar and procurator general of the Order, which required him to return to Rome, where he took up residence in the hospital of St John Lateran.

There was no women's branch of the Camillians, and Louis was convinced that one was needed, to bring feminine qualities to their mission to the sick and aged. In 1891 a meeting with a young woman named Judith Vannini during a retreat led him to invite her to join him in such a venture. She agreed, and with two companions became a Camillian tertiary in 1892, professing private vows the following year and perpetual vows in 1895. This was the birth of the Congregation of the Daughters of St Camillus. Louis wrote the Rules, concentrating on ministry to the sick in the spirit of St Camillus. Judith took the name Josephine in religion and was elected first superior general. (She was beatified on 16 October 1994; 23 Feb.). Trouble—apparently endemic in new women's Orders—arose when Louis was accused of being too intimate with the Sisters and was suspended from acting as their spiritual director and confessor. The accusations were baseless, as both he and Josephine knew, but he preferred to accept injustice rather than defend himself, which he saw as contrary to his vow of obedience. He was further cut off from his foundation when he returned to France in 1898.

In 1900 the Order despatched Louis to Peru, where its house in Lima, which had been separated from the rest of the Order for over a century, had asked to be re-integrated. He went with the title of Official Visitor, expecting to spend only a short time there, but his reforms were so successful that when the time came for him return to Rome, both the archbishop of Lima and the papal nuncio declared him indispensable. His superiors agreed that he should stay, so again he obeyed, and he spent the last twenty-three years of his life in Peru, becoming superior of the house he had reformed. He relinquished this office in 1910 and, aged sixty-nine, devoted himself full time to caring for the sick of Lima (who were many), working, as he said, "ten times harder than I ever used to do in Europe." His working day began at 5 a.m., and his only regret was that there were not forty-eight hours in a day. He set up a hospital run by the Order and established a religious presence in five of the city's public hospitals. He was also much in demand as counsellor and confessor in the archbishop's house, the nunciature, and several religious Congregations. His strength began to fail when he was seventy-five, and he was obliged to reduce his workload. The last three years of his life were a slow approach to death, confined to his room, spending most of his time praying the rosary. He died peacefully at the age of eighty-two, on 23 September 1923.

The ordinary process of Louis' cause was opened in 1959 but ran into difficulties in 1964 and was blocked by the Sacred Congregation for the Doctrine of the Faith (the re-titled Holy Office) in 1966, probably owing to the resurgence of accusations from the early days of the foundation of the Daughters. A more detailed study of his life was then undertaken, resulting in the presentation of five solid volumes containing his own writings and a biography. This time the Congregation raised no objections, and the decree of his heroic virtue was published on 24 April 2000. The cure of Sr Domenico Nieves Paviona, considered terminally ill, was accepted as a miracle through his intervention on 7 July 2001, and was followed by his beatification on 4 November. The Pope called his life "a glorious example of a life totally dedicated to the exercise of charity and mercy toward those who suffer in body and spirit."

His remains had originally been interred in Lima (where an unknown hand carved the words *Apóstol de Lima* on his tomb). In 1948 they were transferred to the provincial house of the Daughters in Buenos Aires, and in 1999, when the path to his beatification had been cleared, they were returned to Rome. They now rest in the chapel of the Daughters' Generalate at Grottaferrata.

His writings are published as *Scritti del Padre Luigi Tezza alle Figlie di S. Camillo* (1998); the biography is in four volumes, dealing with the first twenty-three years of his life (1991), the years 1865–1868 (1993), 1869–1900 (1994), and his last twenty-three years (1995). The website www.camilliani.org/tezza has detailed information on his life, spirituality and the course of his process (but can be obstinate).

The Daughters under Josephine Vannini expanded their work to Belgium, France, and Argentina.

St Pius of Pietrelcina (Padre Pio) (1887–1968)

The most famous stigmatist since the first—St Francis of Assisi (4 Oct.)—was born into a family of agricultural labourers in Pietrelcina, in the Benevento region north-east of Naples, on 25 May 1887. His father's name was Grazio Forgione and his mother's Maria Giuseppina Di Nunzio, though in the village she was generally called "Mama Peppa." He was christened Francesco in the village church of Santa Anna on the day following his birth, and confirmed at the age of twelve by the archbishop of Benevento, Donato Maria Dell'Olio.

He was clothed with the Capuchin habit in 1903, when he was sixteen, at their convent in Morcone, taking the name Pius ("Pio"in Italian) in religion. Ordained priest seven years later, he returned to Pietrelcina to say his first Mass. It was soon after this that he began to experience pains in his hands and feet, and in September 1911 he told his spiritual director that he had "had invisible stigmata for over a year."He was ordered to undergo various medical tests, at the same time confessing that he also felt the pain of Jesus' crown of thorns and scourging.

Pius was exempted from military service—from which religious had no blanket exemption—on the grounds of health, as he had bronchial trouble (suspected to be tuberculosis), and was allowed back to Pietrelcina to convalesce in the pure mountain air. He served as a medical orderly for three months in 1917 but then was again excused on health grounds. He recovered and was called up again in 1918, but again his health collapsed and he was sent back.

This time he was sent to the convent at Giovanni Rotondo, where he was to spend the rest of his life.

On 5 August 1918 Pius experienced "transverberation," meaning that he felt his side being pierced as Jesus' had been with the lance: the wound was visible and bled continually. His stigmata also became visible the following month and were to remain so until they equally mysteriously disappeared during his last Mass. There was no way of keeping this hidden in a century of mass media; nor did the Capuchins attempt to do so. His condition soon became known all over Italy, and thousands flocked to the convent to look at him and attend his Masses. Photographs were taken in which the marks clearly showed, but the Vatican, always cautious with extraordinary manifestations, refused to pronounce on whether they were from God, the product of a psychosomatic disorder, or even fraud aimed at drawing pilgrims to the convent. He was examined by several doctors, who were—not unnaturally—unable to diagnose their origin either.

Pius would go into ecstatic trances while saying Mass, sometimes keeping the crowds who flocked to his Masses for two hours or more. Church authorities became increasingly alarmed and tried first to make him say Mass in private—rescinded after a day owing to mass protest—and then to move him away to Ancona on the Adriatic coast, far from Neapolitan obsession with blood: this plan was withdrawn after a week after further popular protest. All he would say on the subject was that he was "a mystery to myself," but he did suggest that his gifts should produce benefits for others. This came about quite soon, as money from grateful penitents and admirers began to flow in. His community opened a twenty-bed hospital in a disused convent in 1925. Still Church officials treated him with the greatest suspicion: in 1931 he was suspended from all his priestly functions except that of saying Mass, but he was obliged to do this in private. This ban lasted two years, after which popular enthusiasm again won the day and his privileges were restored—except that of hearing women's Confessions, from which he was banned for a further year.

In 1929 Pius had ministered to a dying American woman, and in 1940 her daughter, the wealthy Maria Pyle, provided him with funds to begin a more ambitious hospital project to serve the needs of the remote rural area around San Giovanni Rotondo. The project was delayed by the Second World War but went ahead in 1946, with building work on what was known as the *Casa Sollievo della Sofferenza* ("Home for the Relief of Suffering") started the following year. In the same year the Capuchins opened a convent in Pius' birthplace, Pietrelcina.

The crowds of penitents grew ever larger, so that he was obliged to establish an advance booking system. Vatican suspicions lessened, and Pius was invited to visit Pope Pius XII (1939–1958), who suggested the formation of prayer groups to support the work of the hospital. This was opened in 1956, in the presence of a crowd of 15,000, including many high-ranking church and state officials. Pius was given personal control of the hospital and devised an original regime with "times for prayer and times for science." He planned a whole complex including an international study centre, a hospice for old people, and a cenacle for spiritual exercises. His vision was one of "holistic" treatment long before the concept reached the general consciousness.

In 1959, with his health deteriorating, Pius began broadcasting his spiritual thoughts on the hospital radio after the midday and evening Angelus. He made an apparently miraculous recovery when a statue of Our Lady of Fatima was brought into the hospital—which did not occasion any sort of official inquiry. His recovery was sustained, and in 1966 the tenth anniversary of the foundation was celebrated with an international convention of the prayer groups. On 20 September 1968 huge crowds gathered to mark the fiftieth anniversary of his stigmata. Two days later, as he was saying Mass, some in the congregation noticed that the stigmata had disappeared. It proved to be his last Mass, and he died the following day.

Doctors who examined his body found no trace of the wounds ever having been there, and declared his feet and hands to be "as fresh as those of a child"— which is somewhat odd in itself. The cause for his beatification was opened two months later. Pope John Paul II, elected in September 1978, set up an examination of the charges brought against Pius during his lifetime and found them all to be false. The diocesan process delivered 104 volumes of evidence to the Congregation for the Causes of Saints in 1990, and the beatification ceremony took place on 2 May 1999. The crowds were so great that some 200,000 people could not get into St Peter's Piazza, and had to watch the ceremony on huge screens erected in front of St John Lateran. The pope in his homily said that people saw in Pius "a living image of Christ suffering and risen" and mentioned his stigmata with no hint of doubt, although he concentrated more on Pius' long hours spent in the confessional and his outstanding charity.

In June 2000 a seven-year-old boy, Matteo Pio Colella, the son of a doctor working at San Giovanno Rotondo, was rushed to hospital with galloping meningitis. By nightfall he was in a coma, with loss of function in nine vital organs. His mother and some Capuchin friars of Pius' monastery held a prayer vigil, and in the morning Matteo awoke from his coma to say that he had seen an elderly man with a white beard, dressed in a long brown robe, who had told him, "Don't worry, you will soon be cured." In December 2001 this was accepted as a miracle produced by Pius' intervention, and it cleared the way for his canonization, which took place on 16 June 2002. In his homily on this occasion the pope did not mention the stigmata, referred only briefly to "trials" and his "constant reference to the Cross," and emphasized his prayer life and his charity:

"In fact, the ultimate reason for the apostolic effectiveness of Padre Pio, the profound root of so much spiritual fruitfulness, can be found in that intimate and constant union with God, attested by his long hours spent in prayer and the confessional. He loved to repeat, 'I am a poor Franciscan who prays' ... This fundamental characteristic of his spirituality continues in the 'Prayer Groups' that he founded, which offer to the Church and to society the wonderful contribution of incessant and confident prayer. To prayer, Padre Pio joined an intense charitable activity, of which the 'Home for the Relief of Suffering' is an extraordinary expression. Prayer and charity, this is the most concrete synthesis of Padre Pio's teaching, which today is offered to everyone."

The above is substantially the account in *Butler*, September, pp. 216–9, based largely on Various, *Il grande livro di Padre Pio* (1998), here updated for the canonization. The literature on him is vast, as now is the amount of information on the internet, including graphic descriptions of his grappling with demons, much in the manner of St Antony of Egypt. Studies available in English include, in date order, those by C. M. Carty (1956); N. de Robeck (1960); O. de Lislo (1961); J. McCaffrey (1978); A. Pandiscia (1991); and W. Gallagher (1995).

The Home for the Relief of Suffering now belongs to the Vatican and treats some 60,000 patients each year. It operates as a public hospital within the Italian Health Service and enjoys a high rank as an "Institute for Care and Recovery of a Scientific Character." A new shrine, designed by the celebrated architect Renzo Piano, was inaugurated in July 2004. Circular in plan, with the floor descending in a spiral around the altar in a way designed to echo the valley floor of the surrounding area, the church can hold 8,000 people and is the largest in Christendom after St Peter's, although the architect insists that its arched segments provide intimate spaces for quiet prayer and meditation (*Zenit* interview, 23 July 2004).

24

Bd Anton Martin Slomšek, *Bishop* (1800–1862)

The inscription on the statue of the first Slovene to be beatified, standing in front of the cathedral in his diocese of Maribor, Slovenia, reads, "Anton Martin Slomšek, first bishop of Maribor, awakener of national consciousness, educator, writer." A great admirer of SS Cyril and Methodius (14 Feb.), he is a worthy follower in their footsteps as evangelizer, promoter of national culture, and apostle of church unity.

He was born on 26 November 1800 in the parish of St Martin of Ponikva, near Celje in eastern Slovenia. Slovenia was then a province of the Hapsburg Empire, and St Martin had been a Christian settlement since around the tenth century. He was the eldest child of a relatively prosperous peasant family, farming over fifty hectares of land. His father expected Anton to help from an early age, but his mother persuaded him to allow the child at least to attend Sunday school, led by the curate, Fr Prašnikar. He was clearly the brightest child in the village, and his mother and the curate then sent him to school in Celje, some ten miles away. It was a great step forward for him, but it coincided with the ruin of his family. His mother died giving birth to her eighth child; his father married a woman twenty-seven years his junior and died himself in 1821; his second son took over the farm but proved incapable of running it, and an enforced sale took place. Anton relied increasingly on Fr Prašnikar.

In Celje he was boarding and had to pay for his board and lodging as well as school fees. Fr Prašnikar helped to some extent, and Anton worked as a coach to children of wealthy parents. From grammar school in Celje he moved to the lyceum in the capital, Ljubljana, for some months, and then went to study philosophy at Senj. He had been convinced of his vocation to the priesthood for several years and in 1821 entered the seminary at Celovec (Klagenfurt, now in Austria). Already a fervent devotee of the Slovene language and culture, he found himself in an atmosphere where it was despised. He nevertheless gathered a group of some fifty seminarians together and taught them Slovene. He completed his pastoral and theological courses in three years and was ordained by the bishop of Krško (in south-eastern Slovenia) on 8 September 1824. That same day he began a spiritual diary, dedicated to the bishop, Jakob Pavlić, which he started with quotations from Matthew, Luke, and Galatians, ending the first entry with, "Yet it is no longer I who live, but Christ who lives in me" (Gal. 2:20). He celebrated his first Mass in Olimje, where Fr Prašnikar was by then parish priest, and a week later said Mass in his native Ponikva. He returned to Celovec for a further year of theological studies but refused to stay on to take a doctorate, preferring pastoral work in a parish.

Anton's first post as curate was in a beautiful country area, where he soon became popular with the people, who came considerable distances to hear him preach. But he found his parish priest cold and overbearing and after two years asked for a transfer. The bishop sent him to the village of Nova Cerkev, near Vojnik and not far from his birthplace. He spent two happy years there and was then invited back to Celovec to become spiritual director of the seminary, a post he held for nine years. During this time he began collecting folk songs (and writing his own), which he published as *Songs collected across Carinthia and Styria*. He revived his Slovene-study group, became an expert on the orthography of the language, and published books on this, as well as collections of sermons—in the most famous of which he preached the possession of the mother tongue as a God-given talent, not to be buried in the ground. In his summer vacations he walked widely, as far as Vienna and Salzburg to the north and Zagreb to the east. Wherever he went, he studied the local history and culture.

Anton then applied to return to parish work, as he missed direct pastoral contact with the people. He was appointed to Vuzenica, on the river Drava nor far south of Celovec (then Saldenhofen an der Drau, but now over the border in Slovenia). Radical restoration of the church and priest's house was needed, as well as of liturgy and pastoral care. With the assistance of two curates, he threw himself into all aspects of the work with enthusiasm. At meals with the curates, he insisted they all speak Latin two days a week, German another two, and Slovene the remaining three. He spent as much time as he could with children, and it was during this period that he wrote his Sunday School textbook, *Little Blazey and Agnes in Sunday School*. Written out of a deep understanding of and feeling for children, this was to have a great influence on the future development of education in Slovenia, as well as being translated into Czech and Russian. It was a true textbook of life for country children, with a far wider range of subjects than would be included in "Sunday School" now: the "three Rs", plus German and religion, with instruction in hygiene, botany, astronomy, fruit-growing, and first-aid.

In 1844 the bishop nominated him inspector of schools in the diocese of Lavant (spanning the present Austria–Slovenia boundary), which involved two days' arduous travelling each week. Anton moved to St Andraž (St Andrä in Austria) to cut down the journeys. Wherever he went, he sought to inculcate a new spirit in the schools. To assist in this, he compiled two prayer books for children, one in Slovene and one in German, followed by a book of hymns for schools. He wanted to publish a complete liturgical handbook, with music for hymns and Mass chants throughout the year, but never managed to complete this. He also tried to found a Slovenian publishing house, but the government, fearing this was a manifestation of pan-Slav national feeling, refused to allow it. He did, however, publish the first of a series titled "Little Crumbs," anthologies of notes and thoughts, which became hugely popular and were reprinted for years after his death. He also embarked on a translation of the Bible into Slovene, but got no further than the Pentateuch.

Anton was then appointed town priest of Celje, where he arrived just after the death of Bishop Kutnar of Lavant, who had proposed him for the post. He had hardly begun work when the cardinal archbishop of Salzburg proposed that he should take over the diocese. He reluctantly agreed and left Celje only three months after his arrival there. Great crowds turned out to bid him farewell as he left for Salzburg by the railway that had been built just a few years earlier. He was consecrated on 5 July 1846 and solemnly enthroned in St Andraž a week later, adding Martin to his first name after his sponsor at confirmation and his native parish.

He wrote pastoral letters to his clergy in Latin and to his flock in German and Slovene. Their message was strict enough in terms of faith and morals, but the tone was consistently warm and caring. He was cautious over the revolutions of 1848, advising people to welcome progress but to avoid violence; but nationalist aspirations throughout central Europe encouraged him in his continual concern for Slovene culture. (Slovene intellectuals issued the first political proposal for a united Slovenia.) He took especial care of the education of seminarians and began to promote parish missions, leading some himself, speaking at as many as possible, and inviting the Lazarists into the diocese to conduct them. He raised considerable support in the diocese for the Lazarist missions in Africa and America. In 1851 Anton Martin formed the confraternity of SS Cyril and Methodius to pray and work to overcome disunity among Christians, particularly between Catholics and Orthodox. This received papal approval a year later and spread widely in Europe. In 1856–1857 he undertook an apostolic visitation of the Benedictine monasteries of central Europe, at the request of Pope Pius IX.

Anton Martin's great achievement was to transfer the see from St Andraž, at the very northern edge of the diocese and in German-speaking parts, to Maribor, forty miles to the south-east (now the principal city of eastern Slovenia). This had been proposed several decades earlier but had been vetoed by the emperor in 1832. Anton Martin had the personality and drive to convince the pope and the powers in Vienna that the project should now be carried through. The church of St John the Baptist in Maribor was restored and made the new cathedral, and Anton sang a first solemn Vespers there on 3 September 1859. He negotiated changes in diocesan borders that resulted in some 200,000 Slovenes becoming part of his diocese instead of that of Graz in Austria—not as many as he had wanted, but still a considerable achievement. He founded a seminary and theological school in Maribor, which developed into the present university. And he continued to write: school textbooks, catechisms, liturgical manuals, Slovene history and biographies, amounting to some fifty books published in his lifetime.

By 1862 his health was rapidly failing, and he died of an intestinal complaint on 24 September. His burial in the Chapel of Our Lady of Sorrows was marred by a group of Germanophile youths, who spat on his coffin, shouting, "Take that, you Slovene saint!" In 1941, when the Axis powers invaded, his tomb became a focus of national resistance, and the Nazis gave orders for the coffin to be removed; but it was rescued by partisans and re-buried under the Franciscan church. It was finally laid to rest in the crypt of the newly restored cathedral in 1978, which was the 750th anniversary of the diocese of Lavant. Pope John Paul II beatified Anton Martin in Maribor on 19 September 1999. Bishop Frank Bramberger of Maribor said of him:

> "Teacher and educator, writer and poet, biographer and critic, lover of his mother tongue and fighter for national equality, patriot, speaker and preacher, ecumenical worker and teacher of the Slovene people, priest and bishop—Slomšek's personality is like a mosaic. Each stone has its own colour, but all together provide the image of a saint, that is a person who is open to the breath of the Holy Spirit, who prophetically understands the signs of the times and responds to them, who understands how to use all natural and supernatural means to realize the Kingdom Of God on earth."

In his homily at the ceremony, Pope John Paul II quoted Anton's words spoken at a parish mission: "They say, 'The world has grown old; the human race is adrift; Europe is coming to an end.' Well, yes, if we abandon humanity to its natural course, to its fatal direction. No, if the power from on high that is preserved in the religion of Jesus, in his Church, is poured out anew on all ranks of the human race and restores them to life." Recalling Bishop Anton's example—"He shows that it is possible to be sincere patriots and with equal sincerity to coexist and cooperate with people of other nationalities, other cultures, and other religions"—the Pope urged the young people of Slovenia to be "builders of peace within Europe too!"

His collected works (incomplete) were published in Maribor between 1876 and 1899. His letters have been collected into the Maribor archives (1930–1934). There are biographies in Slovene by F. Kozar (1863) and F. Kovažiž (1935). See also *LThK*, ²IX, 834f; on his liturgical work see S. Krajnk, *L'opera liturgica di A. M. Slomšek nella sua attività pastorale* (1993). The quote from Bishop Bamberger is on www.catholic-forum.co./saints/saintaed.

OCTOBER

1

Bd Luigi Maria Monti, *Founder* (1825–1900)

Born in Bovisio, a small town in the diocese of Milan, Luigi was the eighth of eleven children. His father died when he was twelve, and Luigi learned the craft of woodcarving to produce articles for sale in order to help support his mother and his younger brothers and sisters. As time went on, his workshop drew other devout young men to meet there for evening prayers. They became a regular group, calling themselves The Company of the Sacred Heart of Jesus, but known to local people as The Company of Friars. They led an austere life, cared for the sick and the poor, and strove to reconcile those who had lapsed from the faith—many, in a time of social upheaval and competing ideologies.

Luigi, whom people called "Father" on account of his way of life, though he was never ordained, made a private vow to his confessor, consecrating himself to God and vowing chastity and obedience. This unconventional way of"religious"life brought him and his Company enemies in the town, including the parish priest, who must have felt his position threatened. These delated the Company to the local magistrates, accusing them of political conspiracy against the occupying Austrian forces. Luigi and his companions were sent"on remand" to prison in Desio and spent seventy-two days there before a full investigation into the charges proved them false and procured their release.

Following his spiritual director, Fr Luigi Dossi, Luigi joined the Congregation of Mary Immaculate (founded in 1847 in nearby Brescia by Bd Ludovic Pavoni, 1784–1849; 1 Apr.). He was a novice for six years before deciding that this form of consecration was not right for him, during which time he gained both teaching and nursing experience. He put the latter to heroic use, agreeing to be isolated in the asylum in Brescia with sufferers from cholera during an outbreak in 1855. But, although he admired the Constitutions of the Congregation, he could not feel spiritually at home in it, and he was to write toward the end of his life of the aridity he felt despite endless hours spent in prayer before the Blessed Sacrament, ended only by a vision of Jesus and Mary—who seem to have told him to go back to the way he began.

Fr Dossi's next proposal for his true vocation was an organization dedicated specifically to the care of sick people in Rome. Luigi received this idea enthusiastically and with some of his former Company members and an experienced nurse named Cipriano Pezzini formed a group, which he named The Congregation of the Sons of the Immaculate Conception. They proposed to offer their services to the Santo Spirito Hospital, one of the best known in Europe, but the Capuchin friars who provided chaplains to the hospital were already organizing a group of lay helpers working as a sort of Third Order, and did not particularly want a rival group arriving from the provinces. Brother Luigi, as he was now known, had to ask if his group could be incorporated into the Capuchin organization, to which the friars agreed. They were given practical nursing duties, but Luigi also gained a diploma as a phlebotomist (blood-letter) from La Sapienza University.

Despite the general bureaucratic problems of having new religious movements approved, the Congregation gained the ear of Pope Pius IX (Bd; 7 Feb.), who was always interested in anything to do with the Immaculate Conception— which he had proclaimed as dogma on 8 December 1854 and tended to see as the answer to all the ills of the world—and was also genuinely concerned for the fate of Rome's sick people. He appointed Luigi superior general in 1877. The Brothers worked assiduously, especially during epidemics of typhoid or malaria, to which the area around Rome was much subject until the marshes were drained in the early twentieth century. They went out and started small communities in the countryside, also travelling to isolated farms in the region to provide nursing care.

In 1882 a Carthusian monk from Desio came to see Luigi, saying he had been inspired by Mary Immaculate to do so. He told him that he had four nephews who had been left orphans, and Luigi promptly expanded his mission to open an orphanage in Saronno (north-west of Milan) to cater for them and other orphans, who were received into a family atmosphere and given a parentally loving preparation for life. Luigi continued his unremitting service to the sick and orphans until his death at the age of seventy-five, by when he was exhausted and practically blind, on 1 October 1900. Despite Pius IX's encouragement, the Congregation had still not received official approbation, which was given in 1904 by Pius X (St; 21 Aug.), who stipulated that its members could be ordained so as to provide a priestly ministry from within, adding a sacramental ministry to the forms of help they could provide.

In 1941 the archbishop of Milan, Cardinal Ildefonsus Schuster (beatified, somewhat controversially in view of his relations with Mussolini's Fascist regime, in 1996; 30 Aug.), initiated the diocesan process for Luigi's beatification, which was completed in 1951. He was declared Venerable in 2001, and in 2003 the cure of a Sardinian farmer, Luigi Iecle, was declared miraculous and brought about through Luigi Monti's intercession, clearing the way for his beatification on 9 November 2003. Pope John Paul II held him up as an example of "faithfulness to God's call and to the proclamation of the gospel of charity," who was "entirely dedicated to healing the physical and spiritual wounds of the sick and the orphaned ... a model of solidarity toward the needy ..."He did not mention the fact that he had remained a layman all his life.

2

Bd John Beyzym (1850–1912)

John (Jan) was born in Beyzymy Wielkie, now in the north-western Ukrainian province Volynska' Oblast', (then the Polish province of Volinia), on 15 May 1850. His parents were landowners and he received his early education privately on the family estate. In 1863 an uprising deprived his parents of their land and forced them to separate, and John moved on to secondary school in Kiev. He entered the Jesuit novitiate at Stara Wiés in December 1872. During his novitiate he had an experience that may well have influenced his future choice of mission, accompanying priests visiting the sick during a cholera outbreak in the villages around Kiev. From Stara Wiés he progressed to further studies in theology and philosophy at Kraków, where he was ordained on 26 July 1881.

He was assigned to teach French and Russian in Jesuit schools in Tarnopol and Chyrów. John spent seventeen years teaching and also looking after the school infirmary, although he had asked to go and work among lepers as early as 1879, two years before his ordination. His wish was not granted until 1898, by which time he was already forty-eight years old. The Jesuit general Luis Martín sent him to Madagascar, as he could speak French and there were already French Jesuits working with the lepers there.

He was posted to the leprosarium at Ambahivoraka, in a desert area near the capital, Antananarivo. There 150 victims of the disease lived in conditions of total misery, without adequate food or medical care. They died as often from hunger as from the effects of the disease. John took the radical decision to move into the encampment and live with the lepers—the first priest to take such a step in Madagascar. It was not easy for him: he found the sight and the stench of leprosy repulsive and told his provincial that at times he had even fainted, "for here we don't breathe the scent of flowers but the putrefaction of bodies generated by leprosy." But he was determined to carry on and improve conditions: putting his experience in school infirmaries into effect, he was able to improve medication for the lepers' sores and to introduce elementary hygienic measures, such as clean water. He begged for food in the city, to supplement the inadequate supply of rice provided by the government. The improved diet reduced the average rate of death from five a week to five a year.

State "care" of lepers did not involve any dimension of hope or giving sufferers any reason to live a life guided by principles. John saw that if this was to change, a completely different sort of place from the State hospices had to be provided. He wrote to missionary organizations and magazines in Poland, begging for funds, which began to arrive in a steady stream. He enhanced his appeal in his native country by naming his new project after Our Lady of Czestochowa, inspiring many who had little to give to those who had even less. He left Ambahivoraka in 1903, moved 180 miles south, and began building a hugely ambitious hospital at Marana, near Fianarantsoa, where there was a good water supply and fertile land for growing crops. His only resources were the charitable donations he received from Europe, mainly from Poland, Austria, and Germany. He persevered against seemingly overwhelming odds, and the hospital was finally opened in August 1911. A priest who was also a medical doctor described it as "a colossal task … [but] his trust in God's help was unshakeable." Sisters of the Congregation of St Joseph of Cluny (founded in 1807 by Bd Anne-Marie Javouhey [15 July] and her three sisters) came to staff it. The patients were accorded dignity and equality through wearing uniform, and they worshipped together in the chapel, which had decorations carved by John himself. He was astonished when the lepers from Ambahivoraka arrived, having travelled for a month on foot, determined to be where he was.

He did not live long after the opening of the hospital, dying at Marana on 2 October 1912, but his work lives on after him, and the hospital still functions as a memorial to his tireless work and towering achievement. Since 1964 small houses have been added to the main buildings, where the families of those who are sick can live. He changed public attitudes to leprosy, as well as transforming the lives of sufferers from the disease. He was one of four Poles beatified by Pope John Paul II in his home city of Kraków on 18 August 2002. His homily tied the four together under the common link of mercy, and of John Beyzym he said that he provided "the greatest gift of mercy: bringing people to Christ and giving them the opportunity to know and enjoy his love."

Quote on the hospital from Vatican news service, citing Fr J. Lielet, *Chine, Ceylan, Madagascar* (1912). On the Cluny Sisters see *Orders*, pp. 102–3.

4

Bd Francis Xavier Seelos (1819–1867)

The sixth of twelve children of Mang (named for the local saint) and Frances Schwarzenbach Seelos was born in Füssen, in the Swabia region of Bavaria, 60 miles south of Munich, on 11 January 1819. He was christened Francis Xavier, was confirmed when he was nine, and made his First Communion at the age of eleven, by which time he was determined to become a priest and given to declaring that he would be another Francis Xavier (3 Dec.). His father was a tailor (or textile merchant), and the family was devout, with daily Mass and regular prayers.

He went to grammar school in Füssen, followed by seven years at the Academy of St Stephen in Augsburg, then in 1839 embarked on a philosophy and theology course at Munich university, made possible by a scholarship. After gaining a degree in philosophy (but before completing his theology) Frances Xavier entered the Augsburg diocesan seminary, in September 1842. He had already applied to the Redemptorists, and two months later heard that he had been accepted to train for their mission in the U.S.A. He left the seminary in December and sailed for New York the following March, arriving on 20 April 1843. He joined a small group of priests and brothers working mainly for the German immigrant community. For his novitiate year he was sent to the parish of Saint James in Baltimore, Maryland. The Redemptorists' character was formed by prayer, strict discipline, and mortification. Francis Xavier, who loved the life, was professed on 16 May 1844 and ordained priest on 22 December of the same year.

In August 1845 he was posted to the parish of Saint Philomena in Pittsburgh. The pastor there was John Nepomucene Neumann (canonized in 1977; 5 Jan.), whom he described as "in every respect ... like a remarkable father to me. He has introduced me to the active life; he has guided me as my spiritual leader and confessor." When Neumann was appointed provincial superior of the Redemptorists in the U.S.A., Francis Xavier succeeded him as pastor of Saint Philomena's. The parish was growing rapidly, with three Masses each Sunday in the church, plus another for children in the hall, then catechesis and a conference in the afternoon, followed by Vespers and devotions, with a sermon. He devoted special attention to the school children, as well as spending long hours in the confessional, hearing Confessions from "Whites and Blacks" in German, English, and French besides visiting his parishioners assiduously. He was also Redemptorist novice-master. His reputation spread, and people came in increasing numbers from outside the parish to seek his advice and even physical cures, which often resulted from his praying with the sick.

After nine years in Pittsburgh Francis Xavier was transferred to Baltimore, as parish priest of Saint Alphonsus, with responsibility also for outlying districts served by mission chapels. Again his reputation as a spiritual adviser spread, and people waited two or three hours to confess to him. Working with the Oblate Sisters of Divine Providence, he took pastoral care of the black Catholic community as well. The days were not long enough, as he wrote to his sister (by then also a professed religious): "... from morning to night I am overwhelmed with cares and worries ... White and Negro, German and English, confreres and externs, clerical and lay people, aristocratic men and unworldly nuns, the poor, the sick, ask for my assistance. One wants this, another that. There is no rest." Despite this, "I cannot thank God enough for my vocation."

Exhaustion took a toll on his health, and in 1857 a blood vessel burst in his neck, nearly killing him and forcing him to rest for several weeks. He was moved to Annapolis, Maryland, as parish priest of Saint Mary's and Redemptorist novice-master, but after only two months there he was appointed to Saints Peter and Paul in Cumberland, Maryland, a small but rapidly growing parish with the Redemptorist seminary attached to the church. His gifts of preaching and instructing simply but profoundly again increased his appeal and widened his influence: "Whenever I preach, although my sermons are very simple, people show much pleasure in listening to me with attention, all ears. They never seem to get tired listening to me. Particularly, the catechetical instructions, which I myself willingly give, appear to them very instructive and interesting," he wrote to his sister (adding that his own failures to live up to his teaching prevented him from becoming proud). There were up to seventy seminarians at a time, and he somehow found time to guide their spiritual formation and oversee their general welfare, instilling the "twelve monthly virtues" laid down by the founder, St Alphonsus de'Liguori (1 Aug.), in his *Primitive Rule*.

In 1860 the bishop of Pittsburgh, Michael O'Connor, was due to retire. Supported by many other people, he recommended Francis Xavier to Rome as his successor, saying that, despite being "quite German in character," and lacking Neumann's (by then Bishop of Baltimore) learning, he possibly exceeded him in zeal and piety. Francis Xavier was convinced he lacked the qualities and experience required in a bishop and begged Pope Pius IX in a letter to be excused from "this act of God." Unknown to him, his name had already been removed from the list of possible candidates—at least in part due to anti-German feelings, largely among Irish American Catholics. When he learned he was excused, he gave his seminarians a "free day" and organized a gala celebration of the feast of St Stanislaus (then 7 May, now 11 April), at which he declared, "I would rather be bishop of my students than bishop of Pittsburgh!"

By 1862 Cumberland was threatened by the progress of the American Civil War, and, with seminarians caught in crossfire, Francis Xavier moved the seminary to Annapolis, safer in Union territory. He cared for Confederate prisoners and for wounded Union soldiers. Faced with the problem of seminarians being drafted into the Union army—only priests were exempt—he went to see President Lincoln to ask for them to be excused. His request was denied, but he achieved his aim by the simple expedient of promptly asking the bishop to ordain all his students. By this time, internal dissensions in the Order had led to his dismissal as director of the seminary, for being, allegedly, "too lenient." In 1863 he was appointed superior of the Redemptorist "mission band" and spent the next two years travelling and conducting parish missions, with their traditional Redemptorist emphasis on sermons followed by Confessions, in the states of Connecticut, Illinois, Michigan, Missouri, New Jersey, New York, Ohio, Pennsylvania, Rhode Island, and Wisconsin. Everywhere he went, he brought people into or back to the practice of the faith through his simplicity, cheerfulness, and obvious sincerity.

In 1865 Francis Xavier was recalled from the mission band and appointed to the parish of the Holy Redeemer in Detroit. During his short stay of only ten months he gained the affection of his parishioners, largely through his obvious love for and attention to the poorest and "most abandoned" in the parish. A huge crowd came to say their farewells on the evening before he left for what was to be his last post, in New Orleans. There the Redemptorists were in charge of three parishes: Saint Mary's for German speakers, Saint Alphonsus' for English, and Notre Dame de Bon Secours for French. Francis Xavier had been superior to most of the priests there at one time or another, and so came among friends. He spoke all three languages but worked mainly at St Mary's. He had been there only five weeks when news reached him that his mother had died. He settled once more into his pattern of preaching, catechizing, hearing Confessions, and giving advice.

In September 1867 one of the frequent outbreaks of Yellow Fever hit the city. Francis Xavier worked tirelessly caring for the sick and dying, but caught the virus himself and died on 4 October. He was only forty-eight years old. He was buried in the crypt of St Mary's, next to Brother Wenceslaus Neumann, St John Neumann's brother. The "informative process" of the cause for his canonization was introduced in 1900, but it was not until 1966 that a miraculous cure attributed to his intercession took place. He was beatified on 9 April 2000 in Rome. In his homily at the ceremony, the pope said, "In the various places where he worked, Fr Francis Xavier brought his enthusiasm, spirit of sacrifice, and apostolic zeal. To the abandoned and lost he preached the message of Jesus Christ ... and in the long hours spent in the confessional he convinced many to return to God."

The official biography is *The Cheerful Ascetic*, by Michael Curley, CSsR (1969, n.e. 2002) on which the numerous articles on or linked to the comprehensive website www.seelos.org are based, including a lengthy summary by Thomas Artz, CSsR, with photographs of places associated with Fr Seelos; also "America's Forgotten Saint?" by Carl Hoegerl, CSsR, from *Soul Magazine* (Jan.–Feb., 1999).

5

St Faustina Kowalska (1905–1938)

Helena Kowalska was born in 1905 in the village of Glagowiec, near Lódz in Poland, the third of ten children born to Marianna and Stanislaus Kowalski. Her parents' poverty meant that she received only three years of secondary schooling, from the ages of thirteen to sixteen, before going to work in domestic service in order to support herself and help them. When she was nineteen, against the wishes of her parents, she entered a convent of the Sisters of Our Lady of Mercy as Sister Maria Faustina, to which she later added "of the Blessed Sacrament."

The Congregation ran boarding schools for neglected and maladjusted girls. Faustina was a "co-adjutrix" (a type of lay Sister) and worked in a number of convents as cook, gardener, and porter, usually supervising and training small groups of the girls, to whom she was able to relate easily and effectively. At the same time she developed a deeply spiritual inner life marked by mystical experiences and visions—to which some sources add bilocation, prophecy, stigmata, and the mystical marriage—which she revealed only to her superior and her spiritual director. He ordered her to write an account of her experiences in the form of a diary: but Faustina was virtually illiterate and wrote an ungrammatical and unpunctuated version that required translation to be intelligible. The first translation (which reached Rome in 1958) was badly done and was to delay her cause by many years. Her fellow Sisters seem to have regarded her as an ordinary, hard-working nun with no special attributes except a strong common sense, although some commented, not always approvingly, on her ability to read other people's thoughts and see beyond external posturings.

Faustina's special devotion was to the Divine Mercy, and in one of her visions she saw Our Lord with rays of mercy flowing as streams of multi-hued light from his heart. He named her the apostle and secretary of his mercy, saying, "Today I am sending you with my mercy to the people of the whole world. I do not want to punish aching mankind but … to heal it." He ordered her to paint and distribute the image she had just seen, with the title, "Jesus, I trust in you." The devotion as expounded by Faustina involved the adoration of God's great mercy as seen in his roles of creator, redeemer, and the source of all holiness; it also involved co-operating in the merciful work of Christ and prayer that the whole world would recognize and benefit from this divine mercy. Shortly before her death she believed she was being called by God to found a new Congregation dedicated to spreading her message. She felt, however, that she did not have the ability for such an undertaking, and her illness then put it out of the question.

Faustina died in Kraków of tuberculosis on 5 October 1938, after offering her sufferings for the conversion of sinners. She was beatified in 1993 and canonized on 30 April 2000 by Pope John Paul II, who as a young man had developed a strong devotion to her. Later, as archbishop of Kraków, he had promoted her cause, ordered a better translation of the diary to be made, and was instrumental in persuading the Vatican eventually to lift its prohibition on devotion to the Divine Mercy, a ban apparently imposed because of a lack of theological sophistication and some suspect devotional practices in Faustina's writings—at least in the earlier translation, which was actually condemned as heretical. On the occasion of the canonization, and in accordance with Faustina's wishes, the Pope established the second Sunday of Easter as a universal feast-day dedicated to the Divine Mercy, to be a "perennial invitation to the Christian world to face, with confidence in the divine goodness, the difficulties and trials that await men and women in the coming years."

On the orders of her spiritual director Faustina kept a diary of her spiritual experiences, titled "Divine Mercy in My Soul." Extracts were published in *On the Divine Mercy* (1955); a fuller version is *Divine Mercy in My Soul, The Diary of Sister M. Faustina Kowalska* (1987). Of the many biographies, see M. Winowska, *L'icone de Christ miséricordieux, message de Soeur Faustine* (1973); Sr Sophia Michalenko, *Mercy My Mission: Life of Sister Faustina H. Kowlaska* (1987, republished 1993 as *The Life of Faustina Kowalska*, the authorized biography); and Maria Tarnawska, *Blessed Sister Faustina Her Life and Mission* (1989, 2d edn, 1993), based largely on extracts from the diary. See also *Dict. Sp*, 56 (1974), 719–20, with photographs.

A number of artists have attempted to reproduce her vision of the merciful Savior; the most frequently reproduced image is the rather sentimentalized version painted in 1943 by the Polish artist Adolf Hyla.

9

St Cyril Bertrand Sanz Tejedor and Companions, *Martyrs*
(died 1934)

A general account of the Martyrs of and associated with the Spanish civil war of 1936–1939 is given in the *Butler* July volume (pp. 169–79). The members of this particular group, beatified in 1990 and the first to be canonized (on

21 November 1999), also have an entry on the anniversary of their execution (October, pp. 58–60). The entry here is based partly on the latter, and readers are referred to the former for background information.

These martyrs were Brothers of the Christian Schools, or La Salle Brothers, members of the teaching Order founded by St John Baptist de la Salle (7 Apr.). They were working in Asturias, a mining area in north-western Spain, where support for the reforms brought in by the Second Republic in 1931 was solid among a highly politicized working class. When a new government elected two years later threatened to undo republican labour legislation, feelings ran high, and when a right-wing group, seen by the miners and others as "clerical–fascist,"joined the government in October 1934, the region erupted in armed revolution. The Church had become associated with right-wing policies, particularly on account of its educational policies, which entailed workshops producing goods for sale below the price at which similar goods produced by adult wage-earners could be sold. The object of this was to educate the children of the poor without charging fees, but the perceived effect was to deprive working people of their livelihood, and the Brothers of the Christian Schools were associated with this.

Cyril Bertrand (Cirilo Bertrán, the names he took in religion) Sanz Tejedor was born in Lerma, in the diocese of Burgos in northern Castile, on 20 March 1888 and christened José. He joined the La Salle Brothers and after being professed in 1905 was appointed to a number of schools, which were successively closed down under anti-clerical legislation in the 1920s which forbade religious to run schools. In 1925 he was appointed superior of the community in Santander, where he remained for six years, allowed to run a school that became highly respected throughout the region. In 1933 Cyril Bertrand was invited to take charge of a school in Turón, in Asturias, one of fourteen schools run by the Brothers in the area, attended mainly by children of miners. When the uprising broke out on 4 October 1934, the rebels seized him and the seven other members of his community. These were (with their names in religion in parentheses):

Filomeno López López (Marciano José), born in the province of Guadalajara in 1900. He was encouraged to join the Order by an uncle, but on account of health problems he had to return home. He was re-admitted, but as a non-teaching Brother engaged in manual work. He replaced a Brother who was frightened of the situation in Turón in April 1934.

Claudio Bernabé Cano (Victoriano Pío), born in the province of Burgos in 1905. He had joined the Brothers in 1918 and was an able musician. He was transferred from the community in Palencia for his own safety and had been with the community as choirmaster for a mere ten days.

Vilfrido Fernández Zapico (Julián Alfredo), born in the province of León in 1903. Brought up by a priest uncle after the death of his mother, he first joined the Capuchins in Salamanca but was forced by an illness to return home. He joined the La Salle Brothers at the age of twenty-two and was transferred to Turón, where his strength of character was needed, in 1933.

Vicente Alonso Andrés (Benjamín Julián), born in the province of Burgos in 1908. He joined the Brothers at a young age and had some difficulty with his studies, but he was finally professed in August 1933. Noted for his sense of joy and sound judgment, he worked first at their school in Santiago de Compostela, leaving grieving parents and children when he was moved to Turón.

Héctor Valdivielso Sáez (Benito de Jesús), born in Buenos Aires, Argentina, in 1910. His parents had emigrated there a few years before his birth, but they failed to prosper in Argentina and returned to Spain, where Héctor joined the Brothers. He longed to go back to Argentina as a missionary, and attended the La Salle missionary novitiate at Lembecq-lez-Hal in Belgium as a preparation. Back in Spain, he taught at the Order's school in Astorga before being transferred to Turón. A talented writer and dedicated to the principles of Catholic Action, he is the first Argentinian saint.

Manuel Seco Gutiérrez (Aniceto Adolfo), the youngest member of the community, born in the province of Santander in 1912 and so only twenty-two at the time of his martyrdom. Following the early death of their mother, three sons in the family were brought up by their father to join the La Salle Brothers. He joined in 1928 and took his first vows in 1930. After a year at the College of Our Lady in Valladolid he was moved to Turón in August 1933.

Román Martínez Fernández (Augusto Andrés), born in the province of Santander in 1910. He was left the only male in the household on the death of his father, and his mother strongly resisted his intention to become a religious, but when he fell seriously ill she vowed to Our Lady that she would accept his wish if he recovered. He took his vows in 1932 and was at Palencia when the Brothers were dispersed as a safety measure. He was moved to Turón in 1933, and it was he who addressed the group's last words to the executioners.

The Passionist priest executed with them was **Fr Manuel Canoura Arnau** (Inocencio de la Inmaculada), born in the province of Mondoñedo in 1887. He had joined the Passionists at the young age of fourteen and been ordained priest in 1920. He devoted himself to teaching philosophy and theology in the several schools to which he was sent. He was in Turón simply because he had been staying at the college to hear the students' Confessions prior to the first Friday of the month, which fell on the 5th. He and the eight La Salle Brothers were arrested early in the same morning by members of the self-styled "Revolutionary Committee." They were held in the *casa del pueblo*, while a secret decision to kill them was taken. Four days later they were led out to the cemetery, where a large pit had already been dug, and shot on its edge, together with two government officers. Executioners had to be brought in from outside, since no one from Turón would accept the task.

The rebel leader who gave the order for their execution himself produced an impressive testimony: "The Brothers and the priest listened quietly to the sentence and then walked to the middle of the cemetery at a leisurely yet firm pace. They knew where they were going and went like lambs to the slaughter. It was so impressive that I, hardened as I am, could not help being moved … I think that while walking, and when waiting at the gate, they prayed in a subdued voice." Some months later their bodies were exhumed and taken to Bujedo, where many of them had been trained, to be placed in a mausoleum.

In beatifying and now canonizing groups of victims, generally priests and religious, of the conflict in Spain as martyrs, the Church has taken great care to point to their lack of involvement in politics, and at this canonization ceremony, Pope John Paul II declared: "They are not heroes of a human war, in which they did not participate, but educators of youth. Because of their state as consecrated persons and teachers, they faced their tragic destiny as an authentic testimony of faith, giving the last lesson of their life by martyrdom."

❖

M. Valdizán, FSC, *Los mártires de Turón*, 2 vols. (1985); P. Chico, FSC, *Testigos de la Escuela Cristiana* (1989). *Oss.Rom.* (Spanish weekly edition), 21 November 1999. The website in the Saints Alive series produced by St Thomas Church, Rochester, NY, although claiming copyright, is virtually a word-for-word reproduction of the *Butler* 9 October entry.

10

St Daniel Comboni, *Bishop and Founder* (1831–1881)

The first Catholic bishop of central Africa was born into a poor peasant family at Limone on Lake Garda, in the province of Brescia in northern Italy, on 15 March 1831. His parents, Luigi and Domenica, had eight children, but suffered the exceptional misfortune of seeing six die in infancy and a seventh in childhood, leaving Daniel, born fourth, an only child. Their poverty obliged them to send him away to be educated for free at the religious institute in Verona founded by Fr Nicholas Mazza, dedicated to training priests for the African missions. There Daniel discovered his vocation to the priesthood and also developed his lifelong passion for Africa, nourished by the tales told by returning missionaries. He studied theology and philosophy and was ordained by the bishop of Trent on 31 December 1854.

In 1857 he set out for Sudan with five other missionaries from the institute, taking four months to reach Khartoum. The climate was unbearably hot, the people were destitute, and the work was backbreaking. Daniel embraced it all wholeheartedly, writing back to his parents: "We will have to labour hard, to sweat, to die; but the thought that one sweats and dies for love of Jesus Christ and the salvation of the most abandoned souls in the world, is far too sweet for us to desist from this great enterprise" (quoted on Agenzia Fides site). One of his companions died, but Daniel was the more determined to carry on. He coined the phrase "*O Nigrizia o morte*" ("Negritude or death"), a pointer to the advanced theories of mission he was to develop. Forced by sickness to return to Italy after two years, he set to work on a "plan for the rebirth of Africa," to "save Africa through Africa," a theory of inculturation a century before such a concept became generally acceptable. He believed that Africa would be evangelized through the quality of its people, whom he saw as adults in need of help, rather than as children in need of guidance, as was the paternalistic view common in Europe.

Daniel travelled widely in western Europe—France, Spain, England, Germany, and Austria—preaching his message that European society as well as the Church needed to become far more concerned with Africa. He asked for financial aid but was certainly not envisaging the colonial partition and exploitation that led to politicians still declaring in 2005 that the time has come to eradicate poverty in Africa. He divided the rest of his life between Europe and Africa, making eight journeys in all to "the dark continent." In Italy he founded the first magazine devoted specifically to the missions, named the *Annals of the Good Shepherd*, and in 1867 he founded in Verona the male Comboni Missionaries, known first as the *Istituto delle Missione per la Nigrizia*, which eventually became the Congregation of the Sons of the Sacred Heart in 1894. He followed this in 1872 with a similar Institute for women—the first time it was thought possible for women to work in Africa. This started as the *Istituto delle Pie Madri*, but over time its members became generally known as Comboni Missionary Sisters.

In 1870 Daniel petitioned the bishops gathered in Rome for the First Vatican Council for every local Church to contribute to the African missions—the *Postulatum pro Nigris Africae Centralis*. So that missionaries could become acclimatized to Africa before venturing into its depths, he opened missionary institutes in Cairo. In 1872 he was appointed pro-vicar apostolic of Central Africa, which gave him pastoral responsibility for almost a hundred million people living in Nubia, Egyptian Sudan, and the territory as far south as the Great Lakes. He founded missions in El-Obeid, Khartoum, Berber, Delen, and Malbes. In 1877 he became successively vicar apostolic, titular bishop of Claudioplis, and finally bishop of Khartoum. That year a terrible drought affected Sudan, leading to the deaths of half the population from starvation within a year and decimating the missionaries. Daniel appealed to European leaders and bishops for help and returned once more to Europe to organize an international group of fresh missionaries, whom he assembled in Verona and despatched to Sudan.

He worked to suppress the slave trade, still active in the area, mainly supplying black slaves to Arab countries. Daniel spoke six European languages as well as Arabic and several central African dialects, on which he made notes that contributed greatly to Western understanding of them, and somehow he found time to engage in research into the region and its geography, producing learned monographs on the subject. He also wrote several thousand letters a year, of which a minority have survived and recently been collected in one volume. He made his last journey to Africa in 1880, and his last two years were saddened not only by the deaths of many of his companions but also by calumnies spread about him.

Daniel died on 10 October 1881 in Khartoum and was interred there. Five years later his tomb was desecrated by followers of the fanatically anti-Christian *Mahdi*, or Muslim Messiah (Mohammed Ahmed, 1844–1885), the rebel leader who that same year took Khartoum and killed General Gordon. The diocesan cause of his beatification was introduced in 1928; in 1970 the sudden cure of a Brazilian girl was attributed to his intercession, and this was officially decreed a miracle in April 1995, leading to his beatification by Pope John Paul II in St Peter's Piazza on 17 March 1996. In 2002 the cure of a Muslim living in Khartoum was decreed miraculous, and he was canonized, also in St Peter's, on 5 October 2003.

Material on him and the Comboni Missionaries in English is relatively abundant: L. Cocchi, *Daniel Comboni: Builder of Civilization* (n.d.); J. M. Lozano, *The Spirituality of Daniel Comboni* (n.d.); P. Chiochetta, *Papers for the Evangelization of Africa* (1982); A. Gilli, *History of the Comboni Missionary Institute* (1985); Comboni Missionaries, *The Comboni Missionaries in South Africa, 1924–1994* (1995); F. Perli, *Be My Witnesses: Spirituality for Mission* (1996); and T. Agostini, *The Comboni Missionaries: An Outline History 1867–1997* (2003). His writings are available in Italian: D. Comboni, *Gli Scritti* (1991); also a selection, *Un passo al giorno* (1997); see also D. Agasso, *Un profeta per l'Africa* (1993); A. Montonati, *Il Nilo scorre ancora* (1995); J. M. Lozano, *Vostro per sempre* (1996); and G. Romanato, *Danile Comboni, l'Africa degli esploratori e dei missionarie* (1998). These references, with a thematic selection of his writings, can be found at www.giovaniemissione.it/testimoni/comboniintro. See also "Daniel Comboni, 1831–1881," *World Mission Magazine*, October 2003.

The "Comboni Family," the two Congregations of priests and Sisters, presently work in forty-one countries, serving in hospitals, orphanages, and schools.

18

BB Daudi Okelo and Jildo Irwa, *Martyrs* (died 1918)

The precise date of birth of these two young Ugandan catechists is not known: Daudi is thought to have been born in around 1902 and Jildo in around 1906, making them probably sixteen and twelve years old at the time of their death. Both came from the Acholi tribe, belonging to the Lwo people, who today live mostly in northern Uganda but also in Congo, Kenya, southern Sudan, and Tanzania.

Daudi was born to pagan parents, named Lodi and Amona, in the village of Ogom-Payira, on the Gulu-Kitgum road. Jildo's parents, Okeny and Ato, were also pagan, though his father later became a Christian. He was born in the village of Bar-Kitoba, about eighty miles north-west of Kitgum. In 1915 the Comboni Missionaries (founded by St Daniel Comboni in 1867; 10 Oct.) established a mission in Kitgum, and Daudi and Jildo received instruction there. Daudi was baptized and received his First Communion on 1 June 1916, Jildo five days later, and both were confirmed on 15 October, after which Daudi agreed to be enrolled as a catechist. When the catechist in the village of Paimol died early in 1917, Daudi offered to replace him and was appointed toward the end of the year. The younger Jildo went with him as his assistant. The head of the Kitgum mission, Fr Cesare Gambaretto, warned them of the dangers from tribal rivalry, roaming gangs of slave traders (slaves were still being taken to Arab countries or sold to wealthy locals), hunters for gold, and insurgents against a not over-sensitive British colonial administration. Both insisted that they were not afraid to die.

The catechists' day began with a dawn call on the drums, summoning the catechumens to morning prayer and a question-and-answer session on the basic elements of the catechism—called *Lok-odiku* ("the words of the morning"). During the day the children helped with cattle or crops, and there was another call to prayer and rosary at sunset. Sundays were marked with a longer prayer service. In October 1918 a decision by the district commissioner caused a group of raiders to combine with Muslim extremists and some witch-doctors and turn against the Christian catechists. During the weekend of 18–20 October, five men came before dawn to the hut where Daudi and Jildo were staying, clearly intent on killing them. A village elder tried to fend them off, saying that the catechists were his guests, but the two boys were dragged out, told to give up their work and, when they refused, speared to death, Daudi first and Jildo shortly after, when even the sight of Daudi being killed did not shake his resolve. Daudi's body was left unburied, then dragged a few days later on to an empty termite mound. His bones were collected in 1926 and interred in the mission church in Kitgum. The place where they were killed became known as *Wi-Polo*, meaning "in heaven."

Both were beatified on World Mission Sunday, 20 October 2002. Pope John Paul II held them up to "the entire Christian community as examples of holiness and virtue and as models and intercessors for catechists throughout the world, especially in those places where catechists still suffer for the faith, sometimes facing social marginalization and even personal danger." One such place is still the region their people inhabit, with continued tribal and political violence in northern Uganda and twenty years of persecution of Christians in southern Sudan.

❖

Atlas, Plate 88, F2. See also "St Charles Lwanga and Companions," *Butler*, June, pp. 22–4, for the proto-martyrs of Africa, also from Uganda.

29

Bd Gaetano Errico, *Founder* (1791–1860)

The second of nine children of Pasquale Errico and Marie Marseglia, Gaetano was born on 19 October 1791 in the village of Secondigliano, on the northern fringes of Naples. His father managed a small pasta-making factory, in which Gaetano helped as a child. He felt a vocation to the priesthood when he was fourteen and applied first to the Capuchins and Redemptorists, but was rejected by both on account of his youth. Two years later he was accepted into the diocesan seminary in Naples. Because his parents could not afford the residential fees, he registered as a day-student and walked the five miles there and back each day. He also found time to visit the sick in his parents' parish and to encourage the children in their catechism classes.

Gaetano was ordained in Naples Cathedral on 23 September 1815 and was appointed a schoolteacher. He was an exemplary teacher for twenty years, serving also as parish priest of SS Cosmas and Damian. He made an annual retreat at the Redemptorist house in Pagani (in the diocese of Salerno, south of Naples), and during his retreat in 1818 he had a vision of the founder, St Alphonsus de'Liguori (1696–1787; 1 Aug.), who told him that God wanted him to found a new religious Congregation; he was also to build a new church in Secondigliano and dedicate it to Our Lady of Sorrows. This idea was received with enthusiasm in the village, but when the cost became apparent, the enthusiasm diminished. Gaetano persevered, nonetheless, and against considerable odds the church was completed in twelve years.

He also built a house to serve as the first home of the Congregation-to-be. At first it functioned as a retreat house for priests, whom Gaetano would try to inspire with missionary zeal. He commissioned a sculpture of Our Lady of Sorrows from a famous Neapolitan sculptor, Francesco Versella, and refused to accept it until the sorrowing features were just as he wanted them. Once installed, in May 1835, it immediately became a focus of pilgrimage. On his next retreat he was given to understand that his Congregation was to be dedicated to the Sacred Hearts of Jesus and Mary, which was in accordance with the chief focus of his devotion. The statutes he drew up were approved on 14 March 1836, and he was able to open a novitiate with eight postulants. Papal approval was forthcoming two years later, in 1840 he sought and was granted royal approval, and in 1846 Pope Pius IX issued the Brief granting final approval. The Congregation by this time had several houses in southern Italy, and Gaetano was elected superior general.

Despite a harsh self-imposed regime of fasting and penance, he travelled the whole area, preaching, hearing Confessions, and encouraging frequent Communion. He had a constant care for the sick and excluded, as well as a sharp eye for sinners who needed to be reconciled. Known everywhere as "O superiore," he died on 29 October 1860 at the aged of sixty-nine, whereupon the people of Secondigliano immediately acclaimed him as a saint. He was declared Venerable by Pope Leo XIII in 1876, Pope Paul VI issued the decree of his heroic virtue on 4 October 1874, and Pope John Paul II beatified him on 24 April 2002 after the spontaneous recovery of a man about to undergo emergency surgery in 1952 for a perforated stomach wall, whose wife slipped an image of Gaetano under his pillow and prayed to him, was accepted as a miracle. In his homily the pope said that, "In an age defined by profound political and social change, in opposition to the spiritual rigorism of the Jansenists, Gaetano Errico proclaimed the greatness of the mercy of God, who always calls to conversion those who live under the dominion of evil and sin."

The Missionaries of the Sacred Hearts of Jesus and Mary never grew into a large Congregation and today number only 100 around the world, but they carry out a dedicated mission, especially to the poor and abandoned, in Italy, Slovakia, U.S.A., Argentina, India, and the Philippines. In the U.S.A. their seminarians study at Mount St Mary's at Emmitsburg, Maryland, and they have a novitiate nearby at Fairfield, Pennsylvania. They staff a Hispanic National Parish in Camden, New Jersey, and a "spiritual life centre" in Linwood, New Jersey.

NOVEMBER

11

The Martyrs of Bulgaria (died 11 November 1952)

Three Assumptionist priests are commemorated here, all shot in the central prison of Sofia, capital of Bulgaria, at 11.30 p.m. on the night of 11 November 1952. Also shot with them was the bishop of Nikopol, the Passionist Eugene Bossilkov, who was beatified on 15 March 1998 (*Butler*, Dec., Supplement, pp. 287–9). Two of these three were priests of the Latin rite, the third of the Eastern rite. All were talented, well-educated, good communicators, and influential through their writings, which made the Communist authorities single them out as ringleaders of the "Catholic Organization of Conspiracy and Espionage in Bulgaria,"whose aim was to "subvert, undermine, and weaken the people's democratic power through a coup d'Etat, insurrection, revolts, terrorist acts, crimes, and foreign armed interventions." Faced with such accusations, there could be only one outcome of their show trial.

Bl Josaphat Šiškov, the eldest of the three, was born on 9 February 1884 in Plovdiv in south-central Bulgaria (Philippopolis in classical times). He was christened Robert Matej (Matthew), and the Romanized form of his surname is Chichov. He came from a large and devout family of Latin-rite Catholics and at the age of nine entered the junior seminary of the Augustinians of the Assumption, or Assumptionists (founded in France in 1845 by Fr Emmanuel d'Alzon) at Kara-Agatch, in Edirne (formerly Adrianopolis), just over the border in Turkey. He began his novitiate in 1900, at the age of sixteen, taking the name Josaphat. The following year he was appointed to teach at the seminary, and in 1902 he was transferred to their seminary (St Michael's) in Varna, on the Black Sea coast, where he directed the band and published articles in magazines. After two years there he went to the Catholic university at Louvain in Belgium to complete his philosophy and theology courses. He was ordained on 11 July 1909 at Malines, the seat of the archbishops of Malines-Brussels.

On Josaphat's return to Bulgaria he taught first at the College of St Augustine in Plovdiv and then at St Michael's Seminary in Varna. He was a distinguished and innovative educator, making use of the latest "media" of his time: one of the first typewriters made with Cyrillic characters, a record player, and a film projector. He expanded the seminary to thirty students, raising money by teaching French to Bulgarian teachers, civil servants, and army officers. He started the "St Michael French-Bulgarian Circle," which grew to have 150 members, most of them advanced business students.

A frequent visitor to Varna was the apostolic visitor to Bulgaria, Bishop Angelo Roncalli, the future Pope John XXIII (beatified on 3 Sept. 2000; see 3 June), who often spent vacations at the seminary. Josaphat was also parish priest in Yambol (inland and south-west from Varna) and chaplain to the Oblate Missionary Sisters of the Assumption (also founded by Fr Emmanuel d'Alzon, in 1865), who had been active in schools, hospitals, and orphanages in the area since 1868.

Josaphat wrote articles for the Catholic magazine *Poklonnik* ("The Pilgrim"), introduced devotion to the Sacred Heart, and was a generally hard-working parish priest. In 1949 he was appointed parish priest of the Latin-rite parish in Varna, where he was to stay until he was arrested in December 1951. He was held in undisclosed locations until 29 September 1952, when he was put on trial with the other two Assumptionists, Bishop Bossilkov, and a further thirty-seven priests, religious and lay people.

Bd Kamen Vichev (or Vitchev), the middle one of the three in age, was born on 23 May 1893 in Ustrem, in the south-eastern province of Burgas. He was baptized Petar (Peter) and also studied at Kara-Agatch, spending two years at Phanaraki (on the outskirts of Istanbul) from 1907 to 1909. He joined the Assumptionist novitiate in 1910, taking the name Kamen, and made his final profession in 1912. After six more years of study he was appointed professor at St Augustine's in Plovdiv, and then at the junior seminary of Koum Kapou in Istanbul. He completed his degree studies at Louvain, was ordained at Kadiköy College (in a suburb of Istanbul) on 22 December 1921, and taught theology there until 1925.

From 1927 to 1929 Kamen studied for a doctorate of theology in Rome and Strasbourg, returning to Plovdiv in 1930 to become in due course rector, dean of studies, and philosophy lecturer. The school took Catholic, Orthodox, Jewish, and Muslim students, all of whom lived harmoniously in an atmosphere conducive to ecumenism and inter-faith dialogue. Kamen wrote for learned journals such as *Istina* and the *Review of Byzantine Studies*, and also for scientific journals under various pen-names. In 1948 the authorities closed the college and expelled all foreign religious from Bulgaria. Kamen was one of twenty Bulgarian Assumptionists allowed to remain and was appointed provincial vicar, responsible for overseeing five Eastern-rite and four Latin-rite parishes.

He was arrested on 4 July 1952, accused of being one of the organizers of the conspiracy hatched by "spies for the Vatican and the French [the Assumptionists' French foundation, the priests' specific ties, and their degrees from Louvain probably helped to account for this singling out] ... seeking to foment an imperialist war against the USSR, Bulgaria, and the people's democracies." There was no news of him until the list of "conspirators" was published on 20 September and he was brought to trial with the others on 29 September.

Bd Paul Džidzov (or Djidjov), the youngest of the three, was born in Plovdiv on 19 July 1919. His parents were Latin-rite Catholics and he was baptized Josif (Joseph). He was educated by the Assumptionists, first at St Andrew's School, then from the ages of twelve to nineteen at St Augustine's College, leaving in 1938 to join the novitiate in the Jura region of eastern France, and taking the name of Pavel (Paul). Practical and athletic, he helped in teaching the students at the seminary school. He made his final vows in September 1942 but was then taken seriously ill, which forced him to return to Plovdiv and continue his theology studies on his own. He was ordained in the cathedral on 26 January 1945.

Paul was then posted to Varna, where he continued to study business management and social sciences. He made no attempt to hide his anti-Communist views and was consequently closely monitored by secret service agents. Back in Plovdiv, he became treasurer of St Augustine's during Fr Kamen's tenure as rector and stayed there until the college was closed. Another of the Bulgarians allowed to remain in the country after 1948, he was appointed provincial treasurer and procurator and as such tried to get much-needed funds channelled through the French ambassador—one of the "French connections" behind the accusation, no doubt. He was arrested with Fr Kamen and brought to trial with him and the others.

❖

The trial was held at the Supreme Court in Sofia, and the accused had been tortured in prison beforehand. The outcome was totally foreseeable, and on 3 October 1952, timed for the eve of the opening of the Nineteenth Congress of the Soviet Communist Party, held in Moscow, the three Assumptionist priests were found "guilty of having organized and directed in Bulgaria, from 9 September 1944 [four days after the Soviet invasion] to the summer of 1952, a clandestine organization, a secret service agency of the Pope and of imperialists." They were condemned to "death by firing squad with privation of their rights, confiscating all their properties to the benefit of the State."

It was not until after the fall of the Berlin Wall in 1989 and the consequent opening up of secret archives that what had happened to them between their arrests and their death could be pieced together and the date and place of their death established. Their cause was begun in September 1995, and Pope John Paul II beatified them during his apostolic visit to Azerbaijan and Bulgaria, on 26 May 2002, in the central square of Plovdiv. The Pope stressed the ecumenical heritage of the martyrs, welcoming the presence of the Orthodox metropolitan of Plovdiv, who had asked to take part in the ceremony, and "respectfully greeting" the Muslims present. He also paid tribute to the "memory of the other confessors of the faith who were sons and daughters of the Orthodox Church and who suffered martyrdom under the same Communist regime," adding: "This gesture cannot fail to have an ecumenical character and significance. Perhaps the most convincing form of ecumenism is the ecumenism of the saints and martyrs."

❖

Quotations from Vatican sources, translation slightly adapted. On the Assumptionists see *Orders*, pp. 17, 18. In May 1999 the Bulgarian Supreme Court of Appeal found that the trial contained "glaring violations" and annulled the death sentence, at least on Bishop Bossilkov: see *The Tablet*, 29 May 1999, p. 758. On the background see J. Rothschild, *Central Europe between the Two World Wars* (1974); R. J. Crampton, *Eastern Europe in the Twentieth Century* (1994); further refs. on www.holycross.edu/departments/history/vlapomar/persec. For a list of all killed for their faith under Communist regimes, with photographs and addresses of the promoters of their causes see www.newsaints.faithweb. com/martyrs/East. For an explanation of the icon displayed at the beatification ceremony in place of conventional portraits see www.assumption. edu/magazine/archive/summer2002/icons.

15

Bd Mary of the Passion, *Founder* (1839–1904)

The founder of the Franciscan Missionaries of Mary was born in Nantes, near the mouth of the river Loire in western France, into a noble family named de Chappotin de Neuville, on 21 May 1839, and baptized Hélène Marie Philippine. Her desire to dedicate her life to God first manifested itself during a retreat when she seventeen, but then her mother died, postponing any decision for a while. She entered the Poor Clares in December 1860, and in January 1861 had a visionary experience in which God invited her to offer herself as a victim for the Church and the pope. Shortly after this she became seriously ill and had to leave the convent.

When she had recovered, her confessor recommended the recently founded (in 1857, by Emily d'Outremont d'Hooghvorst) Society of Mary Reparatrix, and she joined them at their convent in Toulouse, taking the habit on 15 August 1864 with the name Mary of the Passion in religion. She was sent to India while still a novice, in March 1865, to Madurai in the southern State of Tamil Nadu (ecclesiastically a Jesuit apostolic vicariate), where the Reparatrix Sisters were working to establish a Congregation of Indian Sisters. Mary took her temporary vows there in May 1866 and was quickly promoted to local superior and then provincial superior, in charge of three convents. These flourished and developed their apostolate, but then dissensions arose, and eventually the situation in Madurai became so divisive that in 1876 Mary and nineteen others left the convent and the Society. They moved to Udagamandalam, near Coimbatore, 120 miles north-west of Madurai, where the Paris Foreign Mission Society (MEP) had established a house two years earlier. They stayed there, becoming a community under the authority of the MEP vicar apostolic, Mgr Joseph Bardou.

In search of Vatican approval for the new community, Mary travelled to Rome in November 1876 and—with perhaps surprising speed—gained Pope Pius IX's approval to found a new specifically missionary Institute, to be named Missionaries of Mary. *Propaganda Fide* suggested France as a fruitful source of new vocations, and she opened a novitiate at Saint-Brieuc in Brittany. Vocations came so fast that planned growth became difficult. Mary went to Rome again in June 1882, and was granted permission to open a house there. While in Rome she was received into the Third Order of St Francis. In March 1883 dissension in the Institute resulted in her deposition as superior. She appealed to Pope Leo XIII, who ordered an inquiry and reinstated her in July the following year.

From then on official approval came speedily: provisional in 1890, with affiliation to the Franciscan family as Franciscan Missionaries of Mary (FMM), with final approval in 1896. Activities increased, with Sisters sent all over the world, regardless of danger. Seven of them were killed during the Boxer uprising in China in 1900: they were canonized among the companions of Augustine Zhao Rong (see 9 July) on 1 October 2000. Mary carried on a constant correspondence with her missionaries, encouraging them all to persevere in the way of holiness. She also wrote a number of treatises on religious formation. By the time she died, on 15 November 1904, there were more than 2,000 Franciscan Missionaries of Mary, spread over four continents and working in eighty-six houses.

The cause of her beatification was opened in San Remo in 1918, and the apostolic process was formally introduced in 1979. The decree on her heroic virtues was promulgated in June 2000, and the healing of a religious suffering from Pott's Disease—tuberculosis of the lungs and spine—was accepted as a miracle brought about by her intercession in March 2002, clearing the way for her beatification on 20 October 2002. In his homily Pope John Paul II commented that, "At the heart of the missionary commitment she placed prayer and the Eucharist, because for her adoration and mission blended to become the same work. Drawing on scripture and the Fathers of the Church, combining a mystical and an active vocation, passionate and intrepid, she gave herself with an intuitive and bold readiness to the universal mission of the Church."

On the Society of Mary Reparatrix see *Orders*, p. 278; on the FMM, *ibid.*, p. 149.

22

Bd Thomas Reggio, *Bishop and Founder* (1818–1901)

This future archbishop of Genoa and founder of the world's first Catholic newspaper was born in Genoa on 9 January 1818, and christened Tommaso (Thomas). His father was no less a personage than the Marquis of Reggio, and his mother's name was Angela Pareto. His aristocratic and relatively wealthy background afforded him a wide culture as well as a solid Christian upbringing.

At the age of twenty, however, Thomas turned his back on a potentially brilliant worldly career and entered the archdiocesan seminary of Genoa. With his background, of course, he could have pursued power through the clerical route, but he abjured any such sentiments, declaring at the time of his ordination in 1841 that he wanted to be a saint and that the way to this was to live "in accordance with the two cornerstones of Christianity: prayer and ascesis." Two years later he was vice rector of the Genoa seminary, moving on to become rector of the one at Chiavari. While he was there, in 1849, he founded, with others, *The Catholic Standard*. While committed to defending the Faith and its basic principles, this was equally committed to objectivity in reporting and to the freedom of the press. It campaigned for Catholics to found a political party, but in the climate of animosity between the Vatican and the recently united Kingdom of Italy (whose constitution was proclaimed in 1861), the pope (Pius IX; 7 Feb.) held that Catholics should not vote and should not take part in the parliamentary process. This decision was promulgated in 1868 and reaffirmed by Pius IX in an audience on 11 October 1874, on the ostensible grounds that a Catholic elected as a deputy to parliament would have to take an oath that could be interpreted as implying approval of the "spoliation of the Holy See." Thomas closed the newspaper without complaining of this verdict, though his sympathies must have been rather with the Moderates, who accused Catholics of failing in their duty to the State by not voting. (It was to be another thirty years before the ban was even modified, let alone lifted, by Pius X.)

In 1877 Thomas was consecrated bishop of Ventimiglia, on the coast of what is now the Italian Riviera, between Monaco and San Remo, but which at the time was an area deeply afflicted with poverty. The new bishop dedicated himself to the service of all, but especially of the poor. Crossing and re-crossing the difficult terrain by mule, he visited the most remote villages, encouraging the parish priests (most of whom had to work in the fields, as their flocks were too poor to support them), inspiring renewal of the liturgy and participation by the faithful through hymn-singing (eighty years before the Second Vatican Council), and providing a sound basis for people's faith through education and catechesis. To assist him in this work he founded the Sisters of St Martha in 1878. The nuns were to follow their patron by serving the poor "with [their] humble hands," finding Christ in the poorest and most needy of all ages. He also held three diocesan synods during his fifteen years as bishop.

In 1887 Thomas was to be found, at the age of sixty-nine, shifting the rubble left by an earthquake with his bare hands, identifiable not by any marks of episcopal rank but by "his patched cassock and his watch hanging from a piece of string" (Vatican). The earthquake left large numbers of orphans, for whom he founded orphanages in Ventimiglia and San Remo to enable them to learn a trade (for which they were paid while in the orphanage) and so improve their prospects of earning a living.

Five years later he asked the pope to relieve him of duties, pleading old age. The pope, by then Leo XIII, responded by appointing Thomas as archbishop of Genoa. He inherited a difficult situation, with an anti-Catholic civic administration added to the normal conditions of stress and poverty inherent in an industrializing city, but he gradually came to occupy a position of counsellor to believers and non-believers alike. He encouraged associations of Catholics, workers and others, and campaigned for reduced working hours and free weekends. In this he was taking a leaf out of the books of free-thinking radicals, who came to admire him for this traditionally un-Catholic approach. He also started a network for immigrants, helping to supply then with official papers and prevent the exploitation that faced "illegals." Behind all his outward activity he led an intensely ascetic and prayerful life—as he had vowed to do many years earlier, at the time of his ordination.

To mark the beginning of the new century—which Catholic Italy dedicated to God and Our Lady—he had a statue of Christ the Redeemer erected on Mount Saccarello, overlooking Ventimiglia. He invited all the bishops of Liguria to attend its dedication, but his health suddenly worsened and he was unable to climb to the statue with them. He died the following year, in the afternoon of 22 November, at Triora. He was beatified by Pope John Paul II on 3 September 2000, in the company of two popes, Pius IX and John XXIII. In his homily at the ceremony, John Paul II called him "a man of faith and culture … sensitive to the many sufferings and the poverty of his people …" His message, the pope continued, "can be summed up in two words: truth and charity."

❖

Oss.Rom., 6 September 2000 and similar sources. On *Non expedit* see *Cath. Encyc.*, vol 11 (1911), available at www.newadvent.org, among many informative sites.

During the Second World War the Sisters of St Martha worked to save many Jewish lives. This was commemorated on 30 August 2000, when an olive tree was planted in the motherhouse, donated by the Italian National Jewish Fund at the request of Emmanuel Pacifici, who had hidden in the nuns' house in Settignano. His father, Ricardo Pacifici, was chief rabbi of Genoa during the war and was deported to Auschwitz, from which he never returned. The Sisters currently number 620 and serve the poor and needy through catechesis, health care, and teaching in Argentina, Brazil, Chile, India, Italy, and Lebanon.

25

BB Louis (1880–1951) and Mary (1884–1965) Beltrame Quattrocchi

Husband and wife have become saints in the history of the Church, usually as martyrs or when both have entered religious life by mutual agreement, but the beatification of Luigi Beltrame Quatrocchi and his wife, Maria Corsini, on 21 October 2001 marked the first time a married couple has been beatified together. The occasion was all the more remarkable because three of their four children were present at the ceremony. This joint beatification fulfilled a long-expressed wish by Pope John Paul II to highlight the fact that holiness is not restricted to religious and priests. For the first time, the "heroic virtue" required was declared to be inherent in many years of married life, not incidental to it. The couple were presented as a "gift" to married couples and an example to them. (There is, it might be noted, a certain irony in the fact that their immediate example—to their children—resulted in three out of the four choosing the clerical or religious life.)

Luigi was born in Catania on 12 January 1880, the son of Carlo and Francesca Quatrocchi; Maria Corsini was born in Florence on 24 June 1881. She was the daughter of an army captain of grenadiers, Angiolo Corsini, and the family had lived in Florence, Arrezzo, and Rome by the time Maria was nine. She started school in Rome at a parish school run by nuns, but when one of the nuns made an insulting remark about the king, Maria's father transferred her to a state-run school. Luigi studied law, in which he took a degree at La Sapienza University in Rome. He then worked as a lawyer with the "tax police," or Inland Revenue. Maria met Luigi in Rome when they were both teenagers, and they were married in the basilica of St Mary Major on 25 November 1905. During the early years of their marriage the parents of both, as well as Maria's grandparents, lived with them.

Maria was initially the more devout of the two: their son Cesare was to describe his father as "a good man, just and honest, but not very practising."

Gradually, however, she converted Luigi to daily Mass, and he developed the habit of saving his "Good morning" to her until the end of Mass, as though to indicate that the day began properly only with it. The first four years of marriage brought three children: Filippo, born in 1906; Stefania, born in 1908 (died in 1993); and Cesare, born in 1909. In 1914, while she was expecting a fourth, Maria's pregnancy developed severe complications, to the point where a leading gynaecologist advised her and Luigi that she had about a five per cent chance of surviving if she continued with the pregnancy and that the baby would die anyway. They refused an abortion without a second thought, and after a very difficult pregnancy mother and daughter both lived. She was christened Enrichetta. The elder sister, Stefania (who joined the Benedictines in Milan in 1927, becoming Sister Maria Cecilia), recalled that when she was about five she and her brothers had seen their father talking to a priest for a long time outside the confessional, holding his head in his hands and weeping; the children were terrified and "prayed as children do." Both boys were later to become priests, the elder, Filippo, as a diocesan priest, using the name Fr Tarcisio, and the younger, Cesare, entering the Trappists in 1924, where he took the name Fr Paolino in religion.

Luigi was a brilliant and successful lawyer, eventually becoming deputy attorney general of Italy. Maria, whose main interests, after her family, were education and music, volunteered as a Red Cross nurse during the First World War, was a prominent member of Women's Catholic Action, and lectured widely to women's lay groups. During the Second World War, they opened their flat in Rome as an acceptance-point and shelter for refugees. After the war, Luigi, a personal friend of politicians such as Alcide de Gasperi and Luigi Gedda, played a prominent part in steering Italy's legal institutions back to democracy after Mussolini's fascism. Describing the atmosphere in the family home, Enrichetta said: "At times they obviously had differences of opinion, but we, their children, were never exposed to these. They solved their problems between them, through conversation, so that once they reached an agreement the atmosphere continued serene." Fr Paolino described it as "supernatural, serene and happy ... but not excessively pious," adding that Maria was originally the more obviously devout of the two, but in later years Luigi "also begun to run, and they both attained high levels of spirituality." He always kept a copy of *The Imitation of Christ* given to him by his mother when he was ten, in which she had written, "Remember that Christ must be followed, if necessary, unto death."

Luigi died on 9 November 1951, at the family home on Via Depreti in Rome, after they had been married for forty-six years. Maria followed him after fourteen years of widowhood, on 26 August 1965, dying in the arms of the youngest daughter, for whom she had been willing to sacrifice her own life some fifty years earlier. Enrichetta repaid her parents by devoting her life to looking after them as they grew older. Their cause was considered jointly because, in the words of the Prefect of the Congregation for the Causes of

Saints, Cardinal José Saraiva Martins, "It was impossible to distinguish their experience of sanctity, lived together so intimately ... [They] made their family an authentic house church, open to life, prayer, witness of the gospel, the social apostolate, solidarity with the poor, and friendship." This raised the question of the date of their commemoration: Pope John Paul II made the original decision that it should be their wedding anniversary, rather than the death of one or the other or two separate dates. He also willingly agreed that the necessary miracle could be shared: this was the inexplicable cure of a young man with a severe circulatory disorder, who went on to become a neurosurgeon in Milan. Their beatification ceremony was supposed to have been held in St Peter's Piazza, but torrential rain forced 40,000 people to crowd into the basilica. The occasion had been made the culmination of celebrations to mark the twentieth anniversary of the pope's encyclical on the family, *Familiaris consortio*. Both sons, the elder of whom had become a monsignor in the diocese of Rome, concelebrated the Mass. The pope concluded his homily at the ceremony by saying that, "An authentic family, founded on marriage, is in itself good news for the world."

Their letters have recently been published in two volumes: *Dal campo base a la velta* (Letters to one another from 1901 to 1940) and *Dialogando con i figli* (letters to their children) (both 2001). There are a number of websites providing the basic information, some with photographs; also a short play with the couple and their children as characters: Martino Redi Maghenazi, *Un' aureola per due: Maria e Luigi Beltrame*, at erreddi.it/fdn/storiabeltrame.htm.

26

St Humilis of Bisignano (1582–1637)

He was the son of Pirozzo and Ginevra Giardino, born on 26 August 1582 at Bisignano, near the city of Cosenza in Calabria, in the poor south of Italy, and was christened Luca Antonio. He is reputed to have been an exceptionally devout child but had to earn his living working on a farm.

Luca made up his mind to become a religious when he was eighteen, but "for various reasons" (Vatican) was obliged to wait nine years until he was finally accepted as a lay brother by the Observant Franciscans in nearby Mesoraca. He made his religious profession on 4 September 1610, being given the name Humilis, which was to prove exceptionally apt. He was illiterate but showed extraordinary powers of assimilating knowledge: "He was also blessed with extraordinary gifts of reading hearts, prophecy, miracles, and, especially, of infused knowledge. Although he was illiterate and without education, he responded to questions on sacred scripture and on any point whatsoever of Catholic doctrine with a precision that astounded theologians" (Vatican). Humilis was subjected to several examinations by panels of experts but could never be found to be in error. This extraordinary quality came to the notice of the Franciscan minister general, Br Benigno Genova, who took Humitis with him on his canonical visitation of convents in Calabria and Sicily. His fame eventually reached the ears of Pope Gregory XV, who summoned him to Rome as a counsellor. He lived there for several years, providing the same service to Pope Urban VIII after Gregory's death, but the Roman climate made him ill, and after spending some time in Naples he returned to Bisignano.

His holiness was as outstanding as his knowledge. Humilis was subject to frequent ecstasies, which earned him the nickname "the ecstatic friar." He became renowned for both his wisdom and his holiness, but remained humble despite the remarkable things that happened to him in his outward and spiritual life. He asked his superiors if he could go on their overseas missions in 1628, but this request was refused, and he continued with his humble, although remarkable, life of prayer and service to the needy.

Humilis died in Bisignano on 26 November 1637. His cause made slow progress, but he was eventually beatified by Pope Leo XIII on 29 January 1882 and canonized by Pope John Paul II on 19 May 2002. The pope declared his example provided "a joyful and encouraging invitation to meekness, kindness, simplicity, and a healthy detachment from the transient goods of this world."

Butler, Nov., p. 214, citing a Life by A. de Vicenza (1872) and classic Franciscan sources. The Vatican biography is longer, but stronger on respectful comment on his character than biographical details.

Bd James Alberione, *Founder* (1884–1971)

The founder of what has grown to be the Pauline Family of religious Congregations was born on 4 April 1884 in San Lorenzo di Fossano in the Cuneo area of northern Italy, the most westerly province of the Piedmont region, and christened Giacomo (James). His parents, Michele Alberione and Teresa Allocco, were farmers, and Giacomo was one of six children. After elementary school in Cherasco he entered the junior seminary in Bra in 1896, encouraged by his parish priest, Fr Montersino, but he was asked to leave (for some sort of disciplinary reason?) in April 1900, and after a gap of six months he moved to the seminary in Alba in October. He was in the habit of rising before dawn to spend time in vigil before the tabernacle, and on the night of 31 December 1900 he felt a sudden call to do something special to serve the people of the new century. What this was to be did not become clear for several years.

James was ordained on 29 June 1907, and after a spell serving as parish priest in Narzole in the Cuneo district and studying for his doctorate in theology was appointed spiritual director of young people and altar servers at the seminary in Alba in October 1908. He spent several happy and successful years directing various aspects of the pastoral work of the seminary, and then in September 1913 first became involved in mass communication, which was to prove the mission he had felt called to carry out, as director of the weekly *Gazzetta d'Alba*. He saw the Church's need to engage with the communications media both in order to defend itself against hostile propaganda from outside and to spread the good news. To this end, he foresaw a Society that would be specifically dedicated to the apostolate of the Word through the written word.

The story of his life from then on effectively becomes that of his foundations. He founded the Society of St Paul, for priests (known as Paulines), assisted by consecrated laymen (Disciples of the Divine Master) on 20 August 1914. The Society received its Constitutions on 5 October 1921, when some of its members took private vows. It was erected into a diocesan Congregation by Bishop Francesco Re of Alba on 23 November of the same year. Its foundation was followed less that a year later by the Daughters of St Paul, co-founded by Mother Thecla Merlo, aged twenty-one at the time, who became their first superior general (now Venerable). Teaching young men, let alone women, to run bookshops and operate printing presses was not universally seen as suitable for religious Congregations, but he persevered and was proved ever more right with the expansion of the "mass media" as the century progressed. The work almost came to a halt when James fell gravely ill in 1923, but he made an apparently miraculous recovery, with the words "Do not be afraid. I am with you. From here I want to enlighten. Be sorry for sin" engraved on his mind and from then on inscribed on the walls of all the Family's chapels. Two more Congregations for women followed during the inter-war years: the Pious Disciples of the Divine Master, co-founded by Sr Scholastica Rivata, in 1924, and the Sisters of Jesus the Good Shepherd (also known as the Pastorelle Sisters) in 1936, with official approval following two years later.

He developed the spiritual formation of his "family members" as well as their practical activities, and it was through a series of weekly meditations on the meaning of being an apostle in the contemporary world that the overall name of "Pauline Family" came into use. He was also responsible for building two imposing churches in Alba, one dedicated to St Paul and one to The Divine Master, and two in Rome, one again of The Divine Master, and the sanctuary of the Queen of Apostles. He established a branch foundation in Rome in 1926, followed by many more in other parts of Italy. The Second World War caused a temporary cessation of physical development, but he used the "break" to refine and develop the spiritual formation underpinning all his endeavours, summed up in the words, "The first concern of the

Pauline family should be holiness of life; the second, holiness of doctrine."
He also masterminded the project for an *Encyclopedia of Jesus the Master*,
which was eventually published in 1959.

James saw that periodicals would be an effective way of spreading the gospel,
with a wider potential than that of books alone. He had issued *Vita Pastorale*
("Pastoral Life"), for priests, since 1912, and in 1931 he began publishing
Famiglia Cristiana ("Christian Family") to promote Christian living in people's
homes. *Madre di Dio* ("Mother of God") followed in 1933,"to reveal to souls the
beauty and grandeur of Mary," then *Pastor bonus* ("Good Shepherd") in 1937,
published in Latin, to help in the formation of priests. *Via, Verità e Vita* ("Way,
Truth, and Life"), dedicated to catechesis, and *Vita in Cristo nella Chiesa* ("Life
in Christ in the Church"), to disseminate appreciation of the liturgy, were added
in 1952, followed by *Il Giornalino* ("The Little Newspaper"), for children.

After the Second World War, in 1947, the Disciples of the Divine Master
became a Congregation with canonical rights. The fortieth anniversary of
the first foundation, in 1954, was the occasion for the publication of a first
biographic study, *Mi protendo in avanti* ("I Strain Ahead"), and a short "charis-
matic history of the Pauline Family," *Abundantes divitiae gratiae suae* ("The
Abundant Gifts of His Grace"). In 1957 the Society held its first general chapter,
at which James was confirmed as superior general. A new Congregation, the
Sisters of Mary Queen of Apostles (or Apostoline Sisters), was founded in 1959,
and in 1960 three associated Secular Institutes, of the Priest Jesus, St Gabriel
Archangel, and Mary Most Holy in her Annunciation, were formed into the
"Pauline Association" by the Roman Congregation for Religious. A fourth, of
the Holy Family, was added later.

From 1962 to 1965 James, as a major religious superior, attended the
sessions of the Second Vatican Council, which he followed with close
attention. On the occasion of the second general chapter of the Society,
in 1969, Pope Paul VI received James and representative Sisters and priests in
audience and presented the papal cross *Pro Ecclesia et Pontifice* to the founder
and the Pauline Family. Of James he said, "Here he is, humble, silent, tireless,
always vigilant, recollected in his thoughts, which run from prayer to action;
always intent on scrutinizing the 'signs of the times,' that is, the most creative
way to reach souls. Our Fr Alberione has given the Church new instruments
with which to express herself, new means to give vigour and new breadth
to her apostolate ..." At this chapter he retired as active superior general but
retained the title of "emeritus."

Two years later the Pope visited him in the afternoon of 26 November 1971
as he lay on his deathbed; he died in the evening, murmuring,"I die ... I pray
for all. Paradise!"The cause of his beatification received the *Nihil Obstat* in 1981;
he was declared Venerable on 25 June 1996; the decree of his beatification was
officially promulgated on 20 December 2002, and he was beatified on 27 April
2003, when the Pope recalled his stated mission"to make Jesus Christ, the Way,

273

the Truth, and the Life, known 'to people of our time with the means of our time.'"

❖

The Daughters of St Paul have a study of aspects of his life and work at www. daughtersofstpaul.com/jamesalberione. *Orders*, pp. 114–15; 324, 326. Article II of the Constitutions of the Paulines require them to "work for the glory of God and the salvation of other souls through the modern media of communication," so the priests and the Sisters have expanded their apostolate to produce and publish new media—cinema, radio, TV, cassettes, video, CDs, internet—alongside books and other printed matter. The priests currently work in twenty-six countries and the Daughters in thirty-five. The Sisters Disciples opened their first house in the U.S.A. on Staten Island in 1947; they are involved in various forms of pastoral ministry and also produce vestments, sculpture, music and printed material.

Bd Gaetana Sterni, *Founder* (1827–1889)

One of six children of Giovanni Battista Sterni and Giovanna Chiuppani, Gaetana was born on 26 June 1827 in Cassola, in the northern Italian province of Vicenza. Her father was administrator of the country property of the noble Venetian family of Mora, and the family lived in relative comfort. When Gaetana was eight, they moved to nearby Bassano del Grappa (about twenty miles north-east of Vicenza and thirty north of Padua: the Vatican describes it as "an ancient and cheerful city"). Then a series of misfortunes drastically affected the family: Gaetana's elder sister, Margherita, died at the age of eighteen, closely followed by her father; her brother Francesco left home to go on the stage, and the family was left in dire financial straits.

Gaetana was forced to grow up before her time and support her mother. She was a devout and sensitive young woman, physically attractive and full of good sense. She attracted the attentions of a young widower with three children, Liberale Conte, who asked her to marry him. She was not yet quite sixteen, but after much consideration she accepted him and soon grew to love him and the children deeply. She was overjoyed when she found that she was expecting a child. Then tragedy struck again: she had a "prophetic" dream that her husband would soon die; this proved true, and after a brief illness he died before their child was born, leaving her heartbroken, widowed with three children, and pregnant before she reached nineteen. The final blows were that her child died a few days after birth and her husband's family demanded that she return his three children to them, which she did, leaving her effectively bereft of all that was most meaningful in her life.

She returned to live with her mother, finding her only consolation in long hours of prayer. She came to realize that she had a vocation to the religious life—something she had not previously in any way suspected—and asked to be received as a postulant by the Canossian Sisters (founded in 1808 by St Magdalen of Canossa; 10 Apr.) in Bassano. After five months in their convent, she had another premonitory dream, this time of her mother's death, which again was proved true within a few days. She was forced to leave the convent to take care of her younger siblings, acting as head of the household for the next six years.

Another premonition was that her true calling was to live among the sick and the poor and help them in any way she could. She had heard Jesus telling her, "I want you among my poor." Gaetana eventually shared this with her confessor, who was fairly dismissive of the notion, but a Jesuit, Fr Bedin, told her to follow the call. There was a hospice for beggars in Bassano, known as the Recovery, and at the age of twenty-six, finally free of family responsibilities, she moved there.

She spent the next thirty-six years there, serving the sick, the dying, and the destitute with total dedication. Many of the beggars had come to be such through their own vices and abuses, but this made no difference to her. When she was thirty-three she took a vow of total devotion to God, and five years later, with two like-minded friends, she formed the nucleus of what became the Congregation of Daughters of the Divine Will, a name indicating their complete willingness to go anywhere and do anything that seemed necessary to accomplish the Lord's will for them. This was in 1865, and the Congregation was approved by the bishop of Vicenza ten years later. The numbers grew and the motherhouse was established in Vicenza. Gaetana died of natural causes in Cassola on 26 November 1889, and her remains were interred in the mother-house.

She was beatified with seven others in St Peter's Piazza on 4 November 2001. In his homily the Pope said that she "learned that the will of God is always love, dedicated herself with untiring charity to the excluded and the suffering. She always treated her brothers and sisters with the kindness and love of the one who serves Christ in the poor."

DECEMBER

2

Bd Liduina Meneguzzi (1901–1941)

Elisa Angela Meneguzzi came from a family of poor farm-workers from Giarre, in the province of Padua in north-eastern Italy. She was born on 21 September 1901. As a child she frequented daily Mass and taught the catechism to other children as soon as she was old enough to do so. At the age of fourteen she went into domestic service, working for wealthy families in the area and also in hotels in the spa town of Abano.

Elisa worked until she was twenty-five and then followed her desire to enter the religious life. She joined the Sisters of the Congregation of St Francis de Sales in Padua, taking the name Liduina in religion. For the next nine years she worked in "support" roles at the boarding school of Santa Croce, where she was housekeeper, sacristan, nurse, and housemistress. Her wish was to serve in overseas missions, and in 1937 this was granted when she was sent to Dirē Dawa in Ethiopia. Ethiopia at the time was under Italian rule following Mussolini's invasion in October 1935 (regarded by many Italian church dignitaries as a crusade to restore the gospel to a country where it had once held sway), and Dirē Dawa was a cosmopolitan city on the only road and railway link between the capital, Addis Ababa, and the coast of the Gulf of Aden at Djibouti. Its inhabitants included Copts, Catholics, Muslims and followers of native religions.

Liduina worked as a nurse in the Parini Hospital, a civic institution that was turned into a military hospital on the outbreak of the Second World War in September 1939. She then cared for wounded soldiers, who came to see her as an "angel of charity." When the city was bombed she helped carry the wounded to shelter, and baptized children dying in the streets. She attended people of all colours and creeds without distinction, telling them all about "Father God" (a concept to which most could subscribe) and his goodness and the reward in heaven awaiting those presently suffering on earth. Muslims— the majority of those she treated—called her "Sister *Gudda*" (meaning "great") and "ecumenical flame."

Her ministry was cut short by cancer. She worked on as her health declined and then underwent surgery, but complications developed, and she died on 2

December 1941. She was buried in the military ceremony at Dirē Dawa, at the request of soldiers she had cared for, but in July 1961 her remains were taken to the Sisters' motherhouse in Padua and interred in the chapel, where they became a focus of devotion.

Liduina was declared Venerable in 1996 and beatified on 20 October 2002, World Mission Sunday. The Decree on her heroic virtue stated that, "The message that Blessed Liduina Meneguzzi brings to the Church and the world today is that of hope and love. A kind of hope that redeems us from our selfishness and from aberrant forms of violence. A kind of love that is a spur to solidarity, to sharing out and to service, following the example of Christ who came not to be served but to serve and to give his life to save all of us." The Pope said at her beatification that, "In the course of her brief but intense life, Sr Liduina poured herself out for her poorer and suffering brothers ..."

9

St Juan Diego Cuauhtlatoatzin (1474–1548)

The story of Juan Diego, beatified in 1990 and canonized on 30 July 2002 at the shrine of the Virgin of Guadalupe outside Mexico City in front of an estimated five million pilgrims, is essentially that of the Virgin of Guadalupe. This apparition of the Virgin delivered a unique message to Juan Diego: that two peoples, the conquered and the conquerors, should be brought together by her actions, working through a powerful symbol. This symbol is the figure of *la morenita*, the "little dark girl" apparently miraculously imprinted on the Mexican Indian's cactus-cloth cloak after he had seen the "lady" who called herself "the ever-Virgin, Holy Mary, mother of the God of Great Truth, Téotl." This took place, according to the tradition, in 1531. There is a relatively early summary account of the events in Juan Diego's language, Náhuatl, and a somewhat fuller one (in Náhuatl but written in the Roman alphabet), the *Nican Mopohua*, from thirty years later. This is the work of Antonio Valeriano, one of the few Indian students privileged to study in the College of Santa Cruz in Tlatelolco (although there is no complete text dating from his lifetime).

Juan Diego himself, whose Indian name, *Cuauhtlatoatzin*, means "talking eagle," is said to have been a childless widower, a very devout convert Christian. This may suggest that he was a convert of Spanish Franciscans, who were the first missionary Order to arrive in Mexico, in 1524. There was an investigation into the "events of Guadalupe," the *Informaciones Guadalupanas*, held in 1666. This produced an account of Juan Diego that states he was born in 1474 in the Tlayacac ward of Cuauhtitlan, fourteen miles north of

Tenochtitlán (now Mexico City). The term used to describe him in the *Nican Mopohua* makes him a "poor Indian," of the lowest social strata above slaves in the Aztec Empire. The Virgin calls him "the most humble of my sons," and he refers to himself as "a nobody … a small rope, a tiny ladder, the tail end, a leaf"—but also calls her "the least of my daughters, my Child," and "my Child, the least, my Child and Lady": only when he is speaking to the bishop does he refer to her as "my Ama, the lady from heaven, Holy Mary, precious mother of God." He worked in the fields and made mats. He was happily married but he and his wife had no children; both had been given Christian names on their conversion (hers was Maria Lucia). He is described as solitary in character, given to frequent penances and to walking the fourteen miles to Tenochtitlán to receive instruction. His wife died in 1529 and he moved to live with his uncle, Juan Bernadino, the one whom Our Lady was to cure of smallpox. After the apparitions he moved to a room attached to the first chapel built on the *cerrito* (little hill) and devoted the rest of his life to telling people the story. He died on 30 May 1548, at the age of seventy-four.

The trouble with this account is that it dates from over 130 years after the apparitions (which the bishop never mentioned), and could just as well be a pious fiction made to round out the story as a "biography" in the modern sense. And the story as told in the *Nican Mopohua*, whether it is regarded as fancy, history, or parable, really needs no embellishment. In outline, it is this:

On 9 December 1531 the Indian was walking past a sacred hill called Tepeyac on his way to Mass when he heard a voice calling him from the hill. He climbed up and found an olive-skinned girl apparently about fourteen years old. She told him to go to the bishop, the Franciscan Juan de Zumárraga, and tell him that she wanted a church built on the spot, in which she would show her compassion to all people, "Because I am your merciful mother and the mother of all nations that live on this earth … There I will hear their laments and remedy and cure all their misfortunes." The misfortunes at the time were mainly suffered by the indigenous Indians, who had seen their culture virtually obliterated under the conquest by Hernán Cortés and his army ten years earlier. During those years, missionaries had arrived who genuinely tried to reach out to the indigenous peoples, to understand their traditions while instructing them in the Catholic faith.

Juan Diego went to the bishop, who was known for his kindness toward the Indians but who told him to come back another day. He returned to Tepeyac and had another conversation with the Virgin, going back to the bishop, who was still unconvinced. The next day Juan went to fetch a priest to visit his uncle, Juan Bernardino, who was in danger of death from smallpox. He avoided Tepeyac as he was in a hurry, but the Virgin came to meet him, promised to cure his uncle, and sent him to gather flowers (described as "roses of Castile," which did not grow in Mexico generally, and certainly not at that height in December) from the hill. She wrapped these in his cloak and told him to go back to the bishop, which he did. When he opened his cloak, the roses tumbled out and the Virgin's image was instantaneously imprinted on his cloak. The next day he led the bishop to the spot and went on to see his uncle, whom he found had been cured at exactly the time the Virgin had promised he would be. The bishop built the chapel and placed the cloak with the image in it, "so that all might see and venerate her precious image."

The importance of the story lies in the message, not the events. It proclaims Mary's central message for all times, that of the *Magnificat*: that God is on the side of the downtrodden, not the mighty. It shows that at least sections of the Church were seeking to convey this message to the *conquistadores* and their successors. It has made Mary the advocate of the poor and the excluded peoples of the New World and the whole world. Her image, described so precisely, gives dignity to threatened indigenous peoples everywhere: she is one of the conquered, whom the conquerors regarded as savages who had to be converted or killed. She states clearly that she is one of them. The result (as expressed by the Mexican bishops in May 2002) was "the beginning of evangelization with a vitality that surpassed all expectations. Christ's message, through his Mother, took up the central elements of the indigenous culture, purified them, and gave them the definitive sense of salvation."

What historical foundations "the Guadalupe event" rests on will inevitably continue to be a matter of debate. The official Church has now pronounced on the historicity of Juan Diego, claiming recent evidence that has come to light. As recently as 1996, however, no less a person than the abbot of Guadalupe, Fr Guillermo Schulenberg, called Juan Diego "a symbol, not a reality" and said that the stories "are sincere, but they spring out of a particular historical context and mentality." The main difficulty is that the account as we have it, a master-piece of story-telling, is Spanish rather than Indian in its approach and appears to be a conscious attempt to transpose the story of the apparition 200 years earlier at Guadalupe in the Extremadura province of Spain (from where Cortés himself and many of his soldiers came) to the Mexican situation of the time. The original has similar details, including the "going back a different way" and the miraculous cure (of a dead boy). The image on the cloak (however it got there) is Spanish in style and its details have precedents: whether it reflects the story or the story is elaborated to accord with the image is impossible to say. What is undeniably extraordinary, however, is that the cloak, or *tilma*, made of maguey cactus fibres, which would not normally be expected to last more than some twenty years, is still intact after nearly 500, as is the image on it, which has no visible brush strokes and—like the Shroud of Turin—defies artistic explanation however and whenever it was produced. It is even claimed that the scene the Virgin was looking at can be seen reflected in her eyes.

In the end, sceptics will always find grounds for doubt, and the devout faithful will always find motives for belief. In the story of Juan Diego and Our Lady of Guadalupe, the Church proclaims that its faith, when it is authentic, is life-giving for all, especially for the "little ones" of the Gospel, whom Mary dignifies in her *Magnificat* and in her appearance as the "little dark girl." The apparitions soon led to the mass conversion of millions of Mexican Indians. The patronage of Our Lady of Guadalupe has been extended over the years: of Mexico City in 1737; of all New Spain in 1746; "Virgin Patroness of Latin America" in 1910; and "Queen of Mexico and Empress of the Americas" in 1945. Her message still needs to be proclaimed, as it was during the canonization ceremony of Juan Diego, at which the archbishop of Mexico City asked the pope to confer his blessing on the Indians, so that their needs and human rights would be recognized, and the pope said that Juan Diego, "in accepting the Christian message without forgoing his indigenous identity, discovered the profound truth of the new humanity, in which all are called to be children of God." Re-stating the message of *la morenita*, he continued: "The noble task of building a better Mexico, with greater justice and solidarity, demands the cooperation of all. In particular, it is necessary today to support the indigenous peoples in their legitimate aspirations, respecting and defending the authentic values of each ethnic group. Mexico needs its indigenous peoples and these people need Mexico!"

The Feast of Our Lady of Guadalupe is 13 December, but St Juan Diego is commemorated on the anniversary of the first apparition, 9 December.

There is an English translation of the *Nican Mopohua* at www.sancta.org/intro. Recent books in English on the significance of Guadalupe include M. C. Bingemer and I. Gebara, *Mary, Mother of God and Mother of the Poor* (1993); J. Rodríguez, *Our Lady of Guadalupe: Faith and Empowerment among Mexican American Women* (1994); D. Brading, *Mexican Phoenix: Our Lady of Guadalupe— Image and Tradition* (2001), with illustrated account of the shrine and discussion of controversies. V.P. Elizondo, *Guadalupe, Mother of the New Creation* (1997); *idem*, La Morenita: Evangelizer of the Americas (6th edn, 1980); "Our Lady of Guadalupe: A Guide for the New Millennium," *St Anthony Messenger* (Dec. 1999); "St Juan Diego: New World Apostle," *ibid*. (July 2002) in which he argues strongly on the basis of new evidence for the historical existence of Juan Diego. Abbot Guillermo Schulenberg's claim that the story is a myth accorded with feminist (including Christian feminist) assertions that *la morenita* represents the triumph of the goddess Tonantzin. An alternative explanation for the (Spanish) title "of Guadalupe" is that the Virgin used the Book of Revelation image of the woman "who crushes the serpent" of herself. In Náhuatl this would be *coatlax-opeuh*, pronounced *quatlasoupay*, which is very similar to *Guadalupe*.

The shrine of Our Lady of Guadalupe receives between twelve and seventeen million pilgrims each year, making it the most visited Christian shrine after St Peter's in Rome. Juan Diego's supposed home at *El Cerrito* has also become a place of pilgrimage since his beatification in April 1990. Like the Virgin, he too has become an intercessor, appealed to often when others have failed to help with family problems or serious illnesses.

10

Bd Marcantonio Durando, *Founder* (1801–1880)

Marcantonio came from a distinguished and wealthy family from Mondovì, forty miles south of Turin, in the region of Piedmont, which during the first half of the nineteenth century was under the domination of Austria. His family was to be heavily involved in the struggle for Italian unification, the *Risorgimento* ("Revival"). His father is described (in Vatican and Vincentian sources) as having "liberal ideas" and being of "lay and agnostic tendencies,""tainted with secularism, even if not always with real anticlericalism." His mother, on the other hand, was pious and devoutly Catholic. She had the greater influence on Marcantonio, the father the greater on his two brothers, Giacomo and Giovanni; the former became minister of foreign affairs in the Rattazzi government of 1862, the latter a general first in the papal and then in the Piedmontese army.

Marcantonio, by contrast, entered the diocesan seminary of Mondovì at the age of fourteen and at seventeen joined the novitiate of the Vincentians (or Congregation of the Mission, founded in 1625 by St Vincent de Paul; 27 Sept.), intending to become a missionary in China. His studies were interrupted in 1822 on grounds of his health and the distress caused by the death of his mother. He was ordained in 1824, but his wish to go to China was not granted by his superiors, who required him to preach parish missions and lead clergy retreats locally. His preaching was eloquent, often reducing his congregations to unrestrained weeping, and his missions brought huge numbers to Confession: in Sommaria, seventeen priests could not keep up with the demand. After six years of demanding work he was appointed superior of the Vincentian house in Turin. Religious life was in need of rebuilding after the suppression of communities under Napoleon, and Vincentian priests had been forced to scatter and to earn their living individually. Marcantonio succeeded in reuniting them and making the Turin house a centre for retreats and conferences for both clergy and laity, and it became a spiritual powerhouse for the whole region of Piedmont.

He invited the Daughters of Charity (also founded by St Vincent, with St Louise de Marillac; 15 Mar.) to Italy. They were enjoying a period of revival after being suppressed during the French Revolution, especially after the Miraculous Medal revelations to St Catherine Labouré (31 Dec.), a novice in the Congregation, in 1830. The first Sisters to arrive were welcomed by Carlo-Alberto (duke of Savoy and king of Sardinia, 1831–1849), and as more arrived they took over the running of both military and civil hospitals. In 1837 Carlo-Alberto himself handed the keys of a huge former Visitandine convent in Turin, San Salvario, to the Daughters of Charity. This became their provincial house. Marcantonio asked them to staff field hospitals during the Piedmontese uprising against the Austrians of 1848 (in which his general brother Giovanni incurred the wrath of Pope Pius IX by leading papal troops across the river Po to oppose the Austrians), and even sent some to the Crimea in 1855 to help look after the war-wounded.

Marcantonio organized the Sisters on the lines originally established by St Vincent and St Louise: Ladies of Charity, the well-to-do who provided financial support, and Daughters, usually from poorer backgrounds themselves, who did the physical work. Living in "Mercy Units" (*Misericordie*), they provided the poor with soup kitchens, clothes, shelter, refuges for abandoned children, basic medical care, nursing homes for the elderly, orphanages, nursery schools, home visits ... The first of these units was established in 1854 and the last in 1879. Marcantonio visited them on a weekly basis, encouraging and providing basic material needs. The units multiplied in number and spread from the centre of Turin to the outskirts and beyond, providing a network of assistance to huge numbers at a time when newly industrializing Turin was experiencing an influx of people seeking work, producing social problems beyond the capacity of the civil administration. Associations of "Children of Mary" (formed according to the revelations to St Catherine Labouré) followed the Mercy Units, catering to the spiritual formation of young people.

In addition to his inspiration and organization of the Mercy Units, Marcantonio had since 1837 been Visitor of the Vincentian province of Lombardy, overseeing seven houses responsible for retreats, parish missions, seminaries, and schools. The archbishop of Turin also made him responsible for overseeing other Congregations: the Sisters of St Joseph, newly arrived in the area; the Sisters of St Ann; the Poor Clares; and the newly founded Repentant Sisters of St Magdalene. In 1865 he founded the Company of the Passion of Jesus the Nazarene, or Nazarene Sisters, which took in young women anxious to lead the religious life but canonically barred—because they had been born outside marriages sanctioned by the Church—from entering other Congregations. The initial object was to offer them a haven and a means to "make saints of" themselves, as he wrote to them at the inception of the community. He then saw a particular need they could answer and entrusted them with tending sick people in their own homes. (The poor ended their lives in hospitals, where they were visited by priests and nuns, while the better-off stayed in their own homes, where they were usually cut off from spiritual ministration, so it was mainly to these that the Nazarenes attended.) The whole scheme was too radical for some of the clergy and caused a canon of the cathedral to exclaim, "If Fr Durando were to come to confess to me, I could not in conscience absolve him." He had added a further six Vincentian houses when religious

Congregations were suppressed in 1866 and their property confiscated. This meant that, in order to keep their work going, the Vincentians (and other Congregations) effectively had to act as private citizens and to buy back their houses with personal funds.

Marcantonio remained on good personal terms with his "liberal" brothers but wrote openly criticizing them for anticlericalism and for their support for restrictive measures against the Church. In 1857 he wrote to Giacomo: "With all my heart I want peace between the government and the Church, and that there should be an end to this uneasiness in which we find ourselves all the time, and an end, in short, to this attacking of the Church and its institutions and its rules, and, in short, that we be allowed to live and breathe." When Rome was occupied by Italian nationalist troops in 1870 and papal temporal possessions were reduced to Vatican City he wrote again: "Reflect, and if your heart disapproves, as I suspect, speak out openly ... I love and wish for the greatness of Italy and, I will say it again, achieved by legitimate means, and I wish for, and see the importance of, absolute independence for the Vatican, intrinsic to, and essential for, its splendour, just as much as for the greatness and unity of Italy."

Foreign missions remained a major concern of Marcantonio, even though he had not been able to go to China himself. He encouraged the Vincentians of his province to apply to serve on the missions. He placed the Vincentians of Genoa in charge of a seminary funded by the wealthy Marquis Brignone Sale with the special purpose of training priests for overseas missions. Marcantonio himself had almost gone to Ethiopia in 1839 with Fr Justin de Jacobis (canonized in 1975; 31 July) but had to stay in Italy as he was likely to be nominated prefect apostolic. He would have been a preferable choice to the two priests he did send, one whom became an explorer and the other a conqueror responsible for Italian colonial expansion into Eritrea.

Marcantonio continued to be actively involved in all his projects until the last year of his life, an eminent figure in the Church and prominent in civil affairs through his family. He had a wide circle of friends and collaborators, was revered by most for his qualities of courtesy and gentleness, but was misunderstood by some who regarded him as autocratic. When he died, at the age of seventy-nine on 10 December 1880, the Vincentians acclaimed him as "a second St Vincent." The diocesan cause of beatification was started in Turin in 1929, and the apostolic process began in Rome in 1940. A miracle obtained through his intercession was accepted in 2001, and Pope John Paul II beatified him on 20 October 2002, saying of him, "He lived the faith with a burning zeal, shunning every kind of compromise or interior tepidity."

The 2002/3 issue of *Vincentiana* is devoted to him; the above is based mainly on the "Short Life" in it by a group of Nazarene Sisters of Turin, trans. T. Davitt, CM.

On the Vincentians see *Orders*, p. 389; on the Daughters of Charity, *ibid.*, p. 89. The Nazarene Sisters still exist, working in Italy and elsewhere.

11

St María Maravillas de Jesús Pidal y Chico de Guzmán (1891–1974)

Born in Madrid on 4 November 1891, María de las Maravillas (Mary of the Marvels) was the daughter of the marquis of Pidal, Luis Pidal y Mon, and his wife, Cristina Chico de Guzmán. At the time of her birth her father, who had previously been minister of agriculture in the Spanish government, was Spanish ambassador to the Holy See. With his brother he had formed the Catholic Union, a political party aimed at upholding Christian principles in public life, which had been championed by Pope Leo XIII as well as most of the Spanish bishops. María thus grew up in an atmosphere of high culture and firm Catholic devotion, and great care was given to her education. She studied languages and general culture, also dedicating herself to charitable works to help poor families. She received her first Communion in 1896 and was confirmed in 1902.

She was deeply influenced by her reading of St Teresa of Avila (15 Oct.) and St John of the Cross (14 Dec.), and made up her mind to become a Discalced Carmelite. She helped to take care of her father in his final illness leading to his death in 1913, but her mother was then reluctant to allow her to enter religious life and effectively postponed her decision for a further six years. She then joined the Discalced Carmelite convent in El Escorial (Philip II's great monastery/palace, north-west of Madrid) in October 1919, making her simple vows in May 1921.

By this time María had already conceived the project of building a convent at Cerro de los Angeles, the hill that marks the exact geographical middle of Spain (just south of Madrid, visible from the railway and road links to Toledo and Aranjuez). This was to be a "living lantern burning in love for and reparation to the Heart of Jesus." There was already a statue of the Sacred Heart there, by which King Alfonso XIII had consecrated the nation to the Sacred Heart on 30 May 1919. On 19 May 1924 María and three other Carmelites from El Escorial installed themselves in a house in the town of Getafe, near Cerro de los Angeles, in order to oversee the construction work; she made her final profession there on 30 May 1924. The work was completed in two years, she was appointed prioress of the community of four in June 1926, and the foundation was formally opened on 31 October. Numbers grew, and this was the first of a number of new "houses of the Virgin" or Teresian Carmelite convents established in Spain. She was careful not to call them a new foundation or a new branch of the Carmelite family, seeing them simply as new establishments following the Discalced reform set in motion by St Teresa.

In 1933 María sent three nuns to a new house at Kottayam, in the southern Indian State of Kerala, and this became the source of other foundations in India. Her position as prioress extended to all the houses of Teresian Carmelites, despite her sense of her own inadequacy and reluctance to exercise authority—perhaps surprising in someone from her background and who had certainly shown her ability to get things done. Like St Angela of the Cross some years before her (canonized with her; see 2 Mar.), she insisted that her convents should be small and poor in furnishing, with bare walls adorned only with Bible verses or writings by the Carmelite saints. Criticized for this on the grounds that they were not "solid" foundations, she replied that it did not matter if they collapsed, since they were only a small part of a great tradition that would go on without them.

On the outbreak of the civil war in July 1936 the nuns had to leave the convent at Cerro de los Angeles and take refuge, initially in Madrid and then near Salamanca. They moved back on the conclusion of the war in 1939 and rebuilt the convent from the total ruin to which it had been reduced in the fighting. Nearby María was responsible for building an estate of 200 houses for working families, with a church and a school for their children. The funds for all this came simply from her trust in Providence and the generosity of patrons, since the nuns lived in total poverty with no fixed source of income other than what they earned by the work of their hands. María herself lived a life of extreme asceticism, spending her nights half in prayer and half sleeping on the floor (which did her health no good). She also suffered from spiritual aridity, known only to her spiritual directors, a long "dark night of the soul" as described by St John of the Cross, whose "nada, nada, nada" ("nothing, nothing, nothing") she applied to herself, calling herself "a sinful nothing," while the impression she gave to others was rather one of purposefulness and joy.

In her later years María restored the convent building at El Escorial and sent nuns to form a new community there, and she also sent nuns to St Teresa's original convent of La Incarnación just outside Avila. She devised the Association of St Teresa to unite all the houses she had started with others living the same ideal. This was officially approved by the Holy See in 1972. Her health weakened in 1974, and she received the last sacraments on 8 December, the feast of the Immaculate Conception. She died in the Carmel of La Aldehuela, near Madrid, three days later, surrounded by the members of her community, repeating the words, "What joy to die a Carmelite!"

She was beatified by Pope John Paul II on 10 May 1998 and canonized by him in Madrid, with four other Spaniards, on 4 May 2003, when the pope described her as "motivated by a heroic faith that shaped her response to an austere vocation, in which she made God the centre of her life."

15

St Virginia Centurione Bracelli, *Founder* (1587–1651)

The daughter of Giorgio Centurione and Lelia Spinola, Virginia was born in Genoa, then an independent republic, on 2 April 1587. Both sides of her family boasted ancient noble lineage. At the age of fifteen, despite her desire for a convent life, her father arranged a marriage for her with Gaspare Grimaldo Bracelli, who was also from a distinguished family but engaged in destroying its fortunes and his health through a life of determined dissipation and heavy gambling. The couple had two daughters, Lelia and Isabella. Virginia did what she could to make her husband mend his ways and pay attention to the duties of fatherhood, but his excesses brought about his early death from tuberculosis at Alessandria, where he had gone in search of a cure, on 13 June 1607, after making a deathbed repentance in response to the pleas of his devoted wife.

Virginia thus found herself widowed at the age of twenty and on the day of her husband's death made a private vow of lifelong chastity, but her father would still not accept her desire for a cloistered life and tried to arrange a second marriage for her. This time she resisted him and refused. She went to live in her mother-in-law's house, took care of her daughters while they were growing up, and began to devote a large part of her time and half her fortune to helping people in need. Her father served a year as doge of Genoa from 1621 to 1622, but he could not persuade her to abandon her way of life, and, once she had arranged suitable matches for her own daughters, she gave herself entirely over to charitable works.

Needs of all sorts became more acute in Genoa with the outbreak of war between the republic and the neighbouring Duchy of Savoy, supported by France, in the autumn of 1624. Unemployment increased, starvation was rife, and many children were orphaned. Virginia found a little girl lying abandoned in the street and took her home with her. She was soon caring for fifteen orphans and then extended her work to take in refugees and abandoned women. Her mother-in-law died in August 1625, and Virginia took over her house as a refuge for street children and young girls in danger of being forced by poverty into prostitution. She merged her efforts with an existing charitable foundation, calling the new foundation "The Hundred Ladies of Protective Mercy for the Poor of Jesus Christ," later modified to become the "Auxiliaries of Ladies of Mercy." War was followed by plague and famine in 1629–1630, and Virginia needed more accommodation to house orphans and the destitute, so she rented the convent of Mount Calvary, which was standing empty, and moved there in April 1631, forming an umbrella organization for all her activities, named

"Works of Our Lady of Refuge on Mount Calvary." Within three years she had taken on two other houses and was caring for 300 beneficiaries. She sought and received official recognition as a charitable institution from the senate of the republic. She trained the young women in her care so that they would have a means of earning their own living, educated her "daughters" to become future teachers, and taught children their catechism.

Virginia had an opportunity to purchase the convent building, but had to refuse owing to the high price asked. Instead, she bought two villas by the hill known as Monte Carignano and established these as the motherhouse of the Institute, completing the foundation with a new annex to the church of Our Lady of Refuge to serve as the chapel. She took her basic concepts from the Constitutions of the Franciscans, divided her "daughters" into those who were clothed as religious and those who were not, with both ranks living together under obedience and a promise (though not a formal vow) to persevere in poverty and chastity. The senate appointed a panel of "Protectors" to supervise and administer the Institute, whose members divided into Sisters of Our Lady of Refuge of Mount Calvary and Daughters of Our Lady on Mount Calvary, both pledged to work for the sick and the needy and to lend their services to the local public hospital, the Pammatone. The work was assisted by prominent Genoese nobles, including Marquess Emmanuele Brignole, who financed the opening of a second house, which led to the Sisters also being known as *Brignoline* ("Brignole Sisters").

Virginia left the governance of the Institute to the Protectors and worked as a humble Sister, spending long hours visiting the sick and begging in the streets morning and evening. Retaining her influence with the government of Genoa, nevertheless, in 1637 she persuaded the senate to place the republic under the protection of the Blessed Virgin and in 1642 encouraged the archbishop, Cardinal Durazzo, to introduce the Forty Hours devotion. She then formed a group of ordinary families to help themselves as far as possible: their sick and disabled were cared for in the Institute's hospital, but able-bodied men were made to find work, women were taught embroidery and knitting, and children were obliged to attend school. This making common cause with the common people alienated many of her former aristocratic and wealthy women patrons, who felt deprived of her company and influenced the senate to withdraw its support in the form of the Protectors, throwing Virginia once more back on her own resources. Despite failing health, she returned to an administrative role, becoming effective superior of the Sisters at Monte Carignano.

Virginia was influential enough, despite having renounced her wealth and position in society, to intervene in disputes between rival factions of nobles and senators, and in 1647 she helped to resolve the conflict between the archdiocese and the senate provoked by the latter's withdrawal of financial support for her Institute. The remainder of her time she continued to devote to all who sought her help. She died at Monte Carignano of natural causes, aged sixty-four, on

15 December 1651. The Daughters spread throughout northern Italy and were the main helpers during epidemics from 1656, when fifty-three of them died nursing the sick, to 1911, when modern medicine led to improved public health. Pope Leo XII invited a group of the Daughters to Rome in 1827, to take charge of the Baths of Diocletian Hospital, and in 1833 Pope Gregory XVI gave them a house on the Esquiline Hill, which became their generalate.

Virginia's cause took a long time to come to fruition, despite her fame of sanctity at the time of her death, but took a giant step forward when her body was exhumed in 1801 and found to be incorrupt. From then on a great popular cult developed and many favours were attributed to her intercession. She was finally beatified by Pope John Paul II in Genoa on 22 September 1985 and canonized by him in Rome on 18 May 2003. She had, the Pope said in his homily, "Disregarding her noble origins … devoted herself to assisting the lowliest with extraordinary apostolic zeal … [She] leaves the Church the witness of a simple and active saint."

Butler, December, pp. 135–6, citing French and German sources, both of which depend on the Vatican information used here; *Orders*, p. 295. The Daughters still have their motherhouse in Rome, while the Sisters retain theirs in Genoa, also running two maternity homes in the area. Both stress the fact that, despite becoming two parallel Congregations through historical chance, their spirit is identical.

28

Bd Catherine Volpicelli, *Founder* (1839–1894)

Caterina (or Katarina; Catherine) was born into a prosperous middle-class family in Naples on 22 January 1839. Educated initially at home, she then attended the Royal College of St Marcellinus, where she acquired a level of culture unusual for a woman of her time. At the age of twenty, on 28 May 1859, she entered the convent of the Perpetual Adorers, where she thought she would be able to find "intimate union with God," but poor health obliged her to leave after six months, and her spiritual counsellor, (Blessed) Ludovico da Casoria, told her that her work would be "the Heart of Jesus."

In 1864, after she had been seriously ill—to the extent that her life was regarded as being in danger and her recovery treated as miraculous—her confessor introduced Catherine to the *Messenger of the Sacred Heart*, the monthly review dedicated to spreading the "apostleship of prayer." She wrote to the editor and received details of the association. She flung herself enthusiastically into spreading it in Naples, becoming its first "messenger" in Italy (*zelatrice,* which involved receiving a diploma) and the central figure of its activities in Naples. She found that it enabled her to cultivate her devotion to the Eucharist and to the Sacred Heart and to build forms of pastoral outreach to everyone. Other "messengers" came to join her, and with her became the first members of a new Institute, of Servants of the Sacred Heart (*Ancelle del Sacro Cuore,* not to be confused with the Congregation of the same name founded by Abbé Victor Braun in France in 1866).

In 1870 Catherine moved out of the family house and established her home and workplace in the Palazzo del Largo Patrone alla Salute. A few years later the cardinal archbishop of Naples, Sisto Riario Sforza, officially made this the Diocesan Centre of the Apostolate of Prayer, but handed its direction to Canon Luigi Caruso. The archbishop and Fr Ludovico da Casoria were frequent visitors, and it became a prominent spiritual focus in the city, with well-known Jesuits giving almost perpetual courses on spiritual exercises.

Four years later the Rule she had written, at the suggestion of Cardinal Sforza, received Vatican approval, and the Institute officially came into being. In November 1879 Catherine and her companions were received in audience by Pope Leo XIII, who asked them to give an account of their activities and their plans, called them "new and in accordance with the needs of the times," and declared: "A new Institute without a habit: that's what is needed." Catherine had a new sanctuary of the Sacred Heart built next to the Palazzo, and this was consecrated by the new archbishop of Naples, Cardinal Guglielmo Sanfelice, in May 1884. It was to be used above all for the perpetual adoration of the Blessed Sacrament, encouraged by the pope as a way of combating the perceived threats of growing atheism and Freemasonry.

The first National Eucharistic Congress was held in Naples in 1891, and Catherine and her Sisters were entrusted with organizing perpetual adoration in the cathedral, making preparations for the general Confession and Communion, and making the vestments. Three years later she died at the relatively early age of fifty-five. Her cause was introduced in 1911, she was declared Venerable by Pope Pius XII in 1945, and in 1999 a miracle attributed to her intercession was recognized, paving the way for her beatification, which took place in Rome on 29 April 2001. The Pope said of her: "She was always able to find in the Eucharist the missionary fervour which impelled her to express her vocation in the Church with … prophetic intentions of promoting the laity and new forms of consecrated life."

The Servants of the Sacred Heart have three levels of belonging: the "Servants" proper, who live in community (and still wear secular dress); the "Little

Servants," or Oblates, who are also consecrated but live with their families; and the "Additionals" (*Aggregati*), who do not take vows but help in any way their situation permits. They have six houses in Italy, most in or near Naples, and run mission houses in Brazil, where a male branch of Servants also operates.

30

Bd Eugenia Ravasco, *Founder* (1845–1900)

The third of six children of Francesco Matteo and Carolina Mozzoni Frosconi, Eugenia was born in Milan on 4 January 1845. Her mother died when she was three years old, and her father moved to Genoa, where two of his brothers lived, in search of work. He took Eugenia's eldest brother and youngest sister with him, leaving the others in the care of relatives in Milan: Eugenia with an aunt, Marietta Anselmi, who brought her up like a second mother and gave her a good grounding in the faith. Her father brought all the children together in Genoa in 1852, but he died three years later, and Eugenia (with other siblings) again found herself in the care of her extended family, this time her aunt and uncle, Elisa and Luigi Ravasco. They already had ten children of their own but were evidently a large-hearted couple and found the resources of time and dedication needed to give their nephews and nieces a good religious education. Eugenia made her First Communion and received the sacrament of Confirmation on the same day, 21 June 1855, at the age of ten.

A devout child, she became deeply attached to the dominant spiritual practices of the time: adoration of the person of Christ present in the Blessed Sacrament in the tabernacle, and devotion to the Sacred Heart of Jesus and the Immaculate Heart of Mary. Not so her eldest brother, Ambrose, who came under the influence of Freemasons, then increasingly influential in generally anticlerical northern Italy. Her uncle had tried to bring him back to the faith, without success, and when he died in 1862, this task fell to the seventeen-year-old Eugenia, whose efforts, even when aided by her aunt Marietta, proved equally unsuccessful. Marietta tried to persuade her to marry, but Eugenia felt sure she was destined to the religious life, and in May 1863 a mission preacher convinced her that she should look for a way of serving others out of dedication to the Sacred Heart.

She found no existing organization that matched her desires and began a mission on her own to poor and abandoned girls, mainly those living on the streets, which generally implied working as prostitutes. Her aunt tried to dissuade her, regarding them as totally unsuitable company for her niece, but Eugenia persevered and gradually won their respect. One person alone, however, could not do all that was needed for them, and like so many other young women of her time, she felt called to start a new religious organization to give them a Christian education. Other young women joined her, and with guidance from Canon (later Archbishop) Magnasco, she founded the Congregation of the Sacred Hearts of Jesus and Mary. Despite scorn in the local press at such a venture by a young woman of twenty-three, and outright opposition from Freemasons and other anticlerical groups, the new foundation grew and the Sisters began opening schools in which future catechists and teachers could be formed.

The Congregation gained diocesan approval in 1882 and the first Sisters, including Eugenia, who became the first mother superior, took perpetual vows in 1884. Although she was by now in poor health, Eugenia travelled extensively, opening new houses in other parts of Italy and also in France and Switzerland. Her Congregation's mission broadened from care and education of young girls to include care of the dying, of prisoners, and of people alienated from the Church. She died in Genoa on 30 December 1900, nine years before the Congregation received pontifical approval. She was declared Venerable on 1 July 2000 and beatified on 27 April 2003. In his homily the Pope spoke of her love for the Hearts of Jesus and Mary and how this produced her passionate devotion to the poor and needy, so that, "With foresight, she was able to open herself to the pressing needs of the mission, with special concern for those who had 'fallen away' from the Church."

Her Congregation, also known as the Ravasco Institute, currently works in three countries in Europe, six in Latin America, in Africa, and in the Philippines. The Sisters run schools and help in parishes and with missions.

CANONIZATIONS IN CHRONOLOGICAL ORDER

With date of Commemoration

Benedict Menni	21 November 1999	24 April
Cyril Beltrand and Companions	21 November 1999	9 October
Jaime Hilario	21 November 1999	18 January
Thomas of Cori	21 November 1999	11 January
Faustina Kowalska	30 April 2000	5 October
Christopher Magallanes and 24 Comps	21 May 2000	25 May
Mary of Jesus Venegas	21 May 2000	30 July
Joseph Mary de Yermo y Parres	21 May 2000	20 September
Augustine Zhao Rog and 119 Comps	1 October 2000	9 July
Josephine Bakhita	1 October 2000	8 February
Katharine Drexel	1 October 2000	3 March
María Josefa Sánchez de Guerra	1 October 2000	20 March
Augustine Roscelli	10 June 2001	7 May
Bernard of Corleone	10 June 2001	12 January
Louis Scrosoppi	10 June 2001	3 April
Rebecca Ar-Rayès	10 June 2001	23 March
Teresa Eustochio Verzeri	10 June 2001	3 March
Joseph Marello	25 November 2001	30 May
Léonie François de Sales Aviat	25 November 2001	10 January
Mary Crescentia Höss	25 November 2001	5 April
Paula Montal Fornés	25 November 2001	26 February
Alphonsus of Orozco	19 May 2002	19 September
Benedetta Frasinello	19 May 2002	21 March
Humilis of Bisignano	19 May 2002	26 November
Ignatius of Santhià	19 May 2002	21 September
Pauline of the Suffering Heart	19 May 2002	9 July
Pius of Pietrelcina	16 June 2002	23 September
Juan Diego	30 July 2002	9 December
Peter de Betancur	30 July 2002	25 April
Jose María Escriva de Balaguer	6 October 2002	26 June
Angela of the Cross	4 May 2003	2 March
José María Rubio y Perlata	4 May 2003	2 May

María Maravillas Pidal y Chico de Guzmán	4 May 2003	11 December
Genevieve Torres Morales	4 May 2003	5 January
Pedro Poveda Castroverde	4 May 2003	28 July
Maria de Mattias	18 May 2003	20 August
Ursula Ledóchowska	18 May 2003	29 May
Virginia Centurione Bracelli	18 May 2003	15 December
Joseph Sebastian Pelczar	18 May 2003	28 March
Arnold Janssen	5 October 2003	15 January
Daniel Comboni	5 October 2003	10 October
Joseph Freinademetz	5 October 2003	28 January

BEATIFICATIONS IN CHRONOLOGICAL ORDER

With date of Commemoration

Antony Martin Slomšek	19 September 1999	24 September
Arcangelo Tadini	3 October 1999	20 May
Diego Oddi	3 October 1999	3 June
Edward Poppe	3 October 1999	10 June
Ferdinand Mary Baccilleri	3 October 1999	13 July
Mariano of Roccacasale	3 October 1999	31 May
Nicholas of Gesturi	3 October 1999	8 June
Andrew of Phú Yên	5 March 2000	26 July
Andrew of Soveral and Comps	5 March 2000	16 July
Maria Stella Mardosewicz and Comps	5 March 2000	1 August
Nicholas Bunkerd Kitbamrung	5 March 2000	12 January
Peter Calungsod	5 March 2000	2 April
Anna Rosa Gattorno	9 April 2000	6 May
Francis Xavier Seelos	9 April 2000	4 October
Mariam Thresia Chiramel Mankidiyan	9 April 2000	8 June
Mariano of Jesus Euse Hoyos	9 April 2000	13 July
Mary Elizabeth Hesselblad	9 April 2000	24 April
Francisco and Jacinta Marto	13 May 2000	20 February
Columba Marmion	3 September 2000	30 January
John XXIII	3 September 2000	3 June
Pius IX	3 September 2000	7 February
Thomas Reggio of Genoa	3 September 2000	22 November
William Joseph Chaminade	3 September 2000	22 January
José Aparicio Sanz and Comps	11 March 2001	22 September
Charles Manuel Rodríguez Santiago	29 April 2001	13 July
Catherine Cittadini	29 April 2001	5 May
Manuel González García	29 April 2001	4 January
Marie-Anne Blondin	29 April 2001	2 January
George Preca	9 May 2001	26 July
Ignatius Falzon	9 May 2001	1 July
Maria Adeodata Pisani	9 May 2001	25 February
Joseph Bilczewski	26 June 2001	20 March
Sigmund Gorazdowski	26 June 2001	1 January

Josaphata Hordashevska	27 June 2001	7 April
The Martyrs of Ukraine	27 June 2001	7 March
Alphonsus Mary Fusco	7 October 2001	6 February
Emily Tavernier	7 October 2001	23 September
Eugenia Picco	7 October 2001	7 September
Ignatius Maloyan	7 October 2001	11 June
Mary Euthymia Üffing	7 October 2001	9 September
Nicholas Gross	7 October 2001	23 January
Thomas Mary Fusco	7 October 2001	24 February
Louis and Maria Beltrame Quatrocchi	21 October 2001	25 November
Bartholomew Fernandes dos Mártires	4 November 2001	16 July
Gaetana Sterni	4 November 2001	26 November
John Antony Farina	4 November 2001	4 March
Louis Tezza	4 November 2001	23 September
María Pilar Izquierdo de Albero	4 November 2001	27 August
Dominic Methodius Trcka	4 November 2001	23 March
Paul Peter Gojdič	4 November 2001	17 July
Artemide Zatti	14 April 2002	15 March
Gaetano Errico	14 April 2002	29 October
Ludovic Pavoni	14 April 2002	1 April
María Romero Meneses	14 April 2002	7 July
María del Tránsito Cabanillas	14 April 2002	25 August
Louis Variara	14 April 2002	1 February
The Martyrs of Bulgaria	22 May 2002	11 November
Juan Bautista and Jacinto de los Angeles	1 August 2002	16 September
Sigmund Felínski	18 August 2002	17 September
John Balicki	18 August 2002	15 March
John Beyzym	18 August 2002	2 October
Santia Szymkowiak	18 August 2002	29 August
Andrew Hyacinth Longhin	20 October 2002	26 June
Daudi Okelo and Jildo Irwa	20 October 2002	18 October
Lyduina Meneguzzi	20 October 2002	2 December
Marcantonio Durando	20 October 2002	10 December
Mary of the Passion	20 October 2002	15 November
Caritas Brader	23 March 2003	27 February
Dolores Rodríguez Sopeña Ortega	23 March 2003	10 January
Juana María Condesa Lluch	23 March 2003	16 January
Ladislaus Battyány-Strattmann	23 March 2003	22 January
Pierre Bonhomme	23 March 2003	9 September
Eugenia Ravasco	27 April 2003	30 December
James Alberione	27 April 2003	26 November
Julia Salzano	27 April 2003	17 May
María Cristina Brando	27 April 2003	20 January

Maria Mantovani	27 April 2003	2 February
Mark of Aviano	27 April 2003	13 August
Marija Petković	6 June 2003	9 July
Ivan Merz	22 June 2003	10 May
Vasil' Hopko	14 September 2003	23 July
Zdenka Cecilia Schelingová	14 September 2003	31 July
Teresa of Calcutta	20 October 2003	5 September
Bonifacia Rodríguez Castro	9 November 2003	8 August
John Nepomucene Zegrí y Moreno	9 November 2003	17 March
Luigi Maria Monti	9 November 2003	1 October
Rosalie Rendu	9 November 2003 ·	7 February
Valentine Paquay	9 November 2003	1 January

ALPHABETICAL INDEX OF ENTRIES